An Integrated Approach to Modern Economics

An Integrated Approach to Modern Economics

Edited by Swena Lesley

Clanrye International
www.clanryeinternational.com

Clanrye International,
750 Third Avenue, 9th Floor,
New York, NY 10017, USA

ISBN: 978-1-63240-680-4

Cataloging-in-Publication Data

An integrated approach to modern economics / edited by Swena Lesley.
p. cm.
Includes bibliographical references and index.
ISBN 978-1-63240-680-4
1. Economics. I. Lesley, Swena.

HB171 .I58 2018
330--dc23

For information on all Clanrye International publications
visit our website at www.clanryeinternational.com

CLANRYE INTERNATIONAL

Printed in China.

Contents

Preface

Economics is the field which studies and analyses the different areas of market which are divided into production, consumption and distribution of various services and products. It has two branches namely microeconomics and macroeconomics. This book includes some of the vital pieces of research work being conducted across the world, on various topics related to economics. The objective of the book is to give a general view of the different areas of the subject, and its applications in different areas. It is a compilation of chapters that discuss the most vital concepts and emerging trends in the field of contemporary economics. It is a vital tool for all researching and studying this field.

After months of intensive research and writing, this book is the end result of all who devoted their time and efforts in the initiation and progress of this book. It will surely be a source of reference in enhancing the required knowledge of the new developments in the area. During the course of developing this book, certain measures such as accuracy, authenticity and research focused analytical studies were given preference in order to produce a comprehensive book in the area of study.

This book would not have been possible without the efforts of the authors and the publisher. I extend my sincere thanks to them. Secondly, I express my gratitude to my family and well-wishers. And most importantly, I thank my students for constantly expressing their willingness and curiosity in enhancing their knowledge in the field, which encourages me to take up further research projects for the advancement of the area.

Editor

1

Oil Price Forecasting Using Crack Spread Futures and Oil Exchange Traded Funds

Hankyeung Choi[1], David J. Leatham[2], Kunlapath Sukcharoen[2]

ABSTRACT Given the emerging consensus from previous studies that crude oil and refined product (as well as crack spread) prices are cointegrated, this study examines the link between the crude oil spot and crack spread derivatives markets. Specifically, the usefulness of the two crack spread derivatives products (namely, crack spread futures and the ETF crack spread) for modeling and forecasting daily OPEC crude oil spot prices is evaluated. Based on the results of a structural break test, the sample is divided into pre-crisis, crisis, and post-crisis periods. We find a unidirectional relationship from the two crack spread derivatives markets to the crude oil spot market during the post-crisis period. In terms of forecasting performance, the forecasting models based on crack spread futures and the ETF crack spread outperform the Random Walk Model (RWM), both in-sample and out-of-sample. In addition, on average, the results suggest that information from the ETF crack spread market contributes more to the forecasting models than information from the crack spread futures market.

KEY WORDS: oil price forecasting, crack spread futures, oil-related exchange traded funds, multivariate GARCH model

[1] Ministry of Strategy and Finance, Sejong Special Self-Governing City, Republic of Korea; [2] Department of Agricultural Economics, Texas A&M University, USA

1. Introduction

Crude oil is an important energy commodity that is vital for most economic activities. Consequently, numerous studies have been devoted to modeling and forecasting crude oil prices. In recent years, the link between the crude oil and refined product markets has been addressed often in the energy economics literature. In particular, several studies have examined the existence of a long-run equilibrium relationship between the prices of crude oil and refined products (Asche, Gjolberg, & Völker, 2003; Gjolberg & Johnsen, 1999; Haigh & Holt, 2002; Lanza, Manera, & Giovannini, 2005; Serletis, 1994). The emerging consensus from these studies is that crude oil and refined product prices are cointegrated. As a result, we should be able to forecast future oil price movements based on information from the refined product markets. However, only a few empirical works have investigated the ability of refined product prices to forecast the price of crude oil (see, for example, Gjolberg & Johnsen, 1999; Lanza et al., 2005; Murat & Tokat, 2009). A deeper understanding of the relationship between the crude oil and refined product markets and of the predictive power of the refined products are indeed worthy of investigation and may carry important implications for energy consumers, producers, investors and policymakers.

Correspondence concerning this article should be addressed to: **Kunlapath Sukcharoen**, Department of Agricultural Economics, Texas A&M University, College Station, TX 77843, USA
E-mail: kunlapath@tamu.edu

In this study, we explore the link between the crude oil spot and refined product derivatives markets and examine the ability of the refined product derivatives prices to predict movements in the crude oil price. In oil and energy markets, the profits of oil refiners, the major participants in the markets, depend largely on the crack spread (the difference between the price of crude oil and the prices of refined products – typically gasoline and heating oil). Because the demand from oil refiners, whose production decisions are tied directly to the crack spread, largely affect the price of crude oil (Verleger, 1982; Verleger, 2011), it is possible that there is a long-run equilibrium relationship between crude oil and crack spread derivatives prices. This study therefore examines the existence of long-run equilibrium price relationships between the crude oil and crack spread derivatives markets. Specifically, we explore the equilibrium price relationships between (i) the OPEC crude oil spot and crack spread futures and (ii) the OPEC crude oil spot and Exchange Traded Fund (ETF) crack spread. The Granger causality is then used to analyze the lead-lag relationship and determine whether the crack spread derivatives prices are useful for forecasting the movements of crude oil spot prices. Finally, we compare the forecasting ability of the two crack spread derivatives with that of a conventional Random Walk Model (RWM).

Our paper contributes to the existing literature by enriching the understanding of the dynamic relationships between crude oil spot and refined product derivatives prices in the following ways. First, unlike many previous studies, we focus on the prices of crude oil spot and crack spread derivatives. With the notable exception of Murat and Tokat (2009), our study is among the first to examine the link between the crude oil spot and crack spread derivatives markets and to investigate oil price forecasting models based on information from the crack spread derivatives markets. Unlike Murat and Tokat (2009), we analyze not only the futures market but also the ETF market. Thus, the findings from this study also have implications regarding which market contributes more to the forecasting models. In addition, while Murat and Tokat (2009) ignore the presence of heteroskedasticity in the residuals, we correct for the time-varying nature of the variance and covariance of commodity prices and returns by utilizing a Multivariate GARCH (MGARCH) model. Second, whereas most of the previous literature, including Murat and Tokat (2009), focuses on either Brent or West Texas Intermediate (WTI) crude oil prices, we investigate the dynamics of the new OPEC Reference Basket (ORB) price. The understanding of the OPEC crude oil price is important given the share of OPEC's crude oil production and exports. The U.S. Energy Information Administration (2014) reports, "OPEC member countries produce approximately 40 percent of the world's crude oil and exports approximately 60 percent of the total petroleum traded internationally." In particular, the study allows us to answer whether the crack spread price data from the U.S. derivative markets can significantly explain OPEC crude oil price movements. In summary, given the limited empirical investigations of the link between the OPEC crude oil spot and refined product derivatives markets, the results from this study should provide useful information for both oil refiners and energy investors regarding portfolio investment and risk management.

The remainder of this paper is organized as follows. Section 2 contains a brief discussion of the theoretical background on predicting oil price movements using crack spread derivatives. Section 3 describes the data. Section 4 presents the methodology used in forming the forecasting models. Section 5 discusses the empirical results, and finally, Section 6 concludes.

2. Predicting oil price movements using crack spread derivatives

The idea of forecasting oil price movements using information from the crack spread futures market is based on two different arguments. The first argument relies on the proposition that the price of crude oil largely depends on the demand from oil refiners (Verleger, 1982; Verleger, 2011). The rationale behind this proposition is that oil refiners are most concerned with the crack spread, and therefore, they cut their levels of production when the price of crude oil is too high compared with the prices of their refined products (i.e., when the crack spread is too low). A decrease in production of refined products will, in turn, lower the price of crude oil through the lower demand for input (Verleger, 2011). This relationship suggests that we should be able to forecast future oil price movements based on information from the crack spread markets. Assuming that the efficient market hypothesis holds,

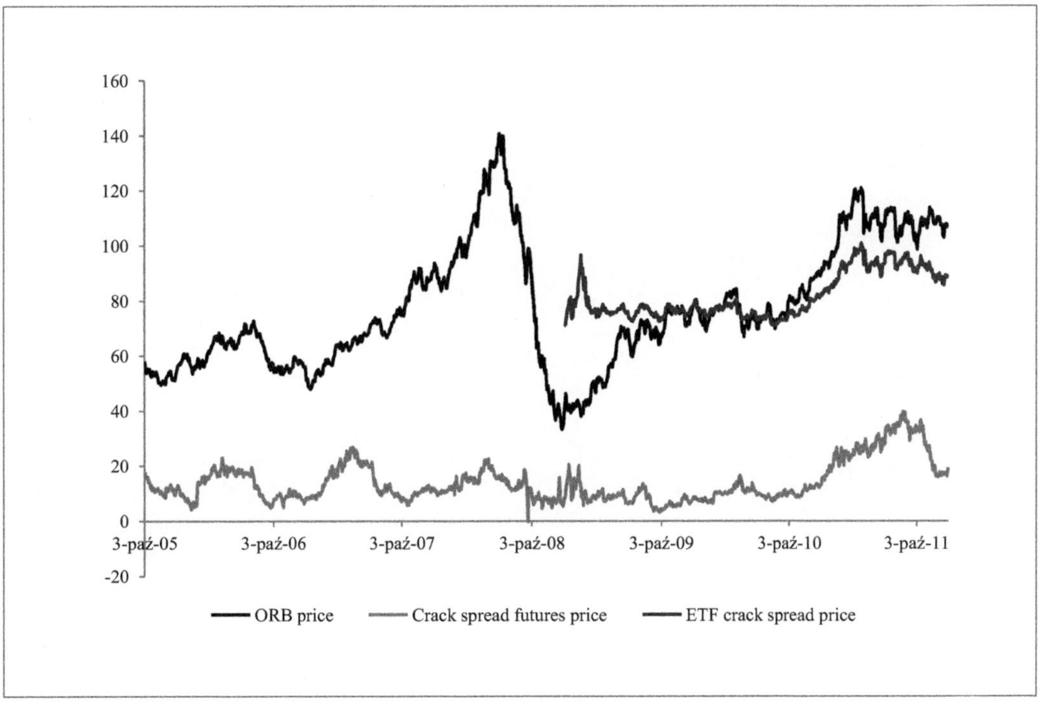

Figure 1. Daily ORB, crack spread futures, and ETF crack spread prices

then the prices of futures contracts based on crack spreads are the optimal forecasts of the crack spreads (e.g., Chinn & Coibion, 2014; Lean, McAleer & Wong, 2010; Ma, 1989). Accordingly, information contained in crack spread futures should at least partially explain future oil price movements.

The second argument relies on the proposition that there is a positive relationship between convenience yield (the benefit from physically holding a commodity rather than holding a futures contract for that commodity) and marginal production costs (Heinkel, Howe, & Hughes, 1990). The reasoning behind this proposition is that, to maximize their profits, oil refiners respond to increased demand through immediate production when the marginal production costs are low and through the stock kept in inventory when the marginal costs of production are high. This strategy implies that when the marginal production costs are relatively inexpensive (expensive), the convenience yields are low (high). Because low marginal costs imply high profit margins or crack spreads, the proposition therefore suggests that there is a negative relationship between the convenience yields and crack spreads. This negative relationship is empirically verified by Edwards and Ma (1992) and Kocagil (2004). Given the Theory of Storage (Kaldor, 1939), commodity spot prices and commodity futures prices are related through the convenience yield. Thus, assuming the efficient market hypothesis, one should expect the existence of a long-run equilibrium relationship between crude oil spot and crack spread futures markets and that variations in crack spread futures can help explain crude oil price movements (see, for example, Asche et al., 2003; Gjolberg & Johnsen, 1999; Haigh & Holt, 2002; Lanza et al., 2005; Murat & Tokat, 2009; Seletis, 1994).

Instead of relying solely on crack spread futures, the recent introduction of derivative-based ETFs allows oil refiners and investors to capture crack spread changes by purchasing equal units of the ProShares UltraShort DJ-UBS Crude Oil ETF (SCO), the United States Gasoline Fund (UGA) and the United States Heating Oil

Fund (UHN) for the 2:1:1 crack spread (which refers to an approximation of the profit margin that oil refiners earn by turning two barrels of crude oil to one barrel of gasoline and one barrel of heating oil) because the price of the SCO fund represents the cost of purchasing two units of oil, where the values of the UGA and UHN funds are the proceeds derived from selling one unit of the respective distillate. Because these funds basically attempt to track the movements of the nearby futures, forwards, options and swap contracts, a positive relationship between crack spread futures and the ETF spread can be expected. Specifically, during the period from January 2009 to December 2011, the correlation coefficient between the daily prices of crack spread futures and the ETF crack spread is 0.9061. Figure 1 clearly shows that the price of the ETF crack spread tracks the price of the crack spread futures fairly well (though they are not exactly the same). Given the positive relationship between the two crack spread derivatives, the ETF crack spread should also contain useful information about future oil price movements. Because the entry barrier in the ETF market is not as strict as in the futures markets, more diverse types of investors (i.e., not only oil refiners and institutional investors) can enter the ETF market, which raises the question of whether the ETF crack spread is better at explaining spot oil price movements than the crack spread futures. Given the recent increased investor interest in oil and refined product ETFs and the convenient trading system, we expect that the ETF market should contribute more to the forecasting models. To the best of our knowledge, no empirical research has yet directly addressed the role of the ETF crack spread in predicting the movements of the crude oil spot price. Therefore, this paper examines the forecasting power of both crack spread futures and crack spread ETFs for the first time.

3. Data

The analysis uses daily closing spot price data for the OPEC Reference Basket (ORB), daily closing futures price data for the front-month crude oil, RBOB regular gasoline, and No. 2 heating oil futures contracts, and daily closing ETF price data for the ProShares UltraShort DJ-UBS Crude Oil ETF (SCO), the United States Gasoline Fund (UGA) and the United States Heating Oil Fund (UHN). Given that the new ORB price was introduced on June 16, 2005, the data for spot and futures prices used in this study cover the period from October 3, 2005 to December 30, 2011. The data for the oil ETFs span the period from January 2, 2009 to December 30, 2011. Data from earlier periods were not used because trading did not begin on the SCO until November 25, 2008. The spot price, futures price and ETF price data are obtained from OPEC, New York Mercantile Exchange (NYMEX), and New York Stock Exchange (NYSE) data mines, respectively.

The closing prices for the three series are available at different times of the day. The closing spot price on a particular calendar date is obtained at 4:00 AM (EST) on the next calendar date. For instance, the Monday closing spot price is available in the early morning on Tuesday. On each trading day, the NYMEX futures closing prices are determined at 2:30 PM (EST), whereas the NYSE ETF closing prices are determined at 4:00 PM (EST). Given the discrepancies in real time, caution must be exercised in modeling and interpreting market relationships on the same calendar date. In particular, on a given calendar date, the futures price and the ETF price data are available before the OPEC crude oil price data. Thus, it would be inappropriate to allow the daily closing ORB price to influence the futures and ETF prices on the same calendar date. This disparity suggests that the model describing the relationship between the crude oil spot and crack spread derivatives should be recursive in nature.

The most common ratio of the crack spread for light oil is 3:2:1 (three crude oil, two gasoline, and one heating oil). However, OPEC crude oil is considered a representative of heavier oil compared with lighter oil such as WTI and Brent. Consequently, the 2:1:1 crack spread is a better description for the case of ORB prices because heavier crude oil usually yields less gasoline than the lighter oil such as WTI. Given that crude oil is quoted in dollars per barrel and refined products are quoted in cents per gallon, gasoline and heating oil prices are converted to dollars per barrel by multiplying the cents-per-gallon price by 42. Accordingly, the 2:1:1 crack spread futures are calculated as

$$crack\ spread\ futures = \left(\frac{1}{2}\times 42\times RB\right)+\left(\frac{1}{2}\times 42\times HO\right)-CL \quad (1)$$

where RB, HO, and CL refer to gasoline futures price per gallon, heating oil futures price per gallon, and crude oil futures price per barrel, respectively. Finally, the 2:1:1 ETF crack spread can be calculated as

$$ETF\ spread = SCO + UGA + UHN \quad (2)$$

where SCO, UGA, and UHN are the prices of the ProShares UltraShort DJ-UBS Crude Oil ETF (SCO), the United States Gasoline Fund (UGA) and the United States Heating Oil Fund (UHN), respectively.

4. Methodology

The aim of the analysis is to examine the contribution of two different derivatives products, crack spread futures and the derivative-based ETF crack spread, in explaining and forecasting crude oil price movements. Because the sample period includes the financial crisis in 2008, we first test for structural breaks in the data. We adopt a Zivot and Andrews (1992) test (hereafter a ZA test) to determine the breakpoint endogenously from the data. The ZA test is a simple modification of an Augmented Dickey-Fuller (ADF) test for unit root in which a dummy variable for a mean shift and/or a dummy variable for a trend shift occurring at each possible break date are added to the ADF test equation. In this study, we use the following ZA model that allows for both a mean shift and a trend shift at each possible break date (T_b):

$$\Delta y_t = \mu + \alpha y_{t-1} + \beta t + \gamma DU_t(T_b) + \theta DT_t(T_b) + \sum_{j=1}^{k} \delta_j \Delta y_{t-j} + \varepsilon_t \quad (3)$$

where

$$DU_t, DT_t = \begin{cases} 1 & if\, t > T_b \\ 0 & otherwise \end{cases}$$

The test assumes no structural break(s) under the null hypothesis of unit root (i.e., $\alpha = 0$). The model is estimated for every possible break date. The candidate break date is then chosen where the one-sided t-statistic of $\alpha = 0$ (against the alternative hypothesis that $\alpha < 0$) in equation (3) is at a minimum (most negative). If the null hypothesis of no break(s) on the selected candidate break date is rejected, we conclude that there is a structural break on that particular candidate break date. After identifying the first breakpoint, the test is reapplied to each subsample until the test fails to detect evidence of an additional break. If structural breaks over the sample period exist, the analysis is also conducted for each sub-sample period to examine possible changes in the relationship between the variables of interest.

Similar to Murat and Tokat (2009), we explore the long-run equilibrium relationships between the crude oil spot and each crack spread derivative using the Error Correction Model (ECM). Given the timing consideration discussed above, the ECM framework is appropriate because the model is specified such that the current daily return in a particular market depends on its own past returns and past returns of the other market. Let s_t denote the log of the crude oil price at time t and cs_t denote the log of the crude oil futures price at time t. According to the Engle and Granger (1987) representation theorem, if both s_t and cs_t are integrated of order one, I(1), but the stochastic error terms are stationary (integrated of order zero, I(0)), the two variables are said to be cointegrated. Cointegration between the two variables could then be established through the error correction representation as

$$\Delta s_t = \alpha_s + \sum_{l=1}^{n} \alpha_{11}(l) \Delta s_{t-l} + \sum_{l=1}^{n} \alpha_{12}(l) \Delta cs_{t-l} + \tau_s ECT_{t-1} + \varepsilon_{s,t} \quad (4)$$

$$\Delta cs_t = \alpha_{cs} + \sum_{l=1}^{n} \alpha_{21}(l) \Delta s_{t-l} + \sum_{l=1}^{n} \alpha_{22}(l) \Delta cs_{t-l} + \tau_{cs} ECT_{t-1} + \varepsilon_{cs,t} \quad (5)$$

where ε_t is the stationary error term, and ECT_{t-1} is the error correction term. τ_s and τ_{cs} are the adjustment coefficients. The ECM for the OPEC crude oil spot and the ETF crack spread follows a similar representation as equations (4) and (5) but with ETF in place of cs. We also conduct Granger causality tests to examine the lead-lag between markets and to determine whether the crack spread derivatives prices are useful for forecasting the movements of crude oil spot prices.

In the forecasting exercise, we also use the MGARCH model, which was introduced by Bollerslev, Engle, and Wooldridge (1998), to account for the presence of heteroskedasticity in the residuals of the estimated ECM. In this study, the constant conditional correlation (CCC) MGARCH model and the dynamic conditional correlation (DCC) MGARCH model are employed. Under the same bivariate error correction model (equations (4) and (5)), following Kroner and Sultan (1993), the conditional variance of the CCC MGARCH model can be specified as

$$\varepsilon_t = \left[\varepsilon_{s,t} \quad \varepsilon_{cs,t}\right]^T \mid I_{t-1} \sim N(0, H_t) \quad (6)$$

where $\varepsilon_{s,t}$ and $\varepsilon_{cs,t}$ are error terms following the GARCH (1,1) model with a zero mean and a conditional covariance matrix H_t with a constant correlation ρ.

$$H_t = \begin{bmatrix} h_{s,t}^2 & h_{scs,t} \\ h_{scs,t} & h_{cs,t}^2 \end{bmatrix} = \begin{bmatrix} h_{s,t} & 0 \\ 0 & h_{cs,t} \end{bmatrix} \begin{bmatrix} 1 & \rho \\ \rho & 1 \end{bmatrix} \begin{bmatrix} h_{s,t} & 0 \\ 0 & h_{cs,t} \end{bmatrix} = D_t R_t D_t \quad (7)$$

$$h_{s,t}^2 = \beta_{0s} + \beta_{1s}\varepsilon_{s,t-1}^2 + \beta_{2s}h_{s,t-1}^2$$
$$(8)$$
$$h_{cs,t}^2 = \beta_{0cs} + \beta_{1cs}\varepsilon_{cs,t-1}^2 + \beta_{2cs}h_{cs,t-1}^2$$

where $h_{s,t}^2$ and $h_{cs,t}^2$ are the conditional variances for the crude oil spot and crack spread futures returns, respectively. The ε_t is a standardized residual vector with a mean zero and a variance of one, which, in this study, is a 2×1 vector of normal, independent, and identically distributed (*iid*) innovation.

Because the assumption of constant correlation may be too restrictive, we also employ the DCC MGARCH model. In contrast to the CCC MGARCH model, the DCC MGARCH model, proposed by Engle (2002), allows a time-varying correlation ρ_t:

$$H_t = \begin{bmatrix} h_{s,t}^2 & h_{scs,t} \\ h_{scs,t} & h_{cs,t}^2 \end{bmatrix} = \begin{bmatrix} h_{s,t} & 0 \\ 0 & h_{cs,t} \end{bmatrix} \begin{bmatrix} 1 & \rho_t \\ \rho_t & 1 \end{bmatrix} \begin{bmatrix} h_{s,t} & 0 \\ 0 & h_{cs,t} \end{bmatrix} \quad (9)$$

$$\rho_t = (1-\lambda_1-\lambda_2)\rho + \lambda_1\rho_{t-1} + \lambda_2\varepsilon_{s,t-1}\varepsilon_{cs,t-1} \quad (10)$$

where ε_t is the standardized disturbance vector, ρ is the unconditional correlation of the standardized residual (ε_t), and λ_1 and λ_2 are parameters that capture the dynamics of a conditional quasi-correlation. λ_1 and λ_2 are nonnegative and satisfy $0 \le \lambda_1 + \lambda_2 < 1$. The MGARCH model for the OPEC crude oil spot and the ETF crack spread follows a similar representation as equations (6) to (10) but with *ETF* in place of *cs*.

Finally, we construct forecasts using a recursive window scheme. One-step-ahead forecasts of crude oil prices are generated dynamically from the in-sample parameter estimates. The forecasting performance of the two crack spread derivatives is then evaluated. A benchmark for evaluating different forecasting models is the random walk model (RWM) without drift. The accuracy of the forecasts obtained from the error correction models is assessed on the basis of the mean-absolute error (MAE) and the root mean-squared error (RMSE):

$$MAE(I) = \sum_{t=1}^{n} \left| \hat{y}_t - y_t \right| / n$$
$$(11)$$
$$RMSE(I) = \sqrt{\sum_{t=1}^{n} \left(\hat{y}_t - y_t \right)^2 / n}$$

where $\hat{y}_t$ is the one-step-ahead forecast of the dependent variable for t = 1, …, n, and y_t is the actual value. For the MGARCH models, the forecasting performance is evaluated by the following modified MAE and RMSE:

$$MAE(II) = \sum_{t=1}^{n} \left| \frac{\hat{y}_t - y_t}{\sqrt{variance_t}} \right| / n$$
$$(12)$$
$$RMSE(II) = \sqrt{\sum_{t=1}^{n} \left(\frac{\hat{y}_t - y_t}{\sqrt{variance_t}} \right)^2 / n}$$

where $variance_t$ is a time-varying conditional variance in the MGARCH model. This method is used for scaling the residuals, which can be thought of as an element of variation that is not explained by the fitted model. The intuition behind this modification is that the MGARCH model could reduce the unexplained variance (or residual) in the ECM; thus, this benefit should also be taken into account. In addition, the Diebold-Mariano (Diebold & Mariano, 1995) test is also conducted to assess whether the differences between the two rival forecasts are statistically significant.

5. Empirical results

Descriptive statistics are presented in Table 1. The presence of skewness, leptokurtosis, and non-normality (implied by the significant Jarque-Bera statistics) in all of the series suggest that the unconditional distributions of the crude oil spot, crack spread futures, and ETF crack spread prices and returns are asymmetric, fat tailed-tailed, and non-normal. Plots of the entire data series for the daily prices and daily log returns are presented in Figures 1 and 2, respectively. As shown in the figures, there are considerable co-movements among the prices and returns. However, the crack

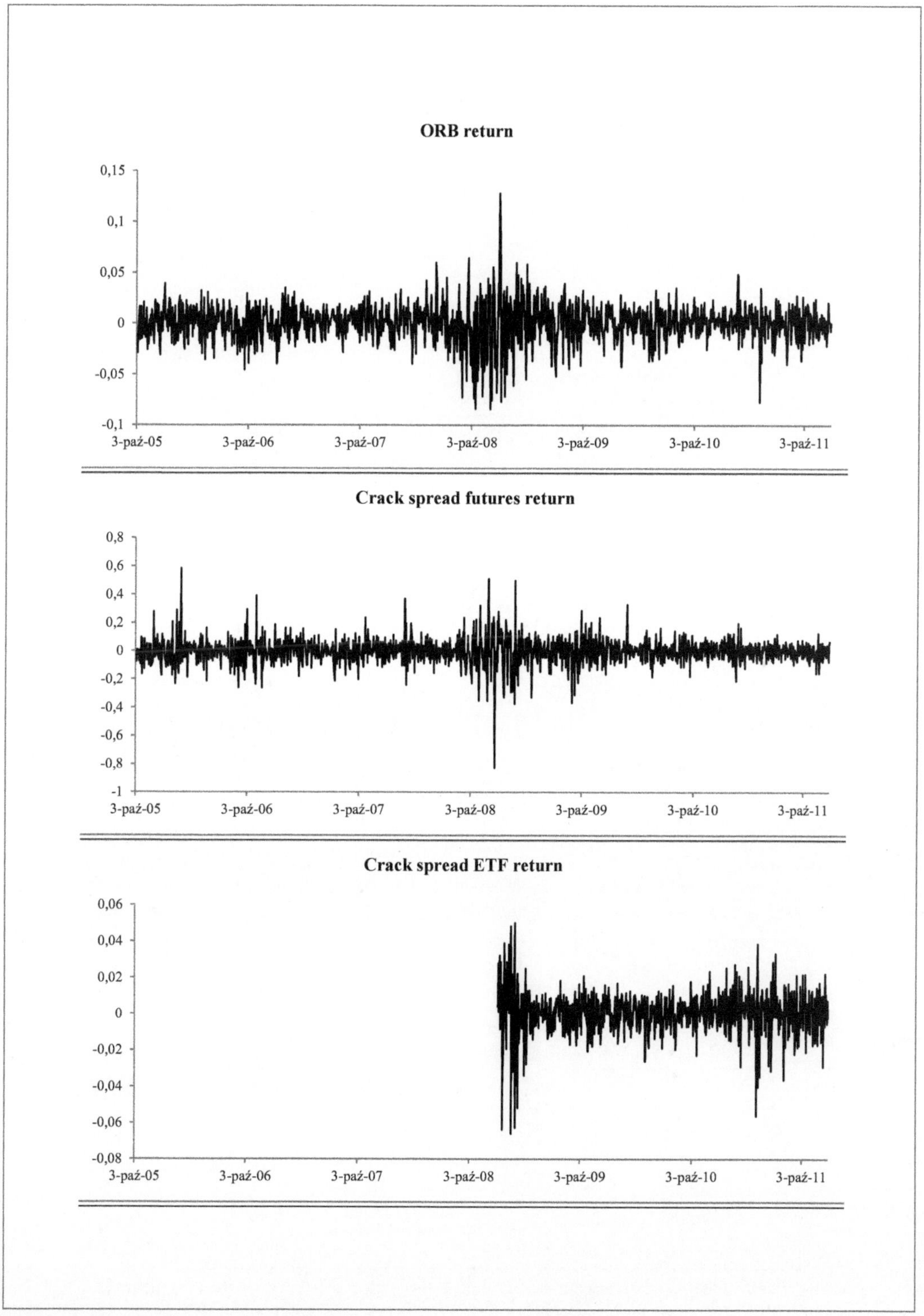

Figure 2. Daily log returns of ORB, crack spread futures, and ETF crack spread

Table 1. Descriptive statistics

	Log price			First difference of log price (return)		
Statistic	**Crude oil spot**	**Crack spread futures**	**ETF crack spread**	**Crude oil spot**	**Crack spread futures**	**ETF crack spread**
Mean	4.3077	2.5145	4.3974	0.0004	0.0001	0.0003
Median	4.2856	2.4348	4.3502	0.0013	0.0024	0.0005
Std. Dev.	0.2892	0.4820	0.0976	0.0178	0.0862	0.0119
Skewness	-0.0163	0.2501	0.6531	-0.3442	-0.2550	-0.7277
Kurtosis	2.3900	2.6487	1.9142	4.1110	9.8810	5.1606
JB test	10.3553	10.3677	80.0621	47.4000	1321.1280	187.5280
(p-value)	(0.0000)	(0.0000)	(0.0000)	(0.0000)	(0.0000)	(0.0000)

Note: The JB (Jarque-Bera) test is a test of whether the series are derived from a normal distribution. The p-value of zero indicates that the null hypothesis "the distribution is normal" is rejected.

Table 2. Unit root tests

	Variable (X) and its first difference (ΔX)	ADF	KPSS
log (crude oil spot)	X	-1.7570	2.6400**
	ΔX	-25.2330**	0.1030
log (crack spread futures)	X	-3.6630*	4.8000**
	ΔX	-28.3740**	0.0370
log (ETF crack spread)	X	-2.2140	3.5100**
	ΔX	-20.6640**	0.0490

Note: The null hypothesis of the ADF tests is the non-stationarity of the series considered, while the null hypothesis of the KPSS tests is the stationarity of the series considered. * and ** imply rejection of the null hypothesis at the 5% and 1% levels, respectively.

Table 3. Johansen Test for Cointegration

	Maximum rank	Trace statistic	5% critical value
crude oil spot and crack spread futures	0	19.7725	15.4100
	1	2.1320	3.7600
crude oil spot and ETF crack spread	0	25.8011	15.4100
	1	1.9651	3.7600

Note: The null hypothesis of the Johansen test is that there is no lesser cointegration equation than the maximum rank level. The cointegrating vector of oil spot and crack spread is $\log(s) - 1.073 \log(cs) - 1.615 = 0$, and the cointegrating vector of oil and ETF is $\log(oil) - 1.756(ETF) + 3.225 = 0$.

Table 4. Wald Test-Granger Causality

Null hypothesis	Whole sample	Period 1	Period 2	Period 3
Δs does not Granger cause Δcs	4.4691*	6.8845**	5.5237*	2.5905
Δcs does not Granger cause Δs	0.8674	1.7873	0.7612	8.6193**
Δs does not Granger cause ΔETF				0.0303
ΔETF does not Granger cause Δs				178.91**

Note: The table reports Wald test statistics. * and ** denote rejection of the null hypothesis at the 5% and 1% levels, respectively.

spread futures prices and returns appear to be relatively more volatile than the ORB and ETF crack spread prices and returns over the period analyzed.

The unit root behavior of the log price and log returns series is then investigated using the Augmented Dickey-Fuller (ADF) and the Kwiatknowski-Phillips-Schmidt-Shin (KPSS) tests. Table 2 shows the unit root test results. The ADF tests show that all of the log prices except the log price of crack spread futures have a unit root, but first-differencing leads to stationarity. Given the observed dynamics of the price and return data, the ADF regressions are run with a trend and a constant for the log price series and with a constant for the return series. The KPSS tests suggest that the log price series are non-stationary, whereas the return series are stationary. In summary, although there is a dispute regarding the stationarity of the crack spread futures, the logarithms of the crude oil and ETF crack spread prices are integrated of order one, I(1). We therefore employ the Johansen's cointegration technique (Johansen, 1988; Johansen, 1991) to test whether the crude oil spot price and its possible predictors (the prices of crack spread futures and the ETF crack spread) are cointegrated. The results are shown in Table 3. The lag length selection is based on the Akaike Information Criterion (AIC), Schwarz Bayesian Information Criterion (SIC) and Hannan-Quinn Information Criterion (HQC). For each pair, the null hypothesis of no cointegrated relationship is rejected, whereas the null hypothesis of having at most one cointegrated relationship cannot be rejected. This result implies that one cointegrating vector exists for each pair; thus, the long-run relationship should be considered when modeling the return dynamics. Therefore, an error correction model (ECM) would be appropriate to model and forecast the dynamic of crude oil prices.

5.1 Structural breaks and causality test

From the results of the ZA test, we identify two structural breaks: one on September 2, 2008 and the other on April 29, 2009. Those dates are consistent with the period of the 2008 financial crisis. In September 2008, Lehman Brothers submitted a bankruptcy petition, and Merrill Lynch was sold to the Bank of America. Additionally, during that month, the global stock markets, including the Dow Jones Industrial Average, the FTSE of England, the CAC40 of France, the Dax30 of Germany, and the Hang Seng of Hong Kong, dropped precipitously. Likewise, the price of oil decreased significantly to 30.28 dollars per barrel, its lowest level since the beginning of the 2008 financial crisis. After April 2009, the global oil market recovered from the price collapse resulting from the financial crisis. Because no further structural breaks are detected, the entire sample period was divided into three sub-periods: sub-period 1 (October 2005 to September 2008), sub-period 2 (October 2008 to April 2009), and sub-period 3 (May 2009 to December 2011). These divisions are denoted as the pre-crisis, crisis, and post-crisis periods.

Based on the detected structural breaks, we conduct a Granger-causality/ block exogeneity Wald test for the OPEC crude oil spot market and the crack spread futures market on the entire sample period and the three sub-sample periods. Because the ETF crack spread data could only be obtained beginning in January

2009, the causality test between the oil spot and ETF crack spread markets is only applied for the post-crisis period. Table 4 reports the Wald test statistics. For the whole sample, we find that the crack spread futures market has no significant impact on the crude oil market, but an impact of the oil spot market on the crack spread futures market is observed. Similar results are obtained for the pre-crisis and crisis periods. For the post-crisis period, however, the dynamic between the two markets is reversed; instead, a unidirectional relationship from the crack spread futures market to the crude oil spot market is detected. This result is consistent with that of Murat and Tokat (2009), who study the relationship between WTI crude oil and the 3:2:1 crack spread futures markets. For the relationship between crude oil spot prices and ETF crack spread prices, the block exogeneity test indicates a strong unidirectional relationship from the ETF crack spread market to the OPEC crude oil market. In summary, in the post-crisis period, the price changes in the crack spread futures and ETF crack spread markets led to future OPEC crude oil spot price changes. This result implies that, for the post-crisis period, the crack spread futures and the ETF crack spread are useful for forecasting the movements of the OPEC crude oil spot prices.

5.2 Estimation of the ECM and MGARCH models

The estimation results from the four alternative error correction models are provided in Table 5. The first three models correspond to the relationship between the crude oil spot and crack spread futures markets during (i) the entire sample period, (ii) the pre-crisis and crisis periods (given the Granger-causality results, these two periods are combined), and (iii) the post-crisis period. The last model corresponds to the relationship between the crude oil spot and ETF crack spread markets during the post-crisis period. The estimated coefficients on the error correction terms (i.e., ECT_{t-1}) of the crack spread futures and ETF crack spread returns are all significant. This result confirms that all of the markets adjust to their long-run equilibrium. The lagged returns of the crack spread futures and ETF crack spread are significant only in the post-crisis period. This result implies that, after the crisis, the current OPEC crude oil return did respond to the returns of those variables in the previous period. The estimation results are consistent with the Granger-causality test results discussed in the previous section and hence confirm that the information provided by the two crack spread derivatives are useful in explaining OPEC crude oil price movements.

To compare and discuss the forecasting performance of the crack spread futures and ETF crack spread, we only focus on the post-crisis data. Taking into account the possibility of heteroskedasticity in the residuals of the estimated error correction models, the Breusch-Pagan (BP) and White tests are used to test for the presence of heteroskedastic disturbances. The results of both tests confirm that the null hypothesis of homoscedasticity is rejected at the 5% significance level for all residuals from the estimated error correction models. Therefore, the multivariate GARCH-type models are applied to account for the time-varying variance characteristic in the data.

The estimation results from the CCC and DCC MGARCH models are provided in Table 6. The sum of the coefficients of *arch(1)* and *garch(1)* are close to 1, implying that shocks cause a high persistence in the volatility. For both the ECM-MGARCH 1 (CCC and DCC models for oil spot and crack spread futures) and ECM-MGARCH 2 (CCC and DCC models for oil spot and ETF crack spread), the sum in the crack spread equation is higher than in the crude oil spot equation. This result suggests that the shock effect of both the crack spread futures and the ETF crack spread is more persistent than the shock effect of the crude oil spot on those two crack spread derivatives. Moreover, the $\lambda_1 + \lambda_2$ estimates of the DCC ECM-MGARCH 2 model are close to (but less than) 1, meaning that a shock can move the correlation away from its long-run average for a considerable amount of time. Therefore, the DCC MGARCH model may capture the variation in the correlation between the crude oil spot and ETF crack spread markets more effectively than the CCC MGARCH model.

Figure 3 presents the conditional correlation of the CCC MGARCH models (the straight line) and the conditional correlation of the DCC MGARCH models (the time-varying line). The correlation between the oil spot and ETF crack spread markets in the CCC model (0.5990) is relatively higher than that between the oil spot and crack spread futures markets (0.1051).

Table 5. Error correction models

	OPEC crude oil and crack spread futures						OPEC crude oil and ETF crack spread	
	ECM 1 (Whole sample)		ECM 2 (2005:10 - 2009:04)		ECM 3 (2009:05 - 2011:12)		ECM 4 (2009:05 - 2011:12)	
	Δs_{t-1}	Δcs_{t-1}	Δs_{t-1}	Δcs_{t-1}	Δs_{t-1}	Δcs_{t-1}	Δs_{t-1}	ΔETF_{t-1}
ECT_{t-1}	-0.0060	0.0197**	-0.0007	0.0166**	-0.0141*	0.0759**	-0.0233**	0.0044*
Δs_{t-1}	0.2455**	0.2869*	0.2401**	0.3180*	0.2569**	0.2742	0.0241	-0.0038
Δcs_{t-1}	0.0043	-0.0022	-0.0031	0.0138	0.0219**	-0.0220		
ΔETF_{t-1}							0.7450**	-0.0113
constant	0.0003	0.0000	0.0001	0.0000	0.0089	0.0002	0.0001	0.0004

Note: * and ** denote rejection of the null hypothesis that the coefficient is not significant at the 5% and 1% levels, respectively.

Table 6. Multivariate GARCH models

		ECM MGARCH 1 (oil spot and crack spread futures) (2009:05 - 2011:12)		ECM MGARCH 2 (oil spot and ETF crack spread) (2009:05 - 2011:12)	
		Δs_{t-1}	Δcs_{t-1}	Δs_{t-1}	ΔETF_{t-1}
CCC	*arch(1)*	0.1759**	0.0805**	0.0624**	0.0260**
	garch(1)	0.5397**	0.8968**	0.8915**	0.9618**
	constant	0.0000*	0.0001*	0.0000*	0.0000
	ρ	0.1051**		0.5990**	
DCC	*arch(1)*	0.1800**	0.0815**	0.0734**	0.0312**
	garch(1)	0.5923**	0.8952**	0.8743**	0.9624**
	constant	0.0000*	0.0001*	0.0000*	0.0000
	λ_1	0.0490		0.0286*	
		0.7083**		0.9218**	

Note: * and ** denote rejection of the null hypothesis that the coefficient is not significant at the 5% and 1% levels, respectively.

In terms of the DCC model, the conditional correlation between the oil spot and crack spread futures markets is low and sometimes negative, while that between the oil spot and ETF crack spread markets is more than 0.5 most of the time. Because the dynamic correlations change strongly over time in both the ECM-MGARCH 1 and ECM-MGARCH 2 models, the DCC model is more appropriate than the CCC

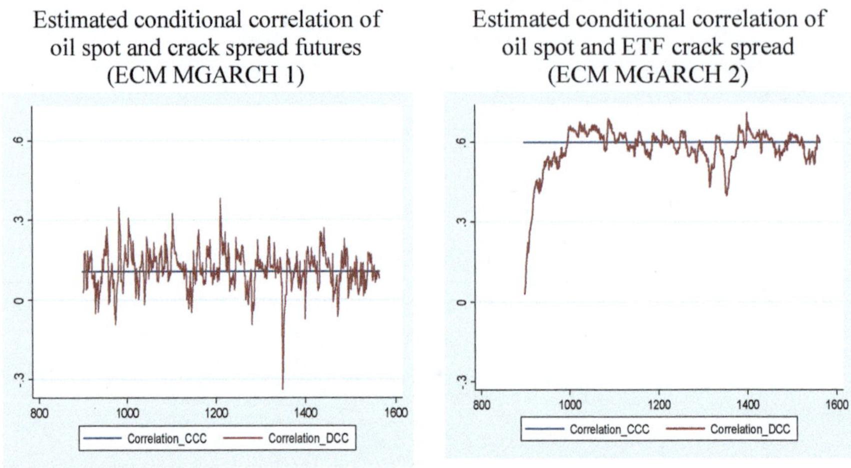

Figure 3. Comparison of unconditional correlations and estimated conditional correlations

model, which assumes constant correlation. Accordingly, only the DCC MGARCH model is used in the forecasting exercise.

5.3 Forecasting performance

The forecasting results are reported in Table 7. For the out-of-sample forecasts, the data are divided into two periods: the first period is from May 2009 to September 2011, and the second period is from October 2011 to December 2011. Based on the ECM and ECM MGARCH models, the forecasting performance of the crack spread futures and the crack spread ETF is evaluated. The RWM is used as a benchmark for evaluating the different forecasting models. We first discuss the forecasting results from the ECMs and then those from the ECM MGARCH models.

Based on the $MAE(I)$ and $RMSE(I)$, the ECMs for crack spread futures and the ETF crack spread outperform the RWM both in-sample and out-of-sample. This result is consistent with that of Murat and Tokat (2009), who show that the ECM for crack spread futures outperforms the RWM in predicting WTI crude oil price movements. Moreover, we find that the ETF crack spread is a better predictor of OPEC crude oil price movements than the crack spread futures both in-sample and out-of-sample. The result of the DM test indicates that these results are significant at the 5% level.

Based on the $MAE(II)$ and $RMSE(II)$, the ECM-MGARCH model for the ETF crack spread shows better in-sample forecasting performance than the model for crack spread futures and the RWM. However, for out-of-sample, it is difficult to derive consistent results between the two instruments. The $MAE(II)$ suggests that the ETF crack spread is a better predictor than the crack spread futures, whereas the $RMSE(II)$ suggests otherwise. Nevertheless, both ECM-MGARCH models outperform the RWM both in-sample and out-of-sample. Overall, the forecasting performance of both the ECM and ECM-MGARCH models confirms that information in both the crack spread futures and the ETF crack spread markets can be used to predict oil price movements. In addition, on average, the ETF crack spread seems to be a better predictor than the

Table 7. Forecasting performance

		In-sample			Out-of-sample		
		CS	ETF	RWM	CS	ETF	RWM
ECM	MAE(I)	0.011023	0.009897	0.011183	0.008965	0.007734	0.009264
	RMSE(I)	0.014365	0.012767	0.014525	0.010914	0.009943	0.011206
ECM MGARCH	MAE(II)	0.781295	0.762333	0.769217	0.684738	0.649659	0.820236
	RMSE(II)	0.999029	0.980128	0.999177	0.836930	0.846540	0.992240

Note: The $MAE(II)$ and $RMSE(II)$ of the RWM are derived by dividing the residual by the time-invariant variance.

crack spread futures. This result is as expected given that the correlation between the oil spot and ETF crack spread markets is relatively higher than that between the oil spot and crack spread futures markets (see Figure 3). A possible explanation for this result may be the institutional differences (such as the magnitude of transaction costs and trading systems) between the futures and ETF markets. Specifically, given that the ETF trading system is accessible to anyone, the ETF market attracts a greater variety of investors (not only oil refiners) and is thus more likely to incorporate new information regarding crude oil spot prices faster than the futures markets, in which most transactions are completed by refinery companies or institutional investors.

6. Conclusion

A number of studies have investigated the dynamics of crude oil spot prices. However, there is lack of research on modeling and forecasting the movements of OPEC Reference Basket (ORB) prices. Accordingly, this study focuses on the dynamics of the OPEC crude oil prices. In response to the emerging consensus that crude oil and refined product (as well as crack spread) prices are cointegrated, we examine the usefulness of the two crack spread derivatives products (namely, crack spread futures and the ETF crack spread) for modeling and forecasting the daily OPEC crude oil spot prices. Specifically, using the Error Correction Model (ECM) and the Multivariate GARCH (MGARCH) model, we explore the long-run relationship between the OPEC crude oil spot market and the two crack spread derivatives markets: the crack spread futures and ETF crack spread markets. We also evaluate the forecasting performance of the two crack spread derivatives with that of the conventional Random Walk Model (RWM).

Based on the two detected structural breaks, we apply a Granger-causality test for the OPEC crude oil spot market and the crack spread futures market on the entire sample period and the three sub-sample periods: the pre-crisis, crisis, and post-crisis periods. A change in the lead-lag relationship between the oil spot and crack spread futures markets is observed over the sub-sample periods. In particular, a unidirectional relationship from the crude oil spot market to crack spread futures is detected for the pre-crisis and crisis periods; however, the relationship between the two markets is reversed in the post-crisis period. The change in this causal relationship may be explained by the increasing need of the oil-related financial market for oil price hedging and investments. Regarding the relationship between the crude oil spot and ETF crack spread markets, the Granger-causality test indicates a strong unidirectional relationship from the ETF crack spread market to the OPEC crude oil market. The results therefore suggest that, in the post-crisis period, both crack spread derivatives may be good predictors of OPEC oil price movements.

In terms of the forecasting performance, we find that the forecasting models (the ECM and ECM-MGARCH models) based on crack spread futures and the ETF crack spread outperform the RWM both in-sample and out-of-sample. Thus, the results confirm that there is valuable information in both the crack spread futures and the ETF crack spread markets. In addition, on average, the ETF crack spread is a better predictor of OPEC crude oil price movements than the crack spread futures both in-sample and out-of-sample. This result suggests that the ETF crack spread market contributes more to the forecasting models than the crack spread futures market.

Our findings provide the following practical implications for policymakers and investors. First, the results suggest that shocks in refined product futures and ETF markets could easily spread to the crude oil spot market, which could impact oil production decisions. Policymakers should therefore design policies to prevent extreme fluctuations in the prices of derivative products caused by speculators. Second, our results suggest that investors could (partly) predict crude oil spot price movements using information flows from the crack spread futures and ETF crack spread markets. In addition, the ETF crack spread price is a better predictor in that the ETF market incorporates new information regarding crude oil spot prices faster than the futures market. Hence, our findings are useful for institutional and individual investors who are interested in understanding and forecasting OPEC crude oil dynamics.

However, our results are not without limitations. First, in comparing the forecasting performance of crack spread futures and the ETF crack spread, only the post-crisis data (the data from May 2009 to December 2011) are used. However, the data used in the forecasting models correspond to the launch of oil and refined product ETFs in approximately 2008 and the change in the lead-lag relationship between crude oil and crack spread futures prices in April 2009. Further study using longer periods of ETF data would be helpful in understanding the relationship between the crude oil spot and crack spread ETF markets. Second, only the 2:1:1 crack spread is evaluated in this study. Other multi-product crack spread variants may also be useful in explaining oil price movements. Finally, our analysis only focuses on forecasting OPEC crude oil prices. The approach can be easily adapted to forecasting other benchmarks of crude oil prices, including WTI (which is considered by Murat and Tokat (2009)), Brent and Dubai. Further research on this subject could lead to improved price forecasts and risk management in oil and refined product markets.

References

Asche, F., Gjolberg, O., & Völker, T. (2003). Price relationships in the petroleum market: an analysis of crude oil and refined product prices. *Energy Economics,* 25 (3), 289-301.

Bollerslev, T., Engle, R. F., & Wooldridge, J. M. (1988). A capital asset pricing model with time-varying covariances. *Journal of Political Economy,* 96 (1), 116-131.

Chinn, M. D., & Coibion, O. (2014). The predictive content of commodity futures. *Journal of Futures Markets,* 34 (7), 607-636.

Diebold, F. X., & Mariano, R. S. (1995). Comparing predictive accuracy. *Journal of Business and Economic Statistics,* 13 (3), 253-265.

Edwards, F. R, & Ma, C. (1992). Futures and options. New York, NY: McGraw-Hill.

Engle, R. F. (2002). Dynamic conditional correlation: A Simple Class of Multivariate Generalized Autoregressive Conditional Heteroskedasticity Models. *Journal of Business and Economic Statistics,* 20 (3), 339-350.

Engle, R. F., & Granger, C. W. J. (1987). Co-integration and error correction: representation, estimation, and testing. *Econometrica,* 55 (2), 251-276.

Gjolberg, O., & Johnsen, T. (1999). Risk management in the oil industry: can information on long-run equilibrium prices be utilized? *Energy Economics,* 21 (6), 517-527.

Haigh, M. S., & Holt, M. T. (2002). Crack spread hedging: accounting for time-varying volatility spillovers in the energy futures market. *Journal of Applied Econometrics,* 17 (3), 269-289.

Heinkel, R., Howe, M., & Hughes, J. S. (1990). Commodity convenience yields as an option profit. *Journal of Futures Markets,* 10 (5), 519-533.

Johansen, S. (1988). Statistical analysis of cointegration vectors. *Journal of Economic Dynamics and Control,* 12 (2-3), 231-234.

Johansen, S. (1991). Estimation and hypothesis testing of cointegration vectors in Gaussian Vector Autoregressive Models. *Econometrica,* 59 (6), 1551-1580.

Kaldor, N. (1939). Speculation and economic stability. *Review of Economic Studies,* 7 (1), 1-27.

Kocagil, A. E. (2004). Optionality and daily dynamics of convenience yield behavior: an empirical analysis. *The Journal of Financial Research*, 27 (1), 143-158.

Kroner, K. F., & Sultan, J. (1993). Time-varying distributions and dynamic hedging with foreign currency futures. *Journal of Financial and Quantitative Analysis,* 28 (4), 535-551.

Lanza, A., Manera, M., & Giovannini, M. (2005). Modeling and forecasting co-integrated relationships among heavy oil and product prices. *Energy Economics,* 27 (6), 831-848.

Lean, H. H., McAleer, M., & Wong, W. K. (2010). Market efficiency of oil spot and futures: a mean-variance and stochastic dominance approach. *Energy Economics*, 32 (5), 979-986.

Ma, C. (1989). Forecasting efficiency of energy futures prices. *Journal of Futures Markets*, 9 (5), 393-419.

Murat, A., & Tokat, E. (2009). Forecasting oil price movements with crack spread futures. *Energy Economics,* 31 (1), 85-90.

Serletis, A. (1994). A co-integration analysis of petroleum futures prices. *Energy Economics,* 16 (2), 93-97.

U.S. Energy Information Administration. (2014, May 6). What drives crude oil prices? Retrieved from http://www.eia.gov/finance/markets/supply-opec.cfm

Verleger, P. K. (1982). The determinants of official OPEC crude oil prices. *Review of Economics and Statistics*, 64 (2), 177-183.

Verleger, P. K. (2011). The margin, currency, and the price of oil. *Business Economics*, 46 (2), 71-82.

Zivot, E., & Andrews, D. W. K. (1992). Further evidence on the great crash, the oil-price shock, and the unit-root hypothesis. *Journal of Business and Economic Statistics,* 10 (3), 251-270.

Acknowledgements

We sincerely thank two anonymous referees for constructive comments and suggestions that improved the contributions and presentation of the paper.

2

Comparing dividend puzzle solutions by Polish, Canadian, Norwegian and American executives

Agata Sierpińska-Sawicz[1]

ABSTRACT This study compares firms' dividend policy antecedents in four countries. The author surveys managers of 230 companies listed on the Warsaw Stock Exchange that paid dividends over the 2001-12 period and compares the findings to survey reports from the USA, Canada, and Norway. The main antecedents of dividend policy in these countries are the level of current earnings, their stability over time, the level of expected earnings and the pattern of past dividends. The last factor is of little importance for Polish managers, as the history of dividend payouts in Polish-listed companies is brief. The establishment of factors that shape the dividend policy in public companies has crucial importance in global financial markets. Investors make cash transfers to markets that ensure a high return on invested capital. Orders from foreign investors generate almost 50% of the turnover on the Warsaw Stock Exchange. Therefore, in their decisions on the division of earnings, Polish companies should be guided by similar considerations as those displayed by companies in developed economies that seek to attract foreign investors. The study expands on the existing survey research on dividends and provides new evidence from managers of companies in Poland.

KEY WORDS: dividend, survey, dividend policy, dividend antecedents, dividend determinants

---

[1]Poznan University of Economics, Poland

Introduction

Dividend policy plays a key role in the distribution of listed companies' net profits, but despite the existence of numerous studies, Brealey, Myers, Allen and Mohanty (2011) list dividends as one of the ten unresolved problems in contemporary corporate finance. The problem of decision-making with regard to dividend payments, described in the literature as the "dividend puzzle" (Black, 1976; Baker, Powell, & Veit, 2002), emphasizes the role of three forces that influence dividend policy: managers, shareholders, and potential investors. Baker, Singleton and Veit (2011) assume that a major reason for this ongoing debate is the heavy reliance on economic modeling approaches and the lack of an in-depth understanding of how investors and managers behave and perceive dividends. Dividend policy continues to attract attention due to its linkage with corporate financing and investing decisions and its impact on shareholder wealth (Baker & Jabbouri, 2016).

The Polish capital market is a unique case in the study of corporate dividends. Since the start of the reg-

Correspondence concerning this article should be addressed to: **Agata Sierpińska-Sawicz,** Poznan University of Economics, Department of Controlling, Financial Analysis and Valuation, al. Niepodleglosci 10, 61-875 Poznań, Poland, E-mail: agata.sierpinska-sawicz@ue.poznan.pl

ulated stock exchange market, the State Treasury has privatized large factories by placing them on the stock exchange, the proceeds from which served to replenish the state budget. However, the Treasury continues to be the majority shareholder in strategic companies in the fuels, energy and mining sectors. Faced with a budget deficit, the Treasury expects to receive dividends from the companies in which it has a stake. Hence, these companies are the main dividend payers in the Polish market (Sierpińska-Sawicz, 2014).

In studying dividend policy, researchers typically rely on two main approaches: managerial surveys and statistical analyses of published financial data. Survey research complements research based on secondary data and provides additional insights into why firms make certain dividend policy decisions (Baker & Weigand, 2015). Data on Polish companies listed on the regulated market are distorted by high inflation and interest rates, especially in the early years of privatization. Therefore, these data are difficult to apply in comparisons with long-term data from highly developed markets. In addition, compared with exchanges in mature economies, the Warsaw Stock Exchange (WSE) is in its early stages of development. Thus, the study presented in this paper relies on the questionnaire method. To provide further insight into how dividends are perceived from a managerial perspective in Poland, the present study surveys managers of dividend-paying firms listed on the WSE.

This study's analysis of the existing literature justifies the proposal of the following hypotheses. H1: The key antecedents of dividend policy in Poland relate to the level of the company's earnings, similar to the impact of earnings in the USA, Canada, and Norway. H2: The antecedents of dividend policy in Poland do not fundamentally differ from those in the USA, Canada, and Norway. Testing these hypotheses is important for the WSE. Almost 50% of the turnover on the WSE stems from orders by foreign investors. Therefore, in their decisions on the division of earnings, Polish companies should be guided by similar considerations as those displayed by companies in developed economies that seek to attract foreign investors.

This research may be most comprehensive study that analyzes Polish managers' assessment of dividends. Subsequently, the outcomes are compared with survey research conducted in the USA, Canada and Norway. The paper contributes to the dividend literature by expanding on the existing survey research on dividends and by providing new evidence from managers of companies in Poland.

Literature review

Lintner (1956) is the first to initiate manager surveys applied to dividend policy studies. His seminal research on US executives reports that the basic premises for dividend payments are the pattern of past dividends and the current level of earnings. Baker and Powell (2000) conduct surveys of CFOs of listed companies on the New York Stock Exchange (NYSE) from three industrial sectors: manufacturing, wholesale/retail groups and utilities. Their findings show that the most important factors influencing dividend payouts are the expected level of future earnings, the pattern of past dividends, the availability of cash and the desire to maintain or increase the share price. The same factors influence managers' dividend decisions for companies listed on the NASDAQ (Baker, Veit, & Powell, 2001).

Baker, Saadi, Dutta, and Gandhi (2007) analyze managers' perceptions of dividends on the Toronto Stock Exchange (TSX). Their findings show that in Canada, the most important factors are the level of current and future earnings, their stability over time and the pattern of past dividends. This tendency holds among financial versus non-financial managers with reference to the four most important antecedents; however, there is an industry effect if the entire ranking is considered (Baker, Saadi, & Dutta, 2008). Lintner (1956) reports that an industry effect may influence firms' corporate dividend policy and investor perceptions of dividends for firms in different industries. For example, firms operating in saturated and mature industries have a higher propensity to pay dividends than do firms in high-growth industries. Based on research in the USA, Canada, the UK, Germany, France and Japan, Denis and Osobov (2008), conclude that the propensity to pay dividends is connected to firms' size, growth opportunities and profitability and is higher among larger, more profitable firms.

Baker, Mukherjee, and Paskelian (2006) explore the perceptions of dividends among Norwegian managers. On the Oslo Stock Exchange (OSE), the most important antecedents other than those connected to earnings include the current degree of financial leverage and liquidity constraints. The pattern of past dividends plays a minor role compared to Anglo-Saxon countries. Kowalewski, Stetsyuk, and Talavera (2007) also do not find support for a persistent pattern of dividend payouts over time for companies listed on the Warsaw Stock Exchange. The authors attribute these outcomes to the underdevelopment of the capital market in Poland. The number of listed companies is relatively small, and most firms have a very short history as a listed public company. Consequently, companies may not care about maintaining stable dividend payout ratios over time and might use other techniques to compete for investors. Nevertheless, consistent with the corporate finance literature, Kowalewski et al. (2007) find that in Poland, larger companies and more profitable firms that do not have good alternative investment opportunities pay more dividends. Also noteworthy is the lower information efficiency and higher volatility of Poland's capital market in comparison to developed markets.

Researchers seem to pay little attention to variables relating to the current state of the economy. In his literature review, Kowerski (2010) states that one of the few exceptions is the study by Marcus and Martin Jacob, which shows the positive global influence of the GDP growth rate on dividend decisions. Kowerski also reports a significant influence of the macroeconomic situation on dividend decisions in Poland. His study shows that in Polish public companies, the personal economic sentiment of managers plays an important role. Management boards' dividend decisions are driven by managers' own appraisal of the current economic situation and not merely by the macroeconomic situation in the previous year.

Research design and methodology

Sample and survey

The research into the antecedents of dividend policy was conducted among a group of companies listed on the regulated market of the WSE that paid out dividends in the period from 2000-2012. The author assumed that companies that had not paid out dividends for over a decade would not be able to earnestly determine the factors that influence dividend policy.

Using the WSE Fact Books for the years 2001-2013, the author generated a list of 271 companies that had paid a dividend at least once during the research time frame. In early 2012, among the selected 271 dividend payers that had declared a dividend during the study period, 39 were no longer listed and 2 had merged with other companies. In the middle of 2012, the survey was therefore sent to 230 companies. The author attached a letter of intent in which the companies received assurances about the confidentiality of the data and a commitment to use the data only for inferences.

The survey was modelled on the questionnaires designed by Baker et al. (2007), with the questions and statements adapted to the Polish reality, and the survey instruments **were extended** to missing factors that appear in other studies for comparison purposes.

The survey contains 3 sections. The first section asks respondents to indicate the importance of 26 factors (F1-F26) in determining their firm's dividend policy. The author uses a five-point equal-interval importance scale where 0=none, 1=low, 2=moderate, 3=high, and 4=very high. The second section contains 7 questions about the background of the respondents and their firms. The third section of the survey asks the respondents to provide their opinion on 37 closed-end statements within 6 areas involving their firms' dividend policy and their explanations for paying cash dividends. The third section is not included in this study.

The first part of the study was conducted in electronic form. The author sent a link to a website from which the survey could be downloaded. The respondents were asked to select the name of their company from an enclosed list. Thus, the respondents had the opportunity to view the list of companies participating in the study. Foreign companies received an English-language version of the questionnaire in PDF format via e-mail.

Two weeks after the questionnaires were dispatched, the companies were sent a reminder requesting completion. As a result of these repeated attempts to obtain responses, the author received 36 completed surveys from listed companies. Each company returned only one survey, of which four surveys were filled out entirely except for the name of the company, but by using the stored IP addresses, they were able to be accurately identified. The percentage of research sample responses (16%) obtained in the first stage of the research was insufficient to make generalizations and formulate propositions designed to verify the initial hypotheses.

Table 1. Structure of the respondents by position

Category of response	No. of responses	Structure, %
Chairperson	18	21.4
CFO	26	31.0
Another board member	8	9.5
Supervisory Board of Audit Committee member	5	6.0
Investor Relations Department	27	32.1
Total	84	100.0

Notes: Adapted from author's own calculations based on the WSE survey results.

In the second stage of the study, the author sent out a paper version of the survey and contacted the companies by telephone to ask them to complete the survey. In addition, the data collection procedure included an offer to send the companies the aggregate survey results so the companies could compare their own dividend policy with the results for the rest of the industry. As a result, over a three-month span, an additional 48 surveys were received, which resulted in a total of 84 complete questionnaires and a total response rate of 36.6%. In line with the pertinent literature, this sample is deemed sufficient to verify the research hypotheses. For example, some studies feature the following response return rates: 32.9% for the NYSE (Baker, Powell, 2000), 29.8% for the NASDAQ (Baker et al., 2001), 27.3% for the Oslo Stock Exchange (OSE) (Baker et al., 2005) and 35.4% for the TSX (Baker et al., 2007).

Considering the characteristics of the respondents in terms of value, the market capitalization of the domestic respondents (82 out of 84 responses) accounts for 71% of the total capitalization of domestic companies listed on the WSE. With foreign companies included (2 out of 84 responses), respondents' capitalization amounts to nearly 50% of the WSE's total market capitalization at the end of 2012 (WSE data). Hence, nearly all the major dividend payers from the study period returned completed surveys. These are large companies with established market positions. A comparison of the antecedents of the dividend policy pursued by the WSE-listed companies with those of companies listed on the OSE, NYSE, NASDAQ and TSX is justified because, as Denis and Osobov (2008) argue, the propensity to pay dividends is higher among larger, more profitable companies whose retained earnings account for a large part of the value of their property. Similar reasoning appears in earlier comparative studies (Baker et al., 2007).

Table 1 presents the structure of the respondents by their position in the firms. The data analysis indicates that 68% of the respondents are directly involved in dividend policymaking, including 63% representing companies' management. While not directly involved in dividend decision-making, over 32% of the respondents must be knowledgeable about their companies' dividend policy in order to communicate with shareholders.

Statistical tests

To test the first hypothesis, the author calculated the arithmetic mean ($\overline{x}$) and standard deviation (s_d) of each of the 26 factors influencing the companies' dividend policy. The author used a t-test for the null hypothesis that the mean response for each of the 26 factors influencing dividend policy equals 0 (no importance). For each factor, the author verified the null hypothesis by testing for the absence of significant differences between the arithmetic mean and the value of 2.0 (average weight of the 5-point scale). This comparison indicates whether the factor is relatively less or more important than the validity referred to as "average".

A chi-square test (for a single sample) was used to estimate whether there is a difference between the observed and anticipated numbers of replies included in each category of validity. To avoid problems caused by too few observed numbers, the 5-point validity scale was converted into a 3-point scale covering the "none/low", "medium" and "high/very high" categories. Particularly noteworthy is the fact that, while almost every factor was assigned very high importance by at least one respondent, at least one of the respondents also considered every factor to have no importance. These findings suggest that the weight that the respondents attributed to each factor influencing their firms' dividend policy differed from a company to company. This outcome can be confirmed by the results of the t-test, which show that the majority of the arithmetic mean values are statistically significantly different from the value of 2.0 (at $p = 0.05$ - 21 factors, at $p = 0.01$ - 20 factors). Thus, the chi-square test analysis confirms the conclusions from the t-test analysis for almost all of the factors. The results of the chi-square test indicate that the numbers of "high/very high" and "none/low" responses are significantly different from the number of "average" responses.

In order to test the second hypothesis to determine whether the ordering of the factors by Polish, Norwegian, Canadian and American managers differs significantly, Spearman's rank correlation coefficients were computed for each separate pair of rankings. The significance of the correlation coefficient was checked using a t-test to verify the hypothesis of the independence of the orderings.

To facilitate comparison of the results, the Polish ranking is purged of some factors that are not present in other research: F23, F24, F25 and F26 for the WSE-OSE (Norway) comparison, 7 factors (F6, F7, F14, F22, F24, F25 and F26) for the WSE-NYSE (US) comparison, 4 factors (F14, F24, F25 and F26) for the WSE-NASDAQ (US) comparison and 4 factors (F14, F24, F25 and F26) for the WSE-TSX (Canada) comparison. For Polish companies and American firms listed on the NYSE, the author merged the level of current (F3) and expected future (F4) earnings into one factor, similar to the study of NYSE managers. After re-ordering the remaining factors of own study for each pair, the author calculated the correlation coefficients in four stages. The resulting correlation coefficients are as follows: for Polish and Norwegian companies, the correlation coefficient is +0.732 and is statistically significant ($t = 4.809$, $df = 20$ and $p = 0.000$). Next, for companies listed on the WSE and NYSE-listed firms, the correlation coefficient is +0.450 and is statistically significant ($p = 2.125$ with $df = 16$, $p = 0.049$). For Polish companies and firms listed on the NASDAQ, the correlation coefficient is +0.516 and is statistically significant ($p = 2.694$ with $df = 20$ and $p = 0.016$). Finally, the correlation coefficient for the rankings of the factors compiled by the managers of Polish and Canadian companies is +0.707 and is statistically significant ($p = 4.475$ with $df = 20$ and $p = 0.000$). These results refute the hypothesis of the independence of orderings for all pairs. Thus, all the rankings of the factors determining dividend payouts in the compared countries are consistent and move in the same direction, thus implying that comparisons between the rankings can be made directly.

Comparison of the hierarchy of the antecedents of dividend policy in the compared countries – survey results and discussion

Table 2 shows the results of the ranking of the factors affecting firms' dividend policy in Poland and the results of the rankings of the same factors by Canadian, Norwegian and American authors (Baker et al., 2000, 2001, 2006, 2007).

In Poland, the most important factors determining dividend payouts are the level of current earnings (F3), their stability over time (F1) and the level of expected future earnings (F4). The data in Table 2 show that respondents from all of the analyzed markets rank the factors relating to earnings among the top five most important factors influencing firms' dividend policy. Dividends are paid from a company's earnings; therefore, companies' dividend policy must take into account, first and foremost, their financial results. Thus, based on the results of the survey, the first hypothesis (H-1) is confirmed.

The analyses included comparisons of the hierarchy of the antecedents of dividend policy between Poland and the other countries examined in the study. In the Norwegian ranking, the first two factors are the same as in Poland. A difference appears only with regard to the third factor for Poland, namely expected future earnings, which occupies fourth place for Norway.

Table 2. Ranking of factors influencing dividend policy in selected countries

Factor		Mean of the sample ($\bar{x}$)	Rank				
			Poland WSE	Norway OSE	USA NYSE	USA NASDAQ	Canada TSX
F3	Level of current earnings	3.27	1	1	1	3	4
F1	Stability of earnings	3.11	2	2	5	2	2
F4	Level of expected future earnings	2.98	3	4,5	1*	4	1
F21	Availability of effective investment incentives	2.80	4	8,5	6	15	11
F11	Liquidity constraints, such as the availability of cash	2.63	5	4,5	7	14	5
F7	Availability of alternative sources of capital	2.50	6	10	-	17	15
F6	Current degree of financial leverage	2.49	7,5	3	-	10	8
F10	Projections about the future state of the economy	2.49	7,5	15,5	17	18	17
F8	Expected rate of return on the firm's assets	2.46	9	7	12	11	10
F26	Shareholders' preferences with regard to receiving dividends on a regular basis	2.41	10	-	-	-	-
F13	Desire to pay out, in the long run, a given fraction of earnings	2.40	11	15,5	8	7	6
F9	Desire to maintain a target capital structure	2.33	12	8,5	10	6	13
F5	Concerns about affecting the stock price	2.24	13	14	3	5	7
F20	Financing considerations such as cost of raising funds externally (debt and equity financing)	2.23	14	12	11	19	14
F2	Pattern of past dividends	2.20	15	11	2	1	3
F15	Existing shareholders' needs, such as the desire for current income	2.20	16	21	9	9	9
F25	Shareholder structure (State Treasury, investment funds, companies, individual investors)	1.94	17	-	-	-	-
F18	Concerns that a dividend change may provide a false signal to investors	1.74	18	18	4	8	12
F22	Signaling incentives such as using dividend changes to convey information to the financial markets	1.65	19	13	-	16	16
F19	Legal rules and constraints such as paying dividends that would impair the capital structure	1.61	20	6	15	12	19
F17	Preference for paying dividends instead of making risky investments	1.51	21	20	18	20	21
F16	Contractual constraints, such as dividend restrictions in debt contracts	1.46	22	19	14	21	20
F24	Tax rates on dividends and capital gains	1.36	23	-	-	-	-
F12	Desire to conform to the industry's payout ratio	1.30	24	17	13	13	18
F23	Stockholder characteristics, such as marginal tax rates of company's current shareholders	1.23	25	-	16	22	22
F14	Desire to conform to the dividend payout ratio of the market as a whole	1.12	26	22	-	-	-

Notes: Adapted from author's own calculations based on the WSE survey and Determinants of corporate dividend policy: a survey of NYSE firms, Financial Practice and Education, 10(1), 29-40 by Baker, Powell (2000); The perception of dividends by Canadian managers: new survey evidence, International Journal of Managerial Finance, 3(1), 70-91 by Baker et al. (2001); How Norwegian Managers View Dividend Policy, Global Finance Journal, 17(1), 155-175 by Baker et al. (2005); and The perception of dividends by Canadian managers: new survey evidence, International Journal of Managerial Finance, 3(1), 70-91 by Baker et al. (2007).
*- in the NYSE study, F3 and F1 were merged and became the level of current and expected earnings.

Norwegian managers rank the current level of financial leverage (F6) third, while in Poland, this factor is ranked seventh. Its high ranking in Norway implies that the respondents are aware that their company's dividend policy is affected not only by the amount of funds available for distribution to shareholders but also by the company's capital structure.

In Canada, the three most important factors are the level of expected future earnings (F4), the stability of earnings (F1) and dividend payouts in previous years (F2). In Poland, the last factor was considered to be of average importance (insignificant difference between the arithmetic mean and the value of 2.0) and was ranked fifteenth place, compared to eleventh for the OSE. The weight that managers attach to future earnings is rational because this factor is strongly connected with cash flow, which is the source of dividend payouts. On the other hand, Poland's top-ranked factor, the level of current earnings (F3), ranks fourth in Canada, and the availability of efficient investment projects ranks eleventh. These results suggest, therefore, that Canadian managers attach more weight than their Polish counterparts to what happened and what will happen to the company's earnings beyond the current performance. An equally important role is played by past dividend patterns, thus confirming that, just as in the USA, Canadian managers highly value continuity and stability of dividend payouts. The low ranking of possible investments as a determinant of dividend policy, coupled with the high weighting of past dividend patterns, provides evidence that Canadian companies are more inclined to follow a predetermined payout policy than to apply a residual policy.

The same conclusion holds for the US stock exchanges. Past dividend payouts are in fact the most important determinant for NASDAQ managers and the second most important determinant for NYSE managers. The perception of this particular determinant seems to mark one of the most important differences between the Polish and Norwegian rankings and the Canadian and American rankings. A conclusion can be drawn from the above that TSX, NASDAQ and NYSE managers make decisions based on the Lintner model more than their Polish colleagues. One should also note that companies operating in these mature markets developed dividend models in past periods, which indicates that the maturity of the capital market also affects firms' dividend policy.

The next two factors, the availability of effective investment incentives (F21) and liquidity constraints (F11), are ranked fourth and fifth on the WSE, while on the Oslo and NYSE stock exchanges, these factors are among the top ten antecedents, although they are relegated to rankings between tenth and twentieth on the remaining two stock exchanges. Liquidity constraints such as the availability of cash (F11) is the fifth most frequently quoted determinant of dividend policy for Polish, Norwegian and Canadian companies. Managers from these three markets exhibit notable coherence in their attitudes. They are aware that companies pay dividends out of existing cash rather than from earnings derived through accrual accounting, and, therefore, it is cash availability that affects a company's ability to pay cash dividends. NYSE managers rank liquidity constraints (F11) as the seventh (out of 22) most important determinant of dividend payouts. In contrast, the perception of these factors (F21, F11) by managers of NASDAQ-listed companies indicates considerable differences of opinion. Liquidity is ranked only as the fourteenth most important factor out of the total of twenty-two factors, and the availability of effective investment incentives, which the Polish market sees as the fourth most important factor, is ranked fifteenth. It is also worth noting evidence of differences of opinion with respect to the last issue among managers of TSX-listed companies, where possible investment incentives are ranked only eleventh.

The availability of alternative sources of capital (F7), which ranks sixth in the Polish survey, occupies a lower place in Norway (10th out of 22). F7 is also considered to be a low weight factor in Canada (15th out of 22) and on the NASDAQ, where it is merely seventeenth (out of 22). This result attests to the fact that Polish managers experience greater difficulty in finding sources of financing than their colleagues in the countries used for comparison, as Polish companies have limited access to the debt market. The Catalyst bond market is still underdeveloped. In the debt structure, bonds account for merely 12% of **the total** debt, while 88% of the debt comes from loans, which are difficult to obtain in an economic downturn. In addition, Poland's interest rates have been much higher than those in other EU countries for the last dozen years. On average, bonds account for 20% of the total corporate debt in the EU, compared to 80% in the US, with loans accounting for only 20% of the total debt (Gałka 2015).

Similarly, predictions of the future health of the economy are treated in Poland as a priority (7th most important out of 26), but less so in Norway (16th out of 22), the USA (NYSE), Canada (17th out of 22) and for NASDAQ-listed firms (18th out of 22). The expected return on assets is of the most importance for Norwegian managers (7th out of 22). In Poland, this determinant ranks ninth, in Canada tenth, eleventh on the NASDAQ and twelfth on the NYSE.

From the point of view of the US markets, the impact of dividends on a company's share price is quite an important factor in firms' dividend policy. Both firms listed on the NYSE and the NASDAQ rank it among the five most important factors. An increase in the company's market value is frequently one of the measures adopted to determine the bonuses of US managers. However, this factor has much less importance for Polish managers, falling outside the top ten factors (13th out of 26), and likewise for Norwegian firms (14th out of 22).

The needs of current shareholders, for example, a desire to acquire current earnings (F15) (9th out of 22), are considered more seriously in the US and Canada than in Poland, where such concerns rank sixteenth. Norwegian managers rank this factor only 21st.

The comparison reveals a difference in managers' approach to the avoidance of false signals to investors by changing the amount of their dividend payouts (F18). NYSE managers rank this factor fourth, that is, as a very important factor in the hierarchy. This result means that the signaling effect, despite affirmation by managers from all four countries of their support for the underlying theory, gains actual recognition only on the New York stock exchange. Respondents from the NASDAQ ranked this factor (F18) eighth and Canadian respondents twelfth. Factor (F18) is afforded the least attention by Polish and Norwegian managers, who rank it eighteenth. In Norway, managers' moderate level of concern about sending a false signal about the condition of the company is probably due to the existence of specific regulations and government control. Norwegian companies experience fewer agency problems than their US counterparts due to a concentrated ownership structure and the large Treasury ownership of listed companies. In Poland, shareholder protections have recently been strengthened with the introduction of class action lawsuits against companies.

Norwegian managers' approach to regulations and legal restrictions on the payment of dividends (e.g., equity depletion) also differs. This factor is ranked sixth in Norway, compared to its much lower ranking by Polish companies (20th out of 26), and its rank of fifteenth on the NYSE, nineteenth on the TSX and twelfth on the NASDAQ. The difference stems from regulatory differences between the countries. As mentioned previously, Norway's centralized government (Baker et al. 2006) has established very strict regulatory standards that exert a strong influence on the business environment in order to afford shareholders broad legal protection.

The least important factors from the perspective of all the surveyed groups are investor characteristics such as marginal tax rates and adjustments to the dividend rate across the market. These factors are ranked at the bottom of all the rankings. Tax issues are therefore not considered significant by the managers.

The calculation of Spearman's rank correlation coefficients (rs) allows a determination of the strength of the links between the Polish hierarchy of antecedents with those identified from research in other countries. The author obtained statistically significant results of rs +0.732 for the comparison between the WSE and the OSE, +0.450 for the comparison between the WSE and the NYSE, +0.516 for the comparison between the WSE and the NASDAQ and +0.707 for the comparison between the WSE and the TSX. These high correlation coefficients generally show that Polish, Norwegian, Canadian and American managers build their rankings of factors affecting firms' dividend policy in much the same way, despite the different characteristics of the companies and the markets in which they operate.

Summary and conclusions

To summarize the discussion of the hierarchy of factors shaping the dividend policy for firms in Poland, the USA, Canada and Norway, one first observes that this hierarchy does not differ significantly. The most important antecedents of dividend policy for companies listed on regulated markets of the countries used for the comparison are the level of current earnings, the stability of earnings and the level of expected future earnings. In addition, on the stock markets of the highly developed economies, the level of dividend payouts from past earnings is at a premium. In Poland, this factor is of secondary importance, as companies have yet to develop a target dividend payout model because their history on the WSE is short. The above findings confirm the first research hypothesis: the most important antecedents of dividend policy involve earnings.

In Poland, Norway and Canada, the availability of cash to pay dividends is an important determinant of the distribution of profit, as it is ranked fifth in the hierarchies. In the US, concerns about the impact of dividends on the share price are ranked fifth, which indicates the importance of shareholder value of the company and the informative function of dividends in that market. In Poland, managers attribute a high level of importance to concerns about the company's growth and ensuring access to the resources needed to finance investment. In the US (NASDAQ), a desire to maintain the target capital structure plays an important role, while on the NYSE, it is the availability of effective investment incentives. Canadian managers, in turn, prize the desire to pay a certain portion of earnings over the long term.

Within the first few most important factors influencing firms' dividend policy in the countries used for comparison, there are not major differences in the hierarchy of importance. The greater the number of factors used, the lower the similarity in the hierarchy of factors. Therefore, the second hypothesis is not fully confirmed. The positions of the remaining antecedents differ in the hierarchies of importance and depend on the market situation and economic conditions in each country.

This article analyzes the factors that drive executives in determining their companies' dividend policy. Areas for further research include the determinants that guide investors when purchasing shares of dividend-paying companies, which would allow a comparison of the determinants of dividend policy from both perspectives – the board's incentives when recommending a dividend level and the number of payouts and the investors who expect income. Private investors and their rationale when purchasing stock should receive particular attention, as they were responsible for 12% of the turnover on the Warsaw Stock Market in 2015 (WSE, 2015b).

References

Baker, H. K., & Powell, G. E. (2000). Determinants of corporate dividend policy: A survey of NYSE firms. *Financial Practice and Education*, 10(1), 29-40.

Baker, H. K., Veit, E. T., & Powell, G. E. (2001). Factors influencing dividend policy decisions of NASDAQ firms. *The Financial Review*, 36(3), 19-39.

Baker, H. K., Powell, G. E., & Veit, E. T. (2002). Revisiting the dividend puzzle: Do all the pieces now fit? *Review of Financial Economics*, 1 (4), 241-261.

Baker, K. H, Mukherjee, T. K., & Paskelian, O. G. (2006). How Norwegian managers view dividend policy. *Global Finance Journal*, 17(1), 155-176.

Baker, K. H., Saadi, S., Dutta, S., & Gandhi, D. (2007). The perception of dividends by Canadian managers: New survey evidence. *International Journal of Managerial Finance*, 3(1), 70-91.

Baker, K. H., Saadi, S., Dutta, S., & Gandhi, D. (2008). How managers of financial versus non-financial firms view dividends: The Canadian evidence. *Global Finance Journal*, 19, 171-186.

Baker, H. K., Singleton, J. C., & Veit, E. T. (2011). *Survey research in corporate finance - bridging the gap between theory and practice*, New York, NY: Oxford University Press.

Baker, K. H, & Weigand, R. (2015). Corporate dividend policy revisited. *Managerial Finance*, 41(2), 126-144

Baker, K. H., & Jabbouri, I. (2016). How Moroccan managers view dividend policy. *Managerial Finance*, 42(3), 270 – 288.

Denis, D. J., & Osobov, I. (2008). Why do firms pay dividends? International evidence on the determinants of dividend policy. *Journal of Financial Economics*, 89(1), 62-82.

Black, F. (1976). The dividend puzzle. *The Journal of Portfolio Management*, Winter, 2(2), 5-8.

Brealey, R. A., Myers, S. C., Allen, F., & Mohanty, P. (2011). Conclusion: What we do and do not know about finance". In R. A. Brealey, S. C. Myers, F. Allen (Eds.), *Principles of Corporate Finance* (10th ed., pp. 866-874). New York, NY: McGraw-Hill/Irwin.

Gałka, T. (2015). *Ewolucja rynku obligacji korporacyjnych w Polsce* [Evolution of corporate bonds market in Poland]. Retrieved from http://www.case-research.eu/sites/default/files/T.Ga%C5%82ka_prezentacja.pdf

Kowalewski, O., Stetsyuk, I., & Talavera, O. (2007). *Corporate governance and dividend policy in Poland* (Discussion Paper No. 702). DIW Berlin, German Institute for Economic Research.

Kowerski, M. (2010). *Wpływ nastrojów gospodarczych przedsiębiorców i konsumentów na decyzje dywidendowe spółek kapitałowych* [The influence of the economic sentiment of enterpreneurs and consumers on corporate dividend decisions], *Barometr Regionalny*, *2*(20), 19-34.

Lintner, J. (1956), Distribution of incomes of corporations among dividends, retained earnings and taxes. *American Economics Review*, 46(2), 97-113.

Sierpińska-Sawicz, A. (2014). Dividend policy of State Treasury Shareholding Companies. *Journal of Economics and Management*, Katowice, 18, 225-241.

Warsaw Stock Exchange (2015a). WSE Fact Books 2002-2013, 2015, Available from www.gpw.pl

Warsaw Stock Exchange (2015b). *Udział inwestorów w obrotach instrumentami finansowymi na GPW* [Investors share in financial instruments trade at WSE], Available from www.gpw.pl/wydarzenia/?ph_tresc_glowna_start=show&ph_tresc_glowna_cmn_id=57483

3

Financial market regulation, country governance, and bank efficiency: Evidence from East Asian countries

Sok-Gee Chan[1], Mohd. Zaini Abd. Karim[2]

ABSTRACT This paper examines the relationship between financial market regulation, country governance and efficiency of commercial banks in East Asian economies during the period 2001-2008 using a two-stage estimation technique. In the first stage, we employ a non-parametric approach—Data Envelopment Analysis (DEA)—to estimate the banks' cost and profit efficiency scores and then Tobit estimation to analyze the impact of financial market regulations and country governance on bank efficiency. The results suggest that commercial banks in East Asia are relatively profit efficient rather than cost efficient. The findings show that countries with more financial freedom and independence are more cost efficient. Moreover, government effectiveness is found to be positively related to bank efficiency. Consistent with economic theory, corruption is negatively related to bank efficiency. Therefore, this study reveals the importance of financial market regulations and country governance as catalysts for efficient banking operations in East Asian economies.

KEY WORDS: bank efficiency; institutional environment; data envelopment analysis; tobit regression; East Asia

---

[1]Department of Finance and Banking, Faculty of Business and Accountancy, Universiti of Malaya, Malaysia
[2]Othman Yeop Abdullah Graduate School of Business, Universiti Utara Malaysia, Malaysia

Introduction

The importance of banks in an economy is undeniable because they serve as the main sources of business financing. An effective and efficient banking system contributes to the effectiveness of monetary policy transmission in developing economies because they rely heavily on bank-based activities due to their underdeveloped capital markets. As a result, the banking system in most developing countries, including East Asian economies, is highly regulated, with the primary objective of establishing a sound and resilient financial system.

According to Mishkin (2000), prudent regulation of the banking industry stems from concerns over issues such as regulation of competition, disclosure requirements, examining and monitoring procedures and restrictions in banking activities, including limitation of asset holdings, capital requirements and separation of banking and other financial activities. Previous studies by Stigler (1971), Johnson, Kaufmann and Shelifer (1997), Besley and Burgess (2004) and Asaftei and Kumbhakar (2008) recognize the importance of government regulations to protect and enhance the

Correspondence concerning this article should be addressed to: **Sok-Gee Chan**, Department of Finance and Banking, Faculty of Business and Accountancy, Universiti of Malaya, 50603 Kuala Lumpur. E-mail: sokgee@um.edu.my

growth of the banking system. Banking regulations aim primarily to reduce banks' exposure to risky assets and thus protect stakeholders from financial runs. Beltratti and Stulz (2009) note that lax regulation could contribute to excessive risk-taking by banks.

Giannone, Lenza and Reichlin (2010) argue that regulation of banking competition is necessary, especially in developing countries because of the increase in the openness of financial markets that could result in higher banking costs. This issue is still open to debate because economic theory presumes that an increase in competition actually fosters efficiency in the banking system as banks tend to find ways of lowering production costs to ensure their long-term survival (Barth, Caprio, & Levine, 2004; Chan & Karim, 2010; Claessens & Laeven, 2004). On the other hand, overly stringent regulation of financial markets might damage banks' performance by preventing them from exploiting economies of scale and scope through a more diversified range of banking products or a larger scale of operations (Barth, Brunmgaugh, & Wilcox, 2000; Barth *et al.*, 2010; Claessens & Klingebiel, 2001). In this context, regulations could lead to an inefficient allocation of resources; in contrast, deregulation enables and encourages banks to take advantage of more efficient production techniques (Evanoff, 1998).

Looking at institutional environments enables us to take into account the quality of a country's governance in affecting the performance of the banking sector. An appropriate legal framework and institutional environment contribute to a country's market development and financial development (Claessens & Laeven, 2004; Demirgüc-Kunt, Laeven, & Levine, 2004). A strong legal framework is crucial for the development of a mature financial system (Beck *et al.*, 2001). Nabi and Suliman (2008) stress the contribution of a legal framework in strengthening banking system, whereas González (2009) argues that a well-functioning market depends on contracts and legal enforceability. Hence, this paper aims to examine the relationship between financial market regulation, institutional environment and efficiency of commercial banks in East Asian economies for the period 2001-2008. In particular, we study the effect of tight banking regulation and countries' governance on bank efficiency.

This paper's contribution to the literature is twofold. First, this is the first study conducted on the Asian region regarding the impact of financial market regulations and institutional environment on bank efficiency. Because the debate about the effects of regulations on banks' performance has been inconclusive to date, this study will further focus on financial market regulations in terms of bank ownership, competition, financial development, banking freedom and monetary policy to determine their effects on both banks' cost and profit efficiency. Second, this paper contributes to the scarce line of literature on the impact of regulation and country governance on bank efficiency.

The rest of the paper is organized as follows. Section 2 provides an overview of financial market regulations and institutional environment in the East Asian region. Section 3 reviews the related literature. Section 4 describes the methodology and data employed in the study. Section 5 presents the results and discusses the findings. Finally, section 6 concludes the paper.

Financial market regulations and country governance in the East Asian region

East Asia—with rapidly growing economies—is one of the most dynamic and important regions in the world. Furthermore, it comprises the second largest economy of China and Japan as the third largest economy in the world. The East Asian financial sector is dominated by commercial banks, which account for up to 80% of the sector. According to many analysts, these banks were considered the heart of the problems leading to the Asian crisis in 1997. Hence, to provide an indication of the competitiveness and openness of this region's banking sector, we look at four specific indicators from the Economic Freedom Network developed by Gwartney, Lawson and Hall (2011), namely, ownership of banks, foreign bank competition, private sector credit and interest rate controls. The index ranges between "0" and "10", with higher ratings assigned to countries with more economic freedom.

Bank ownership is computed based on the percentage of deposits that are privately held by the banks (Gwartney *et al.*, 2011), where a high rating is assigned to countries with large shares of privately held deposits. Table 1 shows that the banking industry in Hong Kong is relatively more competitive than that in the other countries in the region (privately held deposits

Table 1. Indicators of financial market regulation and country governance in East Asian economy, 2001-2008

	Financial Market Regulation				Country Governance			
Country	Ownership of banks	Competition in domestic banking	Interest rate regulations	Credit Market Regulation	Political Stability	Government Effectiveness	Regulatory Quality	Control for corruption
China	1.00	5.15	9.75	6.01	-0.24	0.02	-0.33	-0.49
Hong Kong	10.00	7.91	10.00	9.07	1.00	1.57	1.81	1.58
Japan	6.50	7.52	10.00	8.18	1.09	1.29	1.00	1.18
Korea	6.50	7.90	10.00	8.25	0.36	1.07	0.75	0.44
Taiwan	5.00	6.78	10.00	7.84	0.41	1.10	1.02	0.73

Source: Financial market regulation indicators are obtained from Economic Freedom Network by Gwartney et al. (2011), whereas the country governance indicators are from Kaufmann et al. (2009)

have a rating of 10). The rating indicates that private deposits dominated the deposits from government agencies by 95 to 100%. On the other hand, China is still relatively stringent in its banking operations, with an average bank ownership rating of 1. Privately held deposits only constitute between 10 and 40% of banking assets.

On the other hand, the foreign bank competition index is used to capture the existence of foreign banks in a country's banking industry. This index is calculated based on approved foreign bank applications and foreign banking assets in the country's overall banking sector (Gwartney *et al.*, 2011). Table 1 shows that the index for foreign bank competition on average ranges between 5.15 and 7.91. This finding indicates that the region's economies are still relatively closed to foreign bank participation because foreign bank assets are less than 79%, with license approvals of less than 50% from the overall banking industry. However, the financial markets in East Asia are relatively open because most of the countries exhibit high scores in terms of interest rate regulations. This openness is observed because countries with interest rates determined by market forces, stable monetary policy and positive real deposit and lending rates are assigned higher interest rate regulation ratings (Gwartney *et al.*, 2011). On average, most of the countries, except for China, score an average of 10 in interest rate controls—which means that interest rates are primarily allowed to float in line with market forces with reasonable deposit and lending rate spreads as well as with positive real interest rates, as suggested by Gwartney *et al.* (2011).

Overall, the credit market regulation in East Asia is above average, with an index of between 6.01 and 9.07. Credit market regulation reflects the overall banking industry operation in a country, which includes the country's openness to foreign banking activities, freedom from government control and freedom for interest rates to be determined by market forces. In this case, Hong Kong has an average index of 9.07, which is the highest among all the countries. This high index may be observed because Hong Kong—with its relatively open and well-developed financial market—is the main financial hub in Asia. On the other hand, China's credit market regulation reported an average index of 6.01, which can be attributed to more stringent restrictions in terms of foreign bank participation compared with those instituted in the other countries examined in this study.

The country governance indicators are used to represent the selection, monitoring and replacement process of a government. The indicators also include the effectiveness of government policy implementation and formulation as well as the freedom of the country's citizens in expressing their voices. The governance indicators of Kaufmann, Kray and Mastruzzi (2009) follow a normal distribution, with scores lying between -2.5 and 2.5, where high scores represent favorable outcomes. The four indicators used in measuring a country's governance are political stability and absence of violence; government effectiveness; regulatory quality and control of corruption.

Table 1 shows that China, on average, has a weaker governance than the other countries in the region. Moreover, the index of control of corruption in China is relatively low compared with that of the other countries selected for this study. This situation may result in an inefficient banking and financial market in China because both public and private institutions exercise their power for private gain. In addition, China is rated below average in terms of regulatory quality, with an average of -0.33. This score indicates that the Chinese government is weak in promoting the development of the private sector. On the other hand, Hong Kong has better governance than other countries, which reflects its status as one of the developed countries in the region. Hong Kong's relatively greater financial openness has helped the island become the region's financial center.

Literature review

Studies on environmental factors that affect bank efficiency levels are important for predicting the effects of country variables and regulatory changes on bank performance (Chan & Karim, 2010). Dietsch and Lozano-Vivas (2000) noted that the inclusion of country environmental factors is important in cross-country analyses of bank efficiency. This notion is supported by Beltratti and Stulz (2009), who argued that differences in the regulation of financial institutions are useful in explaining banks' performance, especially during banking crises.

Many economists believe that a free market enhances the efficiency level of firms by allowing for healthy competition (Claessens & Laeven, 2004; Evanoff, 1998). Banks are able to exploit economies of scale and alter their production technology given the country's financial freedom (Evanoff, 1998). Evanoff found that heavy regulation damaged US banks' efficiency level from 1972 to 1987. This finding is supported by Claessens and Klingebiel (2001), who found that greater flexibility in banking operations enabled banks to exploit economies of scale and scope. The authors also found that restrictions in banking activities increased the likelihood that banks would suffer during banking crises. Barth *et al.* (2004) also found that greater regulatory restrictions resulted in a higher probability of banks to suffer during banking crises and that there was a negative relationship between banking restrictions and banking sector development and stability. Similarly, González (2005) found that stricter regulations lead to higher risk-taking incentives by banking institutions, leading to a reduction in charter value and stability of the banking system.

Claessens and Laeven (2004) examined the effects of entry and regulations on banking activities in 50 countries for the period 1994-2001. They found that the entrance of foreign banks and a decrease in restrictions on banking activities resulted in higher competitiveness. The results also suggest that such factors contribute to higher contestability of the banking sectors and eventually help create healthy competition. Barth *et al.* (2004) also found that tighter entry restrictions limited banking contestability and competition and led to lower banking efficiency. These results are supported by Barth *et al.* (2010) in their analysis of bank efficiency in 72 countries for the period 1999-2007. They found that tighter regulations reduced bank efficiency. They also found that greater independence of supervisory authority enhanced bank efficiency level.

However, studies on the effect of regulation on banking performance have not yet reached a consensus. Kalish and Gilbert (1973), in examining the influence of bank regulations in the US, found that regulatory decisions failed to explain the efficiency level of banks. Demirguc-Kunt *et al.* (2004) also found that bank regulations appear to be insignificant in explaining the profitability and banking costs of commercial banks. Pasiouras (2008), in his analysis of the impact of regulations on banks' technical efficiency in 95 countries, found no significant relationship between restrictions on bank activities and efficiency levels.

On the other hand, González (2009) found that restrictions on bank activities by means of market monitoring and better contracting led to an increase in bank efficiency. Demirguc-Kunt *et al.* (2004) also found that stricter bank entry requirements and tighter banking activities contributed to higher net interest margins in the banking system. This finding is supported by Lensink, Meesters and Naaborg (2008), who found that an increase in foreign bank ownership correlated negatively with bank efficiency. González (2009) also found that stricter bank regulations reduced banking risk in poorly developed financial markets. This result was confirmed by Delis, Molyneux and Pasiouras (2009), who found that banking restrictions in 22 transition countries contributed to higher bank productivity. Beltratti and Stulz

(2009) also argued that banks performed better under stronger capital supervision and restrictions.

Political stability, government effectiveness, regulatory quality and control of corruption are also important for banking activities. However, studies on the effects of such factors on bank efficiency are limited. Demirguc-Kunt *et al.* (2004) examined the regulations, market structure, institutions and the cost of financial intermediation in 72 countries. They found that financial intermediation cost was lower in countries with better property rights, stronger contract enforcement and a higher level of judicial efficiency. The authors stressed that such factors help to increase the collateral value of bank loans. This finding is consistent with the results of La Porta *et al.* (1998) and Jappelli and Pagano (2002), who found that good judiciary and legal enforcement contributed to lower credit risk in banking institutions.

Lensink and Meesters (2007) studied the effect of institutional differences on the operating efficiency of commercial banks. They found that better institutions can improve banks' efficiency. They also found that banks in countries with a better institutional environment used technologies more efficiently and hence lowered the cost of operations. Chen (2009) found that commercial banks in 10 Sub-Saharan African countries exhibited higher efficiency scores under more stable economic conditions. This result suggests that stronger legal rights, enforcement of contracts, political stability and government effectiveness contribute positively to bank efficiency.

Al-Obaidan (2009) also examined the impact of monetary stability on commercial banks' technical and scale efficiency in six Gulf Cooperation Council (GCC) emerging economies. He found that higher monetary stability resulted in higher scale efficiency. The result also suggests that the technical efficiency of the commercial banking industry in GCC countries is influenced by monetary stability scores.

Sufian and Habibullah (2010) studied the relationship between institutional environment and bank performance for commercial banks in Malaysia. Using data for both foreign and locally owned commercial banks in Malaysia from 1999 to 2007, the authors found that economic freedom, business freedom, financial freedom and freedom from corruption correlated positively with banks' profitability. However, monetary freedom correlated negatively with banks' profitability, which indicates the importance of the government's role in controlling monetary policy.

However, studies on the effect of institutional factors on bank performance have failed to reach a consensus. Studies by Engerman and Sokoloff (1997), Acemoglu, Johnson and Robinson (2001) and William and Levine (2003) show that better institutional environment resulted in lower bank earnings. However, Borovicka (2007) failed to find any significant relationship between indexes of economic freedom and banking costs in 19 transition economies. He also found that the index concerning banking sector reforms correlated positively with the total costs of the banks, which suggests that banking sector reforms resulted in higher banking costs.

Based on the existing literature, there is to date no consensus regarding the effects of banking regulations and institutional environment on banks' performance. This lack of consensus may persist because most studies have failed to consider the governance setup in the countries under investigation. Researchers may omit governance setup because a country's institutional framework, such as economic freedom and country governance, are better able to reflect true market behavior (Claessens & Laeven, 2003). Hence, according to the theory of industrial organization, it is crucial to consider a country's institutional framework when analyzing firms' performance.

This study will go further by analyzing the effects of financial market regulations and country governance on banks' efficiency. In addition, the studies mentioned above were mostly conducted on developed economies, especially European countries, using cross-country analyses characterized by different regulatory frameworks, thus making it important to control for country governance. Moreover, the results obtained from developed markets and European markets may not be applicable to Asian countries, where the respective banking industries are still highly regulated compared with the developed markets.

Methodology and data

Methodology

This study employed Data Envelopment Analysis (DEA) to estimate the cost and profit efficiency scores. The efficiency scores were then used in the second stage of the study to determine the effects of financial market regulations and country governance on bank efficiency in the selected East Asian countries. DEA is a linear programming approach first initiated by Farrell (1957) and further developed by Charnes, Cooper and Rhodes (1978) based on the concept of Pareto efficiency, whereby the production frontier is constructed using a set of efficient observations. A bank is considered to be Pareto efficient when it is unable to increase any output or reduce input combination without reducing other outputs or increasing the input being utilized in the production process (Chen & Yeh, 2000). DEA is used to empirically measure the relative efficiency of a set of Decision Making Units (DMUs) leading to efficient firms on the frontier.

DEA is a well-known technique for measuring bank efficiency. The method generates efficiency estimates for firms with multiple inputs and outputs. DEA requires no a priori specification of functional forms, unlike the parametric method, and hence does not suffer from independent and identically distributed (iid) problems in the second-stage regression estimation. Furthermore, DEA performs relatively well with a small number of observations. Hence, this method was chosen to estimate cost and profit efficiency scores.

The cost efficiency concept based on DEA estimation is defined as the ability of banks to minimize cost in terms of technical and allocative efficiency. Technical efficiency refers to banks' ability to minimize an input mix given the level of outputs or maximize the output level when a fixed amount of input combination is given. On the other hand, allocative efficiency is defined as the ability of banks to optimally allocate their input mix given the prices of the inputs. Hence, the input price information is an important component in the estimation of cost efficiency.

The cost efficiency for *N* firms (i=1,...,N) is defined as the objective of the firms seeking to minimize cost by using a vector of *p* inputs $x_i = (x_{i1},...,x_{ip}) \notin \Re_{p++}$ given the price of inputs $w_i = (w_{i1},...,w_{ip}) \notin \Re_{p++}$ to produce a vector of *q* outputs $y_i = (y_{i1},...,y_{iq}) \notin \Re_{q++}$. Therefore, the cost efficiency for the *j*th firm can be estimated using Equation (1):

$$\begin{aligned}
&Min \sum_p w_{pj} x_{pj} \\
&s.t. \sum_i \lambda_i y_{iq} \geq y_{jq} \forall q \\
&\sum_i \lambda_i x_{ip} \leq x_{jp} \forall p \\
&\sum_i \lambda_i = 1; \lambda_i \geq 0;\ \mathrm{i} = 1,...,\mathrm{N}
\end{aligned} \qquad (1)$$

The cost efficiency for the *jth* bank is given by the ratio of minimum costs to actual costs and can be estimated using Equation 2:

$$0 \leq CE_j = \frac{\sum_p w_{pj} x^*_{pj}}{\sum_p w_{pj} x_{pj}} \leq 1 \qquad (2)$$

Profit efficiency measures banks' performances in terms of profit maximization. It is more widely acceptable as an economic concept than cost efficiency because it is conceptually broader and combines both the cost and revenue sides in estimating efficiency (Berger & Mester, 1997). The profit function can be further categorized into standard and alternative profit functions to represent the degree of competitiveness in the market. The standard profit function assumes perfect competition in both the input and output markets, whereas the alternative profit function gives banks some control over the prices of outputs. According to Humphrey and Pulley (1997), the alternative profit function is better than the standard profit function in estimating banks' efficiency level because, in practice, banks are able to use their local market power in terms of deposit taking and granting loan, hence giving them some control in setting the prices of deposits and loans. Banks can also differentiate their financial products according to their targeted customers, geographical area and time. Therefore, we estimated profit efficiency using the alternative profit function.

The alternative profit efficiency for the *j*th bank can be expressed as follows:

$$\begin{aligned}
&Max\ R_j - \sum_p w_{jp} x_{jp} \\
&s.t. \sum_i \lambda_i R_i \geq R_j \\
&\sum_i \lambda_i y_{iq} \geq y_{jq} \forall q \\
&\sum_i \lambda_i x_{ip} \leq x_{jp} \forall p \\
&\sum_i \lambda_i = 1; \lambda_i \geq 0;\ \mathrm{i} = 1,...,\mathrm{N}
\end{aligned} \qquad (3)$$

where *R* is the revenue of firm *j*. The alternative profit for the *j*th bank is given by

$$0 \leq APE_i = \frac{R_j - \sum_p w_{jp} x_{jp}}{R^*_j - \sum_p w_{jp} x^*_{jp}} \leq 1 \qquad (4)$$

The variable return to scale (VRS) obtained by setting $\sum_i \lambda_i = 1$ is used in the estimation of both cost and profit efficiency. This approach is used because in practice, banks may not be able to proportionally increase both inputs and outputs simultaneously to be cost and profit efficient.

In the second stage of the analysis, Tobit regression estimation was used to determine the effect of capital market regulations and country governance on banks' cost and profit efficiency. The Tobit regression was estimated based on Equation (5).

$$Eff_{it} = \alpha_{it} + \beta_1 OWN_{it} + \beta_2 COM_{jt} + \beta_3 FD_{jt} + \beta_4 MP_{jt} + \beta_5 PS_{jt} + \beta_6 GE_{jt} + \beta_7 RQ_{jt} + \beta_8 CC_{jt} + \beta_9 SIZE_{it} + \varepsilon_{it} \quad (5)$$

where

Eff_{it} = average cost or profit efficiency scores of bank *i* at time *t* (t= year of study)
OWN_{it} = ownership of bank *i* at time *t*
COM_{jt} = foreign bank competition in country *j* at time *t*
FD_{jt} = private sector credit in country *j* at time *t*
MP_{jt} = interest rate control in country *j* at time *t*
PS_{jt} = political stability in country *j* at time *t*
GE_{jt} = government effectiveness in country *j* at time *t*
RQ_{jt} = regulatory quality in country *j* at time *t*
CC_{jt} = control for corruption in country *j* at time *t*
$SIZE_{it}$ = bank size (natural logarithm of total assets) for bank *i* at time *t*
ε_{it} = error terms for bank *i* at time *t*

Tobit regression analysis was used in this study because of the nature of the dependent variable and given that the efficiency scores are truncated between values of "0" and "1". The ordinary least squares estimators of linear models will be biased and inconsistent in censored data. The Tobit regression was hence suggested to overcome the censored data by Tobin (1958). Nevertheless, Amemiya (1973) noted that the Tobit estimator is biased and inconsistent with the presence of heteroscedasticity and distributional misspecification. Therefore, we estimated the Tobit regression by adjusting for robust standard errors and by using the bootstrap-based approach based on 50 replications for a further robustness check of the model estimation. This method was suggested by Chortareas, Girardone, & Ventouri (2013) because it incorporates the parametric structure and distributional assumptions of the equations. Tobit regression analysis has been widely used in the second-stage estimation of bank efficiency analysis based on the DEA approach (Isik and Hassan, 2003; Sufian and Habibullah, 2010).

Data and definition of variables

The sample examined in this study consists of selected commercial banks in the East Asian region, namely, China, Hong Kong, Japan, Korea, and Taiwan, for the period 2001-2008. The input and output specifications are based on the value-added approach proposed by Berger and Humphrey (1992), with the assumption that banks mostly perform typical businesses in a services industry. This approach considers all assets and liabilities as outputs when it contributes to the bank value added. Berger and Humphrey (1992) indicate that because banks pay out interest to depositors, the deposits are treated as outputs whereas the interest rate is considered the input price in generating the stated outputs. The financial products offered by commercial banks—loans, investment and deposits—are used as the banks' output vector. Hence, the input vectors used in producing the financial products and services are personnel costs, capital cost and cost of loanable funds. In this context, the price of labor was calculated by dividing the total personnel costs by total assets. The price of capital was obtained by dividing the total depreciation of the banks by the total fixed assets. The price of loanable funds was computed by dividing the total interest expenses by the total loanable funds. All input and output vectors employed in this study are reported in USD million.

Table 2 presents the descriptive statistics of the input and output vectors used in this study. The study sample consists of 261 commercial banks from five countries with 1668 observations. The commercial banks had average total assets of USD54,775.01 million, with a standard deviation as high as USD146,678.75 million. Thus, the banks were relatively diverse in terms of their scale of operations. In addition, the banks' average total deposits for the period amount to USD46,535.65 million, which is USD14,947.41 million more than the average total loans given out by the commercial banks. The banks were also able to generate, on average, USD1,587.45 million in interest income compared to an average interest expense of USD651.91 million. Finally, the banks were able to

Table 2. Descriptive statistics of input and output variables

	Total Assets	Deposits	Loans	Investment	Interest income	Interest expenses	Pre-tax profit
				In Million USD			
Mean	54775.01	46535.65	31588.24	20185.50	1587.45	651.91	302.87
Standard Deviation	146678.75	128508.91	78246.50	63156.68	4516.38	1935.31	1620.45
Minimum	3.44	0.70	-18.38	0.00	0.06	0.00	-13601.38
Maximum	1414079.13	1286242.61	683890.72	733634.35	63863.19	25730.00	23788.55
Count	1668	1668	1668	1668	1668	1668	1668

generate an average of USD302.87 million in terms of profit before taxes, although some of the banks did experience losses as high as USD13,601.38 million.

The measure of financial market regulations used in this study consists of bank ownership, foreign bank competition, private sector credit and interest rate control. These dimensions were first formulated by Gwartney *et al.* (2011) to measure the credit situation of a particular country. A high index indicates that banks are free from government control, and hence higher bank efficiency is expected. As highlighted by Claessens and Klingebiel (2001), Barth *et al.* (2004) and Barth *et al.* (2010), banks are able to exploit economies of scale and scope that contribute to higher efficiency levels when they are not subjected to government control.

Ownership of banks was computed based on the percentage of bank deposits held by the privately owned banks. A high index of bank ownership indicates that the country has a larger percentage of deposits held by privately owned banks rather than state-owned banks. Therefore, the country is dominated by privately owned banks rather than state-owned banks. Because decision making in privately owned banks is more independent than in state-owned institutions, we expect higher bank efficiency levels if the country's commercial bank deposits are largely held by privately owned banks.

However, the foreign bank competition index helps to capture foreign banking activities in the region. This index is calculated based on approved foreign bank applications as well as the foreign banking assets in the country's banking sector. Banks are expected to perform better in terms of cost control and profit generation under a competitive environment because foreign bank participation in the banking system contributes to higher contestability of the banking sector, which leads to healthy competition (Claessens & Laeven, 2004). In addition, Clarke *et al.* (2000) and Claessens, Demirgüc-Kunt, & Huizinga, (2001) also suggested that higher foreign bank penetration contributes to higher bank efficiency level by inducing healthy competition in the banking system.

Next, private sector credit provides a measure of the extent of government borrowing relative to private-sector borrowing with the banks. According to Gwartney *et al.* (2011), higher borrowings by the government indicate more central planning wherein the commercial banks are largely controlled by the government, hence resulting in more policy planning rather than profit-maximization decisions. Higher ratings were assigned to countries where private-sector borrowings dominated the markets. In such cases, we expect a positive relationship between private sector credit with bank efficiency level because less policy lending and government control would result in more efficient allocations of resources. Demirgüç-Kunt *et al.* (2004) highlighted that banking systems dominated by state banks are more prone to restrictions in their banking activities, which may affect decisions regarding allocation of resources. This reasoning is supported by Beck, Demirgüç-Kunt and Levine (2006), who suggested that a higher degree of freedom helps stimulate efficiency by enabling banks to better diversify their activities without any restrictions by the government.

The interest rate control index is used to represent the freedom of the market in determining the interest rate level. The higher the interest rate controls are, the more freedom the market has in determining real deposit and lending rates. A positive relationship is expected between market freedom and bank efficiency. According to the classical theory, firms are expected to be more efficient when the prices of their products and services are determined by market forces. Hence, we expect bank efficiency to increase if the pricing of the banks' financial products and services are determined by market forces.

Country governance in terms of political stability, government effectiveness, regulatory quality and control of corruption was extracted from Governance Matters VIII developed by Kaufmann *et al.* (2009). The political stability index measures the perceptions of the likelihood of political instability and politically motivated violence in the country. A high index indicates great political stability and hence a high bank efficiency level. This relationship is observed because political instability affects the allocation of resources in the economy.

Next, government effectiveness reflects the perception of the quality of public services, quality of civil service, freedom from political pressures, quality of policy formulation and implementation, and the credibility of the government's commitment to policy implementation. A high index indicates that the government is effective and committed to the implementation of public policy, which will lead to sustainability and development in economic activities. Government effectiveness is therefore believed to improve bank efficiency because it results in more optimistic economic conditions because the rate of success of an economy depends on good governance (Beck, Demirgüç-Kunt, & Levine, 2003). Moreover, Lensink *et al.* (2008) noted that higher government effectiveness lowers the cost of banking operations because it reduces the level of bureaucracy the banks have to address.

Similarly, regulatory quality captures the quality of the government in formulating and implementing sound policies and regulations to promote private sector development. Again, a high index of regulatory quality means high quality in the formulation of sound policies. This factor is important because soundness and quality in policy formulation enables the country to sustain growth during adverse economic situations and hence increase the efficiency level of banks. Lensink *et al.* (2008) also suggested that regulatory quality effectively reduces the cost of banking activities with increasing effectiveness and predictability of the judiciary system.

Control of corruption index measures the ability of the government and public officials to control corruption in public services, which includes the corruption level between the public administration and citizens, businesses and foreign companies. A high index indicates low corruption in public services and hence high bank efficiency. This relationship is observed because corruption increases the cost of doing business, hence reducing efficiency levels. Furthermore, greater freedom from corruption contributes to more equitable treatment and improves regulatory efficiency (Miller et al., 2010) and consequently promotes better allocation of resources in the economy.

In summary, we expect a positive relationship with a more stable political system, good and effective governance and regulation and a less corrupt environment—key factors that can provide the catalyst for the banking sector to efficiently allocate their resources. As noted by Lensink and Mester (2007), Chen (2009), Al-Obaidan (2009) and Sufian and Habibullah (2010), economic stability increases the collateral value of bank loans and reduces financial intermediation costs, thus leading to higher bank efficiency. Chen (2009) also stressed that better country governance contributes positively to bank efficiency.

Results and discussion

The cost and profit efficiency scores of the commercial banks in the East Asian region are shown in Table 3.

The results of the DEA estimation presented in Table 3 show that commercial banks in the East Asian region are relatively more profit efficient than they are cost efficient. Commercial banks in the Chinese market are relatively cost efficient, with an average efficiency score of 43.7%. This figure indicates that the Chinese banking industry is wasting 56.3% of their input mix. Hence, bank management could further reduce their input mix by at least 56.3% to produce the same level of outputs given the input prices. On the other hand, commercial banks in Japan are relatively more profit efficient, with an efficiency score of 76.1%. This find-

Table 3. Average cost and profit efficiency scores for commercial banks in East Asian from 2001 to 2008

Summary Statistics		Mean	Standard Deviation	Minimum	Maximum	Count
China	Cost	0.437	0.256	0.041	1.000	194
	profit	0.619	0.433	0.190	1.000	194
Hong Kong	Cost	0.280	0.193	0.008	1.000	196
	profit	0.446	0.293	-0.033	1.000	196
Japan	Cost	0.219	0.189	0.011	1.000	706
	profit	0.761	0.170	0.250	1.000	706
Korea	Cost	0.254	0.109	0.092	0.582	105
	profit	0.363	0.096	0.187	0.584	105
Taiwan	Cost	0.261	0.135	0.060	1.000	264
	profit	0.414	0.124	0.146	1.000	264

ing implies that to maximize profit, bank management could further reduce their input mix by another 23.9% with the same level of outputs.

After the efficiency scores were estimated, the unbalanced panel data from a Tobit regression were estimated to determine the effects of credit market regulations and country governance on both the cost and profit efficiencies of commercial banks in the East Asian countries. The Hausman test was used to determine the choice between random- and fixed-effect models. The null hypothesis for the Hausman test states that the individual effects are uncorrelated with the regressors in the estimated model (Hausman, 1978). A high value of the Hausman test statistic favors a fixed-effect model as opposed to a random-effect model, which will result in biased estimators. The reported Hausman statistics for cost and profit efficiency estimation are 39.72 and 45.02, respectively, which indicate that the null hypothesis can be rejected for both models. Hence, the fixed-effect estimation is preferred over the random-effect model.

The Tobit regression estimates are presented in Table 4. The results show that the cost efficiency level of commercial banks in the East Asian countries is more sensitive to country governance. Similarly, the profit efficiency level of the commercial banks in the region is affected by both financial market regulations and country governance.

Next, greater freedom in interest rate regulation was found to be positively related to cost efficiency but negatively related to the profit efficiency level of commercial banks in the region. This result indicates that in countries with more freedom to set their interest rates based on market forces, stable monetary policy, and positive real deposit and lending rates, the banks are more cost efficient. However, the negative relationship between profit efficiency and interest rate regulations might indicate that banks tend to offer better pricing to markets to attract more loans and deposits by earning less profit. This behavior justifies a more competitive market where banks fail to extract economic rent to gain higher profits from the markets. In addition, greater financial freedom may hurt profit efficiency because banks tend to engage in higher risk-taking activities, which might contribute to losses in the capital market, resulting in lower earnings (González, 2005). This reasoning is consistent with the findings reported by Sufian and Habibullah (2010), who found that monetary freedom hurts banks' profitability, which indicates the important roles played by governments in developing countries in controlling monetary policies. This finding is also consistent with the studies of Delis *et al.* (2009) and Beltratti and Stulz (2009).

Political stability and regulatory quality tend to have a negative impact on bank efficiency, which suggests that in a more mature and advanced economy

Table 4. Tobit regression estimates of cost and profit efficiency

	Model 1		Model 2	
Variable	Cost efficiency	Profit efficiency	Cost efficiency	Profit efficiency
Constant	-0.077 (0.268) [-0.29]	-1.529 (0.487) [-3.14]***	-0.077 (0.213) [-0.362]	-1.529 (0.374) [-4.088]***
Bank Size	0.007 (0.014) [0.518]	-0.006 (0.022) [-0.294]	0.007 (0.016) [0.438]	-0.006 (0.024) [-0.250]
Ownership of banks	-0.007 (0.007) [-0.949]	0.000 (0.011) [0.028]	-0.007 (0.006) [-1.167]	0.000 (0.012) [0.030]
Competition in domestic banking	0.001 (0.006) [0.164]	0.020 (0.009) [2.088]**	0.001 (0.006) [0.164]	0.020 (0.007) [2.857]***
Interest rate regulations	0.037 (0.018) [2.030]**	-0.085 (0.029) [-2.928]***	0.037 (0.010) [3.700]**	-0.085 (0.020) [-4.250]***
Credit market regulation	-0.005 (0.020) [-0.253]	-0.028 (0.032) [-0.873]	-0.005 (0.020) [-0.253]	-0.028 (0.031) [-0.903]
Political stability	-0.023 (0.014) [-1.641]	-0.090 (0.022) [-4.005]***	-0.023 (0.022) [-1.045]	-0.090 (0.019) [-4.737]***
Government effectiveness	0.136 (0.042) [3.200]***	0.230 (0.068) [3.399]***	0.136 (0.054) [2.519]**	0.230 (0.058) [3.966]***
Regulatory quality	-0.297 (0.029) [-10.102]***	-0.235 (0.047) [-5.001]***	-0.297 (0.038) [-7.816]***	-0.235 (0.033) [-7.121]***
Control of corruption	0.152 (0.044) [3.413]***	0.179 (0.071) [2.529]**	0.152 (0.058) [2.621]***	0.179 (0.072) [2.486]**
Sigma	0.174 (0.003)	0.285 (0.007)	0.174 (0.005)	0.285 (0.001)
LR Chi2 (9)	314.17***	458.33***	224.32***	487.41
Pseudo R2	0.162	0.287	0.162	0.287
Standard deviation	0.104 (0.002) [54.129]***	0.166 (0.003) [54.107]***	0.104 (0.002) [54.129]***	0.166 (0.003) [54.107]***
Log likelihood function	292.289	569.497	292.289	569.497

This table provides the Tobit regression estimation corrected for robust standard errors (Model 1) and a bootstrap-based model (Model 2) for East Asian commercial banks from 2001 to 2008.

Notes: *** and ** denote significance at the 1% and 5% levels, respectively. Standard errors are shown in parentheses, and test statistics are reported in brackets.

with higher income levels, banks incur higher costs of financing because of higher personnel and capital expenses (Dietsch & Lozano-Vivas, 2000). Moreover, banks in more developed and mature markets tend to be less efficient in controlling their expenditures because they focus more on business expansion. Banks may also become complacent in controlling their operation in a more stable economy, which might lead to the "quiet life" hypothesis introduced by Berger and Hannan (1998). The result is supported by Engerman and Sokoloff (1997), Acemoglu *et al.*, (2001) and William and Levine (2003), who found better institutional environments resulted in lower bank earnings.

Findings have also shown that government effectiveness is positively related to bank efficiency. A country that is characterized by political independence and an efficient government has a more efficient banking sector. The results are supported by Levine, Loayza and Beck (2003), who found that a better institutional environment facilitates greater market and financial development, which lead to higher efficiency of the banking industry. In a similar vein, Lensink and Meesters (2007), in their analysis of institutions and bank performance, found that government effectiveness reduces banks' costs in dealing with bureaucracy. The result is consistent with the work of Chen (2009), who found that government effectiveness resulted in the high cost efficiency of Sub-Saharan African banks. Barth *et al.* (2010) also reported that greater government effectiveness indicated higher institutional quality, which eventually contributed to higher bank efficiency.

The results also show that the ability to control for corruption is positively related to bank efficiency level, demonstrating that the lower the incidence of corruption is, the lower the costs of bribing become and hence the higher the bank efficiency level becomes (Lensink and Meesters, 2007). In addition, corruption may also negatively affect the degree of market competitiveness and lead to inefficient loan offerings (Boudriga, Taktak, & Jellouli, 2009). The result is also consistent with the work of Sufian and Habibullah (2010), who found that freedom of corruption was positively related to banks' profitability in Malaysia.

In general, our results suggest that for any country, the ability to control corruption, improve government effectiveness and institute less stringent regulatory conditions will have positive effects on bank efficiency.

Conclusion

This study examined the effects of financial market regulations and country governance on bank efficiency in East Asian countries. The study period was chosen to span from 2001 to 2008 to reflect the impact of current financial market regulations and country governance on bank efficiency. Non-parametric Data Envelopment Analysis (DEA) was employed to obtain cost and profit efficiency scores. A Tobit unbalanced panel data regression was then estimated to analyze the impact of banking regulations and country governance on bank efficiency.

The results show that commercial banks in the East Asian region are relatively more profit efficient than they are cost efficient. The Tobit regression estimation result indicates that the cost efficiency of commercial banks in East Asia is more sensitive to country governance, whereas profit efficiency is affected by both financial market regulations and country governance.

Greater freedom in setting interest rates was found to be positively correlated with cost-efficiency level, suggesting that countries with more financial freedom and independence are more cost efficient. The result is consistent with the work of González (2005), Delis *et al.* (2009) and Beltratti and Stulz (2009) and Sufian and Habibullah (2010). Furthermore, the results show that government effectiveness is positively related to bank efficiency, again demonstrating that countries with more freedom have more efficient banking systems. The result is consistent with the studies of Levine *et al.* (2003), Lensink and Meesters (2007), Chen (2009) and Barth *et al.* (2010).

However, the results show that political stability and regulatory quality are negatively related to bank efficiency levels. The results are consistent with the work of Engerman and Sokoloff (1997), Acemoglu *et al.*, (2001) and William and Levine (2003). Consistent with economic theory, the ability to control for corruption is positively related to bank efficiency level; supporting the views of Lensink and Meesters (2007), Boudriga *et al.* (2009) and Sufian and Habibullah (2010).

The sample examined herein may be a limitation of this study because it only focuses on commercial banks in East Asian countries. Therefore, future studies may consider extending the study to other Asian countries and comparing the differences in institutional framework among different Asian regions to develop a better economic picture that can be generalized to the entire Asian region. Overall, to create more efficient banks, the results of our study suggest that countries should allow the market determine interest rates with less stringent regulatory conditions.

References

Acemoglu, D, Johnson, S., & Robinson, J. A. (2001). The colonial origins of comparative development: An empirical investigation. *American Economic Review*, 91 (5), 1369-1401.

Al-Obaidan, A.M. (2009). Monetary stability and performance in the commercial banking industry of emerging markets. *International Research Journal of Finance and Economics*, 26, 60-72.

Amemiya, T. (1973). Regression analysis when the dependent variable is a truncated normal. *Econometrica*, 41 (6), 997-1016.

Asaftei, G., & Kumbhakar, S. (2008). Regulation and efficiency in transition: The case of Romanian banks. *Journal of Regulatory Economics*, 33 (3), 253-282.

Barth, J. R., Brunmgaugh, D.R., & Wilcox, J.A. (2000). The repeal of Glass-Steagall and the advent of broad banking. *Journal of Economic Perspective*, 14 (2), 191-204.

Barth, J. R., Caprio, G., & Levine, R, (2004). Bank regulation and supervision: What works best? *Journal of Financial Intermediation*, 13 (2), 205-248.

Barth, J. R., Chen, L., Yue, M., Seade, J., & Song, F. M. (2010). Do bank regulation, supervision and monitoring enhance or impede bank efficiency? Available at, http://ssrn.com/abstract=1579352

Beck, T., Demirgüç-Kunt, A., & Levine, R. (2003). Law, endowments, and finance. *Journal of Financial Economics*, 70 (2), 137-181.

Beck, T., Demirgüç-Kunt, A., & Levine, R. (2006). Bank concentration, competition, and crises: First results. *Journal of Banking and Finance*, 30 (5), 1581-1603.

Beck, T., Demirgüç-Kunt, A., Levine, R., & Maksimovic, V. (2001). Financial structure and economic Development: Firm, industry and country evidence. In A. Demirgüç-Kunt, & R. Levine (Eds.), *Financial structure and economic growth: A cross-country comparison of banks, markets and development* (pp. 202-242). Cambridge, MA: The MIT Press.

Beltratti, A., & Stulz, R. M. (2009). *Why did some banks perform better during the credit crisis? A cross-country study of the impact of governance and regulation* (Working Paper No. 15180). National Bureau of Economic Research.

Berger, A. N., & Hannan, T. H. (1998). The efficiency cost of market power in the banking industry: A test of the "Quiet Life" and related hypotheses. *Review of Economics and Statistics*, 80 (3), 454-465.

Berger, A. N., & Humphrey, D. B. (1992). Measurement of efficiency issues in commercial banking. In A. N. Berger & D. B. Humphrey (Eds.), *Output measurement in the service sectors* (pp. 245-300). Chicago, IL: University of Chicago Press.

Berger, A. N., & Mester, L. J. (1997). Inside the black box: What explains differences in the efficiencies of financial institutions. *Journal of Banking and Finance*, 21 (7), 895-947.

Besley, T., & Burgess, R. (2004). Can labor regulation hinder economic performance? Evidence from India. *Quarterly Journal of Economics*, 119 (1), 91-134.

Borovicka, J. (2007). Banking efficiency and foreign ownership in transition: Is there evidence of a cream-skimming effect? *Financial Stability Report* 13, 68-82

Boudriga, A., Taktak, N. B., & Jellouli, S. (2009). Banking supervision and nonperforming loans: A cross-country analysis. *Journal of Financial Economic Policy*, 1 (4), 286-318.

Chan, S. G., & Karim, M. Z. A. (2010). Bank efficiency and macro-economic factors: The case of developing countries. *Global Economic Review*, 39 (3), 269-289.

Charnes, A., Cooper, W. W., & Rhodes, E. (1978). Measuring the efficiency of decision making units. *European Journal of Operational Research*, 2 (6), 429-444.

Chen, C. (2009) *Bank efficiency in Sub-Saharan African Middle-Income Countries* (Working Paper No. 09/14). International Monetary Fund.

Chen, T. Y., & Yeh, T. L. (2000). A measurement of bank efficiency, ownership and productivity changes in Taiwan. *Service Industry Journal*, 20 (1), 95-109.

Chortareas, G. E., Girardone, C., & Ventouri, A. (2013). Financial freedom and bank efficiency: Evidence from the European Union. *Journal of Banking and Finance*, 37 (4), 1223-1231.

Claessens, S., Demirgüc-Kunt, A., & Huizinga, H. (2001). How does foreign entry affect domestic banking markets. *Journal of Banking and Finance*, 25 (5), 891-911.

Claessens, S., & Klingebie, D. (2001). Competition and scope of activities in financial services. *World Bank Research Observer*, 16 (1), 19-40.

Claessens, S., & Laeven, L. (2004). What drives bank competition? Some international evidence. *Journal of Money, Credit, and Banking*, 36 (3), 563-583.

Clarke, F., Cull, R., Amato, L., & Molinari, A. (2000). On the kindness of strangers? The impact of foreign entry on domestic banks in Argentina" In S. Claessen, M. Jansen (Ed.), *The internationalization of financial services: issues and lessons for developing countries* (pp.331-354). London, UK: Kluwer Law International.

Delis, M. D., Molyneux, P., & Pasiouras, F. (2009). *Regulations and productivity growth in banking* (MPRA Working Paper No. 13891). University Library of Munich, Germany.

Demirgüc-Kunt, A., Laeven, L., & Levine, R. (2004). Regulations, market structure, institutions, and the cost of financial intermediation. *Journal of Money, Credit, and Banking*, 36 (3), 593-622.

Dietsch, M., & Lozano-Vivas, A. (2000). How the environment determines banking efficiency: A comparison between French and Spanish industries. *Journal of Banking and Finance*, 24 (6), 985-1004.

Engerman, S. L., & Sokoloff, K. L. (1997). Factor endowments, institutions, and differential paths of growth among new world economies: A view from economic historians of the United States. In S. Haber (Ed.), *How Latin America fell behind. Essays on the Economic History of Brazil and México, 1800–1914* (pp. 260-304). Stanford, CA: Stanford University Press.

Evanoff, D. D. (1998). Assessing the impact of regulation on bank cost efficiency. *Economic Perspective*, 22 (2), 21-32

Farrell, M. J. (1957). The measurement of productivity efficiency. *Journal of the Royal Statistical Society*, 120 (3), 253-290.

Giannone, D. Lenza, M., & Reichlin, L. (2010). Market freedom and the global recession. *International Monetary Fund Economic Review*, 59 (1), 111-135.

González, F. (2005). Bank regulation and risk-taking incentives: An international comparison of bank risk. *Journal of Banking and Finance*, 29 (5), 1153-1184.

González, F. (2009). Determinants of bank-market structure: Efficiency and political economy variables. *Journal of Money, Credit, and Banking*, 41 (06), 735-754.

Gwartney, J., Lawson, R., Hall, J. (2011). *Economic Freedom of the World: 2011 Annual Report*. Vancouver, BC: Fraser Institute. Retrieved from http://www.freetheworld.com/2011/reports/world/EFW2011_complete.pdf

Hausman, J. A. (1978). Specification tests in econometrics. *Econometrica*, 46 (6), 1251-1271.

Humphrey, D. B., & Pulley, L. B. (1997). Banks' responses to deregulation: Profits, technology, and efficiency. *Journal of Money, Credit, and Banking*, 29 (1), 73-93.

Isik, I., & Hassan, M. K. (2003). Efficiency, ownership and market structure, corporate control and governance in the Turkish banking industry. *Journal of Banking and Finance*, 30 (9-10), 1363-1421.

Jappelli, T., & Pagano, M. (2002). Information sharing, lending and defaults: Cross countries evidence. *Journal of Banking and Finance*, 26 (10), 2017-2045.

Johnson, S., Kaufmann, D., & Shleifer, A. (1997). The unofficial economy in transition. *Brookings Paper on Economic Activity*, 2, 159-239.

Kalish, L., & Gilbert, R. A. (1973). The influence of bank regulation on the operating efficiency of commercial banks. Journal of Finance, 28 (5), 1287-1301.

Kaufmann, D., Kraay, A., & Mastruzzi, M. (2009). *Governance matters VIII: aggregate and individual governance indicators 1996-2008. Policy* (Research Working Paper No. 4978). The World Bank.

La Porta, R., Lopez-de-Silanes, F., Shleifer, A., & Vishney, R.W. (1998). Law and finance. *Journal of Political Economy*, 106 (6), 1113-1155.

Lensink, R., & Meesters, A. (2007). *Institutions and bank performance: A stochastic frontier analysis*. Available at, http://ssrn.com/abstract=965825

Lensink, R, Meesters, A., & Naaborg, I. (2008). Bank efficiency and foreign ownership: Do good institutions matter? *Journal of Banking and Finance*, 32 (5), 834-844.

Levine, R., Loayza, N., & Beck T (2003). Financial intermediation and growth: Causality and causes. *Journal of Monetary Economics*, 46 (1), 31-77.

Miller, T., & Holmes, K. R., Kim, A. B., Markheim, D., Roberts, J. M., & Walsh, C. (2010). *Index of Economic Freedom. Washington*, DC: The Heritage Foundation and Dow Jones & Company, Inc.

Mishkin, F. S. (2000). *Prudential supervision: Why is it important and what are the issues* (Working Paper No. 7926). National Bureau of Economic Research. Retrieved from http://www.nber.org/papers/w7926.pdf

Nabi, M. S., & Suliman, M. O. (2008). *The institutional environment and the banking-growth nexus: Theory and investigation for MENA* (MPRA Working Paper No. 11854). University Library of Munich, Germany.

Pasiouras, F. (2008). International evidence on the impact of regulations and supervision on banks' technical efficiency: An application of two-stage data envelopment analysis. *Review of Quantitative Finance and Accounting*, 30 (2), 187-223.

Stigler, G. J. (1971). The theory of economic regulation. *Bell Journal of Economic Management Science*, 2 (1), 3-21.

Sufian, F., & Habibullah, M. S. (2010). Developments in the efficiency of the Thailand banking sector: A DEA approach. *International Journal of Development Issues*, 9 (3), 226-245.

Sufian, F., & Habibullah, M.S. (2010). Does economic freedom fosters banks' performance? Panel evidence from Malaysia. *Journal of Contemporary Accounting and Economics*, 6 (2), 77-91.

Tobin, J. (1958). Estimation of relationships for limited dependent variables. *Econometrica*, 26 (1), 24-36.

William, E., & Levine, R. (2003). Tropics, germs, and crops: How endowments influence economic development. *Journal of Monetary Economics*, 50 (1), 3-40.

4

Costs of corporate bond issue in coal mining companies

Agata Sierpińska-Sawicz[1], Patrycja Barbara Bąk[2]

ABSTRACT

In Poland, more than 90% of electricity production is based on coal fuel. Meanwhile, the financial situation of the mining industry is quite challenging. Companies in this sector are in debt, generating losses caused by a sharp drop in coal prices and a simultaneous increase in extraction costs that result from descending into lower levels of coal deposits. At the same time, banks are reluctant to loan money because of the risk of a borrowing entity's default. Increasingly, companies are turning to bond issue to maintain their liquidity and finance development projects. However, bondholders impose conditions in the form of covenants that are often difficult to satisfy, and the strictest relate to the level of a company's indebtedness and ability-to-repay-debt financial ratios.

This article discusses bond issue costs. The authors analyze the bond issue programs of three of the four mining companies operating in Poland. The fourth company did not issue any bonds. Bond issue costs are composed of interest payable to investors, issue preparation and support costs, collateralization costs, and the cost of recording and organizing the sale. The main cost involved in bond issuance is the coupon cost, which depends on the company's financial health and its level of indebtedness, the purpose of the issue, its volume, and the type and quality of the safeguards against the risk of loss of funds invested by bondholders. Bonds issued by coal mining companies are assumed mainly by banks, which demand high interest due to the poor financial condition of the issuers. In addition to interest, companies also pay a capital commitment fee, an arrangement fee and a fee for early redemption. Altogether, in relation to the costs of capital raised through a bank loan, the bond issue results in significantly higher costs of raising capital.

KEY WORDS: level of issue, bond rates, cost of bonds, collateral

[1] Poznań University of Economics - Department of Controlling, Financial Analysis and Valuation, Poland; [2] AGH University of Science and Technology - Department of Economics and Management in Industry, Poland

1. Introduction

Funding sources and the costs of their acquisition are of vital importance to the very survival and long-term development of companies in the market. A shortage of funds with which to finance current activity upsets a company's short-term financial equilibrium. Lack of development funds, or an excessively high cost of raising them, causes companies to lose their competitive advantage and, in the final analysis, results in their bankruptcy. The choice of sources of funding is particularly important in the mining industry, whose business development is characterized by prolonged investment cycles and relatively long payback periods, which results from the high capital intensity of mining

Correspondence concerning this article should be addressed to: **Agata Sierpińska-Sawicz**, Poznań University of Economics - Department of Controlling, Financial Analysis and Valuation, Al. Niepodległości 10, 61-875 Poznań, Poland.
E-mail: agata.sierpinska-sawicz@ue.poznan.pl

activities. Due to the long implementation period of investment projects, their phased-type character and uncertainty of future profitability, mining companies have limited access to bank loans for financing investments. The seasonality of the consumption of certain raw materials and fluctuations in commodity prices caused by the economic climate are also significant issues. To finance their activities, mining companies are increasingly turning to debt capital. During the recent economic crisis, which resulted in a dramatic decrease in profits, these companies issued corporate bonds, treating them as an alternative to the hard-to-get bank loans. Additionally, issuance of bonds in tranches is a more flexible funding source than bank loans, which, given the fluctuations in financial results, facilitates companies returning the debt (Sierpińska & Bąk, 2012).

This article presents an issue that is important from both scientific and practical points of view. During periods of drops in commodity prices, Polish raw material companies lose their creditworthiness, making bond issuance an important funding option. However, conditions imposed by bondholders are often too demanding, preventing companies from seeking this source of funding. Companies cut on investment projects and experience problems when completing investments in progress. This not only prolongs the implementation of the investments but also lowers their rates of return. Additionally, companies lose financial liquidity, and in the case of a failure to pay liabilities in a timely manner, they pay the penalty interest, which increases financial costs.

The authors attempt to assess the cost of bond issuance and the conditions that must be met in order for investors to plough their free assets to corporate bonds. The assessment was made by comparing the metrics of bonds to the average cost of issuing bonds on Catalyst market, which is a segment of the Warsaw Stock Exchange.

2. Bond issue level in Poland

The proceeds from the issuance of bonds define a company's debt structure, which is determined by many factors. Undoubtedly, important factors include general economic conditions, inflation, interest rates, tax rates and other factors over which managers have no control but must take into account when selecting sources of funding. Economic conditions, which affect the structure of the debt, are associated with the uncertainty of the demand for products and their prices, the market availability of raw materials and fuels, exchange rate changes, the tax system, and so on. The choice of funding sources is strongly influenced by interest rates because they define the cost of external capital, as well as tax rates that affect the tax shield (Rzeszowski & Sierpińska, 2012). The choice of types of debt is strongly influenced by several factors, including the company's financial standing, financial risk, returns on capital, type of company management, and the specificity of the industry in which the company operates.

Companies decide to raise funds from a bond issue when banks are reluctant to loan money due to the risk of the entities' default. Furthermore, in line with Basel III, in the coming years, banks will be forced to lend in line with the maturities of their deposits. Therefore, they will grant short-term loans when they themselves hold short-term bank deposits. Meanwhile, coal mining companies require long-term resources to implement their investment projects (Cornett et al., 2011). Under these conditions, bond issues become a particularly attractive source of funding.

The proceeds from a bond issue can be used for any purpose. On an ongoing basis, investors do not control compliance with requirements that surround the effectiveness of underlying investment projects. Bonds bring an added value over an extended period by providing an opportunity for the full financing of large investment projects from the proceeds of the issue. Financing can be flexibly attuned to the investment needs of the company. The issuer may divide the issue into tranches to ensure that they match the financing needs of the investment process, set a date for their redemption, and decide on the form of security that it can pledge. Furthermore, bond issues do not preclude simultaneous use of other forms of financing, such as a bank loan or issuance of shares.

During an economic boom, companies are more willing to reach out for capital from the issue of shares. According to the theory of market timing, if entrepreneurs believe that because of a slump, their shares will be undervalued until the market rebounds, they will postpone the decision to raise capital through the stock market. When the market price of shares on the stock market begins to meet the expectations of the

Table 1. Growth in the value of funds raised in Poland through bond issues, loans, factoring and leasing in 2003-2013

Description	2003	2004	2005	2006	2007	2008	2009	2010	2011	2012	2013	2014
Long-term bonds in PLN bn	5.3	7.3	8.9	8.8	13.9	14.9	12.2	17.6	24.3	31.4	37.8	49,8
Growth rate, % previous year =100	-	**137.7**	**121.9**	**98.9**	**157.9**	**107.2**	**81.4**	**144.6**	**137.5**	**129.7**	**120.4**	**131,7**
Loans and credit in PLN bn	126.4	129.2	123.3	127.5	144.4	182.5	233.4	220.4	221.2	264.4	270.3	311,0
Growth rate, % previous year =100	-	**102.2**	**95.4**	**103.4**	**113.3**	**126.4**	**127.9**	**94.4**	**100.4**	**119.5**	**102.2**	**109,8**
Factoring in PLN bn	12.0	13.2	14.2	17.0	30.7	47.9	51.4	64.2	79.4	113.1	131.0	142,8
Growth rate, % previous year =100	-	**110.1**	**107.3**	**119.9**	**180.7**	**155.9**	**107.2**	**125.0**	**123.6**	**142.5**	**115.8**	**109,0**
Leasing in PLN bn	11.1	13.8	16.2	21.7	32.7	32.9	23.0	27.3	31.1	31.2	35.3	42,8
Growth rate, % previous year =100	-	**123.9**	**117.6**	**133.9**	**150.7**	**100.8**	**69.8**	**118.7**	**114.1**	**100.3**	**113.0**	**121,2**

Adapted from Rola obligacji korporacyjnych w finansowaniu przedsiębiorstw sektora górniczego w Polsce. [The role of corporate bonds in financing mining sector companies]. Gospodarka Surowcami Mineralnymi, 29(1), 141-155 by Sierpińska and Bąk (2013); W tym roku spółki będą więcej pożyczać na rozwój. [This year companies will borrow more for development] by Sajewicz (2014). Retrieved from http://archiwum.rp.pl/artykul/1234503-W-tym-roku-spolki-beda-wiecej-pozyczac-na-rozwoj.html; Dane Statystyczne [Statistic Data] by Związek Polskiego Leasingu. (2015). Available from http://www.leasing.org.pl/statystyki/; Statystyki [Statistics] by Polski Związek Faktorów (2015). Available from http://www.faktoring.pl/index.php?page=6&id=2015

company's Board regarding its value, the propensity to issue shares increases (Ritter & Welch, 2002). The opposite trend occurs in periods of an economic downturn or low economic activity in the industry. It is in such circumstances that companies are keen to raise funds from a bond issue. During this period, investors prefer bonds with short maturities of one or two years. Not infrequently, companies roll their debts over, i.e., in place of the redeemed bonds, they place a new issue of a similar value on the market. Through fundraising flexibility, they ensure a steady supply of funds, allowing them to maintain liquidity at an appropriate level (Waśniewski,

2012). The flexibility of bonds is also reflected in the fact that they may include the option of the issuer's early redemption. This is cost effective, especially in periods of expected declines in interest rates. Thus, using funds from the issue of lower priced securities, a company can refinance its debt through an early redemption of higher interest securities. In 2014, a series of interest rate cuts prompted businesses to take advantage of this procedure. Moreover, investors are keen to invest surplus funds in corporate bonds because these offer a higher interest rate than bank deposits.

The amount of bond issues in relation to other sources of funding is presented in Table 1. The figures in the table show that the pace of change that surrounds fundraising through the issue of bonds was highly volatile, becoming increasingly so each year. The largest increase in the value of the issued bonds in the previous year was reported to be 57% in 2007. In 2008 -2014, which was a period of decline in corporate investment, the increase in the value of issues was significant.

During the period 2003-2013, the increase in bank debt was markedly lower than the increase in funds from bond issues. Only 2013 witnessed a nearly 10% increase in debt, compared to an over 30% increase in the value of the issued bonds. Factoring shows a high growth rate. In 2012, companies raised 42.5% more funds through factoring than in the previous year. The proceeds from factoring and partly from bond issues were allocated to the maintenance of financial stability.

Leasing grew at a slower pace, and it was mainly used by companies to pay for fixed assets. During an economic downturn, companies are very wary of investing in the development of production capacity. When demand grows, companies use existing production capacity first, and only then do they increase this capacity, which contributes to the creation of new jobs. However, in raw material companies, investment cannot be postponed due to the long investment cycle of mining projects.

In Poland, bond issuance is not only an option for stable companies, such as energy, construction or telecommunications companies, but also for businesses in high-growth sectors, such as renewable energy, biotechnology, medicine and pharmaceuticals. In a bid to tap into EU funding, these companies must have their own funds to contribute to project implementation, hence their decision to issue bonds. Coal mining companies have been issuing bonds for the previous two years, the proceeds from which have been used to finance both operating activities and development.

3. Research methods and information sources

To assess the costs and conditions of bond issuance for coal mining companies, the authors applied a comparative analysis. Based on data derived from the Catalyst website, analyses conducted by the consultancy firm PwC and the authors' own analyses, the authors assessed the costs of bond issuance to mining companies against the average cost of bond issuance in the Polish debt market. There are four coal mining companies in Poland. The research was conducted in three companies, which account for 75% of the sample. The authors analyzed bond issue programs prepared for Jastrzębska Spółka Węglowa (JSW), Kompania Węglowa and Katowicki Holding Węglowy. However, not every program was implemented, due to the high costs of issuance, program preparation and execution, and additional conditions known as covenants, which markedly reduced the flexibility of the companies. At the end of 2014, interest rates in Poland were down to 2%. By March 2015, the Monetary Policy Council further lowered the rates to 1.5%. Such low interest rates prompted companies to benefit more from the debt market. However, the overly restrictive conditions of bond issuance led two of the companies to abandon this method of borrowing.

The detailed provisions of bond issues were confidential. Therefore, this paper presents the general bond issue conditions of three issuance programs that were prepared for mining companies. By factoring into consideration the specifics of the coal mining companies' operations, these programs allowed one to assess the total cost of this form of fundraising. The terms and conditions of the bond issues were highly determined by the issuer's financial standing. Hence, the financial conditions of three mining companies were examined. Table 2 provides the structure of the companies' assets and liabilities.

As indicated by the data in Table 2, the financial structure of all three surveyed companies began to worsen in 2012. The share of equity in total liabilities decreased. In 2014, Kompania Węglowa had a nega-

Table 2. The structure of assets and liabilities in mining companies issuing bonds in years 2010-2014

Description	2010	2011	2012	2013	2014
KOMPANIA WĘGLOWA					
Asset's structure,%					
Fixed assets,%	68,0	66,6	69,3	74,2	74,8
Current assets,%	32,0	33,4	30,7	25,8	25,2
Liabilities structure,%					
Equity,%	21,0	24,7	13,9	4,9	(4,0)
Liabilities and provisions for liabilities,%	79,0	75,3	86,1	95,1	104,0
KATOWICKI HOLDING WĘGLOWY					
Asset's structure,%					
Fixed assets,%	82,0	83,0	72,1	83,6	83,5
Current assets,%	18,0	17,0	27,9	16,4	16,5
Liabilities structure,%					
Equity,%	29,7	31,9	26,7	24,8	11,6
Liabilities and provisions for liabilities,%	70,3	68,1	63,3	75,2	88,4
JASTRZĘBSKA SPÓŁKA WĘGLOWA					
Asset's structure,%					
Fixed assets,%	70,4	68,2	70,4	74,2	85,1
Current assets,%	29,6	31,8	29,6	25,8	24,9
Liabilities structure,%					
Equity,%	57,2	65,2	62,6	60,2	47,3
Liabilities and provisions for liabilities,%	42,8	34,8	37,4	39,8	52,7

Adapted from Financial Statements 2010-2014 by Kompania Węglowa S.A. (2015). Available from http://bip.kwsa.pl/?id_kat=27; Financial Statements 2010-2014 by Katowicki Holding Węglowy S.A. (2015). Available from http://www.khw.pl/bip/wyniki.html; Investors Relations by Jastrzębska Spółka Węglowa. (2015). Available from http://www.jsw.pl/relacje-inwestorskie

tive level of equity. Total liabilities were 4% higher than total assets, indicating an equity deficiency of 4%. For Katowicki Holding Węglowy, the share of equity decreased from 26.7% in 2012 to 11.6% in 2014. JSW had the best capital structure of all researched companies. Its equity level decreased by 15.3 percentage points, from 62.6% in 2012 to 47.3% in 2014. The companies' losses caused their equity to lessen.

In addition to changes in the structure of financing sources, the explicit worsening of the mining companies' financial situations was revealed by the financial results, which are presented in Table 3. The largest decrease in financial results appeared in 2014. Kompania Węglowa generated a loss of 1 bn PLN. Due to the lack of supplementary capital to cover losses, the loss was 2.7 times larger than the level of equity. In 2014,

Table 3. Financial results of Polish mining companies issuing bonds

Description	2010	2011	2012	2013	2014
KOMPANIA WĘGLOWA S.A.					
Assets (PLN mn)	11 439,7	11 852,0	12 136,0	13 049,4	9 324,2
Equity(PLN mn)	2 408,7	2 877,7	1 682,1	637,8	(368,1)
Sales revenues(PLN mn)	10131,3	11 919,7	10 720,6	9 720,1	7 751,0
Net profit/loss (PLN mn)	30,9	554,5	170,8	(699,0)	(1 005,9)
ROS, %	0,30	4,65	1,59	(9,72)	(12,78)
ROA, %	0,27	4,68	1,41	(5,36)	(10,79)
ROE, %	1,28	19,27	10,15	(109,59)	(273,27)
Katowicki Holding Węglowy S.A.					
Assets (PLN mn)	4 757,3	4 744,7	5 456,2	5 674,5	5 177,2
Equity(PLN mn)	1 421,5	1 514,2	1 458,2	1 483,4	597,8
Sales revenues(PLN mn)	3 597,2	3 807,6	3 644,6	3 647,3	3 389,0
Net profit/loss (PLN mn)	31,3	249,7	58,6	30,4	(496,1)
ROS, %	0,87	6,54	1,61	0,83	(14,64)
ROA, %	0,66	5,26	1,07	0,53	(9,58)
ROE, %	2,20	16,49	4,02	2,05	(82,99)
Jastrzębska Spółka Węglowa S.A.					
Assets (PLN mn)	9 106,1	13 617,0	14 067,1	13 862,0	15 369,3
Equity(PLN mn)	520,6	8 443,4	8 579,0	8 351,6	7 267,5
Sales revenues(PLN mn)	6 172,4	9 378,0	8 821,0	7 632,2	6 814,9
Net profit/loss (PLN mn)	1 158,9	2 086,0	988,1	82,2	(657,1)
ROS, %	18,77	22,24	11,20	0,98	(9,64)
ROA, %	12,73	15,32	7,02	0,59	(4,28)
ROE, %	22,6	24,7	11,52	0,98	(9,04)

Adapted from Financial Statements 2010-2014 by Kompania Węglowa S.A. (2015). Available from http://bip.kwsa.pl/?id_kat=27; Financial Statements 2010-2014 by Katowicki Holding Węglowy S.A. (2015). Available from http://www.khw.pl/bip/wyniki.html; Investors Relations by Jastrzębska Spółka Węglowa. (2015). Available from http://www.jsw.pl/relacje-inwestorskie

the loss for Katowicki Holding Weglowy amounted to nearly 0.5 bn PLN, which accounted for 83% of the company's equity. In the same year, JSW also recorded a loss; however, the decrease in equity was minor compared to the two other companies.

Generated losses caused negative return ratios, loss on assets, loss on equity and loss on sales ratios. For Kompania Węglowa, loss on sales amounted to 9.7% in 2013 and 10.8% in 2014. Loss on equity increased from 109.6% to 273.3%. Based on the legal provisions of the

Table 4. Level of coal extraction, average prices of coal, and average cost of coal extraction in the Polish mining industry

Description	2010	2011	2012	2013	2014	Dynamics,% 2011=100
Coal extraction (thous. Mg)	76153,8	75667,8	79234,2	76466,3	72500,0	95,8
Coking coal price (PLN/Mg)	582,75	811,78	625,70	473,34	410,36	50,60
Steam coal price (PLN/Mg)	246,70	266,93	315,27	267,58	234,39	87,80
Average prices of coal in JSW	498,73	583,26	500,90	386,77	338,95	58,10
Coke price (PLN/Mg)	1028,81	1197,93	970,20	758,50	668,18	55,80
Average price of coal in Poland (PLN/Mg)	298,40	341,30	340,00	292,80	278,70	81,60
Average cost of coal extraction (PLN/Mg)	270,00	286,70	304,60	301,40	312,20	108,90
Accumulation (PLN/Mg)	28,40	54,60	35,70	-8,60	-33,50	161,30

Adapted from Inside Statistics by The Mineral and Energy Economy Research Institute of the Polish Academy of Sciences (2015). Inside Statistics. Available from http://www.min-pan.krakow.pl/en/; Investors Relations by Jastrzębska Spółka Węglowa. (2015). Available from http://www.jsw.pl/relacje-inwestorskie

Commercial Companies Code, this company should file for bankruptcy. For Katowicki Holding Węglowy, loss on sales (negative ROS) accounted for 14.6%, and loss on equity (negative ROE) accounted for 9.6% in 2014. In turn, the return on sales for JSW declined from 22% in 2011 to 9.6% in 2014. In 2011, the company's return on assets amounted to 15%, while return on equity was nearly 25%. In the final examined year, these ratios amounted to 4.3% and 9.0%, respectively. Large fluctuations in the mining companies' financial results and profitability indicate that they have limited access to bank loans. Under these conditions, they turn to a more flexible source of funding, namely bonds.

The decrease in coal prices was the basic reason for the worsening financial results of mining companies (Table 4). In the 5-year analyzed period, the prices of coal were highest in 2011, making that year a benchmark value in the table. The average prices of coal in years 2011-2014 dropped by nearly 20%.

Table 4 also presents the prices of coal that were set by JSW itself, as the company influenced the average prices of coal in Polish mining. JSW extracts coking coal, the price of which is much higher than the price of steam coal. In 2011, coking coal cost up to 812 PLN per tonne, while steam coal was 267 PLN/Mg. In subsequent analyzed years, this price ratio deteriorated. Hence, in 2014, the average price of steam coal amounted to 234 PLN/Mg, whereas the average price of coking coal declined to 410 PLN/Mg. The steam coal extracted by Kompania Węglowa and Katowicki Holding Węglowy had an approximate caloric value; thus, its price oscillated around the same amount.

An important factor influencing the financial results of mining companies was an increase in coal extraction costs. During the analyzed period, the cost reached nearly 9%, which led to losses due to the drop in coal prices. In 2011, accumulation on the sale of one tonne of coal amounted to nearly 55 PLN. Four years later, loss on the sale of one tonne of coal exceeded 33 PLN. Due to shortages of coal resources, mines were forced to dig into lower coal deposit levels, which increased the cost of extraction. Additionally, fixed costs, i.e., salaries and overhead expenses, which do not depend on production scale, accounted for more than half of the extraction costs. In 2014, production declined by 4.2%, causing an increase in the average cost of mining by 3.6%. During this period, companies were unable to explore new extraction walls at lower levels of coal deposits due to the lack of investment funds.

The conducted analysis indicates that, as a result of the large drop in coal prices and increase in extraction costs, mining companies suffered from worsened conditions for raising funds. The terms and conditions of bondholders for capital lending will be presented later in the article.

4. Analysis of bond interest rates on Catalyst market

The primary cost involved in a bond issue is the interest paid to investors. Each type of capital has its own cost level. Hence, differences in the cost of acquisition for a given type of capital afford companies an opportunity to design the best structure of their debt that will be the lowest cost of acquisition (Pratt & Grabowski, 2014).

Depending on the method of interest calculation, one can distinguish the following: bonds with a fixed coupon rate (interest rate), bonds with a variable coupon rate, indexed bonds, and zero-coupon bonds (Golawska-Witkowska, Rzeczycka, & Zalewski, 2006; Sierpińska & Bąk, 2013):

In addition to interest-bearing bonds, which are referred to as classic corporate bonds, issuers also put on the market instruments that offer other benefits, e.g., convertible bonds with a right of conversion into the issuer's shares, and bonds convertible into another entity's shares (Vernimmen et al., 2014).

On the Polish market, the interest rate on bonds is generally determined based on 3M or 6M WIBOR (i.e., interbank market rates), to which a margin is added. In Poland, the most commonly issued bonds are those with a variable coupon rate, with margins ranging from 3.3% to 6.5%. The average margin in 2014 stood at 4.12% above WIBOR (Gałka, 2015).

Throughout the life of the bond, a fixed interest rate is the preferred choice for issuers who do not want to be exposed to the risk of interest rate fluctuations. For issuers, a fixed rate is beneficial when financing investment projects with a low rate of return on capital. This approach will not make investment projects unprofitable during times of significant interest rate hikes. To inspire investor interest in bonds with a fixed interest rate, this rate should take into account future growth expectations, and it should be set at a level that is higher than the prevailing rate at the time of issue. For issuers, bonds with a fixed interest rate are especially attractive at times of low interest rates. However, in a bid to capitalize on interest rate hikes following a period of economic downturn, investors prefer bonds with a variable interest rate.

The size of interest and profit margin for investors is determined by such factors as the company's financial situation, its debt level, recognition in investor circles, market position, scale of operations, the size of the bond issue, its purpose, and the nature and quality of the underlying security. Investors expect a higher margin whenever the proceeds from the issue will be used to finance current operations or repay existing debt. They tolerate lower margins when the funds are used to finance development projects. When determining the interest rate and the profit margin, a key element to take into account is the value and type of security pledged as collateral. Secured bonds may have a lower interest rate, especially when they are backed by a mortgage on the company's property. Considerable impact on the bond's interest rate is exerted by the situation in the financial markets. During a downturn, the risk of issuers' bankruptcy is higher, and hence, issuers must offer higher interest to investors.

The interest rate also depends on whether the issue is made by a public company listed on the capital market, or by a non-public company unknown to a wider circle of investors. The latter company must offer a higher profit margin than the former. The cost of raising capital from a bond issue depends on ratings granted by competent institutions. The lack of such ratings, which are required especially by foreign investors, may increase the cost of raising capital in relation to the costs of capital raised through a bank loan. The bond rating, which is an independent and objective assessment of the credit risk posed by an already indebted entity or one incurring debt in the financial markets, is the responsibility of rating agencies. The issuer's inclusion in a particular group allows investors to gauge their risk premium for investing in bonds issued by a given entity. A high rating confirms an issuer's good financial standing, allowing the issuance of bonds at a relatively low interest rate (Dębski, 2010). The market is dominated by three major rating agencies: Moody's, Standard & Poor's, and Fitch Ratings. The agencies are used by corporations that place high value issues on the international debt market. Due to the high costs involved in obtaining a credit rating, small- and medium-sized companies do not approach such agencies. Instead, they can take advantage of domestic credit rating agencies or the services of consulting firms that specialize in granting non-public credit ratings.

5. Cost of organizing bond issuance on Catalyst market

In addition to the interest paid to investors, the issuer incurs the costs involved in organizing an issue. The issue preparation procedure can engage brokerage firms, investment banks or financial institutions, all of which charge a success fee for placing the issue. With high value issues, the fee varies between 1.5 and 2.0% of the value of the issue, while small value issues cost approximately 4-5%. The time of the bonds' redemption is also important. The longer it is, the higher the fee because buyers for long-term instruments are harder to find. Issue costs depend on whether the sale of bonds is arranged as a private or public placement. A private placement entails lower costs than a public one. The costs are essentially a matter of preparing the documentation and selling the issue. Private placements are carried out through the agency of banks or brokerage houses whose job it is to attract investors. They work in smaller groups than in a public offering; however, finding willing investors may be a greater challenge than in a public offering (Grant Thornton, 2013).

Public issues entail more expenses, including costs for legal and financial advisory and advertising. Companies listed on the stock market are already known to investors, generally lowering the promotion costs of their bonds. Furthermore, the issuer has statutory disclosure obligations to both bondholders and regulators, such as the publication of current and periodic reports, which naturally generate ongoing service costs related to the issue. Analysis of bond issuance costs must not overlook the cost of bond filing. The introduction of securities to the market via Catalyst entails additional fees payable to the stock exchange. However, when a company sells its issue via Catalyst, all transactions on the market are monitored through the involvement of the National Depository of Securities in which the securities are held. Catalyst ensures bond liquidity, which affords the opportunity to exit from the investment. In addition, disclosure requirements imposed on listed companies enhance transparency and reduce risk.

6. Security of bonds noted on Catalyst market

The risk inherent in bonds is reduced by different types of collateral. In practice, bond issues may be fully secured, partially secured or unsecured. The most commonly used security in bond issues is a mortgage on the issuer's real estate or other tangible property, registered liens, debts or securities of other entities. Guarantees given by another entity (usually a bank) may also be used as collateral. The guarantor then takes responsibility for redeeming the bonds at maturity, for which it charges a fee.

Mortgages and liens are the most popular forms of security. Pursuant to the provisions of the Bonds Act, these two forms of security are subject to the appointment of an administrator, without naming specific bondholders. The Polish Catalyst market favors unsecured issues. The reason behind this strategy is that not all companies are willing to pledge their assets as security, especially when they use them as collateral for loans. Companies often reduce debt-related risk by taking on different forms of debt. Unsecured bonds are the first choice of companies that are large, known to the market and financially sound because such good standing provides, in itself, the reassurance of debt repayment. Investors can in fact tolerate moderate risk of failure to redeem bonds and pay interest on an ongoing basis, however, only at the expense of a higher interest rate. Bond security plays a relatively minor role for institutional investors. Rather than on security, these investors are focused on the issuer's financial standing, its level of cash flow generated to service debt, and its ability to redeem the bonds.

Regardless of whether the bonds are secured or not, bond issues are often governed by clauses called covenants, which indirectly reduce the risk to bondholders. Covenants commit the company either to take or refrain from taking certain actions until redeeming the bonds. They may include both bans and orders relating to the financial, legal or asset and investment-related situation of the issuer. Covenants may also relate to additional security, reporting the obligations and ownership structure surrounding the issue. All covenants are aimed at reducing the risk of the issuer's insolvency. In the case of non-compliance, they can result in the investor's right to request early redemption of the bonds (Pauka & Śmieja, 2013a).

According to Smith and Warner (1979), the use of covenants entails additional costs but also diminishes the financing risk and thereby reduces the cost of capital. According to these researchers, an optimal set of covenants exists for any company, ensuring a balance between the costs of implementation and enforcement of covenants and the benefits of reducing the investment risks for external entities (Smith & Warner, 1979). Financial covenants are based on parameters of the assessment of the borrower's financial condition. Billett, King and Mauer (2007) proposed a model consisting of 15 variables measuring the level of covenant restrictiveness and relating it to indebtedness, dividends, restrictions on the disposal of assets, level of investment, restrictions on the issuance of bonds, maintenance of a certain level of earnings, mergers and acquisitions, and maintenance of rating. In agreement with other authors, Śmieja and Pauka (2013b) argue that companies with a larger number of effective covenants are less likely to go bankrupt because their boards must avoid risky decisions, specifically because of covenants. Covenants may also relate to general risk, the condition of the company's industry, or the company's management and changes in its ownership structure.

7. Conditions underlying bond issuance in coal mining companies

To assess the costs and conditions of corporate bond issues in companies of raw materials, the authors have carried out an analysis of selected bond issues in the last two years. Bond issue programs were prepared and implemented by legal and financial advisers. Their work costs approximately 1% of the value of the issues.

Bonds bear interest at WIBOR 3M, plus a margin ranging between 270 and 350 basis points p.a., depending on the tranche. This means that as of the date of issue, interest will be paid on a quarterly basis and will be charged based on the amount of bonds issued and outstanding. In the case of a failure to pay interest in a timely manner, a statutory interest rate (8.5% in 2015) will accrue. This poses a risk of increased costs of capital.

In addition to interest, companies pay a fee for the commitment of capital (for the unused capital made available to the company), which, depending on the tranche, costs 50-70 basis points, an arrangement fee of 80-100 basis points, and a fee of 50-65 basis points for early redemption of the bonds with money raised from other debt instruments. The issuance program provides for the redemption of individual tranches of bonds in the subsequent years of the 2015-2020 period. The largest amount to be redeemed falls in the last two years of the program, increasing the total costs of such issues.

The series of floating-rate bonds issued are secured at 110-130% of their value. Therefore, the full amount of the issue and interest on capital are secured. The bonds are secured by a mortgage on the issuing company's property, plant and equipment, registered pledges on receivables held in accounts kept by banks (underwriters), registered pledges on receivables from major long-term agreements for the supply of coal, pledges on coal stocks, and guarantees by subsidiaries. Collateral pledged by the Treasury is used when the issuer is an entity owned by the Treasury. Bond issues made by Kompania Węglowa and Katowicki Holding Węglowy featured this type of collateralization.

The terms and conditions of the bond issue also contain covenants governing the company's disposal of assets, the level of its debt, the conditions of bond redemption, its compliance with financial ratios, and management's obligations to ensure the audit of financial statements and the application of certain accounting principles.

The most commonly used financial ratios, which are defined in the terms and conditions of issue, include the net debt/EBITDA ratio, the Debt Service Coverage Ratio (DSCR) and Projected Cash Flow.

In the issues under consideration, the Net Debt/EBITDA ratio ranges from 2.0 to 3.5. When the metric stands at 2.0, the net debt (debt less cash holdings) should not exceed the generated operating profit plus depreciation and amortization by more than a factor of two. Once the ratio is exceeded, bondholders often demand the payment of financial penalties. For coal mining companies, the level of this ratio may depend on how these companies account for certain business operations. Companies using IAS, a reporting requirement to which listed companies are subject, record the exchange difference on exported raw materials as part of their basic sales revenues, while exchange differences on the importation of materials are recorded as operating costs. In companies recording business operations pursuant to the provisions of the Accounting Act, these differences are recognized in financial revenue and finance costs. This indicates that some of the results of operations are not accounted for in the operating profit. Therefore, it would be necessary either to adjust the operating profit so that it accounts for elements of financial revenue and finance costs, or determine the operating profit starting with gross profit.

Another acute problem related to meeting the standards set by this ratio concerns fund allocation. If the proceeds from the issuance are used to finance current operations, then asset depreciation will not increase, leading to an excessive rise in the Net debt/EBITDA ratio, although the debt level will not rise. On the other hand, debt financing through a bond issue increases depreciation, thus improving the ratio. This ratio should be differentiated and depends on the allocation of funds from the bond issue. The ratio level of 2.0, as required by investors, seems to be too high, posing the risk of non-compliance. The risk is even more acute in raw material companies due to the high volatility of commodity prices on world markets. For example, a decline in coal prices caused the coal companies to generate losses. In certain companies, EBITDA is less than the level of depreciation. Companies can maximize the value of depreciation by charging extraordinary depreciation costs for the closure of mines. However, they will reduce their net profit, which may increase the risk of immediately calling in the debt. The solution to this problem depends on the specific conditions of the bond issue, which are of a confidential nature. Often the terms and conditions of the bond issue stipulate that the company shall be subject to a penalty for failure to comply with financial ratios, which increases the costs of bond issuance. The total cost of the bond issue may then be much higher than the cost of a syndicated loan. The company may comply with the net debt/EBITDA ratio requirement by controlling the level of its debt. However, under difficult market conditions, this could lead to loss of liquidity. In addition, the impossibility of taking on extra debt to complete a project that is already in progress may lead to huge losses due to a breach of contracts for the supply of raw materials. This is clearly illustrated by the problems posed by the delay in completion of the gas terminal in the port city of Świnoujście. Therefore, the terms and conditions of bond issuance should provide for the net debt/EBITDA ratio to be within a reasonable range, rather than at a fixed level, accounting for the nature of the coal companies' business, the seasonality of coal consumption, and fluctuations in financial results due to cyclical changes in the price of coal. When the interest is accrued on a quarterly basis, the net debt/EBITDA ratio is calculated on the last day of each quarter until the redemption date; and when interest is accrued semi-annually, the ratio is calculated on the last day of each half-year. Bondholders usually demand that the calculations be made on the basis of audited values that originate in financial statements, furthering that the annual values of this ratio be verified by an auditor reviewing the annual financial statements.

The second parameter laid down in the terms and conditions of bond issues mandates that DSCR be between 1.1 and 1.3. DSCR is a ratio of cash available to service the debt to the amount of debt consisting of interest and principal, or a given tranche redeemed in a given quarter. A debt level of 1.3 means that if the company is to timely meet its other obligations, e.g., remuneration or materials and services payables, the funds available to service the debt should be 30% higher than the amount to be repaid by the company. As in the case of the previous ratio, this ratio is subject to audit. The method of its calculation must be in accordance with a formula set forth in the bond agreement, and it must be submitted to the Payments Agent, who controls the level of the indicators laid down in the terms and conditions of the bond issue during the accrual of interest.

The third parameter, called the Projected Cash Flow ratio, is laid down within the range of 1.1 to 1.3. This metric measures the relationship between revenues from contracts pledged as security for the bonds and the maximum amount of the bond issue program. It is determined based on values projected at least 1.5-2.0 years ahead. Once its value is fixed at 1.3, it must not fall below that number. With the ratio set at this level, it can be concluded that the conditions of the issue are difficult to satisfy, but everything depends on the method of calculating the values that are the basis for its calculation. If the issue is secured by mortgages on property, plant and equipment, these assets must be valuated, and their future value disclosed in future periods in line with market conditions prevailing at the future time. Hence, it is assumed that the proceeds generated by the collateral should be at least 20-30% higher than the value of the issuance program. In the face of the economic downturn and uncertainty about future economic circumstances, changes in property prices typically lead bondholders to require different forms of security and demand the proceeds from the sale of products manufactured by the company. However, the allocation of funds from current revenues generated by sales of products carries a risk of shortage of funds that are needed to meet liabilities that enable restoration of production processes. This risk is particularly high in the coal mining industry, where employee salaries account for approximately 55% of coal production costs. A failure to pay company employees in a timely manner leads to social unrest and additionally creates political risk because coal mining companies are state-owned. The problem will not be solved by the privatization companies because this will increase risk in the area of energy security.

Limitations imposed by the terms and conditions of bond issuance also concern the level of investment that companies can undertake before the bond's maturity, disposal of assets held, permissible debt level or transfer of funds to subsidiaries. Regulations in these areas differ for each analyzed issue. For example, the provisions governing property, plant and equipment fix the amount of assets that can be sold or put to use by other entities. Such provisions can hinder the use of funds from the sale of assets to service debt. In the face of declining performance, companies could use leaseback more widely in order to retain their ability to redeem individual tranches of bonds, but they do not have the freedom to dispose of their own assets. In addition, bondholders want to have priority over shareholders for access to funds that are generated to service debt. Hence, the limiting conditions of bond agreements often contain provisions concerning the allocation of profit. In such cases, for the period from bond issuance until its redemption, the dividend policy must incorporate provisions that stipulate that the company shall not pay dividends higher than a specified amount, e.g., 30% of any of the generated profit, or the company shall not pay them at all if its profits fall below a specified amount. These provisions are the result of projected cash flows and a need to comply with the above-mentioned financial ratios at a level mandated by bond contracts.

8. Summary

For mining companies, it must be emphasized that raising funds from bond issue is more expedient than bank loans. The prolonged cycle of implementing investment projects lasts for several years. Thus, companies can flexibly adjust the issue tranches to their financial needs and investment realization phases. Terms and conditions of bond issue for the mining industry were compared to average terms of bond issuance on Catalyst market, where average bond interest rates amounted to WIBOR 3M, plus a 3-6% margin. This markup was due to issuance of unsecured bonds that were of higher risk than covered bonds.

Issue programs prepared for mining companies assumed variable interest rates at WIBOR 3M, plus a margin of 2.7 to 3.5%. On Catalyst market, the costs of preparing the issue for larger offers ranged from 1.5 to 2% of the total value of the issue. For mining companies, the latter oscillated near 2%. Besides these two cost components, mining companies had to pay a capital commitment fee of 1.5 to 0.7% (depending on the tranche), an arrangement provision of 0.8 to 1%, and a fee of 0.5 to 0.65% for early redemption when using funds raised from other debt instruments. Issued bonds are secured at the level of 110 to 130% of the total value of the issue by different types of collateral, such as mortgages on the issuer's tangible property, registered pledges on receivables from major long-term agreements for the supply of coal, pledges on coal stocks, and guarantees by subsidiaries. Additionally, several strict covenants were created, relating to the level of indebtedness monitored by ratios: EBITDA (2.0-3.5) and DSCR (1.1-1.3), as well as to restrictions on profit distribution, governing the company's disposal of assets or funds transferred to subsidiaries. Meeting the overly restrictive expectations of bondholders led companies to withdraw from issuing certain tranches of bonds.

References

Billett, M. T., King, T. D., & Mauer, D. C. (2007). Growth opportunities and the choice of leverage, debt maturity, and covenants, The Journal of Finance, *62*(2), 697-730.

Cornett, M. M., McNutt, J. J., Strahan, P. E., & Tehranian, H. (2011). Liquidity risk management and credit supply in the financial crisis, *Journal of Financial Economics, 101*(2), 297-312.

Dębski, W. (2010). Rynek finansowy i jego mechanizmy. [Financial Market and its mechanisms]. Warszawa: Wydawnictwo Naukowe PWN.

Gałka, T. (2015). Ewolucja rynku obligacji korporacyjnych w Polsce [Evolution of corporate bonds market in Poland]. Retrieved from: http://www.case-research.eu/sites/default/files/T.Ga%C5%82ka_prezentacja.pdf

Golawska-Witkowska, G., Rzeczycka, A., & Zalewski, H. (2006). Zarządzanie finansami Przedsiębiorstwa [Corporate Finanance Managment]. Bydgoszcz: Oficyna Wydawnicza Branta.

Grant Thornton (2013, December). Catalyst Report – Summary and Growth Perspectives (2nd Ed.). Retrieved from http://www.gpwcatalyst.pl/pub/files/materialy_do_pobrania/Catalyst%20Report%20December%202013%20FINAL.pdf

Jastrzębska Spółka Węglowa. (2015). Investors Relations. Available from http://www.jsw.pl/relacje-inwestorskie

Katowicki Holding Węglowy S.A. (2015). Financial Statements 2010-2014. Available from http://www.khw.pl/bip/wyniki.html

Kompania Węglowa S.A. (2015). Financial Statements 2010-2014. Available from http://bip.kwsa.pl/?id_kat=27

Pauka, M., & Śmieja, N. (2013a). Zastosowanie konwentów w warunkach emisji obligacji – badania empiryczne wśród emitentów z branży developerskiej w Polsce [Using debt covenants of put options embedded in bonds- an empirical research among bond issuers from real estate development industry in Poland]. Zeszyty Naukowe Uniwersytetu Szczecińskiego, Finanse, Rynki Finansowe, Ubezpieczenia, *62*, 399-409.

Polski Związek Faktorów. (2015). Statystyki [Statistics]. Available from http://www.faktoring.pl/index.php?page=6&id=2015

Pratt, S. P., Grabowski, R. J. (2014). Cost of capital: applications and examples (5th ed). Hoboken, New Jersey, NJ: Wiley.

Ritter, J. R., Welch, I. (2002), A. Review of IPO activity, pricing and allocations. *The Journal of Finance, 57*(4), 1795-1828.

Rzeszowski, P., Sierpińska, M. (2012). Financing structure of enterprises in the metal industry in Poland between 2000 and 2010. *Contemporary Economics, 6*(3), 66-75.

Sajewicz, M. (2014, March 14). W tym roku spółki będą więcej pożyczać na rozwój. [This year companies will borrow more for development]. Retrieved from http://archiwum.rp.pl/artykul/1234503-W-tym-roku-spolki-beda-wiecej-pozyczac-na-rozwoj.html

Sierpińska, M., Bąk, P. (2012). Financial structure of mining sector companies during an economic slowdown. *Archives of Mining Sciences, 57*(4), 1089-1100.

Sierpińska, M., Bąk, P. (2013). Rola obligacji korporacyjnych w finansowaniu przedsiębiorstw sektora górniczego w Polsce [The role of corporate bonds in financing mining sector companies]. Gospodarka Surowcami Mineralnymi, *29*(1), 141-155.

Smith, C.W., Warner J. B. (1979). On financial contracting: An analysis of bond covenants. Journal of Financial Economics, *7*(2), 117-161.

Śmieja, N., & Pauka, M. (2013b). Analiza kowenantów w obligacjach korporacyjnych emitowanych przez niebankowe spółki z branży finansowej. [Covenants analysis in corporate bonds issued by the debt collection firms]. Annales Universitatis Mariae Curie-Skłodowska, Sectio H Oeconomia, *47*(3), 551-561.

Vernimmen, P., Quiry, P., Dallocchio, M., Le Fur, Y., Salvi, A. (2014). Corporate Finance. Theory and Practice (4th ed.). John Wiley & Sons. West Sussex, UK.

The Mineral and Energy Economy Research Institute of the Polish Academy of Sciences (2015). Inside Statistics. Available from http://www.min-pan.krakow.pl/en/

Waśniewski, P. (2012). Wpływ zakresu ujawnień na identyfikację ryzyka kredytowego inwestycji w obligacje korporacyjne. [Influence of exposure range on credit risk identification in corporate bonds investments]. Zeszyty Naukowe Uniwersytetu Szczecińskiego, Finanse, Rynki Finansowe, Ubezpieczenia, *50*, 511-526.

Związek Polskiego Leasingu. (2015). Dane Statystyczne [Statistic Data]. Availabel from http://www.leasing.org.pl/statystyki/

5

Developing Countries as New Growth Poles of Post-Crisis Global Economy

Elena Popkova[1], Svetlana Meshkova[2], Evgeniya Karpunina[3], Elena Karpushko[4], Marina Karpushko[5]

ABSTRACT

This article is devoted to the search for a solution to overcoming the consequences of the global financial and economic crisis and the development of a post-crisis global economy. The purpose of this article is to determine perspectives and directions for the development of new growth poles in a post-crisis global economy and to develop tools for overcoming the consequences of the crisis and facilitating the global economic system entry into a new level of economic growth. The article uses the proprietary methodology for the calculation of "underdevelopment whirlpools," which analyzes the dynamics of economic growth of the most prominent countries in this group and their ability to overcome "underdevelopment whirlpools" and transform into new growth poles for the global economy following the global financial crisis. The use of calculation tools for "underdevelopment whirlpools" determines the prospective of developing countries' transformation into new growth poles in a post-crisis global economy. China, Japan, Brazil, Russia, and India are such poles at present, and they will strengthen their positions in the near future. For this, the research offers the following perspective and directions for the development of new growth poles in a post-crisis global economy for the increase in rates and quality (stability and sustainability) of economic growth: an emphasis on the real sector development of the economy, realization of transnational cluster initiatives, and active creation and implementation of innovations into production. As tools for overcoming the consequences of the crisis and the global economic system entering a new level of economic growth, the author developed the mechanism of post-crisis global economy development.

KEY WORDS: growth poles, global financial and economic crisis, post-crisis phenomena, innovations, global economy

[1]Volgograd State Technical University, Russian Federation, [2]Perm Institute of Economics and Finance, Russian Federation, [3]G.R. Derzhavin Tambov State University, Russian Federation, [4] Volgograd State University of Architecture and Civil Engineering, Russian Federation, [5]Perm National Research Polytechnic University, Russian Federation

Introduction

Over several decades, the global economy has shown stable growth and development. However, despite positive forecasts, 2008 was marked by the global financial crisis, the consequences of which – unemployment, inflation, and reduction of economic growth – influenced even the most economically developed countries.

At present, the global economic system is in post-crisis conditions. To overcome the current recession, it is necessary to reconsider traditional approaches to the provision of economic growth and search for new sources of growth. In this context, it is necessary to focus on the gradual restructuring trends of the global economy.

Correspondence concerning this article should be addressed to: **Elena Popkova,** Volgograd State Technical University, 28 Lenina St. Volgograd 400000 Russian Federation. E-mail: elenapopkova@yahoo.com

Developed countries, which occupy leading positions in the global economy, have almost depleted their potential for further development and realization of strategies to preserve these positions. Indeed, they are overcome in this aspect by developing countries, which possess significant potential for development. Most importantly, the motivation to search for new solutions and actualize new ideas, i.e., the creation and implementation of innovations, is led by developing countries.

Innovations have been a moving force of the global economy, not only over the past few decades but throughout the entire history of mankind. Research has shown that the implementation of innovations has allowed previous global crises to be overcome, which is why it is believed that the consequences of the recent financial and economic crisis will be overcome with the help of innovations.

Therefore, it is necessary to focus on sources of innovations, determine the best direction for their use, and create favorable conditions for their implementation into production. It is very likely that country-incubators of innovations will become new growth poles of the global economy in the short term.

Before the crisis, the USA and the EU were the growth poles of the global economy – they have demonstrated the highest rates of economic growth over the past 35 years and have made the greatest contribution to the formation of the global GDP. China, Japan, Brazil, Russia, and India can potentially take their place after the crisis because the total GDP of these countries exceeds the U.S. GDP, and the economy of these countries is based on the real sector of production, which shows the highest stability and sustainability levels as well as innovation potential.

This research offers a hypothesis in which the conditions of the global economic system functioning were changed cardinally due to the global financial and economic crisis, and the previous growth poles of the global economy are not capable of providing the desired effect, which necessitates the search for new growth poles and the development of working mechanisms in the post-crisis global economy to overcome the long recession.

The purpose of the article is to verify the proposed hypothesis, determine directions for development and new growth poles for the post-crisis global economy, and develop tools to overcome the consequences of the crisis and the global economic system's entry into a new level of economic growth.

Literature Review

The theoretical basis of the research is composed of fundamental works in the study of the sense, notion, and meaning of economic growth for socio-economic systems by authors such as (Pogosov, 2015; Odhiambo, 2015; Zeira & Zoabi, 2015), among others. Economic growth is a process involving the increase in the production capabilities of an economy (Leonida et al., 2015) and can be expressed quantitatively, measured by the increase in GDP growth rates (Sarracino & Bartolini, 2015), and qualitatively, changing the structure of the economy (González-Pernía & Peña-Legazkue 2015). The development of modern economic systems is impossible without economic growth (Choi & Shin, 2015; Lee & Oh, 2015). Therefore, economic growth influences the development of any socio-economic system (Castiglione, Infante, & Smirnova, 2015).

This article also uses material from recent studies that analyze the peculiarities, factors, and conditions of global economic development at present and the growth poles of various economic systems, among which studies by (Bere, 2015; Kolomiets, 2015; Smékalová, Hrabinová, & Habuda, 2014), among others, can be distinguished. The most important peculiarity of modern global economic development is its orientation toward building and developing market relations (Dymskill, 2013) and establishing priorities for the development of the service sphere, which is one of the most important growth poles of the modern global economic system (Ravuri, 2012). The most important factors of global economic development are the globalization and integration of various economic systems (Christofakis & Papadaskalopoulos, 2011), as well as the creation and implementation of innovations for the production activities of business structures (Fuseini & Kemp, 2015).

While conducting research, the author found studies on the foundations of the functioning of the modern global economy and the trends of its development in the past and prospective views, including studies by (Docquier & Machado, 2015; Ilie & Jaradat, 2015; Yakovleva, Azarova, & Titova, 2015), among others. The modern global economic system is based on the principles of the increase in cooperation between its members (Wirtz, Tuzovic, & Ehret, 2015), which is expressed in the processes of regionalization and the international division of labor (Čaušević, 2015). The most important tendencies of the global economic system development include the transnationalization of business (Klinov, 2015), the growth of production factor flows at an international scale (Kornev, Maksimtsova, & Treshchina, 2015), the increase in global economic problems, which require joint solutions by all countries around the world (Pulselli et al., 2015), and the acceleration of crisis phenomena distribution in all member countries regarding integration associations and the global economic system (Dudin & Frolova, 2015).

The author uses research materials by various authors in study of crises in economic systems as well as the sense and peculiarities of the global financial crisis that began in 2008, including (Aytaç, Rankin, & İbikoğlu, 2015; McMaster, 2015; Rodriguez, Turmo, & Vara, 2014; Zhao, Jiang & Li, 2015), among others. An economic system crisis is a temporary violation of processes that take place in the system (Heinrich, Kobayashi, & Bryant, 2016). Economic crises are of different depths and durations (Guttmann, 2015). The most important peculiarities of the global financial crisis, which began in 2008, are the strengthening of risk components in the financial sphere of the economy due to the active implementation of financial innovations in recent years (Galbraith, 2012), the unprecedented scale of the crisis (Capello, Caragliu, & Fratesi, 2015), and structural shifts in the global economic system as a result of the crisis (Hieronymi, 2016).

Method

The theoretical basis of the research is composed of fundamental works on the notion, sense, and meaning of economic growth for socio-economic systems by authors such as (Castiglione et al., 2015; Choi & Shin, 2015; González-Pernía & Peña-Legazkue, 2015; Lee & Oh, 2015; Leonida et al., 2015; Odhiambo, 2015; Pogosov, 2015; Sarracino & Bartolini, 2015; Zeira & Zoabi, 2015), among others.

This study also uses material from recent research that is devoted to the analysis of the peculiarities of the factors and conditions of current global economic development and the growth poles of various economic systems, among which it is possible to distinguish the works of (Bere, 2015; Christofakis & Papadaskalopoulos, 2011; Dymskill, 2013; Fuseini & Kemp, 2015; Kolomiets, 2015; Ravuri, 2012; Smékalová et al., 2014), among others.

While conducting research, the author found studies on the foundations of the functioning of the modern global economy and past trends and prospective development, among which are studies by (Čaušević, 2015; Docquier & Machado, 2015; Dudin & Frolova, 2015; Ilie & Jaradat, 2015; Klinov, 2015; Kornev et al., 2015; Pulselli et al., 2015; Wirtz et al., 2015; Yakovleva et al., 2015).

The author also uses materials from the research of various authors on economic system crises and the sense and peculiarities of the 2008 global financial crisis. These include the works by (Aytaç et al., 2015; Capello et al., 2015; Galbraith, 2012; Guttmann, 2015; Heinrich et al., 2016; Hieronymi, 2016; McMaster, 2015; Rodriguez et al., 2014; Zhao et al., 2015).

To determine new growth poles in a post-crisis global economy, this research uses a proprietary methodology to calculate "underdevelopment whirlpools," which is described in detail in numerous publications by E. G. Popkova that include examples and detailed calculations (Popkova et al., 2013a; 2013b; Popkova & Tinyakova, 2013a; 2013b; 2013c; Popkova et al., 2015), etc.

The methodology of "underdevelopment whirlpools" was developed by the author of this article, Professor Elena G. Popkova, and it is her own development and has been successfully applied over many years. The effectiveness of this methodology was proved by multiple studies in various countries around the world.

An analysis of the "underdevelopment whirlpools" supposes a determination of two key parameters: the depth of the whirlpool and the speed of being drawn into the whirlpool. First, a model country is determined, which leads other countries in the contribution to the global GDP formation and the most important growth pole of the global economy before the 2008 global financial crisis.

The depth of the "underdevelopment whirlpool" is then calculated through a determination of the time lag in the country based on the "model country" regarding the GDP level. For this purpose, the correspondence of the GDP level in the examined country for the selected

Table 1. Table for determining the depth and speed of countries falling into "underdevelopment whirlpools" and perspectives for overcoming these whirlpools

Country	Year	V	Y	Dwhirlpool	Swhirlpool
1	1,2,...,n	V1,2,...,n	Y1,2,...,n	Year-Y	Dwhirlpool2-Dwhirlpool1
2	1,2,...,n	V1,2,...,n	Y1,2,...,n	Year -Y	Dwhirlpool2-Dwhirlpool1
...	...	...	...	...	...
n	1,2,...,n	V1,2,...,n	Y1,2,...,n	Year -Y	Dwhirlpool2-Dwhirlpool1

year to the level of the GDP of the "model country" in one of the previous years is determined.

As a result, the difference between the selected year and the year in which the GDP level of the "model country" coincided with the GDP level in the studied country is determined. The resulting difference reflects the depth of the "underdevelopment whirlpool." The speed of being drawn into the "underdevelopment whirlpool" is determined as the difference between the depths of the "underdevelopment whirlpool" in the current year and the previous year.

Table 1 uses the following legend:

V – GDP per capita;

Y – year in which the country model had the same GDP per capita;

Dwhirlpool – depth of the "underdevelopment whirlpool";

Swhirlpool – speed of being drawn into the "underdevelopment whirlpool."

With regard to the analysis of the growth poles of the post-crisis global economy, this methodology is expected to determine the dynamics of economic growth of top leading countries and trends regarding their overcoming "underdevelopment whirlpools," taking leading positions instead of the ones lagging behind in contributing to the formation of the global GDP and their transformation into new growth poles of the global economy following the global financial crisis.

Results

Before the 2008 global financial crisis, the growth poles of the global economy were the U.S. and countries in the EU, which have demonstrated the highest rates of economic growth and contributed the most to the formation of the global GDP over the last 35 years.

The crisis in the global economy deepened the gap between developed and developing countries in the global economic system, which led to larger migration flows into EU countries. This may be a reason for some countries to leave the EU and further weaken its positions.

It is also possible to suppose that the financial sphere, which has been a growth pole for the U.S. economy in recent decades, depleted its possibilities. Financial speculations were the main cause for the recent financial crisis, which demonstrated their high risk component and incapacity for the provision of stable economic growth.

In this context, the economic growth of industrial countries by means of industrial production and development of the real sector of the economy attracts a significant amount of attention. Such countries include China, Japan, Brazil, Russia, and India, which occupy leading positions in the global GDP rankings of countries and increasingly contribute to the formation of gross global product.

Several decades ago, these countries did not attract any attention in view of economic development and were far from leading positions in international rankings. However, they have made major advances and continue to develop. Figure 1 shows the dynamics of GDP of the USA, Japan, Russia, Brazil, and India over the past 35 years.

With the help of the calculation methodology for "underdevelopment whirlpools," let us view the process of development of these countries (Tables 2, 3).

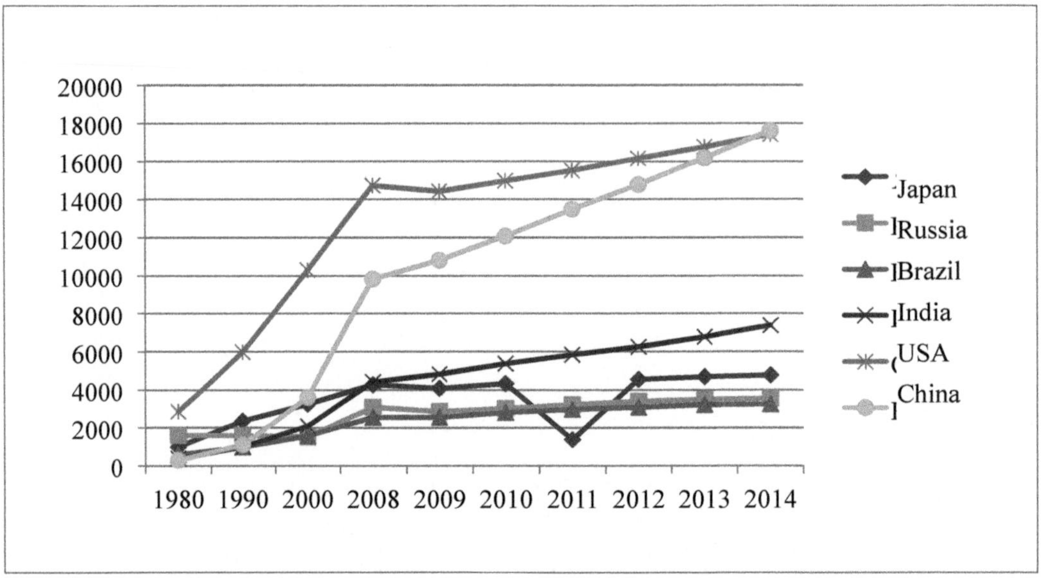

Figure 1. GDP dynamics of the USA, Japan, Russia, Brazil, and India from 1980 to 2014.
Source: IMF (2015)

Table 2. Results of the calculation of "underdevelopment whirlpools" in China and determination of perspectives of its transformation into a new growth pole of the post-crisis global economy

Country	Year	V, USD billion	Y	Dwhirlpool	Swhirlpool
China	1980	298.4	1970	10	-
	1990	1,091.2	1975	15	5
	2000	3,608.3	1983	17	2
	2008	9,826.8	1999	9	-8
	2009	10,813.8	2001	8	-1
	2010	12,085.5	2004	6	-2
	2011	13,482.1	2005	6	0
	2012	14,789.5	2008	4	-2
	2013	16,173.3	2012	1	-3
	2014	17,617.3	2014	0	-1

The model country is the USA, which has been a key growth pole in the global economy in recent decades. China has the highest indicators of GDP among the countries in the world, so it is advisable to view it separately.

Japan, Brazil, Russia, and India also demonstrated high rates of economic growth in recent decades. However, they cannot separately compete with current global leaders, so it is advisable to group them and view their total contribution to the formation of the global GDP.

Table 3. Results of the calculation of "underdevelopment whirlpools" in Japan, Brazil, Russia, and India and the determination of perspectives of their transformation into a new growth pole of the post-crisis global economy

Countries	Year	V, USD billion	Y	Dwhirlpool	Swhirlpool
Japan, Brazil, Russia, India, SAR	1980	3,549.0	1982	-2	-
	1990	5,955.1	1990	0	2
	2000	8,453.2	1996	4	4
	2008	14,329.9	2007	1	-3
	2009	14,328.0	2007	2	1
	2010	15,522.5	2011	-1	-3
	2011	13,432.1	2005	6	7
	2012	17,272.7	2014	-2	-8
	2013	18,172.9	2015	-2	0
	2014	18,955.0	2016	-2	0

As observed from Table 2, at the beginning of the viewed period in 1980, China lagged behind the USA by 10 years in terms of economic development. In 1990, the depth of the "underdevelopment whirlpool" grew by 15 years, and in 2000, by 17 years. However, given the crisis conditions, in 2008, the gap between the GDP levels of China and the USA was reduced to 9 years.

Afterward, under the conditions of the post-crisis global economy, a negative speed of being drawn into the "underdevelopment whirlpool" is observed, and this pressure of the underdevelopment whirlpool is overcome. In 2014, the Chinese GDP exceeded the GDP of the USA ($17,617.30 billion versus $17,418.90 billion).

As observed from Table 3, the total GDP of Japan, Brazil, Russia, and India at the beginning of the viewed period in 1980 exceeded the American GDP. However, in 2000, an "underdevelopment whirlpool" appeared, the depth of which constituted 4 years. Beginning in 2014, the total GDP of these countries exceeds the GDP of the USA.

The use of calculation tools for "underdevelopment whirlpools" allowed for the determination of turning the countries that lagged behind into new growth poles of the post-crisis global economy. China, Japan, Brazil, Russia, and India are such poles now, and according to the IMF forecast, will strengthen their positions in this role in the near future.

To this end, the research offers the following prospective directions for the development of new growth poles of the post-crisis global economy to increase the rates and quality (stability and sustainability) of economic growth:

- emphasis on the development of the real sector of the economy, which is necessary for the provision of sustainable development;
- the realization of transnational cluster initiatives, which is oriented toward the increase in economic growth rates;
- the active creation and implementation of innovations into production, which is important for positive economic development.

Let us view the above proposals in detail. An emphasis on the development of the real sector of the economy supposes an industrial direction of new growth poles in the post-crisis global economy. This does not mean that the development of the sphere of services and agriculture should not be given any attention – the importance of these spheres is not diminished but rather moves into the background, making way for the production sphere.

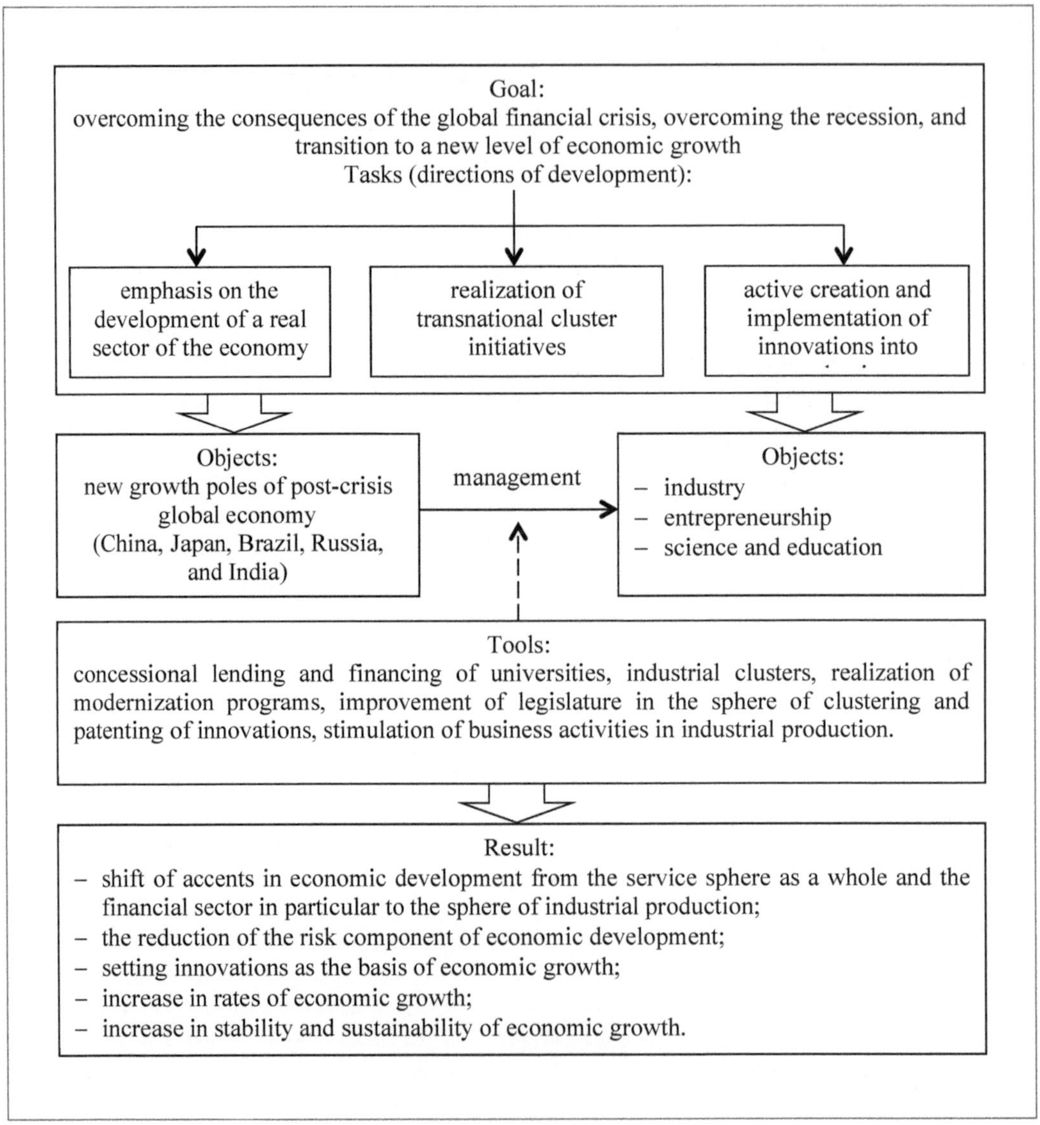

Figure 2. Mechanism of development of the post-crisis global economy

The realization of transnational cluster initiatives is oriented toward the determination of strong transnational connections and the further integration of growth poles into the global economic system. To withstand international competition, companies from these countries have to combine efforts and cooperate within transnational clusters.

The active creation and implementation of innovations into production supposes the development of research and education. The development of science will lead to the creation of multiple inventions and innovational technologies. Information on new knowledge should be distributed throughout the entire economy to successfully commercialize innovations and ensure their quick implementation into production.

An increase in the educational level will stipulate the creation of highly qualified human resources that are capable of using the newest technologies and equipment, which will create favorable conditions for the modernization of the production sector and the formation of industrial enterprises, which are highly competitive in the global markets.

As tools for the realization of the current potential of the global economic system for overcoming the consequences of the global financial crisis, overcoming the recession, and transitioning to a new level of economic growth, this research offers the following mechanism of development for the post-crisis global economy (Fig. 1).

As observed from Fig. 1, the proposed mechanism is oriented at overcoming the consequences of the crisis and the global economic system's transition to a new level of economic growth. The objective of the mechanism is to develop new growth poles of the post-crisis global economy (China, Japan, Brazil, Russia, and India).

The objective of the mechanism in terms of developing the real sector of the economy is developing industries. In terms of the realization of transnational cluster initiatives, the objective is entrepreneurship, and for the active creation and implementation of innovations into production, the objective is increased research and education.

To achieve the set goal for the realization of the prospective directions of the development of new growth poles in the post-crisis global economy, a special tool is used. For the development of the production sector of the economy, it is advisable to use the following tools to stimulate the state:

- the provision of subsidized credits for the modernization of equipment;
- the stimulation of business activities in industrial production.

For realization of cluster initiatives, the following tools should be used:

- the provision of financial resources to clusters under concessional terms;
- the improvement of laws in the clustering sphere.

For development of research and education, the following tools should be used:

- improvement of the system for patenting innovational technologies;
- increased financing of universities, scientific research and developments, and the active provision of budgets in universities to popularize higher education and increase its accessibility.

The expected and most probable results of the realization of the mechanism are the shift in emphasis in economic development from the service sphere on the whole and the financial sector in particular to the sphere of industrial production, the reduction of risk components in economic development, the establishment of innovations into the basis of economic growth, the increase in rates of economic growth, and the increase in stability and sustainability of economic growth.

Conclusion

Thus, due to the use of the analysis methodology of "underdevelopment whirlpools" and the study of the development dynamics of the most promising countries, the proposed hypothesis is proven in which it is determined that the new growth poles of the post-crisis global economy are China, Japan, Russia, Brazil, and India.

The shift of the emphasis in the global economic system confirms the expediency of the use of new development mechanisms for overcoming the consequences of the crisis and the provision of the new quality of growth in the global economy, which include the mechanism developed by the authors of this study.

As a result of this research, it is possible to conclude that, like any system, the global economy can change its structure; however, this requires new approaches to its analysis. Despite the wide diversity of the corresponding methods, this type of analysis is difficult to model and forecast.

The developed tools allow countries to overcome the consequences of the global financial crisis and use the crisis as stimulation for development, without which there are no stimuli for new knowledge, and the implementation of innovations does not proceed.

The crisis also demonstrated the mistakes of state management and the non-effectiveness of previous methods of stimulation for economic growth and development. A new vector of growth in the global economy should be an industry that develops in a stable manner, and the poles of growth should be countries with industrial foci.

Despite the practical direction, the results of this study are limited by the theoretical consideration of the problem of overcoming the post-crisis phenomena in the global economy, determination of new poles of growth, and development of tools for maximal use of poles to transition the global economic system to a new level of economic development.

In conducting further research on the global economy's departure from a post-crisis state, researchers should focus on checking the results of this research with experiments and comparing the expectations for the establishment of China, Japan, Brazil, Russia, and India as new growth poles of the global economy. The practical use of the developed tools should be emphasized.

Further development of the theory and methodology of the "underdevelopment whirlpools" should base its validity on the example of countries that have not yet been the objects of the research of "underdevelopment whirlpools" to determine its universality and effectiveness.

This research was conducted with financial support of the Russian Humanitarian Scientific Fund, Project No. 15-22-01011: "Theoretical and methodological foundations of the marketing provision for the innovational development of intellectual resources of the Republic of Belarus and the Russian Federation under the conditions of economic integration (by the example of creation of universities of the entrepreneurial type)."

This research was conducted with financial support from the Ministry of Education and Science of the Russian Federation, Project No. 2797: "Formation of the system of scientific and production clusters in regions of Russia."

References

Aytaç, I. A., Rankin, B., & İbikoğlu, A. (2015). The social impact of the 2008 global economic crisis on neighborhoods, households, and individuals in Turkey. *Social Indicators Research*, *124*(1), 1-19.

Bere, R. C. (2015). Institutional structures in the growth pole policy from Romania. *Administratie si Management Public, 2015*(24), 64-86.

Capello, R., Caragliu, A., & Fratesi, U. (2015). Global trends and the economic crisis: Future alternative European growth strategies. *Technological Forecasting and Social Change, 98*, 120-136.

Castiglione, C., Infante, D., & Smirnova, J. (2015). Environment and economic growth: is the rule of law the go-between? The case of high-income countries. *Energy, Sustainability and Society, 5*(26), (n.d.) DOI: 10.1186/s13705-015-0054-8.

Čaušević, F. (2015). Globalization, Southeastern Europe, and the world economy. Abington, UK: Routlege.

Choi, K. H., & Shin, S. (2015). Population aging, economic growth, and the social transmission of human capital: An analysis with an overlapping generations model. *Economic Modelling, 50*, 138-147.

Christofakis, M., & Papadaskalopoulos, A. (2011). The growth poles strategy in regional planning: The recent experience of Greece. *Theoretical and Empirical Researches in Urban Management, 6*(2), 5-20.

Docquier, F., & Machado, J. (2015). Global competition for attracting talents and the world economy. *World Economy, 39*(4), 530-542.

Dudin, M. N., & Frolova, E. E. (2015). The balanced scorecard as a basis for strategic company management in the context of the world economy transformation. *Asian Social Science, 11*(3), 282-288.

Dymskill, G. (2013). The problem of power in finance in India and Brazil: From targets of opportunity to poles of self-reinforcing growth? In B. Dasgupta (ed.), Non-mainstream dimensions of global political economy: Essays in honour of Sunanda Sen, (pp. 45-67). Abington, UK: Routlege.

Fuseini, I., & Kemp, J. (2015). A review of spatial planning in Ghana's socio-economic development trajectory: A sustainable development perspective. *Land Use Policy, 47*, 309-320.

Galbraith, J. K. (2012). Inequality and instability: A study of the world economy just before the great crisis. Inequality and Instability: A Study of the World Economy Just Before the Great Crisis. Oxford, UK: Oxford University Press.

González-Pernía, J. L., & Peña-Legazkue, I. (2015). Export-oriented entrepreneurship and regional economic growth. *Small Business Economics, 45*(3), 505-522.

Guttmann, R. (2015). Chronic macro-economic and financial imbalances in the world economy: A meta-economic view. *Revista de Economia Politica, 35*(2), 203-226.

Heinrich, T., Kobayashi, Y., Bryant, K. A. (2016). Public opinion and foreign aid cuts in economic crises. *World Development, 77*, 66-79.

Hieronymi, O. (2016). The crisis of international finance, the Eurozone and economic growth. In S. P. S. Rossi, & R. Malavi (Eds.), Financial crisis, bank behaviour and credit crunch (pp. 3-18). Berlin: Springer.

Ilie, C., & Jaradat, M. (2015). Co-operation in the world economy. *Quality - Access to Success, 16*, 168-173.

International Monetary Fund (IMF) (2015). World Economic Outlook. GDP by Country 1980-2014. Retrieved from http://knoema.ru/tbocwag/gdp-by-country-1980-2014

Klinov, V. G. (2015). The evolution of long waves in the world economy. *Studies on Russian Economic Development, 26*(3), 285-294.

Kolomiets, G. M. (2015). Risk management as a factor of sustainable development of the world economy. *Actual Problems of Economics, 165*(3), 43-49.

Kornev, A. K., Maksimtsova, S. I., Treshchina, S. V. (2015). Experience in world industrial development and the reindustrialization of the domestic economy. *Studies on Russian Economic Development, 26*(5), 460-469.

Lee, S., Oh, D. W. (2015). Economic growth and the environment in China: Empirical evidence using prefecture level data. *China Economic Review, 36*, 73-85.

Leonida, L., Patti, D. M. A., Marini, A., Navarra, P. (2015). Political competition and economic growth: A test of two tales. *Economics Letters, 135*, 96-99.

McMaster, R. (2015). The "illusion" or "paradigm blindness" of economics: Ethical challenges to economic thought from the financial crisis. Marx, Veblen, and the Foundations of Heterodox

Odhiambo, N. M. (2015). Government expenditure and economic growth in South Africa: An empirical investigation. *Atlantic Economic Journal, 43*(3), 393-406.

Pogosov, I. A. (2015). Factors of long-term economic growth: Scientific and technical progress and capital intensity of production. *Studies on Russian Economic Development, 26*(5), 423-433.

Popkova, E. G., Akopova, E. S., Budanova, I. M., & Natsubidze, A. S. (2013a). The directions of transition of economic systems to new quality of economic growth. *World Applied Sciences Journal, 26*(9), 1180-1184.

Popkova, E. G, Zubakova, N. N., Bogdanov, D. V., Yakovleva, E. A, & Nebesnaya, A.Y. (2013b). Measurement of economic growth as a factor of development of strategies of economic transformation. *World Applied Sciences Journal, 25*(2), 264-269.

Popkova, E. G., & Tinyakova, V. I. (2013a). New quality of economic growth at the present stage of development of the world economy. *World Applied Sciences Journal, 24*(5), 617-622.

Popkova, E. G., & Tinyakova, V. I. (2013b). Dialectical methodology of analysis of economic growth. *World Applied Sciences Journal, 24*(4), 467-475.

Popkova, E. G., & Tinyakova, V. I. (2013c). Drivers and contradictions of formation of new quality of economic growth. *Middle East Journal of Scientific Research, 15*(11), 1635-1640.

Popkova, E. G., Yurev, V., Stepicheva, O., & Denisov, N. (2015). Transformation and concentration of intellectual capital as a factor of economic growth in the modern economy. *Regional and Sectoral Economic Studies, 15*(1), 53-60.

Pulselli, F. M., Coscieme, L., Neri, L., Regoli, A., Sutton, P. C., Lemmi, A., & Bastianoni, S. (2015). The world economy in a cube: A more rational structural representation of sustainability. *Global Environmental Change, 35*, 41-51.

Ravuri, E. D. (2012). Assessing the growth pole phenomenon in Venezuela: The case of Ciudad Guayana. In M. J. Williams, J. J. Anderson (eds.), Urban Development: Strategies, Management and Impact (pp. 77-89). New York, NY: Published by Nova Science Publishers Inc.

Rodriguez, A., Turmo, J., & Vara, O. (2014). Financial crisis and the failure of economic theory. Abington, UK: Routlege.

Sarracino, F., & Bartolini, S. (2015). The dark side of Chinese growth: Declining social capital and well-being in times of economic boom. *World Development, 74*, 333-351.

Smékalová, L., Hrabinová, S., & Habuda, M. (2014). Spatial distribution of competitiveness support in the Slovakia in relation to growth poles and small and medium enterprises. *Scientific Papers of the University of Pardubice, Series D, Faculty of Economics and Administration, 21*(30), 95-106.

Wirtz, J., Tuzovic, S., & Ehret, M. (2015). Global business services: Increasing specialization and integration of the world economy as drivers of economic growth. *Journal of Service Management, 26*(4), 565-587.

Yakovleva, E. A., Azarova, N. A., & Titova, E. V. (2015). Innovation as a vector of regional economic development and a necessary condition for the progress of the world economy. *Asian Social Science, 11*(20), 90-96.

Zeira, J., & Zoabi, H. (2015). Economic growth and sector dynamics. *European Economic Review, 79*, 1-15.

Zhao, X., Jiang, X., & Li, Z. (2015). The impact of the economic crisis on the financial performance of multinational corporations. *International Review of Economics and Finance, 37*, 55-68.

6

Tolerable Level of Corruption for Foreign Direct Investment in Africa

Anselm Komla Abotsi[1,2], Tongyai Iyavarakul[1]

ABSTRACT Corruption has become endemic in many African countries and is difficult to eradicate completely; therefore, reducing corruption to a tolerable level that will not deter foreign investors must be the aspiration of all political leaders and stakeholders. This study tries to identify the level of corruption that is tolerable to foreign investors, which is referred to as the Tolerable Level of Corruption for Investment (TLCI). The study proposes that below the TLCI, corruption plays the role of "sand in the wheels of commerce" and thus has a negative impact on FDI inflows, but above the TLCI, corruption functions to "grease the wheels" and has a positive impact on FDI inflows. The study is based on secondary data collected from the World Bank World Development Indicators. Using a dynamic panel data estimation technique while controlling for other variables, the estimated TLCI in Africa is -0.27 on the control of corruption scale, which ranges from approximately -2.5 (weak) to 2.5 (strong). Therefore, all African leaders and stakeholders, especially in countries that fall below the TLCI, should intensify their efforts in the fight against corruption to reduce corruption in their respective countries to at least the TLCI to attract foreign investors.

KEY WORDS: corruption, tolerable level of corruption for investment, foreign direct investment, institutions

[1] National Institute of Development Administration - Department of Development Economics, Bangkok, Thailand;
[2] University of Education, Winneba - Department of Economics, Ghana

1.0 Introduction

In 2013, global economic growth slowed to 2.9 percent – the lowest rate since 2009. Apart from two regions in which growth did not slow between 2012 and 2013 (South Asia and East Asia) all other regions lost momentum in growth. Labor markets have been affected by the slowdown in economic growth. The International Labour Organization (ILO, 2014) reports that in North Africa, the economic growth rate in 2013 proved too low to generate sufficient employment opportunities for a rapidly growing population, and the unemployment rate of 12.2 percent in 2013 remained the highest in the world. The report also indicated that in sub-Saharan Africa, paid employment opportunities are scarce, and the vulnerable employment rate, 77.4 percent in 2013, remained the highest of all regions (ILO, 2014). Economic growth has traditionally been attributed to the accumulation of human and physical capital and increased productivity arising from technological innovation. It must be emphasized that economic growth, even when it is accompanied by high degree of mechanization, generates employment opportunities at least indirectly if not directly. An abundant body of literature considers the employment-GDP

Correspondence concerning this article should be addressed to: **Anselm Komla Abotsi**, National Institute of Development Administration - Department of Development Economics, 118 Moo3, Sereethai Road, Klong-Chan, Bangkapi, Bangkok 10240, Thailand. E-mail: agrivetent@gmail.com

relationship (known as Okun's Law) and the employment elasticity of growth (Piacentini & Pini, 2000; Kapsos, 2005; Seyfried, 2005). Economists generally agree that FDI inflows lead to an increased rate of economic growth (Wijeweera, Villano, & Dollery, 2010). Particularly in developing countries, FDI inflows should exert positive effects on economic growth because these countries suffer from low productivity and capital stock deficiencies (Johnson, 2006).

Neoclassical theory predicts higher marginal returns to the factor that is relatively scarce. Thus, capital should flow from rich countries to Africa – where capital is relatively scarce. For example, the rates of return on FDI were 7 percent globally and higher in both developing (8 percent) and transition (13 percent) economies than in developed countries (5 percent) in 2012 (UNCTAD [United Nations Conference on Trade and Development], 2013). Nevertheless, the UNCTAD (2010) indicates that FDI flows into Africa decreased to $59 billion in 2009, which represents a 19 percent decrement. FDI flows fell further to $55 billion in 2010, which represent 9 percent decrement, and FDI saw a third year of decline in 2011. Both economic theory and empirical studies support the notion that FDI inflows lead to future profits. Beyond the profit motive are various other factors that encourage potential foreign investors to invest in certain countries. Some of these factors include market demand conditions, trade restrictions, investment regulations, labor costs and transportation costs. Specifically, it has been argued that a strong policy and regulatory regime, appropriate institutions, good infrastructure, and political and economic stability are important for attracting FDI inflows (Mwilima, 2003). A non-policy factor that plays a role in the attraction of FDI into a country is its level of institutional quality. Most research on the effect of institutional quality on FDI inflows reveals that countries that have weak institutions, especially high corruption and unreliable legal systems, tend to receive less FDI (Gastanaga, Nugent, & Pashamiova, 1998; Wei, 2000b). African countries still suffer from varying levels of negative perceptions from the outside world despite all the pro-FDI policies implemented to encourage FDI inflows. Factors contributing to these include corruption and political instability due to internal conflict, external conflict, military involvement in politics and religious tension. Over the years, the majority of African countries scored a 3.0 or below on the corruption perception index rating produced by Transparency International. For example, 87% of the countries in Africa scored a 3.0 or below in the years 2011, 2009 and 2008; 83% in 2010; and 77% in 2012. These percentages are alarming. The findings of Treisman (2000) suggest that fighting corruption in many countries has proved so difficult because it greatly varies between countries. Because of the difficulty of eradicating corruption, reducing its prevalence to a tolerable level must be the aspiration of all political leaders and stakeholders. In 2012, the number of countries that scored a 3.0 or below fell to 77%. In the same the year, however, Africa reversed the downward trend in FDI, exhibiting a 5 percent increase in FDI inflows to $50 billion. This gives an indication that there is a level of corruption that is tolerable to investors. Notwithstanding perceptions of corruption levels, FDI continues to flow to some countries, which also supports the idea of a level of corruption that is tolerable to investors. This level of corruption will likely not deter potential investors from investing in Africa. As corruption cannot be completely eradicated, reducing it below a threshold that can be accommodated by investors is a realistic goal for African leaders. In this study, this threshold is referred to as the Tolerance Level of Corruption for Investment (TLCI). This research not only seeks to establish that corruption generally has a negative impact on FDI inflows to Africa but also to show that there is a threshold (TLCI) below which corruption is expected to have a positive impact on FDI inflows to Africa. The TLCI will motivate leaders in Africa to try to control corruption in their countries to levels that will not deter FDI inflows because corruption is difficult if not impossible to eradicate completely. This will lead to an increase in economic growth and reduce both unemployment and poverty on the African continent. The TLCI will also serve as a guide for potential investors in selecting the African countries in which to invest. This study makes a further modest contribution to the empirical literature on the relationship between corruption and FDI inflows to Africa.

Using a dynamic panel data estimation technique while controlling for other variables, the estimated TLCI in Africa is -0.27 on the control of corruption scale, which ranges from approximately -2.5 (weak) to 2.5 (strong). This paper continues with a literature review on FDI and corruption as well as other determinants of FDI as control variables. These variables include the GDP growth rate, GDP per capita, trade openness, natural resources and political stability, economic stability and growth prospects, and infrastructure facilities. This is followed by a presentation of the methodology deployed in the study. The rest of the paper presents the results, discussion, and finally, the conclusion.

2.0 Literature review

Both policy and non-policy factors have been identified as drivers of FDI inflows in the literature (Fedderke & Romm, 2006). Policy factors include openness, product market regulations, labor market arrangements, corporate tax rates, trade barriers, and infrastructure. Non-policy factors include corruption, market size of the host country, distance/transport costs, factor endowments, and political and economic stability (Mateev, 2009). The framework on Multinational National Enterprises (MNEs) posits that firms invest abroad to look for three types of advantages: Ownership (O), Location (L), and Internalization (I); hence, it is called the OLI framework. A firm can use its specific advantages in the foreign country to earn a higher marginal profit or decrease its marginal cost compared to its competitors (Dunning, 1973; 1980; 1988). The institutions in the domestic country have the potential to attract MNEs depending on whether, given the existing institutions, the foreign firm can capitalize on its location advantage. Internalization theorists opine that FDI occurs when the benefits of internalization outweigh its cost (Fina & Rugman, 1996). Firms therefore exploit their ownership and location advantages to minimize their transaction costs. One area of institutions of the domestic country that has generated much interest in recent times is corruption. Public corruption according to Svensson (2005) is the misuse of public office for private gain, which includes the sale of government property, kickbacks in public procurement, bribery and embezzlement of government funds.

Differences among countries with respect to the extent of corruption may depend on the degree to which officials compete against each other to sell mutually substitutable benefits to private agents (Shleifer & Vishny, 1993). Svensson (2005) found the highest levels of corruption to be associated with developing or transition countries. Corruption has become endemic in many African countries and is difficult to eradicate completely. Countries with strong institutions are expected to reduce or maintain corruption at a tolerable level to attract investors. The "grease the wheels" hypothesis is more prominent in the early economics literature, with much emphasis on the effects of corruption on efficiency (e.g., Leff, 1964; Leys, 1965; Huntington, 1968). The "grease the wheels" hypothesis suggests that an inefficient bureaucracy creates a major impediment to economic activity, so some "grease" money may be needed to circumvent this impediment. Beck and Maher (1986) and Lien (1986) suggested that corruption can increase efficiency because inefficient regulations constitute an obstacle to investment which can be removed by bribing bureaucrats. Some studies (Egger & Winner, 2005) found positive short- and long-run impacts of corruption on FDI, which supports the position of Leff (1964). There is some current empirical evidence in support of the "grease the wheels" hypothesis (Vial & Hanoteau, 2010). Corruption may be beneficial in a second-best world by alleviating the distortions caused by ill-functioning institutions. However, some economists are of the view that corruption would tend to reduce economic growth (Shleifer & Vishny, 1993). This negative impact of corruption is viewed as "sand in the wheels of commerce" (Cuervo-Cazurra, 2008). Malfunctioning government institutions have been contended to constitute severe obstacles to investment, entrepreneurship, and innovation by many economists (Mauro, 1995). The malfunctioning of government institutions affects the adoption of available technologies and the productivity of physical capital, and this in turn affects the returns to firms' investments. In highly corrupt countries, managers are unable to improve the technology of their firms because most of their efforts are geared toward engaging public officials to get things done; thus, the returns to their investments dwindle due to inefficiency. Transnational corporations are not able to exploit their ownership or location advantages, and this does not motivate these transnational corporations to invest in the potential host country. Earlier studies on corruption and firm efficiency found corruption to negatively affect the efficiency of firms

(Dal Bo & Rossi, 2007; Picci, 2005; Yan & Oum, 2011). Moreover, studies elsewhere show that corruption actually deters foreign direct investment (Aizenman & Spiegel, 2002; Barassi & Zhou, 2012; Cuervo-Cazurra, 2006; 2008; Habib & Zurawicki, 2002; Hakkala, Norback, & Svaleryd, 2008; Javorcik & Wei, 2009; Voyer & Beamish, 2004; Wei, 2000b).

At low levels, corruption is seen as "greasing the wheels", and at high levels, it is seen as "sand in the wheels of commerce". This study argues that in countries in which bureaucratic regulations are cumbersome, corruption might be a means to achieve certain benefits by foreign investors; thus, they are motivated to invest in those countries. In such countries, corruption is expected to have a positive impact on private investment. However, when corruption goes beyond the paying of bribes to levels of malfunctioning government institutions, corruption is expected to have a negative impact on private investment. In such countries, corruption may deter foreign investment. The corruption variable is captured as the perception of corruption in the public sector of the host country and is expected to have both negative and positive effects on the inflows of FDI into a country depending on the levels of institutional quality and corruption.

2.1 GDP growth rate and GDP per capita

The economics literature indicates that FDI has led to economic development of the host country because FDI in*fl*ows facilitate the acquisition of valuable tangible and intangible assets, such as enhanced technology, managerial skills, expertise, innovation capability, capital formation and related physical assets (Liu, Shu, & Sinclair, 2009; Vu, Gangnes, & Noy, 2008; Wang, 2009). Elsewhere, market size has been predicted to be a positive and significant determinant of FDI flows (Garibaldi et al., 2002; Nunes, Oscategui, & Peschiera, 2006; Sahoo, 2006). This is because larger consumer markets translate into more potential consumption and thus enhanced trade. Market size is generally measured by Gross Domestic Product (GDP) or GDP per capita. The real GDP growth rate is used in the literature to represent a country's economic track record and as an indicator of profitable investment opportunities (Anyanwu, 2012). On the one hand, FDI inflows cause economic growth, and on the other hand, economic growth attracts FDI inflows, thus leading to bicausality issues and endogeneity problems. Although GDP has been used in the literature as a determinant of FDI inflows, this study intends to use the lag of the GDP growth rate, as this is a better indicator of FDI inflows to avoid endogeneity problems. Also included in the analysis is the effect of GDP per capita on FDI inflows. In this study, high previous-year GDP growth rates and GDP per capita of the host country are expected to attract more FDI.

2.2 Trade openness

Trade openness refers to the sum of exports and imports of goods and services into a country and gives an indication of how liberalized a country is in terms of trade. The impact of trade openness on economic growth can be positive and significant mainly due to the accumulation of physical capital and technological transfer as a result of FDI inflows. Therefore, trade openness is an important vehicle for technological spillovers. According to Eicher (1999), Lee (1993) and Young (1991), openness to trade also stimulates domestic investment by encouraging competition in domestic and international markets and generating higher returns on investment through economies of scale. Trade openness is generally a positive and significant determinant of FDI inflows (Asiedu 2002; Sahoo 2006). Trade openness is captured as trade as a share of GDP and it is expected to facilitate the flow of FDI into the host country.

2.3 Natural resources and Political stability

FDI attraction to Africa can also be influenced by the availability of natural resources on the continent. Jadhav (2012) suggest that resource-seeking FDI is motivated by the availability of natural resources in host countries. This resource seeking remains a relevant source of FDI for various developing countries. Studies have shown that natural resources play vital roles in overall attraction of FDI to Africa (Asiedu, 2002; 2005; Dupasquier & Osakwe, 2006). In Africa, countries that have natural resources were more attractive than those without such resources (Asiedu, 2005). According to North and Weingast (1989) and Li (2009), democratic institutions may have a positive influence on FDI, but the presence of natural resources in host countries may affect the FDI-democracy relationship (Asiedu & Lien, 2011). Asiedu and Lien (2011) found that democracy facilitates FDI inflows to countries where the share of natural resources of total exports is low, but it has a negative effect on FDI inflows to countries where exports are dominated by natural resources. This implies that the influence of natural resources and political stability on FDI has to be determined empirically.

2.4 Economic stability and Growth prospects

Economic stability has been found to be a positive indicator of FDI inflows (Mateev, 2009). A country that has stable macroeconomic conditions with high and sustained growth rates is expected to have more FDI inflows than a more volatile economy (Ranjan & Agrawal, 2011). Proxies for the macroeconomic stability of a country include GDP growth rates, industrial production index values, interest rates, and inflation rates (Dasgupta & Ratha, 2000). High inflation rates are associated with economic disarray and lower purchasing power, so inflation risk becomes an important factor in long-run investment plans. Inflation has been found to have a negative relation with FDI inflows though its magnitude is much smaller (Ranjan & Agrawal, 2011).

However, research on the influence of exchange rates on FDI inflows has shown varied results. While Kyereboah-Coleman and Agyire-Tettey (2008) posit that the volatility of the real exchange rate has a negative influence on FDI inflows, Jeon and Rhee (2008) show that FDI inflows have significant association with both the real exchange rate and expected exchange rate changes. Nonetheless, Brahmasrene and Jiranyakul (2001) and Dewenter (1995) find no statistically significant relationship between the level of the exchange rate and FDI inflows (Anyanwu, 2012). When a country's currency depreciates, foreign investors take advantage of the ability to purchase assets at a reduced cost. Investment in countries whose currencies face high depreciation is relatively less expensive. Therefore, it is expected that a high inflation rate in the host country attracts less FDI, while higher pressure to depreciate the exchange rate of the host country attracts more FDI.

2.5 Infrastructure facilities

The importance of infrastructure development to attracting FDI inflows cannot be ignored. Studies by Musila and Sigue (2006) and Dupasquier and Osakwe (2006) show that FDI in Africa is dependent on the development of infrastructure. Similar results were obtained by Kersan-Skabic and Orlic (2007) in the Western Balkan countries and Botric and Škuflić (2006) in Southeast European countries. This shows that embarking on infrastructure development provides an opportunity for countries to attract FDI inflows. Some studies (Ranjan & Agrawal, 2011) used an infrastructure index (INFREX) constructed by considering electric power consumption (kwh per capita), energy use (kg of oil equivalent per capita) and telephone lines, and these had similar results. Infrastructure in this study is captured by telephone lines per 100 population and is expected to lead to greater FDI inflows and, hence, to have a positive impact on FDI inflows.

3.0 Methodology

3.1 Data

With the exception of the control of corruption index, the variables used in this study are based on secondary data collected from the World Development Indicators for 2012. The frequency of the data is annual, and it is available from 1996 to 2012 for 50 countries in Africa. The control of corruption index is drawn from the Worldwide Governance Indicators DATABANK (World Bank, 2013b) This variable is used in determining the impact of corruption on FDI inflows to Africa. This index is chosen not only because of its authenticity but also because of its free availability on the internet. The control of corruption index is one of the six dimensions of governance included in the Worldwide Governance Indicators.

3.2 Data Analysis

In order to meet the objectives of the study, a dynamic panel data estimation technique is used.

Several studies have found lagged FDI to be correlated with current FDI (Asiedu, 2013), so in this study, a new estimator for dynamic panel data models based on a simple transformation of the dependent variable (FDI) is deployed. This dynamic panel model includes endogenous and exogenous variables in addition to the lagged dependent variable. The transformation is achieved by moving the lagged dependent variable to the left hand side and applying the System GMM estimator to the transformed model. The System GMM estimator is chosen over the Difference GMM estimator because it is consistent and asymptotically more efficient, although it is known to perform poorly in finite samples, especially when the variance ratio is high and when the dependent variable is highly persistent. The System GMM estimate also has an advantage over the Difference GMM with respect to variables that exhibit "random walk" or are close to random-walk variables (Baum, 2006; Bond, 2002; Roodman, 2006; 2007). According to Efendic, Pugh and Adnett (2009), because model specifications including macroeconomic variables are known in economics to be characterized by random walk statistical generating mechanisms, the System GMM approach seems more suitable. Empirical research with dynamic models shows that the System GMM is a good estimator, or at least better than the Difference GMM, which is severely downward biased (Hoeffler, 2002; Nkurunziza and Bates, 2003; Presbitero, 2005). Moreover, Roodman (2006) suggests that it is better to avoid Difference GMM estimation, which has a weakness of magnifying gaps if one works with an unbalanced panel .

The general model is of the form presented in equation (1).

$$y_{it} = \alpha y_{i,t-1} + x_{it}'\beta + \varepsilon_{it} \qquad (1)$$

where $\varepsilon_{it} = u_i + v_{it}$, for i = 1,..., N and t = 2,..., T, with $|\alpha| < 1$. The disturbance term ε_{it} has two orthogonal components, which are the fixed effects u_i and the idiosyncratic shocks v_{it}. $E(u_i) = E(v_{it}) = E(u_i v_{it}) = 0$ for i = 1,..., N and t = 2,..., T.

The framework for evaluating the associations among FDI, corruption, and other determinants of FDI is presented in equation (2).

$$y_{it} = \beta_1 + \beta_2 x_{it} + \beta_3 x_{it}^2 + \omega z_{it} + \alpha_1 y_{i,t-1} + \varepsilon_{it} \qquad (2)$$

where y_{it} is a measure of FDI in country i at time period t, $y_{i,t-1}$ is a measure of FDI in country i at time period $t-1$, x_{it} is an index of the control of corruption in country i at time t, x_{it}^2 is the squared index of control of corruption in country i at time period t, z_{it} are control variables in country i at time period t, β_1, β_2, β_3, α_1 and ω are parameters to be estimated, and finally, ε_{it} denotes the disturbance term. StataCorp 2013 is the statistical software used in the data analysis.

3.3 Model One: The System GMM Model of FDI

The benchmark FDI equation in a linear form, with a constant term, is presented in equation (3).

$$\begin{aligned}
&FDI_PerGDP_{it} = \\
&= \beta_1 + \beta_2 Control_of_Corruption_{it} + \\
&+ \beta_3 Control_of_Corruption_Sqr_{it} + \\
&+ \beta_4 Trade_PerGDP_{it} + \beta_5 GDP_Per_Capita_{it} + \\
&+ \beta_6 Natural_resource_{it} + \beta_7 Political_stability_{it} + \\
&+ \beta_8 Inflation_Consum_Prices_{it} + \\
&+ \beta_9 Exchange_Rate_PerUS_{it} + \\
&+ \beta_{10} GDP_Growth_PerAnnual_{it-1} + \\
&+ \beta_{11} Telephone_lines_{it} + \beta_{12} FDI_PerGDP_{it-1} + \\
&+ Time(Dummies) + \varepsilon_{it} \qquad (3)
\end{aligned}$$

The net FDI inflow per GDP is used as the dependent variable in the estimation of the system dynamic model. In addition to the variable of interest, control of corruption and its squared values are included as independent variables, and other control variables were carefully chosen based on previous research and data availability for the selected period. These control variables include trade openness, GDP per capita, natural resources, political stability, inflation rate, exchange rate, the lag of GDP growth rate and telephone lines per 100 population of the host countries. To find out whether FDI inflow to Africa was affected by time-related shocks, time dummies were included.

The control of corruption variable is defined as perceptions of the extent to which public power is exercised for private gain, including both petty and grand forms of corruption, as well as "capture" of the state by elites and private interests (World Bank, 2013b). The control of corruption variable is transformed from its original scale, which ranges from approximately -2.5 (weak) to 2.5 (strong), to a new scale ranging from 0 to 100 for computational purposes and to allow for easy interpretation of the results. The following formula was used: $x = (a + 2.5) * 20$, where x is value of the transformed variable, and a refers to the value of the original scale. This means that the higher a country is on the scale, the better the governance performance against corruption and thus the lower the level of corruption. Therefore, countries scoring low on the scale are relatively more corrupt. A similar transformation was performed for the political stability index, which 'reflects perceptions of the likelihood that the

Table 1. Correlation Matrix of Variables used in the Study

	FDI_PerGDP	Control of Corruption	Control of Corruption Sqr	Trade PerGDP	Natural resource	Inflation Consum Prices	Exchange Rate PerUS	FDI PerGDP (lagged one year)	GDP Growth PerAnnual (lagged one year)	Telephone lines per100people	GDP Per Capita	Political stability	2007 (dummy)	2008 (dummy)	2009 (dummy)	2010 (dummy)
FDI_PerGDP	1															
Control of Corruption	-0.0481	1														
Control of Corruption Sqr	-0.0416	0.9824*	1													
Trade PerGDP	0.3830*	0.1087*	0.1392*	1												
Natural resource	0.2221*	-0.5300*	-0.4845*	0.3457*	1											
Inflation Consum Prices	-0.0107	-0.1022*	-0.0846*	0.0778*	0.0847*	1										
Exchange Rate PerUS	0.1244*	-0.0794*	-0.1007*	-0.0955*	-0.045	-0.0164	1									
FDI PerGDP (lagged one year)	0.3592*	-0.0945*	-0.0694	0.2984*	0.2534*	0.0257	0.1201*	1								
GDP Growth PerAnnual (lagged one year)	0.2810*	-0.0873*	-0.063	0.1592*	0.2824*	-0.0577	-0.0144	0.2832*	1							
Telephone lines per100people	-0.012	0.5080*	0.5373*	0.2382*	-0.1743*	-0.0475	-0.1051*	-0.0148	-0.0339	1						
GDP Per Capita	0.0384	0.2583*	0.3132*	0.3710*	0.2329*	-0.0401	-0.1300*	0.0567	0.0741*	0.6644*	1					
Political stability	0.0286	0.6769*	0.6422*	0.2718*	-0.2647*	-0.1292*	0.0589	-0.0248	-0.0047	0.4374*	0.4357*	1				
2007 (year dummy)	0.033	-0.0029	-0.0049	0.0467	0.0424	-0.0224	0.0343	0.0025	0.0135	0.0183	0.0228	0.0194	1			
2008 (year dummy)	0.0341	0.0018	0.0019	0.061	0.0628	-0.0132	0.0126	0.033	0.043	0.0195	0.0302	0.0154	-0.0625	1		
2009 (year dummy)	-0.0051	0.0027	0.0011	-0.0103	-0.0065	0.0015	0.0256	0.0341	0.0033	0.0234	0.0286	0.0202	-0.0625	-0.0625	1	
2010 (year dummy)	0.0315	0.0033	0.0035	0.0194	0.0184	-0.0221	0.0374	-0.0051	-0.0613	0.0235	0.0192	0.0065	-0.0625	-0.0625	-0.0625	1

government will be destabilized or overthrown by unconstitutional or violent means, including politically motivated violence and terrorism' (World Bank, 2013b). Trade openness refers to the sum of exports and imports of goods and services measured as a share of the gross domestic product. Natural resources refer to total natural resource rents, which include the sum of oil, natural gas, coal (hard and soft), mineral, and forest rents. Inflation, as measured by the consumer price index, reflects the annual percentage change in the cost to the average consumer of acquiring a basket of goods and services that may be fixed or changed at specified intervals. The official exchange rate refers to the exchange rate determined by national authorities or to the rate determined in the legally sanctioned exchange market. It is calculated as an annual average based on monthly averages (local currency units relative to the U.S. dollar). GDP growth rate refers to annual percentage growth rate of GDP at market prices based on constant local currency, and the aggregates are based on constant 2005 U.S. dollars. Telephone lines are fixed telephone lines that connect a subscriber's terminal equipment to the public switched telephone network and that have a port on a telephone exchange. Finally, GDP per capita is the gross domestic product divided by the midyear population (World Bank, 2013a). The correlation matrix (Table 1) indicates significant correlations among some independent variables. It is expected that the existence of correlations among the independent variables will lead to multicollinearity in the estimation, but the statistical nature of panel data estimation addresses the collinearity problems (Ranjan & Agrawal, 2011). Therefore, the inclusion of these variables in the model would not increase the variance of the coefficient estimates because this will render the coefficient estimates unstable.

The two-step estimator is deployed in the estimation because the standard covariance matrix is robust to panel-specific autocorrelation and heteroskedasticity and is thus asymptotically efficient. Control of corruption and trade openness are treated as endogenous and all other independent variables as strictly exogenous. The endogeneity of these variables is controlled for by including their lagged forms as regressors by using internal instruments (lagged levels and lagged differences). It is also less probable that control of corruption and trade openness explain changes in the other independent variables strictly treated as exogenous. No external instruments are used. In this panel, there are 50 countries (N) that are analyzed over a period of 17 years (T), which means there are more countries (N) than years (T). It has been argued by many authors that dynamic panel models are especially designed for situations wherein T is smaller than N to control for dynamic panel bias (Baltagi, 2008; Baum, 2006; Bond, 2002; Roodman, 2006; 2007; Sarafidis, Yamagata, & Robertson, 2009).

3.4 Dynamic Panel Model

Nerlove (2002) argues that economic behavior is inherently dynamic, and thus, most econometrically interesting relationships are explicitly or implicitly dynamic. A simple dynamic model regresses y_{it} on polynomial in time. Adjustment might be partial: the current year's outcome depends on the previous year's outcome, i.e., includes lags of y. Bond (2002) is of the view that when coefficients on the lagged dependent variables are not of direct interest, allowing for dynamics in the underlying process may be crucial for recovering consistent estimates for the other parameters. The inclusion of lags of dependent variables is a parsimonious way of accounting for the effects of explanatory variables in the past and can also help to remove serial correlation in the disturbance term (Beck & Katz, 1996). Dynamic panel models are useful when the dependent variable depends on its own past realizations. In addition, models including lagged dependent variables can also control, to a large extent, for many omitted variables.

Once a lagged dependent variable is included as part of the panel model specification, there is a violation of strict/strong exogeneity because the lagged dependent variable, which is one of the regressors, is correlated with past values of the error term. The correlation of the idiosyncratic error term v_{it} with the lagged dependent variable $y_{i,t-1}$ at time t + 2 is the source of the strict exogeneity. There is also a violation of the weaker condition of no contemporaneous correlation of the regressors with the composite error term $(\varepsilon_{it} = u_i + v_{it})$. When y_{it} is correlated with the fixed effects in the error term, it gives rise to "dynamic panel bias" (Nickell, 1981). The endogeneity problem renders the estimators inconsistent and inferences from the estimated model less accurate.

3.5 The GMM Estimator

The panel dynamic model takes the following form (equation (4)) where y exhibit state dependence:

$$y_{i,t} = \alpha y_{i,t-1} + \beta' x_{i,t} + \varepsilon_{i,t} \quad (4)$$

where $\varepsilon_{it} = u_i + v_{i,t}$, $E(\varepsilon|Z) = 0$, β is a column vector of coefficients, y and ε are random variables, x is a column vector of k regressors, z is column vector of j instruments, and $j \geq k$. X, Y, and Z represent matrices of N observations for x, y and z, respectively. The empirical residuals are $\hat{E} = Y - X\hat{\beta}$. According to Roodman (2009), the problem in estimating this model is that all the instruments are theoretically orthogonal to the error term, which means $E(z\varepsilon) = 0$. Forcing the corresponding vector of empirical moments $E_N(z\varepsilon) \equiv \left(\frac{1}{N}\right) Z'\hat{E}$ to zero generates a system with more equations than variables if $j > k$. This renders the specification over-identified.

The solution to this problem in econometrics is normally the use of instrumental variables (IV). Roodman (2009) suggest two ways to solve this endogeneity problem. One is the use of Difference Generalized Method of Moments (D-GMM) to transform the data to eliminate the fixed effects. The Difference GMM refers to the removal of the individual-specific and unobserved effect in a dynamic panel model by taken the first difference of the linear dynamic panel regression. The sequential exogeneity and the zero serial and cross-section correlation of ε_{it} in the first-differenced linear dynamic panel regression imply that moment conditions $E(y_{i,t-s}\Delta\varepsilon_{it}) = 0$ for all i, t and $s = 2, \ldots\ldots, \infty$ hold. The past levels of the dependent variable serve as instruments for the current first differences of the dependent variable. Difference GMM (D-GMM) is ascribed to Arellano and Bond (1991). The other is the use of System Generalized Method of Moments (S-GMM) to instrument the lag of the dependent variable $y_{i,t-1}$ as well as any other similarly endogenous variables with variables that are uncorrelated with the fixed effects. The System GMM follows the Difference GMM estimation procedure with an additional assumption ($E(\Delta y_{i,t-s}[\alpha_i + \varepsilon_{it}]) = 0$ for all i, t and $s = 2, \ldots\ldots, \infty$), leading to an additional set of moment conditions to leverage. System GMM (S-GMM) is ascribed to Blundell and Bond (1998). S-GMM therefore necessitates lagged changes in the dependent variable to be valid instruments for the level of the lagged dependent variable in the level equation. Though more assumptions are involved with System GMM than Difference GMM, System GMM achieves greater efficiency once these assumptions hold. Moreover, because the System GMM uses the level version of the dynamic panel model together with the differenced version, the effects of time-invariant regressors can be estimated in contrast to Difference GMM in which they are differenced out. The system estimator uses the first difference of all the exogenous variables as standard instruments and the lags of the endogenous variables to generate the GMM-type instruments as described in Arellano and Bond (1991) and includes lagged differences of the endogenous variables as instruments for the level equation.

3.6 Specification Testing in Dynamic Panel Models

Specification testing in dynamic panel models is conducted to address problems of over-identification restrictions and serial correlation. This is accomplished by using the standard Sargan and Hansen J test for over-identification restrictions and Arellano-Bond test for autocorrelation. Roodman (2009) explains that if the model is over-identified, a test statistic for the joint validity of the moment conditions falls out of the GMM framework. The vector of empirical moments $(\frac{1}{N})Z'\hat{E}$ is randomly distributed over 0 under the null of joint validity. Under the null hypothesis that all instruments are uncorrelated with u, the test has a large-sample $\chi^2(r)$ distribution, where r is the number of over-identifying restrictions. The null in both of these tests is that all of the instruments are valid and the alternative is that some subsets are not valid. Roodman (2009) indicates that Sargan-Hansen statistics can also be used to test the validity of subsets of instruments via a "difference-in-Sargan/Hansen" test, which is also known as a C statistic. The Sargan-Hansen test reports two test statistics after estimation – with and without a subset of suspect instruments under the null of joint validity of the full instrument set.

3.7 Testing for Residual Serial Correlation

The degree of serial correlation of the residual term in either Difference GMM or System GMM will determine the validity of any instruments used based upon the dependent variable. The set of valid instruments based upon the dependent variable changes once the residual term is serially correlated. The lags of the change in the dependent variable greater than or equal to 1 are valid instruments for the level equation with the System GMM framework and lags of the dependent variable greater than or equal to 2 are valid instruments for the differenced equation with the Difference GMM framework. The full disturbance term $(\varepsilon_{it} = u_i + v_{it})$ contains fixed effects and is presumed autocorrelated, so the estimators are designed to remove this source of problem. If the ε_{it} _ are serially independent, then $E(\Delta \varepsilon_{it} \Delta \varepsilon_{it-1}) = E[(\varepsilon_{it} - \varepsilon_{it-1})(\varepsilon_{it-1} - \varepsilon_{it-2})] = -E[\varepsilon^2_{it-1}] = -\sigma^2_{\varepsilon}$. Thus, first order serial correlation would be expected. It is, however, not expected that there be any second order serial correlation, (i.e., $E(\Delta \varepsilon_{it} \Delta \varepsilon_{it-2}) =$ $= E[(\varepsilon_{it} - \varepsilon_{it-1})(\varepsilon_{it-2} - \varepsilon_{it-3})] = 0$. One should therefore test for second order serial correlation because its presence indicates a specification error. The idiosyncratic disturbance term v_{it} is related to $\Delta v_{i,t-1}$ mathematically via the shared $v_{i,t-1}$ term, so a negative first order serial correlation is expected in differences meaning that its evidence is of no importance. Therefore, to check for first order serial correlation in levels, it is important to check for second order correlation in differences as well, as this will detect correlation between the $v_{i,t-1}$ in Δv_{it} and the $v_{i,t-2}$ in $\Delta v_{i,t-2}$. Therefore, serial correlation of order l in levels is checked by looking for correlation of order $l+1$ in difference (Roodman, 2009). These tests lose power when the number of instruments i is large relative to the cross section sample size n. The rule of thumb is to keep the number of instruments less than or equal to the number of groups so that when the ratio r of the sample size to the number of instruments is less than one, $ratio = \frac{n}{i} < 1$, the assumptions underlying the two procedures may be violated.

3.8 The Estimation of Tolerable Level of Corruption for Investment

Relationships between two economic variables are predicted to be non-monotonic in various economic theories. A popular empirical test of such theories, according to Plassmann and Khanna (2003), is to estimate an equation using a polynomial of the variable that is supposed to have the non-linear relationship. Once the estimated turning point of the equation is well within the range of the data, this is an indication that the true relationship is non-monotonic. To empirically estimate the Tolerable Level of Corruption for Investment, a power term of the control of corruption index is introduced into the dynamic model to estimate the level of corruption that attracts FDI inflows to Africa. With the addition of the quadratic term, one bend is modeled in the regression. The response variable in this study is foreign direct investment, net inflows (% of GDP) labeled as FDI PerGDP and the variables, Control of Corruption and Control of Corruption Sqr are the control of corruption index and its square, respectively. The TLCI is obtained by estimating the equation and taking the derivative of the estimated equation with respect to the control of corruption variable. Suppose the following is the estimated equation (5):

$$\hat{y}_{it} = \hat{\beta}_1 + \hat{\beta}_2 x_1 + \hat{\beta}_3 x_1^2 + \ldots \tag{5}$$

where $\hat{\beta}_2$ and $\hat{\beta}_3$ are estimators of the parameters β_2 and β_3, respectively. Taking the derivative w.r.t. x_1 yields equation (6):

$$\frac{\delta \hat{y}_{it}}{\delta x_1} = \hat{\beta}_2 + 2\hat{\beta}_3 x_1 = 0 \tag{6}$$

Solving this equation gives the turning point of the relationship reflecting an inverse U-shape if $\hat{\beta}_2 < 0$ and vice versa. The coefficient $\hat{\beta}_3$ tells both the direction and steepness of the curvature (a positive value indicates the curvature is upwards while a negative value indicates the curvature is downwards). This means that the turning point is given by $\varphi = -\frac{\hat{\beta}_2}{2\hat{\beta}_3}$, which is referred to as the threshold point or the Tolerable Level of Corruption for Investment.

3.9 Test of the U-Shaped Relationship

The control of corruption variable scale ranges from approximately -2.5 (weak) to 2.5 (strong), which means that the higher a country is on the scale, the better governance performance against corruption and, thus, the smaller the level of corruption. Therefore, countries scoring low on the scale are relatively more corrupt and expected to attract less FDI, and countries scoring high on the scale are relatively less corrupt and thus expected to attract more FDI. Therefore, at low scores, corruption is expected to have negative impact on FDI inflow, and at high scores, corruption is expected to have a positive impact on FDI inflow. This accounts for the U-shaped relationship.

Most works on turning points use the criteria that if both $\hat{\beta}_1$ and $\hat{\beta}_2$ are significant and if the implied extreme point is within the data range, then they have found a U-shaped relationship. Lind and Mehlum (2007) hold these criteria as sensible but postulate that they are neither sufficient nor necessary and argue that these criteria are too weak. According to Lind and Mehlum (2007), to properly test for the presence of a U-shaped relationship on some interval of values, we need to test whether the relationship is decreasing at low values within this interval and increasing at high values within the interval. Assuming that ε_{it} ~ NID (0, σ2), a test based on likelihood ratio principle (Sasabuchi, 1980) takes the form:

For min(x)

$$H_0: \quad \beta_2 + \beta_3 f'(x_l) \geq 0$$

$$H_1: \quad \beta_2 + \beta_3 f'(x_l) < 0$$

For max(x)

$$H_0: \quad \beta_2 + \beta_3 f'(x_h) \leq 0$$

$$H_1: \quad \beta_2 + \beta_3 f'(x_h) > 0$$

Rejection of the null hypotheses in both cases is a confirmation of a U-shaped relationship. This test gives the exact necessary and sufficient conditions for the test of a U shape. An equivalent test, according to Lind and Mehlum (2007), involves constructing a confidence interval for the minimum point and determining whether the confidence interval is contained within the interval $[x_l, x_h]$. Both tests will be used in this study to confirm a U-shaped relationship and hence the threshold point or the Tolerable Level of Corruption for Investment.

4.0 Results

4.1 Descriptive statistics

The descriptive statistics of the variables deployed in the study are presented in Table 2. All the variables have values ranging from 727 to 877, as the highest observations. The period under study is from 1996 to 2012. Variables obtained from Worldwide Governance Indicators (control of corruption and political stability) have data missing for three years (1997, 1999, & 2001), and this accounts for those variables having the lowest number of observations. Telephone lines have highest number of observations, which gives an indication of the level of infrastructure development in Africa. The mean GDP per capita is 1688.28, and the standard deviation is 2591.61, which shows that the observations are widely dispersed. Also worthy of mention are the mean exchange rate (714.10) and standard deviation of 1857.42, which shows high fluctuation of exchange rate within the period of observation. The mean of inflation rate is 20.10, and the standard deviation of 158.95 also indicates high fluctuation of inflation rate within the period of observation. The variables with the lowest dispersion include FDI inflow, control of corruption, trade openness, natural resource, GDP growth and telephone lines.

4.2 Empirical Results of the Dynamic Panel Model

The results of the dynamic panel model estimated including endogenous and exogenous variables in addition to the lagged dependent variable are presented in Table 3. The FDI net inflow per GDP is used as the dependent variable in the estimation of the FDI model. The control of corruption variable and its squared values as well as other control variables are used as independent variables. The two-step estimator is deployed in the estimation, with control of corruption and trade openness variables treated as endogenous and all other independent variables treated strictly as exogenous. No external instruments are used.

4.3 Model Specification Diagnostics Test

The validity of the estimated results in System GMM depends on the statistical diagnostics tests. The results indicate that the specification pass the Hansen J-statistic test for Over-Identifying Restrictions

Table 2. Descriptive Statistics of Variables in the Dynamic Model

Variable	Observation	Mean	Std. Dev.	Min	Max
FDI PerGDP	805	4.874661	10.38533	-82.8921	145.202
Control of Corruption	727	38.05282	11.91438	8.800001	75
Control of Corruption Sqr	727	1589.774	994.3457	77.44002	5625
Trade PerGDP	797	77.11778	37.27615	17.85861	275.2324
Natural resource	863	15.36953	18.02374	0.003196	100.3669
Inflation Consum Prices	797	20.9961	158.9528	-9.79765	4145.107
Exchange Rate PerUS	859	714.0977	1857.418	0.010014	19068.42
FDI PerGDP (lagged one year)	805	4.874661	10.38533	-82.8921	145.202
GDP Growth PerAnnual (lagged one year)	848	4.807308	7.160985	-32.8321	106.2798
Telephone lines per100people	877	3.499723	5.821433	0.000236	33.11384
GDP Per Capita	851	1688.275	2591.605	53.09856	14901.35
Political stability	728	38.95907	19.05746	-16.4	73.8

(OIR), confirming that the instrument can be considered valid. If the model is well specified, it is expected that the null hypothesis of no autocorrelation of the second order AR(2) is not rejected, and therefore, the Arellano-Bond test for serial correlation supports the validity of the model specification (Basu, 2008). As the number of instruments (47) is less than the number of groups (50), the assumptions underlying the two procedures are not violated. The 47 instruments came from the restriction to use two lags for levels and two for differences in the data (i.e., the restriction is set to (2 2) in *xtabond2*).

The two-step estimates that report the Hansen J-statistic test yield theoretically robust results (Roodman, 2006). The Hansen J-statistic tests the null hypothesis of correct model specification and valid over-identifying restrictions, i.e., the validity of instruments. The rejection of the null hypothesis means that either or both assumptions are violated. Baum (2006) argues that the Hansen J-test is the most commonly used diagnostic in GMM estimation for assessment of the suitability of the model. The Hansen J-test of over-identifying restrictions does not reject the null at any conventional level of significance ($p = 0.188$), giving an indication that the model has valid instrumentation. The difference-in-Sargan/Hansen test, also known as the C-test (Baum 2006; Roodman, 2006), is used to test the validity of subsets of instruments (i.e., levels, differenced, and standard IV instruments). It estimates the System GMM with and without a subset of suspect instruments enabling investigation of the validity (i.e., exogeneity) of any subset of instruments as well as their contribution to "the increase in J-test" (Roodman, 2007). The null hypothesis of the model diagnosis test, which states that the specified variables are proper instruments, i.e., the set of examined instruments is exogenous with p-value 0.471 for GMM differenced instruments and 0.137 for system instruments cannot be rejected. This shows that the exogeneity of any GMM instruments used, i.e., levels and differenced instruments, are valid instruments. Similarly, the null hypothesis of the model diagnosis test states that the specified variables are proper standard "IV" instrument subsets cannot be rejected.

Efendic et al. (2009) posits that the check for the "steady state" assumption suggested by (Roodman,

2006) can also be used to investigate the validity of instruments in System GMM. This assumption requires a kind of steady state in the sense that deviations from long-term values are not systematically related to the fixed effects. The estimated coefficient on the lagged dependent variable in the model should indicate convergence by having a value less than (absolute) unity otherwise System GMM is invalid (Roodman, 2006). The results show that the estimated coefficient on the lagged dependent variable (FDI_PerGDP_1) is 0.468, which means that the steady-state assumption holds. The Wild Chi-square test of joint significance reports that the null hypothesis that independent variables are jointly equal to zero (p=0.000) at any conventional level of significance may be rejected. Based on the various statistical tests that have been conducted, there is enough evidence to conclude that the examined statistical tests satisfy the key assumptions of System GMM estimation and that this model is an appropriate statistical generating mechanism.

4.4 Interpretation and discussion of results

The results of the estimated System GMM are presented in Table 3. Depending on the sign (+/-) of the estimates, a one-unit increase of the independent variable will lead to either an increase or decrease of the dependent variable with a magnitude determined by the corresponding coefficients. All variables with positive estimates have positive impact on the dependent variable, and those with negative estimates have negative impact on the dependent variable. The results show that control of corruption is negative and highly significant while the square of control of corruption is positive and highly significant. The control of corruption scale ranges from approximately -2.5 (weak) to 2.5 (strong) which mean that the higher the score of the country, the less corrupt it is. Thus, at low scores, corruption has a negative impact on FDI inflows, and at high scores, corruption has a positive impact on FDI inflows. This gives an indication that below certain level of corruption, a country is able to attract foreign direct investment, and beyond that level, potential investors are no longer motivated to invest in that country. Potential foreign investors in Africa are very sensitive to the perception of corruption in the host country. This confirms the evidence from earlier studies that corruption deters foreign direct investments (Aizenman & Spiegel, 2002; Barassi & Zhou, 2012; Cuervo-Cazurra, 2006, 2008; Habib & Zurawicki, 2002; Hakkala et al., 2008; Javorcik & Wei, 2009; Voyer & Beamish, 2004; Wei, 2000a).

With exception of inflation, as expected, and GDP per capita, all the other control variables are positive. In addition, with the exception of natural resource, telephone lines and political stability, all the other control variables are significant. The results by Jadhav (2012) on FDI show that traditional economic determinants are more important than institutional and political determinants of FDI. Most of the FDI in the BRICS economies are motivated by a market-seeking purpose. The findings also shows that trade openness is a positive and significant determinant of FDI inflow. The results show that a 1-unit increase in the percentage of trade openness to the GDP of a country leads to 4.13% increase in the percentage of FDI inflow to GDP of that country supporting the assertion that trade liberalization leads to increased FDI inflow (Anyanwu, 2012; Asiedu, 2002; Ranjan & Agrawal, 2011; Sahoo, 2006). The results also show that a 1-unit increase in inflation leads to -1.59% decrease in the percentage of FDI inflow to GDP. The higher the volatility of the inflation rate, the more unstable is the macroeconomic environment of the host country and lower is the FDI inflow to that country. This results is consistent with Ranjan and Agrawal (2011) who found inflation to have a negative relation with FDI inflow though its magnitude is very less. Similarly, a 1-unit increase in previous year's GDP growth rate leads to 1.54% increase in the percentage of FDI inflow to GDP. This shows that because GDP growth rate represent a country's economic track record it is an indicator of profitable investment opportunities to the outside world. This finding is consistent with earlier assertion that market size is a positive and significant determinant of FDI flows (Garibaldi et al., 2002; Nunes et al., 2006; Sahoo, 2006). Contrary to expectations, GDP per capita have a negative and significant association with FDI inflows, but this finding is consistent with earlier findings (Dauti, 2008). The results show that a 1-unit increase in GDP per capita leads to 0.04% decrease in the percentage of FDI inflow to GDP. These results suggest that foreign investors may prefer growing economies to large economies, so they are attracted to African countries whose economies grow. As GDP per capita

Table 3. Results of the Dynamic System GMM Estimation

VARIABLES	FDI_PerGDP
Control of Corruption	-0.533***
	(0.142)
Control of Corruption Sqr	0.00599***
	(0.00146)
Trade PerGDP	0.0413***
	(0.00708)
Natural resource	0.0154
	(0.0141)
Inflation Consum Prices	-0.0159***
	(0.00323)
Exchange Rate PerUS	0.000689***
	(4.19e-05)
FDI PerGDP (lagged one year)	0.468***
	(0.0133)
GDP Growth PerAnnual (lagged one year)	0.0154**
	(0.00757)
Telephone lines per100people	0.0262
	(0.0538)
GDP Per Capita	-0.000370***
	(8.92e-05)
Political stability	0.00470
	(0.0159)
2007 (dummy)	1.225***
	(0.167)
2008 (dummy)	0.904***
	(0.205)
2009 (dummy)	-0.793***
	(0.158)
2010 (dummy)	0.911***
	(0.189)
Constant	9.905***
	(3.058)

Table 3. Results of the Dynamic System GMM Estimation (Continued)

VARIABLES	FDI_PerGDP
OIR test (p-value)	0.188
Arellano-Bond test for AR(1)	0.059
Arellano-Bond test for AR(2)	0.331
Number of instruments	47
Observations	537
Number of groups	50

Note: Standard errors in parentheses
*** $p<0.01$, ** $p<0.05$, * $p<0.1$

can also be thought of as a proxy for labor costs, this means foreign investors desire countries with relatively cheap labor costs. Alsan, Bloom and Canning (2006) posits that GDP per capita may reflect both market size and cost effects. The exchange rate is found, as expected, to have positive impact on FDI inflows. The results show that a 1-unit increase in exchange rate leads to 0.07% increase in the percentage of FDI inflow to GDP in the host country. High exchange rate value relative to the US dollar in the host country accrue to the advantage of the foreign investor because this implies a depreciated currency leads to reduced cost of investment in the host country. It is worth mentioning that natural resources, telephone lines (infrastructural development) and political stability, although not significant, have the expected sign.

The global economy experienced a severe recession inflicted by a massive financial crisis and acute loss of confidence in 2009. Economies around the world have been seriously affected by the financial crisis and slump in activity. FDI inflows to Africa have suffered recently in the wake of the global economic crisis. To determine whether FDI inflow to Africa was affected by time-related shocks, time dummies were included. The inclusion of time dummies in the specification is likely to improve the statistical diagnostics as a result of potential heterogeneous cross-section dependence and also to remove universal time-related shocks from the error term (Efendic et al., 2009; Sarafidis et al., 2009). The time dummy variables used to capture universal time-related shocks before and after the global economy recession are mainly significant. The dummy for 2009 is negative and highly statistically significant, and this finding suggests that FDI inflow to Africa suffered a time-related shock in 2009 due to the severe global economic recession.

4.5 The estimated Tolerable Level of Corruption for Investment

The results in Table 4 show that at certain level of corruption of the host country, investors are motivated to invest in that country, but below that level, investors decline to invest in that country. Estimating the level of corruption that is likely to attract potential investor to Africa is very important not only to African leaders but to all (new and old) potential investors in Africa. This level of corruption is the TLCI of a country, which will determine whether FDI is likely to flow to a country. The coefficient $\hat{\beta}_2$ of the control of corruption variable tells both the direction and steepness of the curvature. As $\hat{\beta}_2$ is a positive value, it indicates that the curvature is upwards but less steep. The turning point is 44.51, and it is highly statistically significant with 95% confidence interval between 37.20 at the minimum and 51.81 at the maximum, as shown in Table 4.

Before the turning point can be used for any analysis, it is prudent to test for its precision and ensure its robustness. The usual criteria used by most researchers is that if both $\hat{\beta}_1$ and $\hat{\beta}_2$ are significant and if the

Table 4. The Turning Point Estimate

FDI_PerGDP	Coef.	Std. Err.	z	P>z	[95% Conf. Interval]	
Turning point	44.50556	3.726251	11.94	0.000	37.20225	51.80888

Table 5. Joint Hypothesis Test Results

FDI_PerGDP	Coefficient
$H_0: \beta_1 + \beta_2 f'(x_l) \geq 0$	-0.42765*** (0.1184)
$H_0: \beta_1 + \beta_2 f'(x_h) \leq 0$	0.365239*** (0.0940)

Note: Standard errors in parentheses
*** p<0.01, ** p<0.05, * p<0.1

implied extreme point is within the data range, then they have found a U-shaped relationship. This test is satisfied in this study because the results in Table 3 show both the control of corruption and the square of control of corruption are significant. However, these criteria, though sensible, are neither sufficient nor necessary and are too weak, as argued by Lind and Mehlum (2007).

Lind and Mehlum (2007) posit that to properly test for the presence of a U-shaped relationship, on some interval of values, we need to joint test whether the relationship is decreasing at low values within this interval and increasing at high values within the interval. The results of the combined test (Table 5) with null hypothesis $H_0: \beta_1 + \beta_2 f'(x_l) \geq 0$ and/or $\beta_1 + \beta_2 f'(x_h) \leq 0$ rejects the null hypothesis and confirms a U-shaped relationship on the observed data range. This test gives the exact necessary and sufficient conditions for the test of a U shape. The confidence interval ($37.20225 \leq \varphi \leq 51.80888$) for the turning point is contained within the observed data range, which further confirms this U-shaped relationship.

Once the exact necessary and sufficient conditions for the test of a U-shaped relationship are satisfied, it can be safely stated that the estimated TLCI for Africa is 44.51. This figure translates to -0.27 on the original control of corruption scale, which ranges from approximately -2.5 (weak) to 2.5 (strong). This means that all African countries falling below the TLCI (the figure -0.27) are less likely to attract FDI inflow. All the countries falling below the TLCI are above the threshold of corruption, and those falling above the TLCI are conversely below the threshold of corruption. This result shows that corruption has a negative effect on FDI when corruption is below the TLCI and a positive effect when above. This finding seems to support the finding by Cuervo-Cazurra (2008) that pervasive corruption has a larger negative influence on FDI in transition economies, while arbitrary corruption has a lower negative influence on FDI. Specifically, the findings in this study are consistent with research by Cole, Elliott and Zhang (2009) on the determinants of province-level FDI in China, which found that foreign capital prefers to locate in regions in which the government has made more effort to fight corruption and the local government is considered to be more efficient. Barassi and Zhou (2012) used non-parametric methods to show that

Table 6. Countries with Corruption Level above TLCI

2009	index	2010	index	2011	index	2012	index
Botswana	0.92	Botswana	1.00	Botswana	0.99	Botswana	0.94
Cape Verde	0.77	Cape Verde	0.80	Cape Verde	0.87	Cape Verde	0.81
Ghana	0.03	Ghana	0.06	Ghana	0.05	Ghana	-0.09
Lesotho	0.16	Lesotho	0.18	Lesotho	0.18	Lesotho	0.11
Madagascar	-0.19	Mauritius	0.65	Mauritius	0.59	Mauritius	0.33
Mauritius	0.63	Morocco	-0.18	Namibia	0.31	Namibia	0.32
Namibia	0.25	Namibia	0.32	Rwanda	0.43	Rwanda	0.66
Rwanda	0.13	Rwanda	0.46	Seychelles	0.26	Seychelles	0.33
Seychelles	0.31	Seychelles	0.29	South Africa	0.04	South Africa	-0.15
South Africa	0.14	South Africa	0.09	Tunisia	-0.22	Tunisia	-0.18
Swaziland	-0.20	Swaziland	-0.17				
Tunisia	-0.11	Tunisia	-0.15				

the impact of corruption on FDI stock is not homogenous. The results of this study complement the findings of Barassi and Zhou (2012), which show that for the top percentile of FDI stock distributions, the impact of corruption on FDI may not be negative after controlling for other relevant factors, such as MNEs' location choice, market size, and factor costs between 1996 and 2003.

In 2009 and 2010, twelve countries exhibited corruption levels above the TLCI, but this number was reduced to 10 in 2010 and 2012 (Table 6). Madagascar fell out in 2010, 2011 and 2012, while Morocco appeared only in 2010. These countries are within the Southern, Western, Eastern and Northern African regions. Conspicuously missing is the Central or Middle Africa region. This finding therefore serves as a wakeup call to all countries below the TLCI to intensify their efforts to reduce the level of corruption in their respective countries to at least the TLCI. The confidence interval ($37.20225 \leq \varphi \leq 51.80888$) for the TLCI translates to ($-0.64 \leq \varphi \leq 0.09$) on the original control of corruption scale. Therefore, countries that fall within this range can be referred to as transition countries.

5.0 Conclusion

Many empirical studies have examined the influence of corruption on economic growth at the country level, but only a few have looked at the effects of the level of corruption on FDI inflows. The quality of institutions or level of corruption in the domestic country has the potential to attract foreign direct investment depending on whether the foreign firm can exploit its location advantage (Abotsi, 2015) within the existing institutions. As corruption cannot be completely eradicated, reducing it to a threshold that can be accommodated by investors must be the goal that African leaders endeavor to achieve. This threshold is referred to as the Tolerable Level of Corruption for Investment in this study. Using a dynamic panel data estimation technique while controlling for other variables, the estimated tolerable level of corruption in Africa is -0.27 on the control of corruption scale, which ranges from approximately -2.5 (weak) to 2.5 (strong). Since 2009, only 12 African countries had control of corruption scores equal to or above the TLCI. This means that the level of corruption in majority of African countries goes beyond merely receiving bribes to malfunctioning of government institutions. Therefore, all African leaders and stakeholders, especially in countries that fall below the TLCI, should intensify their efforts in the fight against corruption to reduce the level of corruption in their respective countries to at least the TLCI to attract FDI to enhance their development. This TLCI will also guide potential investors in selecting which African countries to invest in.

This study's limitations result from the nature and availability of the data deployed in the study. The frequency of the data is annual, and it spans from 1996 to 2012 for 50 countries in Africa with data missing for three years (1997, 1999, & 2001). More robust results would have been obtained if these data were available and included in the analysis. Another limitation to this study is the assumption that foreign investors choose a country based solely on the level of corruption of the host country because there are other country business risks and individual-specific shocks that investors take into consideration before an investment decision is made. It is recommended that in measuring corruption, researchers should endeavor to disaggregate corruption into its various components, such as bribes, kickbacks, and malfunctioning state institutions, because this will not only help stakeholders make informed decision in anticorruption policy formulation but also help them to know where to direct these policies.

References

Abotsi, A. K. (2015). Foreign Ownership of Firms and Corruption in Africa. *International Journal of Economics and Financial Issues*, 5 (3), 647–655.

Aizenman, J., & Spiegel, M. (2002). *Institutional efficiency, monitoring costs, and the investment share of FDI* (Working Paper No. 9324). The National Bureau of Economic Research. Retrieved from http://www.nber.org/papers/w9324

Alsan, M., Bloom, D. E., & Canning, D. (2006). The Effect of Population Health on Foreign Direct Investment Inflows to Low- and Middle-Income Countries. *World Development*, 34 (4), 613–630.

Anyanwu, J. C. (2012). Why Does Foreign Direct Investment Go Where It Goes ?: New Evidence From African Countries. *Annals of Economics and Finance*, 13 (2), 425–462.

Arellano, M., & Bond, S. (1991). Some Tests of Specification for Panel Data: Monte Carlo Evidence and an Application to Employment Equations. *Review of Economic Studies*, 58 (2), 277–297.

Asiedu, E. (2002). On the Determinants of Foreign Direct Investment to Developing Countries: Is Africa Different? *World Development*, 30 (1), 107–119.

Asiedu, E. (2005). Foreign Direct Investment in Africa: The Role of Natural Resources, Market Size, Government Policy, Institutions and Political Instability. *World Economy*, 29 (1), 63–77.

Asiedu, E. (2013). *Foreign Direct Investment, Natural Resources and Institutions* (Working Paper). International Growth Centre. Retrieved from http://www.theigc.org/wp-content/uploads/2014/09/Asiedu-2013-Working-Paper.pdf

Asiedu, E., & Lien, D. (2011). Democracy, Foreign Direct Investment and Natural Resources. *Journal of International Economics*, 84 (1), 99–111.

Baltagi, B. H. (2008). *Econometric Analysis of Panel Data* (4th ed.). Chichester, UK: John Wiley & Sons Ltd.

Barassi, M. R., & Zhou, Y. (2012). The Effect of Corruption on FDI: A Parametric and Non-Parametric Analysis. *European Journal of Political Economy*, 28 (3), 302–312.

Basu, S. R. (2008). *A new way to link development to institutions, policies and geography*. Retrieved from http://unctad.org/en/Docs/itcdtab38_en.pdf

Baum, F. C. (2006). *An Introduction to Modern Econometrics Using Stata*. College Station, TX: Stata Press.

Beck, N., & Katz, J. N. (1996). Nuisance vs Substance: Specifying and Estimating Time-Series- Cross-Sectional Models. *Political Analysis*, 6 (1), 1–36.

Beck, P. J., & Maher, M. W. (1986). A Comparison of Bribery and Bidding in Thin Markets. *Economics Letters*, 20 (1), 1–5.

Blundell, R., & Bond, S. (1998). Initial Conditions and Moment Restrictions in Dynamic Panel Data Models. *Journal of Econometrics*, 87 (1), 115–143.

Bond, S. (2002). *Dynamic Panel Models: A Guide to Micro Data Methods and Practice* (Working Paper No. 09/02). Centre for Microdata Methods and Practise.

Botric, V., & Škuflić, L. (2006). Main Determinants of Foreign Direct Investment in the Southeast European Countries. *Ransition Studies Review*, 13 (2), 359–377.

Brahmasrene, T., & Jiranyakul, K. (2001). Foreign Direct Investment in Thailand, What Factors Matter? *Proceedings of the Academy for International Business*, 1 (2), 13–25.

Cole, M. A., Elliott, R. J. R., & Zhang, J. (2009). Corruption, Governance and FDI Location in China: A Province-Level Analysis. *The Journal of Development Studies*, 45 (9), 1494–1512.

Cuervo-Cazurra, A. (2006). Who Cares about Corruption? *Journal of International Business Studies*, 37 (6), 803–822.

Cuervo-Cazurra, A. (2008). Better the Devil You Don't Know: Types of Corruption and FDI in Transition Economies. *Journal of International Management*, 14 (1), 12–27.

Dal Bo, E., & Rossi, M. A. (2007). Corruption and Inefficiency: Theory and Evidence from Electric Utilities. *Journal of Public Economics*, 91 (5-6), 939–962.

Dasgupta, D., & Ratha, D. (2000). *What Factors Appear to Drive Private Capital Flows to Developing Countries and How Does Official Lending Respond?* (Policy Research Working Paper No. 2392). The World Bank.

Dauti, B. (2008). *Determinants of Foreign Direct Investment inflow in South East European Countries - Panel Estimation* (MPRA Working Paper No. 18273). University Library of Munich, Germany.

Dewenter, K. L. (1995). Do Exchange Rate Changes Drive Foreign Direct Investment? *The Journal of Business*, 68 (3), 405–433.

Dunning, J. H. (1973). The Determinants of International Production. *Oxford Economic Papers*, 25 (3), 289–336.

Dunning, J. H. (1980). Toward an Eclectic Theory of International Production: Some Empirical Tests. *Journal of International Business Studies*, 11 (1), 9–31.

Dunning, J. H. (1988). The Eclectic Paradigm of International Production: A Restatement and Some Possible Extensions. *Journal of International Business Studies Issue*, 19 (1), 1–31.

Dupasquier, C., & Osakwe, P. N. (2006). Foreign Direct Investment in Africa: Performance, Challenges, and Responsibilities. *Journal of Asian Economics*, 17 (2), 241–260.

Efendic, A., Pugh, G., & Adnett, N. (2009). *Institutions and Economic Performance: System GMM Modelling of Institutional Effects in Transition.* European Journal of Political Economy, 27 (3), 586-599.

Egger, P., & Winner, H. (2005). Evidence on Corruption as an Incentive for Foreign Direct Investment. *European Journal of Political Economy*, 21 (4), 932– 952.

Eicher, T. S. (1999). Trade, Development and Converging Growth Rates: Dynamic Gains from Trade Reconsidered. *Journal of International Economics*, 48 (1), 179–198.

Fedderke, J. W., & Romm, A. T. (2006). Growth Impact and Determinants of Foreign Direct Investment into South Africa, 1956-2003. *Economic Modeling*, 23 (5), 738–760.

Fina, W., & Rugman, A. M. (1996). A Test of Internalization Theory and Internationalization Theory: The Upjohn Company. *Management International Review*, 36 (3), 199–213.

Garibaldi, P., Mora, N., Sahay, R. and Zettelmeyer, J. (2002). *What Moves Capital to Transition Economies?* (Working Paper No. 02/64). International Monetary Fund. Retrieved from https://www.imf.org/external/pubs/ft/wp/2002/wp0264.pdf

Gastanaga, V. M., Nugent, J. B., & Pashamiova, B. (1998). Host Country Reforms and FDI Inflows: How Much Difference Do They Make? *World Development*, 26 (7), 1299–1314.

Habib, M. & Zurawicki, L. (2002). Corruption and Foreign Direct Investment. *Journal of International Business Studies*, 33 (2), 291–307.

Hakkala, K. N., Norback, P., & Svaleryd, H. (2008). Asymmetric Effects of Corruption on FDI: Evidence from Swedish Multinational Firms. *The Review of Economics and Statistics*, 90 (4), 627–642.

Hoeffler, A. E. (2002). The Augmented Solow Model and the African Growth Debate. *Oxford Bulletin of Economics and Statistics*, 64 (2), 135–158.

Huntington, S. P. (1968). *Political order in changing societies*. New Haven, CT: Yale University Press.

International Labour Office. (2014). *Global Employment Trends 2014 Risk of a jobless recovery ? Global Employment Trends 2014. Risk of a jobless recovery ?* Geneva: International Labour Office. Retrieved from http://www.ilo.org/wcmsp5/groups/public/---dgreports/---dcomm/---publ/documents/publication/wcms_233953.pdf

Jadhav, P. (2012). Determinants of Foreign Direct Investment in BRICS Economies: Analysis of Economic, Institutional and Political Factors. *Procedia - Social and Behavioral Sciences*, 37, 5–14.

Javorcik, B. S., & Wei, S. J. (2009). Corruption and Cross-Border Investment in Emerging Markets: Firm-Level Evidence. *Journal of International Money and Finance*, 28 (4), 605–624.

Jeon, B. N., & Rhee, S. S. (2008). The Determinants of Korea's Foreign Direct Investment from the United States, 1980-2001: An Empirical Investigation of Firm Level Data. *Contemporary Economic Policy*, 26 (1), 118–131.

Johnson, A. (2006). *The Effects of FDI Inflows on Host Country Economic Growth* (Working Paper No. 58). The Royal Institute of technology. Centre of Excellence for studies in Science and Innovation. Retrieved from https://static.sys.kth.se/itm/wp/cesis/cesiswp58.pdf

Kapsos, S. (2005). *The Employment Intensity of Growth: Trends and Macroeconomic Determinants* (Working Paper No. 2005/12). International Labour Organization.

Kersan-Skabic, I., & Orlic, E. (2007). Determinants of FDI in CEE, Western Balkan Countries (Is Accession to the EU Important for Attracting FDI?). *Economic and Business Review*, 9 (4), 333–350.

Kyereboah-Coleman, A., & Agyire-Tettey, K. F. (2008). Effect of Exchange-Rate Volatility on Foreign Direct Investment in Sub-Saharan Africa: The Case of Ghana. *The Journal of Risk Finance*, 9 (1), 52–70.

Lee, J. W. (1993). International Trade, Distortions, and Long-Run Economic Growth. *IMF Staff Papers*, 40 (2), 299–328.

Leff, N. H. (1964). Economic Development through Bureaucratic Corruption. *American Behavioral Scientist*, 8 (3), 8–14.

Leys, C. (1965). What Is The Problem About Corruption? *Journal of Modern African Studies*, 3 (2), 215–230.

Li, Q. (2009). Democracy, Autocracy, and Expropriation of Foreign Direct Investment. *Comparative Political Studies*, 42 (8), 1098–1127.

Lien, D. H. D. (1986). A Note on Competitive Bribery Games. *Economics Letters*, 22 (4), 337–341.

Lind, J. T., & Mehlum, H. (2007). *With or Without U? - The appropriate test for a U shaped relationship* (MPRA Working Paper No. 4823). University Library of Munich, Germany.

Liu, X., Shu, C., & Sinclair, P. (2009). Trade, Foreign Direct Investment and Economic Growth in Asian Economies. *Applied Economics*, 41 (13), 1603–1612.

Mateev, M. (2009). Determinants of Foreign Direct Investment in Central and Southeastern Europe: New Empirical Tests. *Oxford Journal*, 8 (1), 133–149.

Mauro, P. (1995). Corruption and Growth. *Quarterly Journal of Economics*, 110 (3), 681–712.

Musila, J.W., & Sigue, S. P. (2006). Accelerating Foreign Direct Investment Flow to Africa: From Policy Statements to Successful Strategies. *Managerial Finance*, 32 (7), 577–593.

Mwilima, N. (2003). *Foreign Direct Investment in Africa. Africa Labour Research Network Report*. Retrieved from http://www.sarpn.org/documents/d0000883/P994-African_Social_Observatory_PilotProject_FDI.pdf

Nerlove, M. (2002). *Essays in Panel Data Econometrics*. Cambridge: Cambridge, UK: Cambridge University Press.

Nickell, S. J. (1981). Biases in Dynamic Models with Fixed Effects. *Econometrica*, 49 (6), 1417–1426.

Nkurunziza, J. D. & Bates, R. H. (2003). *Political Institutions and Economic Growth in Africa* (Working Paper 2003-03). Centre for the Study of African Economies. University of Oxford. Retrieved from http://econwpa.repec.org/eps/dev/papers/0409/0409028.pdf

North, D. C., & Weingast, B. R. (1989). Constitutions and Commitment: The Evolution of Institutional Governing Public Choice in Seventeenth-Century England. *Journal of Economic History*, 49 (4), 803–832.

Nunes, C. L., Oscategui, J., & Peschiera, J. (2006). *Determinants of FDI in Latin America* (Working Paper No. 252). Department of Economics. Pontifical Catholic University of Peru. Retrieved from http://departamento.pucp.edu.pe/economia/images/documentos/DDD252.pdf

Piacentini, P., & Pini, P. (2000). Growth and Employment. In M. Vivarelli, & M. Pianta (Eds.), *The Employment Impact of Innovation: Evidence and Policy* (pp. 44-76). London, UK: Routledge.

Picci, L. (2005, June). Corruption measurement and control: towards a unified approach. *Paper Presented at IV Global Forum on Fighting Corruption, Brasılia.*

Plassmann, F., & Khanna, N. (2003). *Assessing the Precision of Turning Point Estimates in Polynomial Regression Functions. Econometric Reviews*, 26 (5), 503- 528.

Presbitero, A. F. (2005). *The Debt-Growth Nexus: a Dynamic Panel Data Estimation* (Working Paper No. 243). Department of Economics. Marche Polytechnic University.

Ranjan, V., & Agrawal, G. (2011). FDI Inflow Determinants in BRIC Countries: A Panel Data Analysis. *International Business Research*, 4 (4), 225–263.

Roodman, D. (2006). *How To Do xtabond2: An Introduction to "Difference" and "System" GMM in Stata* (Working Paper No. 103). Center for Global Development. Retrieved from http://www.nuffield.ox.ac.uk/users/bond/file_HowtoDoxtabond8_with_foreword.pdf

Roodman, D. (2007). *A Short Note on the Theme of Too Many Instruments* (Working Paper No. 125). Center for Global Development. Retrieved from http://www.cgdev.org/files/14256_file_Instruments.pdf

Roodman, D. (2009). How to do Xtabond2: An Introduction to Difference and System GMM in Stata. *The Stata Journal*, 9 (1), 86–136.

Sahoo, P. (2006). *Foreign Direct Investment in South Asia: Policy, Trends, Impact and Determinants* (Discussion Paper No. 56). Asian Development Bank. Retrieved from http://www.adb.org/sites/default/files/publication/156693/adbi-dp56.pdf

Sarafidis, V., Yamagata, T., & Robertson, R. (2009). A Test of Cross-Section Dependence for a Linear Dynamic Panel Model with Regressors. *Journal of Econometrics*, 148 (2), 149-161.

Sasabuchi, S. (1980). A Test of a Multivariate Normal Mean with Composite Hypotheses Determined by Linear Inequalities. *Biometrika*, 67 (2), 429–439.

Seyfried, W. (2005). Examining the Relationship between Employment and Economic Growth in the Ten Largest States. *Southwestern Economic Review*, 32, 13-24.

Shleifer, A., & Vishny, R. W. (1993). Corruption. *Quarterly Journal of Economics*, 108 (3), 599–617.

Svensson, J. (2005). Eight Questions About Corruption. *Journal of Economic Perspectives*, 19 (3), 19–42.

Treisman, D. (2000). The Causes of Corruption: A Cross-National Study. *Journal of Public Economics*, 76 (3), 399–457.

UNCTAD. (2010). *Investing in a Low-Carbon Economy*. Retrieved from http://unctad.org/en/Docs/wir2010_en.pdf

UNCTAD (2013). *Global Value Chains: Investment and Trade for Development*. Retrieved from http://unctad.org/en/ PublicationsLibrary/wir2013_en.pdf

Vial, V. & Hanoteau, J. (2010). Corruption, Manufacturing Plant Growth, and the Asian Paradox: Indonesian Evidence. *World Development*, 38 (5), 693–705.

Voyer, P.A., & Beamish, P. W. (2004). The Effect of Corruption on Japanese Foreign Direct Investment. *Journal of Business Ethics*, 50 (3), 211–226.

Vu, T. B., Gangnes, B., & Noy, I. (2008). Is Foreign Direct Investment Good for Growth? Evidence from Sectoral Analysis of China and Vietnam. *Journal of the Asia Pacific Economy*, 13 (4), 542–562.

Wang, M. (2009). Manufacturing FDI and Economic Growth: Evidence from Asian Economies. *Applied Economics*, 41 (8), 991–1002.

Wei, S. J. (2000a). How Taxing is Corruption on International Investors. *The Review of Economics and Statistics*, 82 (1), 1–11.

Wei, S. J. (2000b). Local Corruption and Global Capital Flows". *Brookings Papers on Economic Activity*, 20 (2), 303–346.

Wijeweera, A., Villano, R., & Dollery, B. (2010). An Econometric Analysis of Economic Growth and FDI Inflows. Economic growth and FDI inflows: a stochastic frontier analysis. *Journal of Developing Areas*, 43 (2), 143-158.

World Bank. (2013a). *World Development Indicators*. Washington, DC: World Bank.

World Bank. (2013b). *Worldwide Governance Indicators.* Washington, DC: World Bank. Retrieved from http://info.worldbank.org/governance/wgi/index.aspx#home

Yan, J. & Oum, T. H. (2011). *Effects of Government Quality and Institutional Choice on the Eficiency of the U.S. Commercial Airports.* Available at http://dx.doi.org/10.2139/ssrn.1956182

Young, A. (1991). Learning by Doing and the Dynamic Effects of International Trade. *Quarterly Journal of Economics*, 106 (2), 369–405.

7

Global Innovational Networks: Sense and Role in Development of Global Economy

Egor V. Dudukalov[1], Natalia D. Rodionova[2], Yana E. Sivakova[3], Elena Vyugova[4], Irina V. Cheryomushkina[5], Elena G. Popkova[6]

ABSTRACT

The starting point for this research is the authors' hypothesis that global innovational networks play an important role in the development of the modern global economy because they stimulate international cooperation in the innovational sphere, the translation of knowledge in the global economic system, and general scientific and technological development and production development.

The purpose of this article is to verify this hypothesis, conduct a complex study on the phenomenon of global innovational networks, and determine their purpose and role in the development of the modern global economy. The methodological basis of this research is founded on the logical modeling of economic systems and methods of structural and functional, systemic, and problem analysis.

In the process of the research, the authors studied examples of global innovational networks created based on modern Europe that include countries from all over the world, namely, Horizon 2020, ERA.Net RUS, and Eurocores (European Collaboration Research). The authors also conducted complex analysis of statistical information on various global innovational networks, the dynamics of the quantity of innovational projects, realized participation in global innovational networks, and the significance of the global innovational indexes of countries of Western Europe (Great Britain, Germany, France, and Italy), Central and Eastern Europe (Czech Republic, Poland, Hungary, and Latvia) and Russia in 2005-2014.

The authors provide a sense of global innovational networks, including their peculiarities and advantages; build a structural and logical model of the global market of innovations; and determine the role of global innovational networks in the development of the modern global economy.

KEY WORDS: global innovational networks, globalization, global economy, economic development

[1]Russian Presidential Academy of National Economy and Public Administration, Russia; [2]Rostov State Economic University (RINH), Russia; [3]Institute of Management - Branch of Russian Presidential Academy of National Economy and Public Administration, Russia; [4]Institute of Economics and Finance, Russia; [5]Voronezh State University of Engineering Technologies, Russia; [6]Volgograd State Technical University, Russia

Introduction

As the global economy develops, it acquires more and more new members. Under the influence of integration processes, modern businesses have taken various forms. One of the most vivid manifestations is the emergence of transnational corporations in the 20th century, which currently have strong positions in the global economic system. As the concept of innovational economic development in the global economy has expanded, new members – global innovational networks – have appeared. These networks were selected as the object of this research.

Correspondence concerning this article should be addressed to: Elena G. Popkova, Volgograd State Technical University, 28 Lenina St., Volgograd, Russian Federation. E-mail: elenapopkova@yahoo.com

Global innovational networks are a form of international cooperation among enterprises in the sphere of scientific research and development for the creation of innovational technologies and their implementation in production. They can be created in any sphere of economic activity. Their members could include entrepreneurial structures, R&D institutes, and other subjects of economic activities of any ownership form. The organizational structure of global innovational networks differs depending on the specifics of the sphere and its subjects.

In the case of the registration of patents based on joint international developments within global innovational networks, network members possess equal rights to them. Overall, the activities of global innovational networks are regulated by international norms of law. It should be noted that recent initiators and members of global innovational networks have included representatives of developing countries. Joint projects, which are conducted with close cooperation within such networks, provide innovational development of the economies of all network members.

The authors of this research offer a scientific hypothesis that global innovational networks play an important role in the development of the modern global economy because they stimulate international cooperation in the sphere of innovation, the translation of knowledge in the global economic system, and general scientific, technical and production development. The purpose of the article is to verify this hypothesis, conduct a complex study of the phenomenon of global innovational networks, and determine their sense and role in the development of the modern global economy.

Literature review

The theoretical basis of the research comprises the works of various authors in the spheres of analyzing the consequences of the globalization of economic activities, the functioning of transnational corporations, and other international entrepreneurial structures; studying the tendencies of development of international business at modern stage; studying the issues of international production and sales cooperation; studying the transformation of national business environments and business societies and the formation of global business; and determining perspectives for the further expansion of international movement of production factors. Many researchers have publications on this topic (Bagwell, 2015; Lan, 2015, & Thauer, 2015). The globalization of the world economy has led to transnational corporations, which conduct their business activities at the international scale (Eberlein, Abbott, Black, Meidinger, & Wood, 2014). Transnational businesses strive to place their production in countries with the cheapest natural and human resources (Porter, 2014), through which the least developed countries receive investments and opportunities for development (Lee, Ryu, & Kang, 2014).

This research is based on studies by modern authors in the spheres of studying the sense of the phenomenon of global innovational networks, their differences from other players in the international markets, the specifics of the organization of their activities and the cooperation of members in such networks and studying the issues of cooperation in global innovational networks with the governments of the countries in which they are represented and specific aspects of their activities, including taxation, crediting, and investments (Chaminade & Plechero, 2015; Cooke, 2013; Herstad, Aslesen, & Ebersberger, 2014; Liu, Chaminade, & Asheim, 2013; Ribeiro et al., 2014; Schøtt, Cheraghi, Rezaei, & Vang, 2014; Silva & Klagge, 2013; van Egeraat & Kogler, 2013).

Global innovational networks are global centers of innovational activities that accumulate new knowledge and stimulate their implementation in the production activities of business structures (Liu et al., 2013). They ensure innovational activity in the global economy; therefore, they often receive tax subsidies and credit resources (Silva & Klagge, 2013). The governments of various countries strive to attract global innovational networks and create them based on their own economies (Cooke, 2013).

The article also uses the works of economists devoted to the analysis of tendencies and factors of development of the modern global economy and the determination of new vectors of its growth and the influence of globalization and integration on the development of the global economy. They study various aspects of globalization of specific markets and spheres of the economy, the functioning and development of integration associations, international cooperation in solving global economic problems of humankind, and the process of overcoming crisis phenomena in the global economy (Čaušević, 2015; Docquier & Machado, 2015; Ilie & Jaradat, 2015; Klinov, 2015; Larionova, Suslova, Povorina, & Vinogradova, 2015; Vinogradova, Kulyamina, Koroleva, & Larionova, 2015; Wirtz, Tuzovic, & Ehret, 2015; Yakovleva, Azarova, Titova, 2015). The most important tendencies of development of the modern global economy are those of integration and disintegration (Kornev, Maksimtsova, & Treshchina, 2015), the growth of contradictions of individual and collective development in countries of the global economy (Pulselli et al., 2015), and the development of international economic cooperation to solve common economic problems (Dudin & Frolova, 2015).

To understand the sense of development of the global economy, the authors use the studies of various authors, devoted to theoretical, methodological and practical aspects of the provision of economic growth, the modeling of the development of socio-economic systems under modern economic conditions, the analysis of disproportions of economic development of countries and the overcoming of them through the creation and implementation of innovations, concepts of innovational development of modern economic systems, high-quality aspects of the provision of sustainable economic growth, and the development of the global economy (González-Pernía & Peña-Legazkue, 2015; Leonida, Maimone Ansaldo Patti, Marini, & Navarra, 2015; Odhiambo, 2015; Pogosov, 2015; Popkova, Yurev, Stepicheva, & Denisov, 2015; Sarracino & Bartolini, 2015; Zeira & Zoabi, 2015). The provision of stable and sustainable economic growth and development require orientation towards the achievement of common (global) goals (Choi & Shin, 2015), a cautious attitude towards existing resources and the environment (Lee & Oh, 2015), and the protection of interests of society within the realization of state economic policy (Castiglione, Infante, & Smirnova, 2015).

A literature review on the topic of the research showed that despite the large number of publications in the sphere of globalization and development of the global economy, the specifics of the activities and influence of global innovational networks, which are a phenomenon of the modern global economic system, on global economic processes have not been studied. This predetermines the necessity for further research in this sphere aimed at determination of the sense of global innovational networks and their role in the development of the global economy – which is studied in this article.

Method

The methodological basis of this research comprises the method of logical modeling of economic systems and the methods of structural, functional, systemic, and problem analysis. This methodology was selected due to, first the novelty of the objects of the research and the lack of statistical information on the current state, tendencies, and dynamics of development of the global innovational networks, which makes the use of methods of economic analysis impossible, and, second, the possibility of conducting full study on the sense and role of global innovational networks in the development of the global economy with the help of these methods.

The work also uses the following general methods of scientific research: induction, deduction, synthesis, and formalization. Due to the use of these methods, the scientific character of this research is ensured. The work is based on the hypothetico-deductive principle. The work is conducted within the concepts of innovational development of an economy, globalization and integration of the global economy, and the transnationalization of business.

Results

There are several dozens of global innovational networks in the world that unite various countries on R&D and the creation of innovational products. Let us view examples of global innovational networks that are created based on modern Europe and include countries from all over the world. One of the largest global innovational networks is Horizon 2020, which is oriented at the realization of many international innovational projects in the period of 2014-2020. The total budget of the projects constitutes more than EUR 80 billion (European Commission, 2015).

Another well-known global innovational network is ERA.Net RUS, which is a platform for the cooperation of countries of the EU and the Russian Federation in innovational and other spheres as follows: the protection of the environment, industrial production, the social sphere, medicine, etc. The total budget of realized innovational projects within ERA.Net RUS is more than $25 million (ERA.Net RUS Plus, 2015).

Table 1. Dynamics of quantity of innovational projects realized within participation in global innovational networks and values of global innovational index of countries of Western, Central, and Eastern Europe and Russia in 2005-2009

Countries	Year/Indicators									
	2005		2006		2007		2008		2009	
	Q	I	Q	I	Q	I	Q	I	Q	I
Countries of Western Europe										
Great Britain	448	0.08	574	0.10	396	0.07	885	0.16	1,008	0.18
Germany	427	0.18	423	0.18	266	0.11	715	0.30	616	0.26
France	389	0.25	357	0.23	256	0.16	407	0.26	530	0.34
Italy	419	0.38	291	0.26	228	0.20	395	0.35	448	0.40
Countries of Central and Eastern Europe										
Czech Republic	75	0.09	80	0.11	85	0.08	91	0.17	97	0.20
Poland	55	0.05	60	0.05	65	0.03	71	0.09	78	0.08
Hungary	34	0.38	37	0.34	40	0.25	44	0.39	48	0.51
Latvia	28	0.32	32	0.22	37	0.18	42	0.30	48	0.34
Russia										
Russia	3	0.02	5	0.03	6	0.04	10	0.06	17	0.10

Source: Adapted from "The Global Innovation Index 2015: Effective Innovation Policies for Development" by Dutta, Bernard, Reynoso, Lanvin and Wunsch-Vincent (2015).

Note:

Q – quantity of innovational projects realized within participation in global innovational networks;

I – value of global innovational index.

Another interesting global innovational network is Eurocores (European Collaboration Research), which includes 68 innovational enterprises from 24 countries of Europe. Within Eurocores, multiple scientific and research conferences are held, and many innovational projects are realized, the total budget of which constitutes more than EUR 50 billion (European Science Foundation, 2009).

These examples of global innovational networks were created around large European investment funds that conduct wide circles of research, concentrated around the most perspective spheres of science – nanotechnologies, breakthrough medicine technologies, etc. – and, despite their global coverage, have many members from the regions in which they were created.

The sense of global innovational networks consists of the unification of efforts of innovational enterprises and R&D centers from various countries for the joint conduct of scientific research and creation of innovations. The most important peculiarities that determine the specifics and nature of the activities of global innovational networks are the following:

- the activities of global innovational networks have an innovational character – their acceptance of enterprises and R&D centers from several countries of the world;
- global innovational networks feature the realization of large projects that are characterized by a high complexity and require special infrastructure and large investments;
- projects realized within such networks usually have large social significance, have a revolutionary direction in science and are held in top-priority spheres of activities;
- global innovational networks are created for a certain period of time, have a clear goal, and cease to exist (or are re-organized) after its achievement;
- the initiator of network creation is, as a rule, a large investment fund that is interested in conducting scientific research.

Table 2. Dynamics of quantity of innovational projects realized within participation in global innovational networks and values of global innovational index of countries of Western, Central, and Eastern Europe and Russia in 2010-2014

Countries	Year/Indicators									
	2010		2011		2012		2013		2014	
	Q	I	Q	I	Q	I	Q	I	Q	I
Countries of Western Europe										
Great Britain	1,347	0.24	1,800	0.32	2,405	0.43	3,214	0.58	4,294	0.99
Germany	796	0.33	1,029	0.43	1,329	0.56	1,718	0.72	2,220	0.92
France	600	0.39	679	0.44	768	0.49	869	0.56	984	0.85
Italy	487	0.44	529	0.47	574	0.52	624	0.56	677	0.79
Countries of Central and Eastern Europe										
Czech Republic	104	0.26	110	0.35	118	0.47	126	0.63	134	0.82
Poland	85	0.10	93	0.13	101	0.17	110	0.22	120	0.69
Hungary	52	0.58	56	0.66	61	0.74	67	0.84	73	0.76
Latvia	55	0.37	62	0.41	71	0.44	81	0.48	93	0.77
Russia										
Russia	25	0.15	31	0.18	39	0.23	46	0.27	53	0.66

Source: Adapted from "The Global Innovation Index 2015: Effective Innovation Policies for Development" by Dutta, Bernard, Reynoso, Lanvin and Wunsch-Vincent (2015).

Note:

Q – quantity of innovational projects realized within participation in global innovational networks;

I – value of global innovational index.

Due to these peculiarities, global innovational networks have the following advantages:

- the attraction of investments for the realization of complex, high-risk, and long-term innovational projects, which, as a rule, is difficult during the performance of such projects on a national scale;
- the possibility of the creation of unique and costly infrastructure, necessary for the conduct of full-scale R&D projects;
- the unification of resources and leading specialists from several countries, due to which the volume of innovational capital exceeds the possibilities of other members of the global market of innovations by several times.

Based on statistical information of for global innovational networks, the authors of this research determined (Table 1-2) and graphically presented (Fig. 1-6) dynamics of the quantity of innovational projects realized within participation in global innovational networks and the values of the global innovational index of countries of Western Europe (Great Britain, Germany, France, and Italy), Central and Eastern Europe (Czech Republic, Poland, Hungary, and Latvia), and Russia in 2005-2014.

The analysis of dynamics of the above indicators made it possible to determine the tendency of expansion of countries' cooperation in the creation of global innovational networks, which leads to an increase in the value of their global innovational index. The number of innovational projects realized through participation in global innovational networks selected for the study of countries of Western Europe increased 10 times over the past 10 years. The annual increase was 10-15%. The value of the global innovational index increased proportionally from 0.08-0.25 to 0.85-0.99.

The quantity of innovational projects realized through participation in global innovational networks selected for the study of countries of Central and Eastern Europe increased 2 times over the past 10 years.

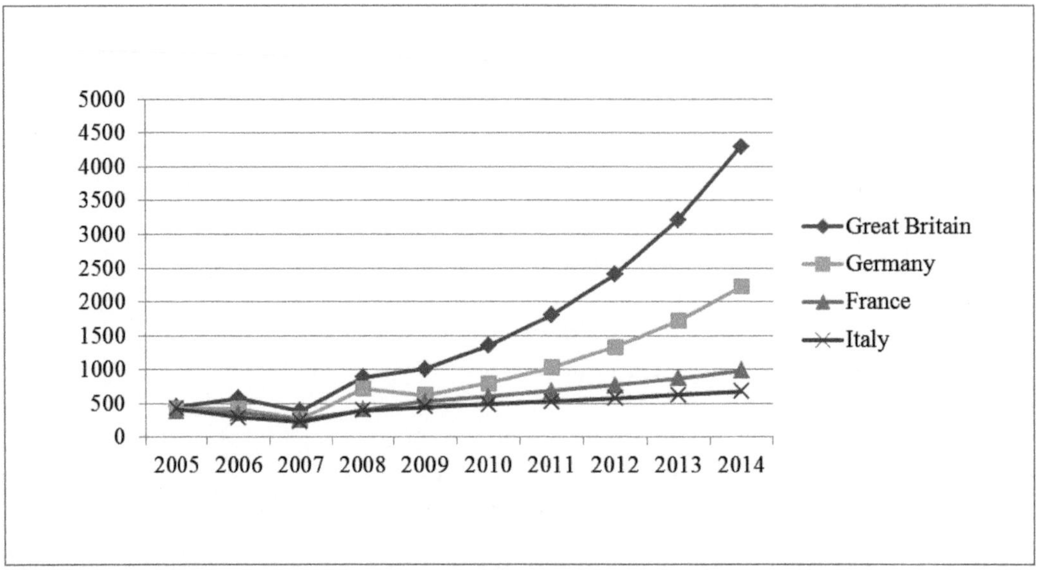

Figure 1. Number of innovational projects of countries of Western Europe realized within participation in global innovational networks in 2005-2014
Adapted from "The Global Innovation Index 2015: Effective Innovation Policies for Development" by Dutta, Bernard, Reynoso, Lanvin and Wunsch-Vincent (2015).; "Funded innovation projects" by ERA.Net RUS Plus (2015); "EUROCORES Scheme European Collaborative Research. Final Activity Report" by European Science Foundation (2009).

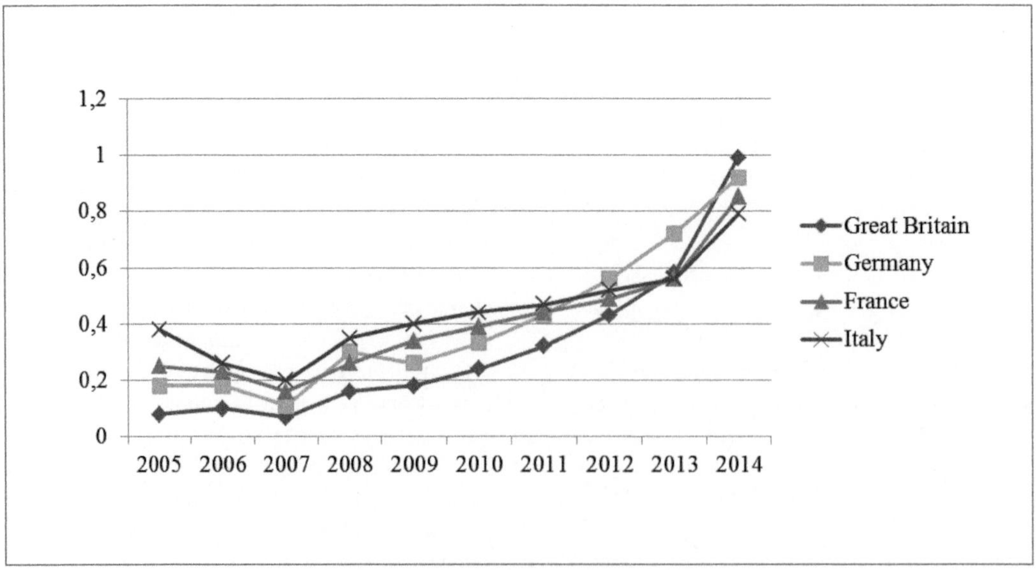

Figure 2. Global innovational index of countries of Western Europe in 2005-2014
Adapted from "The Global Innovation Index 2015: Effective Innovation Policies for Development" by Dutta, Bernard, Reynoso, Lanvin and Wunsch-Vincent (2015).; "Funded innovation projects" by ERA.Net RUS Plus (2015); "EUROCORES Scheme European Collaborative Research. Final Activity Report" by European Science Foundation (2009).

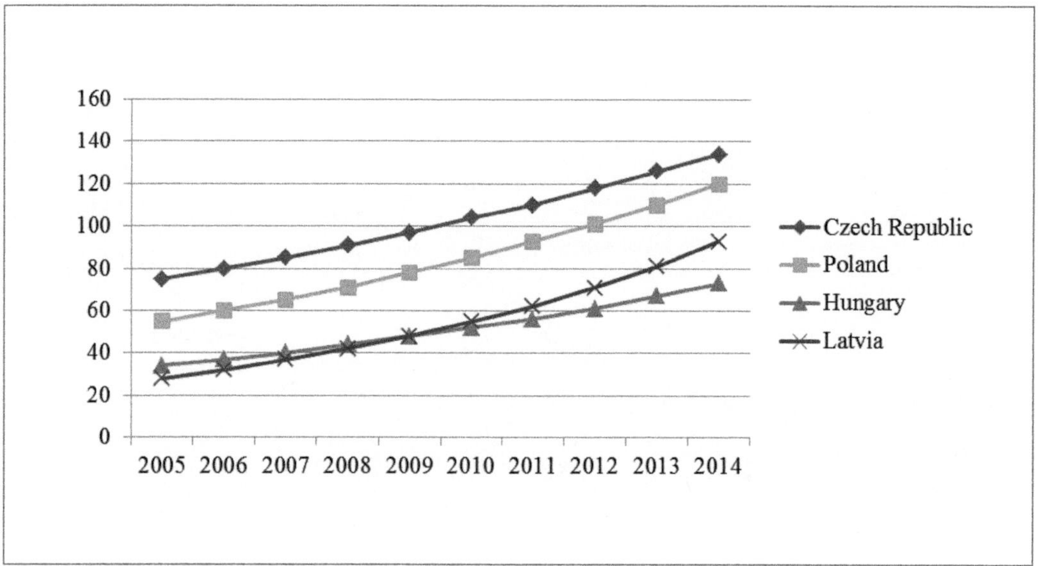

Figure 3. Number of innovational projects of countries of Central and Eastern Europe realized within participation in global innovational networks in 2005-2014
Adapted from "The Global Innovation Index 2015: Effective Innovation Policies for Development" by Dutta, Bernard, Reynoso, Lanvin and Wunsch-Vincent (2015).; "Funded innovation projects" by ERA.Net RUS Plus (2015); "EUROCORES Scheme European Collaborative Research. Final Activity Report" by European Science Foundation (2009).

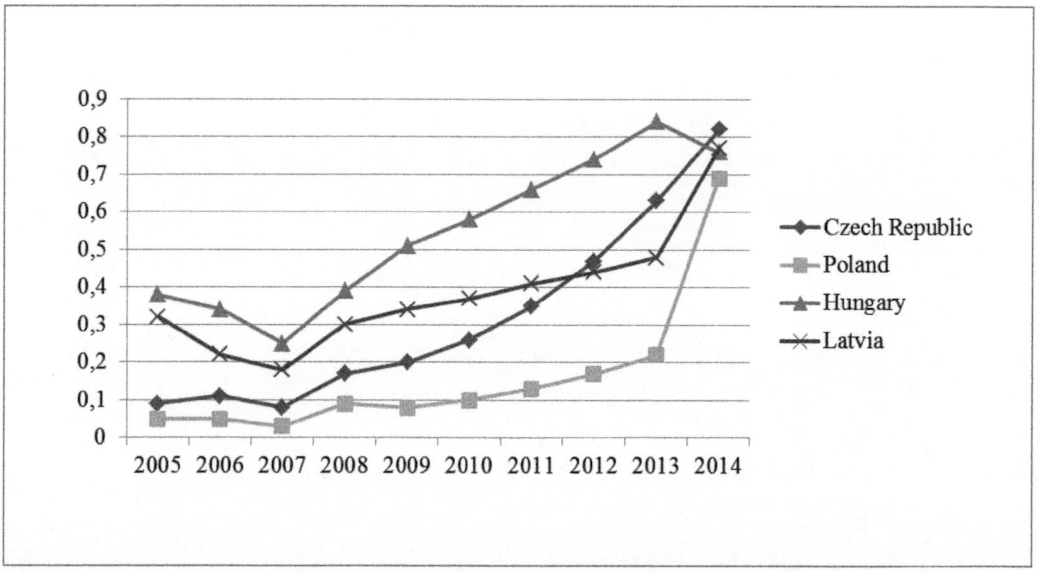

Figure 4. Global innovational index of countries of Central and Eastern Europe in 2005-2014
Adapted from "The Global Innovation Index 2015: Effective Innovation Policies for Development" by Dutta, Bernard, Reynoso, Lanvin and Wunsch-Vincent (2015).; "Funded innovation projects" by ERA.Net RUS Plus (2015); "EUROCORES Scheme European Collaborative Research. Final Activity Report" by European Science Foundation (2009).

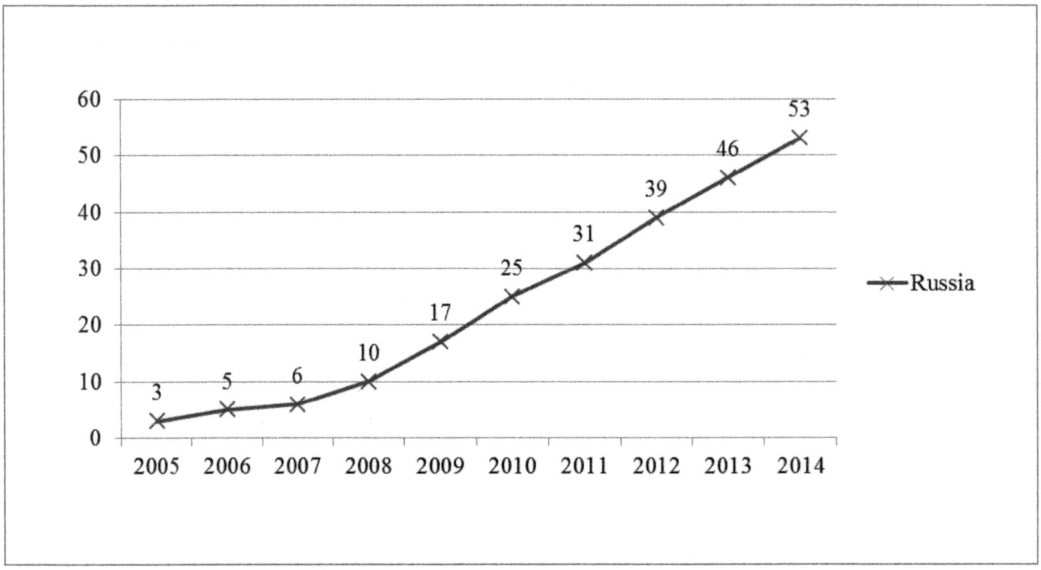

Figure 5. Number of innovational projects of Russia realized within participation in global innovational networks in 2005-2014
Adapted from "The Global Innovation Index 2015: Effective Innovation Policies for Development" by Dutta, Bernard, Reynoso, Lanvin and Wunsch-Vincent (2015). ; "Funded innovation projects" by ERA.Net RUS Plus (2015); "EUROCORES Scheme European Collaborative Research. Final Activity Report" by European Science Foundation (2009).

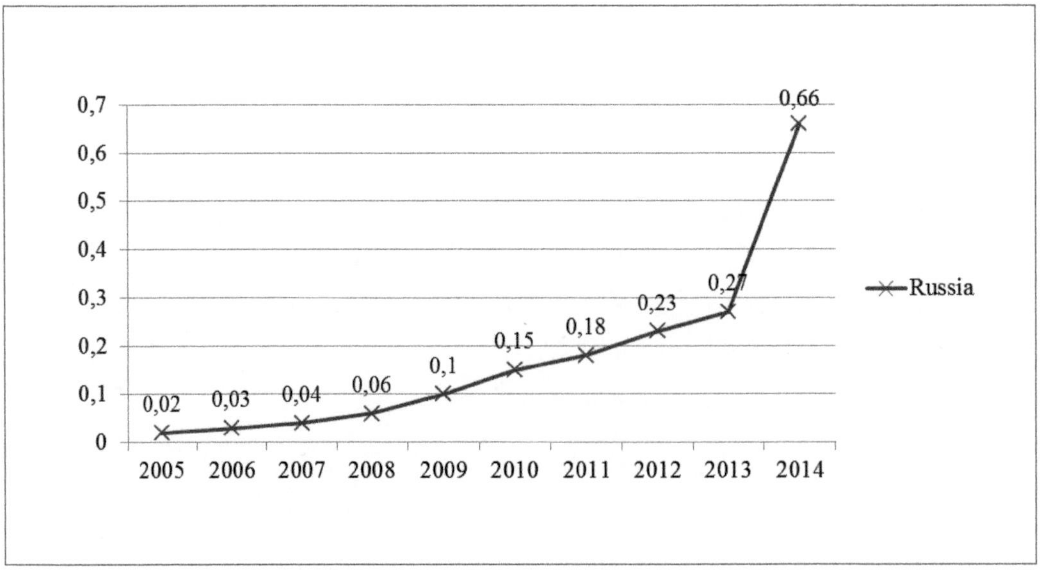

Figure 6. Global innovational index of Russia in 2005-2014
Adapted from "The Global Innovation Index 2015: Effective Innovation Policies for Development" by Dutta, Bernard, Reynoso, Lanvin and Wunsch-Vincent (2015). ; "Funded innovation projects" by ERA.Net RUS Plus (2015); "EUROCORES Scheme European Collaborative Research. Final Activity Report" by European Science Foundation (2009).

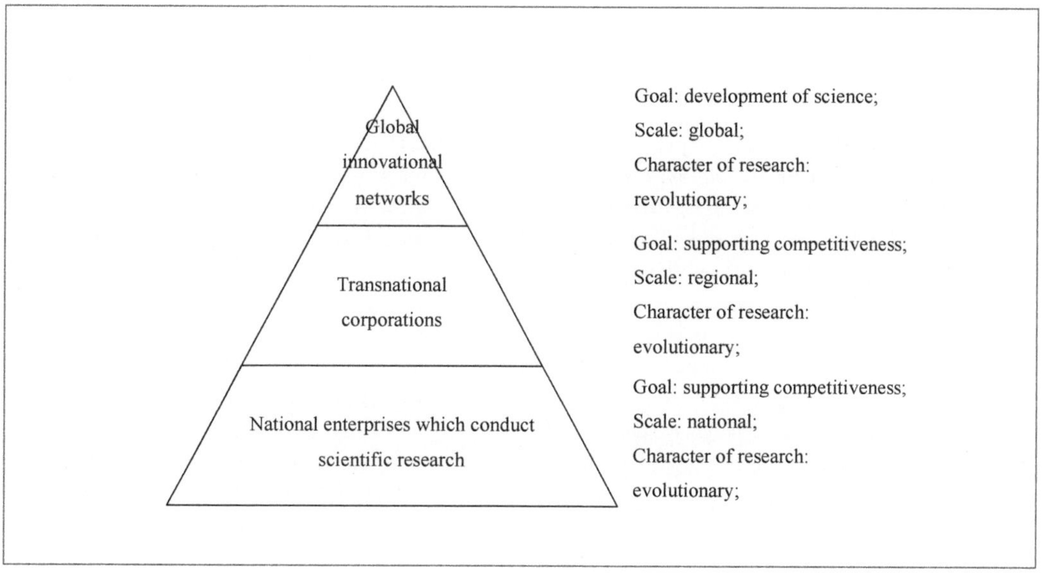

Figure 7. Structural and logical model of global market of innovations

The annual increase was 6-8%. The value of the global innovational index increased proportionally from 0.05-0.09 to 0.75-0.85.

The largest growth in the quantity of innovational projects realized through participation in global innovational networks was found for Russia. Over the past 10 years, it grew 17 times. The annual growth was 25-30%. The value of the global innovational index increased proportionally from 0.02 to 0.66. To determine the position and role of global innovational networks in the development of the modern global economy, let us view the proprietary logical model of the global market of innovations (Fig. 7).

As seen from Fig. 7, the global market of innovations is founded on national enterprises that conduct scientific research. They create most of the innovations. This is necessary for supporting their competitiveness in domestic markets. Their research is focused on a national scale, has an evolutionary character, and aims at slight improvements in manufactured products. Their budget is no more than several thousands of dollars.

Transnational corporations are also in the center of the global market of innovations. They conduct scientific research to support their competitiveness, but in the international markets. Their research has regional coverage and is focused on the regions in which their main centers are located. Their research has an evolutionary character and aims at the significant improvement of manufactured products. The budget of their research may reach several millions of dollars.

On the top of the global market of innovations, there are global innovational networks. They do not seek to support the competitiveness of their members but rather strive for breakthroughs in modern science. They conduct research at the global scale. The character of their research is revolutionary because they are aimed not at the perfection of usual products but at the creation of completely new technologies and development of completely new products. The budget of global innovational networks can be billions of dollars.

Because of the structural and functional analysis of the compiled logical model, it is possible to conclude that global innovational networks are drivers of innovational development in the global economy. Being a locomotive of modern scientific research, they create a scientific and technological base for the research and development of innovational products by transnational corporations and national innovational enterprises.

Conclusion

The offered hypothesis was proven, and the authors concluded that global innovational networks play an important role in the development of the modern global economy. With vast scientific research, they create a technical and methodological basis for the research and development of innovational products by transnational corporations and national innovational enterprises.

The complex study of the phenomenon of global innovational networks made it possible to determine that they consisted of the unification of efforts of innovational enterprises and R&D centers from various countries for joint conduct of scientific research and creation of innovations.

The most important peculiarities that determine the specifics and characteristics of the activities of global innovational networks are the international character of activities, the realization of large projects, the revolutionary direction of R&D, clear goal setting, and initiation by large investment funds. The advantages of global innovational networks are the attraction of significant investments, the creation of unique infrastructure, and a large volume of innovational capital.

It should be concluded that although the fact that the share of the global market of innovations constitutes 3-5% of the global GDP in quantitative terms, in qualitative terms, this market stimulates the development of the global economic system because it provides fuller satisfaction of global public needs, stimulates the effectiveness of the use of existing resources, and increases the sustainability of the development of the global economy.

The limitations of the conducted research include the limited selection of countries and global innovational networks, due to which, not all the peculiarities and advantages of their activities could be determined. As a direction of further research in this sphere, global innovational networks based around Asian, African, American, and Australian investors could be studied to determine common regularities of their development.

References

Bagwell, S. (2015). Transnational entrepreneurship amongst Vietnamese businesses in London. *Journal of Ethnic and Migration Studies, 41*(2), 329-349.

Castiglione, C., Infante, D., Smirnova, J. (2015). Environment and economic growth: is the rule of law the go-between? The case of high-income countries. *Energy, Sustainability and Society, 5*(26). doi:10.1186/s13705-015-0054-8.

Čaušević, F. (2015). *Globalization. Southeastern Europe, and the World Economy*. London, UK: Routledge.

Chaminade, C., Plechero, M. (2015). Do regions make a difference? Regional innovation systems and global Iinnovation networks in the ICT Industry. *European Planning Studies, 23*(2), 215-237.

Choi, K. H., Shin, S. (2015). Population aging, economic growth, and the social transmission of human capital: An analysis with an overlapping generations model. *Economic Modelling, 50*, 138-147.

Cooke, P. (2013). Qualitative analysis and comparison of firm and system incumbents in the new ICT global innovation network. *European Planning Studies, 21*(9), 1323-1340.

Docquier, F., Machado, J. (2015). Global Competition for Attracting Talents and the World Economy. *The World Economy, 39*(4), 530-542.

Dudin, M. N., Frolova, E. E. (2015). The balanced scorecard as a basis for strategic company management in the context of the world economy transformation. *Asian Social Science, 11*(3), 282-288.

Dutta, S., Bernard, A. L., Reynoso, E. R., Lanvin, B., & Wunsch-Vincent, S. (2015). The Global Innovation Index 2015: Effective Innovation Policies for Development. In S. Dutta, B. Lanvin, & S. Wunsch-Vincent (Eds.), The Global Innovation Index 2015. Effective Innovation Policies for Development (pp. 3-39). Ithaca, NY: Cornell University. Retrieved from https://www.globalinnovationindex.org/userfiles/file/reportpdf/GII-2015-v5.pdf

Eberlein, B., Abbott, K. W., Black, J., Meidinger, E., Wood, S. (2014). Transnational business governance interactions: Conceptualization and framework for analysis. *Regulation and Governance, 8*(1), 1-21.

ERA.Net RUS Plus (2015). Funded innovation projects. Retrieved from http://www.eranet-rus.eu/_media/ERANet_RUS_Plus_Funded_Innovation_projects.pdf

European Science Foundation (2009). EUROCORES Scheme European Collaborative Research. Final Activity Report. Retrieved from http://www.esf.org/index.php?eID=tx_nawsecuredl&u=0&g=0&t=1446044498&hash=dc9073a6c14ce8bc53e5f3258a62d570d48430de&file=fileadmin/be_user/activities/EUROCORES/EUROCORES_Scheme/EUROCORES_Scheme_documents/EUROCORES%20Final%20Report-%20%28modified%2020-nov-09%29.pdf

European Commission. (2015). Horizon 2020. The EU Framework Programme for Research and Innovation. Retrieved from http://ec.europa.eu/programmes/horizon2020

González-Pernía, J. L., Peña-Legazkue, I. (2015). Export-oriented entrepreneurship and regional economic growth. *Small Business Economics, 45*(3), 505-522.

Herstad, S. J., Aslesen, H. W., Ebersberger, B. (2014). On industrial knowledge bases, commercial opportunities and global innovation network linkages. *Research Policy, 43*(3), 495-504.

Ilie, C., Jaradat, M. (2015). Co-operation in the world economy. *Quality - Access to Success, 16*, 168-173.

Klinov, V. G. (2015). The evolution of long waves in the world economy. *Studies on Russian Economic Development, 26*(3), 285-294.

Kornev, A. K., Maksimtsova, S. I., Treshchina, S. V. (2015). Experience in world industrial development and the reindustrialization of the domestic economy. *Studies on Russian Economic Development, 26*(5), 460-469.

Lan, S. (2015). Transnational business and family strategies among Chinese/Nigerian couples in Guangzhou and Lagos. *Asian Anthropology, 14*(2), 133-149.

Larionova A. A., Suslova I. A., Povorina E.V., Vinogradova M. V. (2015). Formation of tourist image of the region. *Mediterranean Journal of Social Sciences, 6*(3), 261-266.

Lee, J. Y., Ryu, S., Kang, J. (2014). Transnational HR network learning in Korean business groups and the performance of their subsidiaries. *International Journal of Human Resource Management, 25*(4), 588-608.

Lee, S., Oh, D. W. (2015). Economic growth and the environment in China: Empirical evidence using prefecture level data. *China Economic Review, 36*, 870, 73-85.

Leonida, L., Maimone Ansaldo Patti, D., Marini, A., Navarra, P. (2015). Political competition and economic growth: A test of two tales. *Economics Letters, 135*, 96-99.

Liu, J., Chaminade, C., Asheim, B. (2013). The geography and structure of global innovation networks: A knowledge base perspective. *European Planning Studies, 21*(9), 1456-1473.

Odhiambo, N. M. (2015). Government expenditure and economic growth in South Africa: An empirical investigation. *Atlantic Economic Journal, 43*(3), 393-406.

Pogosov, I. A. (2015). Factors of long-term economic growth: Scientific and technical progress and capital intensity of production. *Studies on Russian Economic Development, 26*(5), 423-433.

Popkova, E. G., Yurev, V., Stepicheva, O., Denisov, N. (2015). Transformation and concentration of intellectual capital as a factor of economic growth in the modern economy. *Regional and Sectoral Economic Studies, 15*(1), 53-60.

Porter, T. (2014). Technical systems and the architecture of transnational business governance interactions. *Regulation and Governance, 8*(1), 110-125.

Pulselli, F. M., Coscieme, L., Neri, L., Regoli, A., Sutton, P. C., (...), Bastianoni, S. (2015). The world economy in a cube: A more rational structural representation of sustainability. *Global Environmental Change, 35*, 41-51.

Ribeiro, L. C., Kruss, G., Britto, G., Bernardes, A. T., da Motta e Albuquerque, E. (2014). A methodology for unveiling global innovation networks: patent citations as clues to cross border knowledge flows. *Scientometrics, 101*(1), 61-83.

Sarracino, F., Bartolini, S. (2015). The dark side of Chinese growth: Declining social capital and well-being in times of economic boom. *World Development, 74*, 333-351.

Schøtt, T., Cheraghi, M., Rezaei, S., & Vang, J. (2014). Innovation embedded in entrepreneurs' networks in private and public spheres: A global study focusing on China and Denmark. *International Journal of Entrepreneurship and Small Business, 23*(1-2), 145-167.

Silva, P. C., Klagge, B. (2013). The evolution of the wind industry and the rise of Chinese firms: From industrial policies to global innovation networks. *European Planning Studies, 21*(9), 1341-1356.

Thauer, C. R. (2015). In need of meta-governance: Business networks of transnational governance. *Israel Law Review, 48*(2), 189-218.

Van Egeraat, C., Kogler, D. F. (2013). Global and regional dynamics in knowledge flows and innovation networks. *European Planning Studies, 21*(9), 1317-1322.

Vinogradova, M. V., Kulyamina, O. S., Koroleva V. A., Larionova A. A. (2015). The Impact of Migration Processes on the National Security System of Russia. *Mediterranean Journal of Social Sciences, 6*(3), 161-168.

Wirtz, J., Tuzovic, S., & Ehret, M. (2015). Global business services: Increasing specialization and integration of the world economy as drivers of economic growth. *Journal of Service Management, 26*(4), 565-587.

Yakovleva, E. A., Azarova, N. A., Titova, E. V. (2015). Innovation as a vector of regional economic development and a necessary condition for the progress of the world economy. *Asian Social Science, 11*(20), 90-96.

Zeira, J., Zoabi, H. (2015). Economic growth and sector dynamics. *European Economic Review, 79*, 1-15.

8

The Mega Distributed Lag Model

Mario Arturo Ruiz Estrada[1], Evangelos Koutronas[2], Ross Knippenberg[3]

ABSTRACT This paper attempts to describe the graphical behavior of the distributed lag model in an infinite coordinate space. The "mega distributed lag model" (MDL) is a mathematical framework that can examine the simultaneous interrelationships between all involved variables. The multidimensional graphical setting simultaneously reveals all non-linear exposure—response dependencies and delayed effects between lagged and dependent variables—which two-dimensional figures overwhelmingly fail to capture. Under the Omnia Mobilis assumption, each distribution lag function is indexed with respect to time and space. The Mega distributed lag model observes multiple trends in full motion, the final output (determinant) of which is called "the JIM-coefficient". Hence, this paper tries to analyze different approaches of lag distribution models that can help in the construction of our new model. The mega distributed lag model" (MDL) is moving from the uses of the classic 2-dimensional and 3-dimensional graphical modeling to a multidimensional graphical modeling in Econometrics. Finally, this model is an extension of those explored earlier in the field of econographicology.

KEY WORDS: Econographicology, Distributed lag model, Multi-Dimensional graphs and Multi-Dimensional geometry

[1] University of Malaya - Economics, Malaysia; [2] University of Malaya - Social Security Research Centre (SSRC), Malaysia;
[3] American Veterinary Medical Association - Economics, United States

1. Introduction

Dynamic specification attempts to capture the hidden dynamics derived by the observed time-series data in a postulate theoretical model (Hendry, Pagan, & Sargan, 1984). The general approach in a trend stationary process has been to de-trend the series and to model the de-trended series as distributed lag or autoregressive distributed lag (ADL) models. A lag distribution function gives a magnitude of the coefficient of a lagged explanatory variable, expressed as a function of the lag, and extra information is injected into the estimation procedure. Estimation and inference concerning the long-run properties of the model are then carried out using standard asymptotic normal theory. A wide variety of specifications has been suggested for this purpose, including arithmetic, inverted V, Almon, Shiller, harmonic geometric, Pascal, rational, gamma, and exponential (Kennedy, 1998). A distributed-lag model is a dynamic model in which the effect of a regressor x on y occurs over time rather than all at once. Based on a Hendry-style (Hendry et al., 1984) autoregressive distributed lag equation (see Appendix A), considered the general form of one dependent variable and one explanatory variable, the model takes the form

$$y_t = \alpha + \beta(L)x_t + u_t = \alpha + \sum_{s=0}^{\infty} \beta_s x_{t-s} + u_t \quad (1)$$

Correspondence concerning this article should be addressed to: **Mario Arturo Ruiz Estrada**, University of Malaya - Economics, KL 53600, Malaysia. E-mail: marioruiz@um.edu.my

where x_t is exogenous for t= 1,...,T, and u_t is the stationary error term, i.i.d. $(0, \sigma^2)$. This form is very similar to the infinite-moving-average representation of an ARMA process, except that the lag polynomial on the right-hand side is applied to the explanatory variable x rather than to a white-noise process ε. The individual coefficients β_s are called lag weights and collectively comprise the lag distribution. They define the pattern of how x affects y over time.

The distributed lag concept was known among economists through the pioneering work of Irving Fisher (1930) on the relationship between the nominal interest rate and the expected inflation rate. However, its application in econometrics was launched by Koyck's (1954) geometric distributed lag model in a study of investment. The geometric distributed lag model was based on the notion of adaptive expectations hypothesis. It could estimate the autoregressive model with an auto-correlated error. One disadvantage of this lag structure is that coefficients of the lagged explanatory variables continually decline; they cannot first rise and then decline, a pattern thought by many to be a priori attractive and one that should not be ruled out of consideration. One way of addressing this problem is to allow unrestricted coefficients on the first few lagged variables and then impose a geometric pattern (Kennedy, 1998). The above mechanism was extensively applied in numerous empirical studies: Cagan's (1956) study of monetary aspects of hyperinflation; Friedman's (1957) study of consumption behavior; Nerlove's (1958a) study of supply and demand decisions (cobweb model); Solow's (1960) study of consumption behavior; and Jorgenson's (1966) study of investment.

At about the same time, Almon (1965) provided a polynomial generalization of Fisher's (1937) arithmetic lag distribution. In this technique, the n coefficients of the lagged explanatory variables are assumed to lie on a polynomial of order r. This allows for a flexible lag structure reduction in the number of the parameters that require estimation if r+1 is less than n. It can be viewed as imposing a specific set of linear constraints on OLS estimation. Several studies have investigated the effects of misspecifying the lag length or polynomial degree in the Almon lag model (Frost, 1975; Harper, 1977; Schmidt & Sickles, 1975; Schmidt & Waud, 1973; Terasvirta, 1976; Thomas, 1977; Trivedi, 1970; Trivedi & Pagan, 1979).

Almon polynomial lag distribution was later extended further by Shiller (1973). Shiller's distributed lag is a variant of this in which these restrictions are stochastic, incorporated via the mixed estimation technique; the coefficients of the lagged explanatory variable lie close to, rather than on, a polynomial. The main problem with the Almon lag is determining n and r; pretesting is usually employed for this purpose, resulting in estimators with unknown properties.

Mitchel and Speaker (1986) introduced a reduced form of the model via a linear transformation of the polynomial lag model, estimated the reduced-form parameters, and recovered estimates of the structural parameters via an inverse linear transformation of the reduced-form parameter estimates. The so-called polynomial inverse lag model has flexible shape and can be easily estimated linearly as long as the lag operator is invertible (the polynomial roots inside/outside the unit root circle) (Kasparis, 2008). Other forms of dynamic specification considered in the literature included the partial adjustment model (Eisner & Strotz, 1963; Nerlove, 1958b) and the multivariate flexible accelerator model (Treadway, 1971) and Sargan's (1964) work on econometric time series.

The most known parameterization of the (ADL) model is the error-correction model (EC). The use of an error correction mechanism for non-stationary variables is equivalent of performing co-integration (Dickey & Fuller, 1981). By differencing and forming a linear combination of the non-stationary data, all variables are transformed equivalently into an EC model with stationary series only (Hassler & Wolters, 2006). Phillips (1954; 1957) introduced EC models to economics. Sargan (1964) used them to estimate structural equations with auto correlated residuals, and Hendry popularized their use in econometrics in a series of papers. A survey on specification, estimation and testing of EC models is given by Alogoskoufis and Smith (1995).

Current literature, however, has identified three major shortcomings (Kim, Fraser, & Hyndman, 2010). First, point estimates of the long-run response are often extremely disparate (Askari & Cummings, 1977; Marquez & McNeilly, 1988). Second, the sampling variability of the long-run response estimator is difficult to estimate accurately (Li & Maddala, 1999). Third, the long-run response estimator can be severely biased, especially in small samples (Focareli, 2005; Pesaran & Zhao, 1999). Among the alternative distributed lag models is a particularly interesting paper published by Grace Wahba (1969), with a chapter entitled "The estimation of the coefficients in a multidimensional distributed lag model". In it, she proposes a multi-dimensional theoretical framework scheme for the general distributed lag model. It is based on the use of matrices and vectors to trace the multi-dimensional effects of the various lags, so the idea of a multi-dimensional focus for the distributed lag model is nothing new. However, the multi-dimensional distributed lag model proposed by Wahba lacks a multi-dimensional visualization to illustrate the behavior of which it speaks. Instead, Wahba's paper utilizes the same 2-dimensional graphical model as its predecessors, and, in doing so, fails to incorporate the dynamic behavior of multidimensional variables as a whole.

2. The Mega Distributed Lag Model

The mega distributed lag model function is formed by a combination of variables, each classified into four levels. Each classification level may contain infinitely–many variables. From largest to smallest, these classifications are: general-variables (GV), sub-variables (SV), micro-variables (MV) and JI-variables (JIV) (see expression 2.5). Each classification varies constantly at different rates. From a graphical perspective, the drawback of a typical distributed lag model is that a researcher can visualize it only in a two-dimensional coordinate space. While this gives a simple representation of the relationship between two variables, the visualization is too restricted to be of use. Namely, the two-dimensional representation ignores the simultaneous interrelationships between all variables, which could adversely affect the analysis. Visualization of the mega distributed lag model function requires the use of a multi-dimensional coordinate space. The most suitable multi-dimensional coordinate space is called the mega distributed lag model, which is alternately called "the infinity coordinates space (specific approach)" (See Figure 1). The application of the infinity coordinates space (specific approach) can help to visualize a large number of distributed lag functions simultaneously in a single image.

Using a large number of distributed lag functions in different spaces in the infinity coordinates space (specific approach) comes with some prerequisite conditions: first of all, we refer to a single point plotted on an infinite dimensional coordinates space (specific approach) as a "T-dot". Second, two T-dots cannot occupy the same space at the same time. Third, each T-dot refers into its general-space, sub-space and micro-space, respectively. Fourth, different T-dots can represent different intervals or units of time. These times are followed by partial times and constant times, with the type of time being related by the plot of the T-dot to its micro-space. For example, the moment in which the T-dot is initially plotted can be considered partial time, but after plotting the second T-dot, the first T-dot then reverts to constant time. The fifth and final condition is that each micro-space keeps its specific distributed lag function (see Figure 2) according to the general-space and sub-space (see Expression 2.5).

Each distributed lag function in the mega distributed lag model is indexed by time, starting from general-space "0", sub-space "0" and micro-space "0". From there it increases by one unit until we arrive to the general-space "∞", sub-space "∞" and micro-space "∞" (see Figure 2). All lag distributed functions in different micro-spaces under different general-space and sub-space levels apply the *Omnia Mobilis*, "Everything is moving", assumption (Ruiz Estrada, 2011a; 2011b). This assumption allows a large number of variables to be simultaneously observed in our multi-dimensional analysis, as opposed to the *ceteris paribus* assumption, which keeps variables constant. Recall that each general-space is formed by an infinite number of sub-spaces, and each sub-space is formed by an infinite number of micro-spaces, and finally each micro-space has an infinite number of T-dots (see Figures 1 and 2). Usually, the T-dots originate from the JI-variables. If we join each individual T-dot by a straight line into each one's respective micro-space, this creates a scatter graph that shows the trend of any distributed lag function. Additionally, recall that the mega distributed lag model consists of infinitely many micro-spaces, each of which shows different distrib-

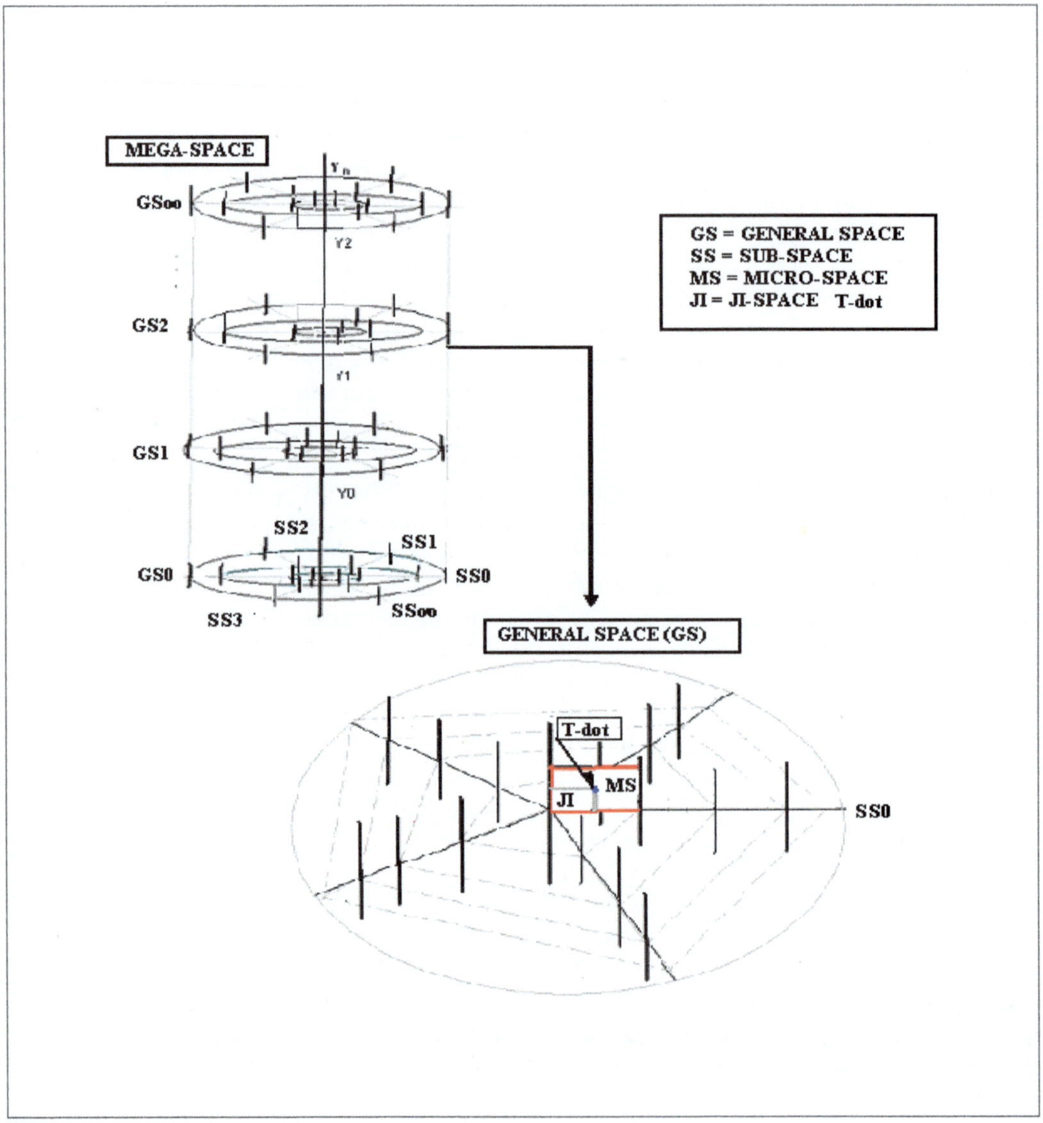

Figure 1. The Infinity Coordinate Space (Specific Approach)

uted lag functions to simultaneously observe multiple trends in full motion (see Figure 2).

The final output of the mega distributed lag model is based on the result of a single determinant (Δ) from a matrix with m rows and n columns (see Expression 2.6). This matrix accounts for the final results of all distributed lag functions from different micro-spaces under different general levels and sub-levels of analysis. The final output (determinant) is labelled "the JIM-coefficient". This JIM-coefficient is a measure encompassing all of the information from the analysis, and so can be

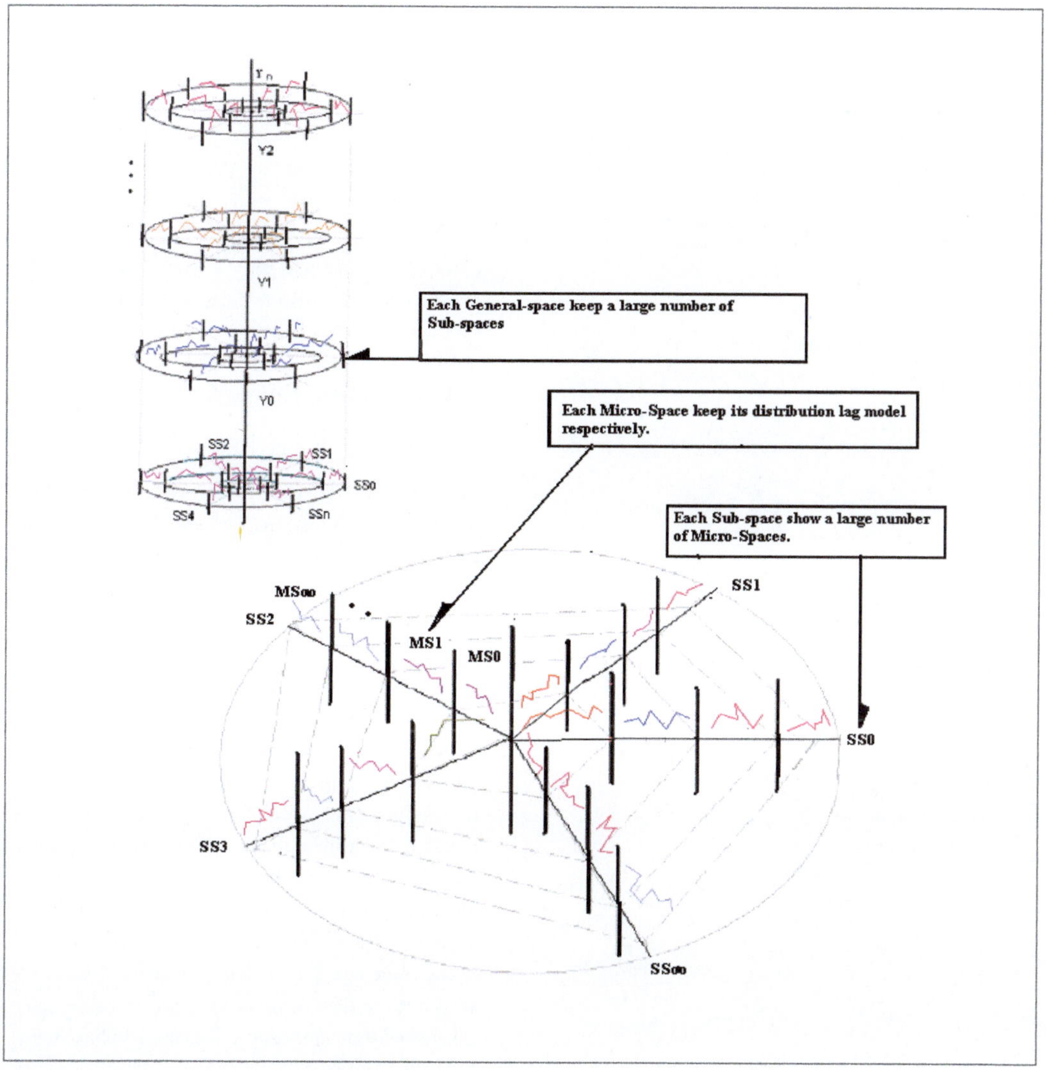

Figure 2. The Mega Distributed Lag Model

considered the final result from the mega distribution lag model.

<u>**General-Space "n"**</u>

$$Y^{n}_{tp(GV:SV:MV:JIV)} = \alpha_{(GV:SV:MV:JIV)} + \beta^{L0}_{(GV:SV:MV:JIV)} X^{tp/0}_{(GV:SV:MV:JIV)} + \beta^{L1}_{(GV:SV:MV:JIV)} X^{tp/1}_{(GV:SV:MV:JIV)-1} + \dots + \beta^{L\infty}_{(GV:SV:MV:JIV)} X^{tp/\infty}_{(GV:SV:MV:JIV)-n} + u^{tk}_{(GV:SV:MV:JIV)} \quad (2.1)$$

Where

$JIV = \{0, 1, 2 \dots \infty\}$

$n = \{0, 1, 2 \dots \infty\}$

Therefore,

$$E/U^{tk}/ = K_o \quad (2.2)$$

$$Var(U^{tk}) = \sigma^{i}_{(GV:SV:MV:JIV)} \quad (2.3)$$

$$Cov(U^{tk}, U^{tk}_{s}) = \sigma^{i}_{(GV:SV:MV:JIV)} \quad (2.4)$$

General model

General-Space 0

Sub-Space 0:

$$SV_0=Y^{0}{}_{tp(0:0:0)}=\alpha_{(0:0:0)+}\beta^{L0}{}_{(0:0:0:0)}X^{tp/0}{}_{(0:0:0:0)}+\beta^{L1}{}_{(0:0:0:1)}X^{tp/1}{}_{(0:0:0:1)-1}+$$
$$+\ldots+\beta^{L\infty}{}_{(0:0:0:\infty)}X^{tp/\infty}{}_{(0:0:0:0:\infty)-n}+u^{tk}{}_{(0:0:0)}\circledR\ldots\circledR$$

$$Y^{0}{}_{tp(0:0:1)}=\alpha_{(0:0:1)+}\beta^{L0}{}_{(0:0:1:0)}X^{tp/0}{}_{(0:0:1:0)}+\beta^{L1}{}_{(0:0:1:1)}X^{tp/1}{}_{(0:0:1:1)-1}+$$
$$+\ldots+\beta^{L\infty}{}_{(0:0:1:\infty)}X_{tp/\infty(0:0:1:\infty)-n}+u^{tk}{}_{(0:0:1)}\circledR\ldots\circledR$$

$$Y^{\infty}{}_{tp(0:0:\infty)}=\alpha_{(0:0:\infty)+}\beta^{L0}{}_{(0:0:\infty:0)}X^{tp/0}{}_{(0:0:\infty:0)}+\beta^{L1}{}_{(0:0:\infty:1)}X^{tp/1}{}_{(0:0:\infty:1)-1}+$$
$$+\ldots+\beta^{L\infty}{}_{(0:0:\infty:\infty)}X^{tp/\infty}{}_{(0:0:\infty:\infty)-n+}\,u^{tk}{}_{(0:0:\infty)}\ldots$$

.

.

Sub-Space ∞:

$$SV_\infty=Y^{*}{}_{tp(0:\infty:0)}=\alpha_{(0:\infty:0)+}\beta^{L0}{}_{(0:\infty:0:0)}X^{tp/0}{}_{(0:\infty:0:0)}+\beta^{L1}{}_{(0:\infty:0:1)}X^{tp/1}{}_{(0:\infty:0:1)-1}+$$
$$+.+\beta^{L\infty}{}_{(0:\infty:0:\infty)}X^{tp/\infty}{}_{(0:\infty:0:\infty)-n}+u^{tk}{}_{(0:\infty:0)}\circledR\ldots\circledR$$

$$Y^{0}{}_{tp(0:\infty:1)}=\alpha_{(0:\infty:1)+}\beta^{L0}{}_{(0:\infty:1:0)}X^{tp/0}{}_{(0:\infty:1:0)}+\beta^{L1}{}_{(0:\infty:1:1)}X^{tp/1}{}_{(0:\infty:1:1)-1}+$$
$$+\ldots+\beta^{L\infty}{}_{(0:\infty:1:\infty)}X^{tp/\infty}{}_{(0:\infty:1:\infty)-n}+u^{tk}{}_{(0:\infty:1)}\circledR\ldots\circledR$$

$$Y^{\infty}{}_{tp(0:\infty:\infty)}=\alpha_{(0:\infty:\infty)+}\beta^{L0}{}_{(0:\infty:\infty:0)}X^{tp/0}{}_{(0:\infty:\infty:0)}+\beta^{L1}{}_{(0:\infty:\infty:1)}X^{tp/1}{}_{(0:\infty:\infty:1)-1}+$$
$$+\ldots+\beta^{L\infty}{}_{(0:\infty:\infty:\infty)}X^{tp/\infty}{}_{(0:\infty:\infty:\infty)-n}+u^{tk}{}_{(0:\infty:\infty)}$$

.

.

General-Space ∞

Sub-Space 0:

$$SV_0=Y^{*}{}_{tp(\infty:0:0)}=\alpha_{(\infty:0:0)+}\beta^{L0}{}_{(\infty:0:0:0)}X^{tp/0}{}_{(\infty:0:0:0)}+\beta^{L1}{}_{(\infty:0:0:1)}X^{tp/1}{}_{(\infty:0:0:1)-1}+$$
$$+.+\beta^{L\infty}{}_{(\infty:0:0:\infty)}X^{tp/\infty}{}_{(\infty:0:0:0:\infty)-n}+u^{tk}{}_{(\infty:0:0)}\circledR\ldots\circledR$$

$$Y^{0}{}_{tp(\infty:1:1)}=\alpha_{(\infty:1:1)+}\beta^{L0}{}_{(\infty:1:1:0)}X^{tp/0}{}_{(\infty:1:1:0)}+\beta^{L1}{}_{(\infty:1:1:1)}X^{tp/1}{}_{(\infty:1:1:1)-1}+$$
$$+\ldots+\beta^{L\infty}{}_{(\infty:1:1:\infty)}X^{tp/\infty}{}_{(\infty:1:1:\infty)-n}+u^{tk}{}_{(\infty:1:1)}\circledR\ldots\circledR$$

$$Y^{\infty}{}_{tp(\infty:\infty:\infty)}=\alpha_{(\infty:\infty:\infty)+}\beta^{L0}{}_{(\infty:\infty:\infty:0)}X^{tp/0}{}_{(\infty:\infty:\infty:0)}+\beta^{L1}{}_{(\infty:\infty:\infty:1)}X^{tp/1}{}_{(\infty:\infty:\infty:1)-1}+$$
$$+.+\beta^{L\infty}{}_{(\infty:\infty:\infty:\infty)}X^{tp/\infty}{}_{(\infty:\infty:\infty:\infty)-n+}\,u^{tk}{}_{(\infty:\infty:\infty)}\ldots$$

.

.

Sub-Space ∞:

$$SV_\infty=Y^{*}{}_{tp(\infty:\infty:0)}=\alpha_{(\infty:\infty:0)+}\beta^{L0}{}_{(\infty:\infty:0:0)}X^{tp/0}{}_{(\infty:\infty:0:0)}+\beta^{L1}{}_{(\infty:\infty:0:1)}X^{tp/1}{}_{(\infty:\infty:0:1)-1}+$$
$$+.+\beta^{L\infty}{}_{(\infty:\infty:0:\infty)}X^{tp/\infty}{}_{(\infty:\infty:0:\infty)-n}+u^{tk}{}_{(\infty:\infty:0)}\circledR\ldots\circledR$$

$$Y^{0}{}_{tp(\infty:\infty:1)}=\alpha_{(\infty:\infty:1)+}\beta^{L0}{}_{(\infty:\infty:1:0)}X^{tp/0}{}_{(\infty:\infty:1:0)}+\beta^{L1}{}_{(\infty:\infty:1:1)}X^{tp/1}{}_{(\infty:\infty:1:1)-1}+$$
$$+.+\beta^{L\infty}{}_{(\infty:\infty:1:\infty)}X^{tp/\infty}{}_{(\infty:\infty:1:\infty)-n}+u^{tk}{}_{(\infty:\infty:1)}\circledR\ldots.\circledR$$

$$Y^{\infty}{}_{tp(\infty:\infty:\infty)}=\alpha_{(\infty:\infty:\infty)+}\beta^{L0}{}_{(\infty:\infty:\infty:0)}X^{tp/0}{}_{(\infty:\infty:\infty:0)}+\beta^{L1}{}_{(\infty:\infty:\infty:1)}X^{tp/1}{}_{(\infty:\infty:\infty:1)-1}+$$
$$+.+\beta^{L\infty}{}_{(\infty:\infty:\infty:\infty)}X^{tp/\infty}{}_{(\infty:\infty:\infty:\infty)-n}+u^{tk}{}_{(\infty:\infty:\infty)} \qquad (2.5.)$$

$$\Delta=\begin{pmatrix} GV_0=SV_0\circledR SV_1\circledR\ldots\circledR SV_{\infty\ldots} \\ . \qquad\qquad\qquad . \\ . \qquad\qquad\qquad . \\ . \qquad\qquad\qquad . \\ GV\infty=SV_0\circledR SV_1\circledR\ldots\circledR SV_{\infty\ldots} \end{pmatrix} \qquad (2.6.)$$

Variables:

GV = General variable, SV = Sub-variable, MS = Micro-variable, JIV= JI-variable, tp = Partial Time, tk = Constant Time, ® = Window refraction

3. Concluding Remarks

In conclusion, previous attempts at graphing multi-dimensional behavior in the distributed lag model have stopped at two dimensions. Because of this, we advocate the use of an alternative general distributed lag model, which we call "the mega distributed lag model". This paper has developed the framework for extending those representations of distributed lag models to an arbitrarily large number of dimensions. The advantage of doing so is to aid in the identification of abnormally strong relationships between the lagged variables and the dependent variable, which two-dimensional figures overwhelmingly fail to capture. Multi-Dimensional Coordinate Space framework treats each dimension uniformly at the cost of coarse representation (Ruiz Estrada, 2011b), enabling us to delve deeper into understanding the behavior of an infinite distributed lag model. Hence, the 2-dimensional Cartesian coordinate plane and the 3-dimensional coordinate space are limited in their ability to visualize a large number of variables simultaneously in the same graphical space and time framework.

References

Almon, S. (1965). The distributed lag between capital appropriations and net expenditures *Econometrica, 33*(1), 178-196.

Alogoskoufis, G., & Smith, R. (1995). On error correction models: Specificaton, interpretation, estimation. In L. Oxley, D. A. R. George, C. J. Roberts & S. Sayer (Eds.), *Surveys in Econometrics* (pp.139-170). Oxford, UK: Blackwell Publishers.

Askari, H., & Cummings, T. (1977). Estimating agricultural supply response with Nerlove Model: A Survey *International Economic Review, 18*(2), 257-292.

Cagan, P. (1956). The monetary dynamics of hyperinflation. In M. Friedman (Ed.), *Studies in the quantity theory of money* (pp. 25-117). Chicago, IL: University of Chicago Press.

Dickey, D. A., & Fuller, A. W. (1981). Likelihood ratio statistics for autoregressive time series with a unit root. *Econometrica, 49*(4), 1057-1072.

Eisner, R., & Strotz, R. H. (1963). Determinants of business investment. In Commission on Money and Credit. American Bankers Association (Eds.), *Impacts of Monetary Policy* (pp. 59-337). Englewood Cliffs, NJ: Prentice-Hall.

Fisher, I. (1930). *The theory of interest*. New York, NY: Kelley and Millman.

Fisher, I. (1937). Note on a short-cut method for calculatin distributed lags. *Bulletin de l'Institut International de Statistique, 29*, 323-327.

Focareli, D. (2005). Bootstrap bias-correction procedure in estimating long-run relationships from dynamic panels, with an application to money demand in the euro area. *Economic Modelling, 22*(2), 305-325.

Friedman, B. M. (1957). *A Theory of the consumption function*. Princeton, NJ: Princeton University Press.

Frost, P. A. (1975). Some properties of the Almon lag technique when one searches for degree of polynomial and lag. *Journal of the American Statistical Association, 70*(351a), 606-612.

Harper, C. P. (1977). Testing for the existence of a lagged relationship within Almon's method. *Review of Economics and Statistics, 59*(2), 204-210.

Hassler, U., & Wolters, J. (2006). *Autoregressive distributed lag models and cointegration. Allgemeines Statistisches Archiv, 90*, 59-74.

Hendry, D. F., Pagan, A. R., & Sargan, J. D. (1984). Dynamic Specification. In Z. Griliches & M. Intriligator (Eds.), *Handbook of Econometrics* (Vol. II, pp. 1025-1100): Amsterdam: North Holland.

Jorgenson, D. W. (1966). Rational distributed lag functions. *Econometrica, 34*(1), 135-149.

Kasparis, I. (2008). *A Simple Proof for the Invertibility of the Lag Polynomial Operator*. (Discussion Paper No. 2008-06). University of Cyprus. Department of Economics.

Kennedy, P. (1998). *A Guide to Econometrics* (3rd ed.). Cambridge, Massachusetts, MA: The MIT Press.

Kim, J., H., Fraser, I., & Hyndman, R. J. (2010). *Improved Interval Estimation of Long Run Response from a Dynamic Linear Model: A Highest Density Region Approach* (Working Papers 2010.06). School of Economics. La Trobe University.

Koyck, L. M. (1954). *Distributes lags and investment analysis*. Amsterdam: North Holland.

Li, H., & Maddala, G. S. (1999). Bootsrap variance estimation of non-linear functions of parameters: An application to long-run elasticities of energy demand. *The Review of Economics and Statistics, 81*(4), 728-733.

Marquez, J., & McNeilly, C. (1988). Income and price elasticities for exports of developing countries. *The Review of Economics and Statistics, 70*(2), 306-314.

Mitchell, D. W., & Speaker, P. J. (1986). A Simple, flexible distributed lag technique: The polynomial inverse lag. *Journal of Econometrics, 31*(3), 329-340.

Nerlove, M. (1958a). Adaptive expectations and the cobweb phenomena. *Quarterly Journal of Economics, 72*(2), 227-240.

Nerlove, M. (1958b). *Distributed Lags and Demand Analysis* (Agriculture Handbook No. 141). Agriculture. Washington, D.C.: U.S. Department of Agriculture.

Pesaran, M. H., & Zhao, Z. (1999). Bias reduction in estimating long-run relationships from dynamic heterogeneous panels. In C. Hsiao, K. Lahiri, L. F. Lee & M. H. Pesaran (Eds.), *Analysis of panels and limited dependent variables: A volume in honour of G. S. Maddala* (pp. 297-321). Cambridge, UK: Cambridge University Press.

Phillips, A. W. (1954). Stabilization policy in a closed economy. *Economic Journal, 64*(254), 290-323.

Phillips, A. W. (1957). Stabilization policy and the time form of lagged responses. *Economic Journal, 67*(266), 265-277.

Ruiz Estrada, M. A. (2011a). Policy modeling: Definition, classification and evaluation. *Journal of Policy Modeling, 33*(4), 523-536.

Ruiz Estrada, M. A. (2011b). Multi-Dimensional coordinate spaces. *International Journal of the Physical Sciences, 6*(3), 340-357.

Sargan, J. D. (1964). Wages and prices in the United Kingdom: A study in econometric methodology. In P. E. Hart, G. Mills & J. K. Whitaker (Eds.), *Econometric Analysis for National Economic Planning* (pp. 25-54). London, UK: Butterworths.

Schmidt, P., & Sickles, R. (1975). On the Efficiency of the Almon Lag Technique. *International Economic Review, 16*, 792-795.

Schmidt, P., & Waud, R. N. (1973). The Almon Lag Technique and the Monetary versus Fiscal Policy Debate. *Journal of American Statistical Association, 68*(341), 11-19.

Shiller, R. J. (1973). A distributed lag estimator derived from smoothness priors. *Econometrica, 41*(4), 775-788.

Solow, R. (1960). On a family of lag distributions. *Econometrica, 28*(2), 393-406.

Terasvirta, T. (1976). A note on bias in the Almon distributed lag estimator. *Econometrica, 44*(6), 1317-1322.

Thomas, J. J. (1977). Some problems in the use of Almon's technique in the estimation of distributed lags. *Empirical Economics, 2*(3), 175-193.

Treadway, A. B. (1971). The rational multivariate flexible accelarator. *Econometrica, 39*(5), 845-855.

Trivedi, P. K. (1970). A note on the application of Almon's method of calculating distributed lag coefficients. *Metroeconomica, 22*(3), 281-286.

Trivedi, P. K., & Pagan, A. R. (1979). Polynomial distributed lags: A unified treatment. *Economic Studies Quarterly, 30*, 37-49.

Wahba, G. (1969). Estimation of the Coefficients in a Multidimensional Distributed Lag Model. *Econometrica, 37*(3), 398-407.

Appendix A

Consider the autoregressive distributed lag model of order p and q, ADL (p, q), defined for a scalar variable y_t as

$$y_t = \alpha + \sum_{i=1}^{p} \gamma_i y_{t-i} + \sum_{i=0}^{q} \beta_i x_{t-i} + \eta_t \quad (A1)$$

where η_t is a scalar independent white noise and x_t is a K-dimensional column stationary variable vector process. The sequence $\{\eta_t\}$ is a white-noise process if for each period t,

$$E(\eta_t) = E(\eta_{t-1}) = \ldots = 0$$

$$E(\eta_t^2) = E(\eta_{t-1}^2) = \ldots = \sigma^2$$

$$E(\eta_t \eta_{t-s}) = E(\eta_{t-j}\eta_{t-j-s}) = 0 \text{ for all } \eta$$

As long as the error term η_t is a white noise process, the ADL model can be estimated consistently by ordinary least squares. Using the lag operator L applied to each component of a vector, $L^k x_t = x_{t-k}$ (lag of a constant: $L\alpha = \alpha$), it is convenient to define the lag polynomial $\gamma(L)$ and the vector polynomial $\beta(L)$

$$a(L) = \alpha$$

$$\gamma(L) = (1 + \gamma_1 L + \gamma_2 L^2 + \ldots + \gamma L^p)$$

$$\beta(L) = (\beta_0 + \beta_1 L + \beta_2 L^2 + \ldots + \beta_q L^q)$$

Rearranging the lag polynomial $\gamma(L)y_t$, equation (A1) takes the straightforward form

$$\gamma(L) y_t = a + \beta(L) x_t + \eta_t \quad (A2)$$

Equation (A2) implies that the current value of y depends on all previous values of a, x, and η. The dynamic effects correspond to the lag weights of the infinite moving average representation

$$\frac{\partial y_{t+i}}{\partial x_t} = \frac{\partial y_t}{\partial x_{t-i}} = \beta_i \quad (A3)$$

Note that the first equation in (A3) requires that the time-series relationship between y and x be stationary, so we can think of β_i either as the effect of current x_t on future y_{t+i} or as the effect of past x_{t-i} on current y_t. In order to obtain stability, it is maintained that

$$\gamma(\varphi) = 0 \Rightarrow |\varphi| > 1 \, \forall \varphi \in N \quad (A4)$$

Under this condition there exists an absolutely summable infinite expansion of the inverted polynomial $\gamma^{-1}(L)$:

$$\gamma^{-1}(L) = \frac{1}{\gamma(L)} = \sum_{j=0}^{\infty} \gamma_j^* L^j, \qquad \sum_{j=0}^{\infty} |\gamma_j^*| < \infty \quad (A5)$$

Invertibility of $\gamma(L)$ hence yields the following representation:

$$y_t = \frac{\beta(L)}{\gamma(L)} x_t + \psi_t, \qquad \gamma(L)\psi_t = \eta_t \quad (A6)$$

where η_t has a stable autoregressive structure of order p. Expanding $\gamma^{-1}(L)$ provides an infinite distributed lag representation,

$$y_t = \left(\sum_{j=0}^{\infty} \gamma_j^* L^j\right)\left(\sum_{j=0}^{q} \beta_j' L^j\right)' x_t + \psi_t = \sum_{j=0}^{\infty} \omega_j' x_{t-j} + \psi_t \quad (A7)$$

where ω_j are the vectors of dynamic multipliers derived by the method of indetermined coefficients. The vector of long-run multipliers of the ADL (p, n) model may therefore be easily computed from:

$$\xi = \frac{\beta(1)}{\gamma(1)} = \sum_{j=0}^{\infty} \omega_j \quad (A8)$$

By re-arranging the x's one obtains with $\Delta = 1 - L$:

$$y_t = \sum_{i=1}^{p} \gamma_i y_{t-i} + \gamma(1)\xi' x_t - \sum_{i=0}^{q-1}\left(\sum_{j=i+1}^{q} \beta_j\right)' \Delta x_{t-i} + \psi_t \quad (A9)$$

where y_t is related to its own past, to contemporaneous x_t and differences Δx_{t-i}. This is called the error correction model (ECM).

9

Scenarios of Business Development in the Agricultural Machinery Market Under Conditions of International Trade Integration

Tatiana N. Litvinova[1], Galina A. Khmeleva[2,3], Lilia V. Ermolina[4], Tatiana V. Alferova[5], Irina V. Cheryomushkina[6]

ABSTRACT The purpose of the article is to identify and analyze scenarios of business development in the agricultural machinery market under conditions of international trade integration using the case of present-day Russia and to determine the need for state support for domestic production. As a methodological provision, we use the scenario analysis method adapted by the authors for the determination and analysis of possible scenarios of business development in the agricultural machinery market under conditions of international trade integration. From the research results, the authors conclude that the Russian agricultural machinery market develops dynamically under the influence of multiple favorable factors and positive tendencies, which include a population's income growth, increases in crop areas of farm crops, and state agricultural machinery modernization programs, among other. In view of recent events in the currency market, Russian manufacturers of agricultural machinery are presented with better opportunities to export their products. The performed analysis of features of the Russian agricultural machinery market under conditions of international trade integration shows that increased demand and market prices are probable and that this could lead to enterprise income growth. From our scenario analysis of business development in the agricultural machinery market under conditions of international trade integration, we identify the absence of an urgent need for state interference in market processes in the Russian market for agricultural machinery in the next five years.

KEY WORDS: business development, agricultural machinery market, international trade integration, scenario analysis

[1]Volgograd State Agricultural University, Russia, [2]Samara State University of Economics, Russia,
[3]Samara National Research University, Russia, [4]Samara State Technical University, Russia,
[5]Perm State National Research University, Russia, [6]Federal State Budget Educational Institution of Higher Education "Voronezh State University of Engineering Technologies", Russia

Introduction

Through international trade integration, markets grow and entrepreneurs travel beyond national limits. Under such conditions, the level and nature of competition in national markets changes, resulting in intensive fluctuations in market prices and changing demand volumes and preferences.

The agricultural machinery market is no exception – as integration processes in the global economy change, foreign suppliers appear in agricultural machinery markets, increasing competition and promoting the division of influence spheres and market structure changes.

Correspondence concerning this article should be addressed to: Tatiana N. Litvinova, Volgograd State Agricultural University, Department of Management, Senior Lecturer, 11 Consular St., Volgograd, Russia, 400081 E-mail: litvinova1358@yandex.ru

As a result, consumers can choose from a large variety of products and manufacturers of agricultural machinery can start to compete with one another for sales even more, leading to a reduction in general market prices and in buyer power growth.

Countries focused not only on meeting national demand but also on the preservation of national production face serious problems related to the reduction of competitiveness between domestic manufacturers, which cannot compete with global companies that have accumulated substantial financial and human resources and that employ superior technologies and equipment.

An inevitable result of a country's integration into the global economy pertains to the dilemma between consumer and manufacturer interests. Countries that prioritize consumers' interests risk becoming less productive and face problems related to economic security.

Countries that prioritize manufacturers' interests must interfere with market processes and expend public welfare in supporting domestic manufacturers. There is a risk of creating conditions that are too favorable for domestic manufacturers under which there are no incentives for development, spurring manufacturers' incapacities to adapt to new economic conditions and to compete in global markets.

This is why in developing state policies that support domestic manufacturers, it is necessary to develop a clear understanding of perspectives on business development in the agricultural machinery market under conditions of international trade integration without violating market mechanisms through state regulation.

This allows one to first identify the need for such interference and to second identify the most central avenues of regulation needed to achieve maximum effects with minimal expenditures. Consequently, the examination of perspectives of business development in the agricultural machinery market under conditions of international trade integration is feasible.

The purpose of the article is to identify and analyze scenarios of business development in the agricultural machinery market under conditions of international trade integration using the example of present-day Russia and to outline the need for state support for domestic production.

Literature review

Economic mechanisms, preconditions, and methodological aspects of business development in the agricultural machinery market under modern economic conditions have been studied in multiple works, including (Bortolini, Cascini, Gamberi, Mora, & Regattieri, 2014a; Huang, Yun, You, & Wu, 2011; Liu Hu, Jetté-Nantel, & Tian, 2014; Staus & Becker, 2012; Yakymenko, 2013; Yu, Leng, & Zhang, 2012; Zhovnovach, 2014). In the agricultural machinery market, machinery and agricultural equipment is bought and sold (Muzlera, 2014). The following main segments of the agricultural machinery market can be identified: agricultural goods, combine harvesters, cultivators, walking tractors, plows, drill machines, and mowing machines, among others. (Bortolini, Mora, Cascini, & Gamberi, 2014b). The agricultural machinery market is central for national food security, as it creates infrastructure needed for agriculture development (Morozova, Litvinova, Rodina, & Prosvirkin, 2015).

Integration processes in the current global economy based on various forecasts and possible future change scenarios have been presented in the following works: (Anderson & Valenzuela, 2011; Dasgupta, Pitigala, & Gourdon, 2012; Golub & Hertel, 2008; Palamarchyk, 2013; (Qobo, 2012, Sung, Delgado, Peña, & Paladino, 2013). Integration involves closing of national economic systems (Bryant & Javalgi, 2014) while preserving their capabilities for self-regulation and self-development (Kobrin, 2015). Within integration processes of the global economy, international standards and norms of economic activities appear in addition to international organizations that control their observation (Wirtz, Tuzovic, & Ehret).

Peculiarities of business activities under conditions of international trade integration and global competition for enterprises operating in various countries and economic spheres have been examined in (Antonakakis & Tondl, 2014; Ganushchak-Yefimenko, 2013a; Ganushchak-Yefimenko, 2013b; Gong & Kim, 2013). Under conditions of international trading integration, entrepreneurs are presented with opportunities to enter new foreign markets (Bull, 2014). At the same time, foreign rivals appear in national markets (Wirtz et al., 2015). On the whole, strengthening competition is an integral component of integration processes in the global economic system (GonÇalves & Madi, 2013).

Table 1. Tree of scenarios

Situation	Scenario (S)	Probability of scenario (P)
	$S_{1\ price}$	$P_{1\ price}$
Market price fluctuations	$S_{2\ price}$	$P_{2\ price}$
	...	...
	$S_{n\ price}$	$P_{n\ price}$
	$S_{1\ demand}$	$P_{1\ demand}$
Changes in demand volumes and product sales	$S_{2\ demand}$	$P_{2\ demand}$
	...	...
	$S_{n\ demand}$	$P_{n\ demand}$

Table 2. Final scenario analysis table

Scenarios of market development	Changes in prices and demand	Probability	Price, RUB (P)	Volume of sales, items (V)	Financial results, RUB million (FR)
Most probable scenario	S_{price}	P_{price}(max)	P_1	V_1	P_1* P_{price}(max)* V^1* P_{demand}(max)
	S_{demand}	P_{demand}(max)			
...	...	...	...	...	...
Least likely scenario	S_{price}	P_{price}(min)	P_5	V_5	P_5* P_{price}(min)* V_5* P_{demand}(min)
	S_{demand}	P_{demand}(min)			

Problems related to agricultural machinery market functioning under conditions of international trade integration and national agricultural machinery market state regulation for support purposes are outlined in the following works: (Clapp & Helleiner, 2012; Khafizova, Galimardanova, & Salmina, 2014; Mulatu & Wossink, 2014; Vošta, 2014; Yushkevych, 2013). Under conditions of international trade integration, national markets of agricultural machinery face intensifying competitive struggles (Solovchuk, (2015) that foreign enterprises often win, compromising national food security (Gnedenko & Kazmin, 2015). To protect national manufacturers, states regulate the development of agricultural machinery markets by providing tax subsidies and more favorable conditions for the economic activities of national manufacturers (Morozova & Litvinova, 2014).

Our analysis of existing scientific works in this research area shows that these works examine specific aspects of the specified problem, leaving the necessity to conduct complex research on business development scenarios in agricultural machinery markets under conditions of international trade integration to address existing gaps and to formulate a comprehensive and objective understanding of future business activities in agricultural machinery markets.

Method

As a methodological provision, the scenario analysis approach adapted by the authors is applied to iden-

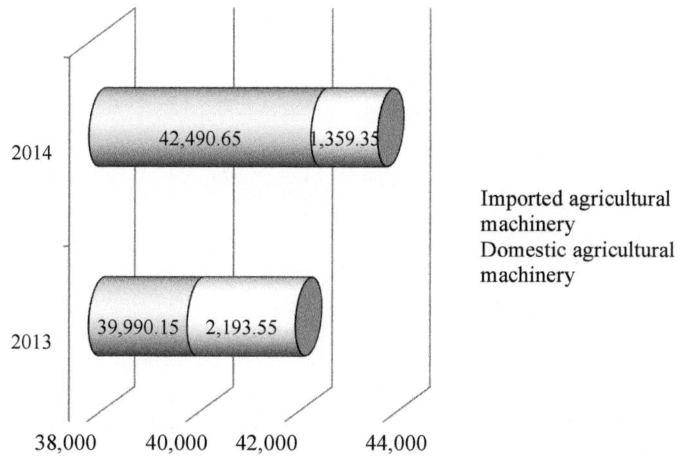

Figure 1. Dynamics and structure of the Russian agricultural machinery market in 2013-2014
Source: Adapted from "Manufacture of agricultural machinery in Russia in January-March 2015" by Agroinfo. Retrieved from http://agroinfo.com/proizvodstvo-selxoztexniki-v-rossii-v-yanvare-marte-2015-goda-1507201504

tify and analyze possible development scenarios of business in the agricultural machinery market under conditions of international trade integration. This approach is designed to identify factors that influence the agricultural machinery market.

On the basis of the determined factors, possible market price and sales volume changes and potential scenarios for such conditions are determined. Each scenario is assigned a possible probability value through expert evaluation through an analysis of market tendencies and factors of market development. As a result, a tree of scenarios was created (Table 1).

From probability scenarios of prices and demand changes, scenarios for the market as a whole and for businesses in this market were formed. The most likely scenario involves price and demand development with maximum probability. Then, scenarios of market development involving price reductions and demand change probability were formulated.

For each business development scenario, average market prices and total volumes of sales in the market were determined. From these data, balanced financial results (profits) were calculated as a product of the price and probability of changes under this scenario and of the volume of sales and probability of such a change under this scenario (Table 2).

The results of the scenario analysis identify future tendencies of business development in the market on the basis of an analysis of factors that influence this market. This methodology allows for the economic modeling and forecasting of market changes through mathematical instruments, ensuring the generation of precise and reliable results.

Results

Before presenting the results of the scenario analysis, let us outline the most important factors of business development in the agricultural machinery market under conditions of international trade integration. The most important of these is foreign competition.

According to data drawn from analytical and consulting company ACM-Holding, in 2014, the agricultural machinery market of Russia reduced by 3.8% relative to 2013. The total volume of agricultural machinery sales for January-December of 2014 amounted to 43,850, with only 1,316 involving Russian machines (market share – 3.1%).

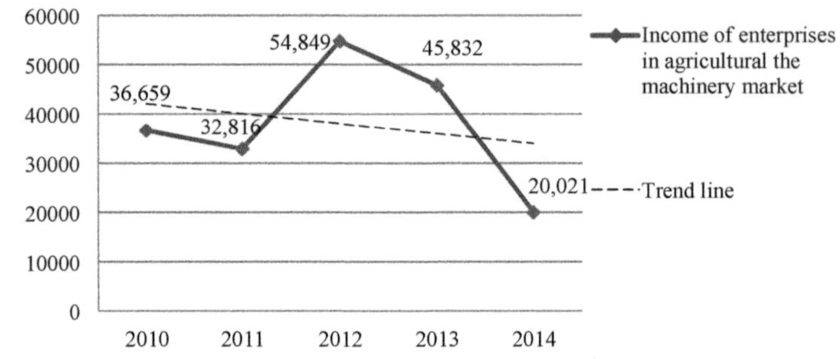

Figure 2. Enterprise profits in the agricultural machinery market from 2010-2014 in RUB million
Adapted from "Russia in numbers. Scientific research and innovations 2015: Bulletin of Rosstat" by Rosstat (2015). Retrieved from http://www.gks.ru/free_doc/doc_2015/rusfig/rus-15.pdf

In 2014, the agricultural machinery market underwent an increase in the market share of imports of new foreign-branded agricultural machinery, which grew from 26.1% to 39.0%, and import shares of used agricultural machinery grew from 7.1% to 8.2% in natural form; imports of used agricultural machinery grew by 10.7%, to 3,590 items.

Overall, sales of imported agricultural machinery (used and new) grew by 36.6%, increasing from 15,200 to 20,700 items (Agroinfo, 2015). The dynamics and structure of the Russian agricultural machinery market from 2013-2014 are shown graphically in Fig. 1.

Fig. 1 shows that the share of imported products in the Russian agricultural machinery market increased in 2014, posing potential losses in domestic production.

Another important feature of the development of the Russian market for agricultural machinery pertains to the growth in population income. As agricultural products and agricultural machinery are complementary goods, increased consumer demand for agricultural products increases demand for agricultural machinery from agricultural manufacturers.

Due to tendencies toward eco-product popularization, agricultural enterprises re-orient their activities toward such forms of production. To do so, new equipment from agricultural machinery manufacturers must be purchased.

Another factor that has affected the development of the Russian agricultural machinery market is Russia's Doctrine of Food Security to 2020, which calls for an increase in farm crop areas. This has also increased demand for agricultural machinery (Larionova, Suslova, Povorina, & Vinogradova, 2015).

These factors also include Russian state programs for the modernization of agricultural machinery on the basis of national strategies of economic modernization. This has increased demand for agricultural machinery. From such increased demand under market forces, agricultural machinery prices will increase.

Recent trends in financial markets have led to the depreciation of the Russian ruble and have made the export of Russian agricultural machinery more profitable. In turn, Russian agricultural machines present price advantages, and despite their lower quality and weaker branding relative to foreign rivals, they are of interest to foreign customers, allowing Russian agricultural machinery manufacturers to compete successfully in foreign markets (Vinogradova, Kulyamina, Koroleva, & Larionova, 2015).

A focus on exports will likely ensure the preservation of Russian agricultural machinery production even with a loss of positioning in the domestic market. However, when planning state strategies for the support of national production, it is not expedient to rely on the moods of players in financial markets alone,

Table 3. Tree of changes in prices and demand in the Russian agricultural machinery market under conditions of international trade integration

Situation	Scenario		Probability of scenario
Fluctuations in market prices	Increase in prices	by 5%	0.3
		by 10%	0.5
	Prices are unchanged		0.1
	Reduction of prices	by 3%	0.06
		by 5%	0.04
Changes in the volume of demand and in product sales	Increase in demand	by 5%	0.4
		by 10%	0.3
	Demand is unchanged		0.2
	Reduction of demand	by 3%	0.07
		by 5%	0.03

Table 4. Final table for the scenario analysis of business development in the agricultural machinery market under conditions of international trade integration

Scenario	Changes in prices and demand		Probability	Price, RUB	Volume of sales, items	Financial results, RUB million
Most likely scenario	Increase of prices	by 10%	0.5	502,237.17	46,042	4,624.85
	Increase in prices	by 5%	0.4			
Highly probable scenario	Increase in prices	by 5%	0.3	479,408.21	48,235	2,081.18
	Increase in prices	by 10%	0.3			
Scenario with moderate probability	Prices are unchanged		0.1	456,579.25	43,850	400.42
	Demand is unchanged		0.2			
Unlikely scenario	Reduction of prices	by 3%	0.06	442,881.87	42,534	79.12
	Reduction of demand	by 3%	0.07			
Least likely scenario	Reduction of prices	by 5%	0.04	433,750.29	41,657	21.68
	Reduction of demand	by 5%	0.03			

as these moods change and the Central Bank of the Russian Federation imposes active monetary policies aimed at strengthening the national currency (Popkova, Yurev, Stepicheva, & Denisov, 2015).

Our analysis of the development of the Russian agricultural machinery market under conditions of international trade integration shows that increased demand and price levels in this market are to be expected, and so it is possible to anticipate enterprise profit growth. Enterprise profit dynamics in the agricultural machinery market for 2010-2014 are shown in Fig. 2.

Fig. 2 shows that over the last five years, there has been overall decline in enterprise profits in the agricultural machinery market. Despite 67% growth occurring in 2012, this was followed by a rapid decline of 64% in 2014. Profits declined by 45% over five years (RUB 16,638 million).

From our analysis of statistical information on the Russian agricultural machinery market, it is possible to conclude that in 2014, sales volumes in the market involved 43,850 items of machinery that earned RUB 20,021 million for enterprises in this market. Thus, the average annual price for agricultural machinery amounted to RUB 456,580. Comparison results for the tree of price change and demand scenarios for the Russian agricultural machinery market under conditions of international trade integration are shown in Table 3.

Table 3 shows that the most likely scenarios involve price increases of 10% (0.5) and 5% (0.3) as well as increased demand of 5% (0.4) and 10% (0.3). Price and demand declines of 5% are the least probable (0.04 and 0.03, respectively). Scenarios of Russian agricultural machinery market development under conditions of international trade integration for the next 5 years (until 2020) are shown in Table 4.

Table 4 shows that the most likely scenario involves price growth of 10% and growth in demand of 5%. For this condition, the average market price of an agricultural machinery item will be RUB 502,237.17, the volume of sales in the market will amount to 46,042 items, and agricultural machinery manufacturer profits (financial results) will amount to RUB 4,624.85 million. This scenario does not involve state support for manufacturers of agricultural machinery.

A scenario involving a price increase of 5% and increased demand of 10% is highly probable. Then, the average annual price of an agricultural machinery item will be RUB 479,408.21, the volume of market sales will amount to 48,235 items, and agricultural machinery manufacturer profits (financial results) will amount to RUB 2,081.18 million. This scenario does not involve state regulation of the Russian agricultural machinery market.

A scenario of moderate probability involves fixed price and demand levels in the Russian agricultural machinery market and a financial value of RUB 400.42 million. Conditions involving an insignificant reduction of prices and demand of 3% is unlikely. In this case, the average market price for agricultural machinery will decrease to RUB 442,881.87. Sales volumes will amount to 42,534 items with financial results equal to RUB 79.12 million.

The least probable scenario would involve a significant decline in demand and prices for agricultural machinery of 5%. Under such conditions, the price for an item of agricultural machinery would decline to RUB 433,750.29, sales volumes would amount to 41,657 items, and profits would amount to RUB 21.68 million. If this scenario is realized, full-scale state interference and agricultural machinery market development for stimulating demand and support for national production will be necessary.

Conclusion

Our research results show that the Russian agricultural machinery market develops dynamically under the influence of multiple favorable factors and positive tendencies, including population income growth, the expansion of farm crop areas, and state programs for agricultural machinery modernization, among others. In view of recent trends in the currency market, Russian manufacturers of agricultural machinery have been better able to export their products.

The results of our scenario analysis of business development in the agricultural machinery market under conditions of international trade integration show that there will be no urgent need for state interference in Russian agricultural machinery market processes in the next five years, as according to our forecasts, this market will likely witness increased demand and market prices to 2020, which should result in significant profits.

Under such conditions, spending assets of state budgets to elicit additional support for national production is not effective. However, for the realization of the least probable scenarios, which assume reduced price levels, sales volumes and profits, state regulation of the Russian agricultural machinery market will be necessary.

The results of the present study are limited by a number of factors affecting our forecasts of Russian agricultural machinery market development under conditions of international trade integration. Despite our thorough analysis of possible influencing factors, such factors are difficult to interpret and require further study; the precise treatment of their effects is also difficult to achieve. Therefore, our results should closely, but not fully, reflect real processes.

Further research in this area may involve monitoring the Russian agricultural machinery market to 2020 to identify realized scenarios, to verify the precision of formulated forecasts, and to identify additional factors shaping this market under conditions of international trade integration for the purposes of formulating new forecasts and increasing their precision.

References

Agroinfo. (2015, June 15). Manufacture of agricultural machinery in Russia in January-March 2015. (2015). Retrieved from http://agroinfo.com/proizvodstvo-selxoztexniki-v-rossii-v-yanvare-marte-2015-goda-1507201504/

Anderson, K., Valenzuela, E. (2011). Agricultural policy as a barrier to global economic integration. In M. N. Jovanović (Ed.), *International Handbook on the Economics of Integration* (Vol. 3, pp. 225-239). Cheltenham, UK: Edward Elgar Publishing.

Antonakakis, N., Tondl, G. (2014). Does integration and economic policy coordination promote business cycle synchronization in the EU? *Empirica, 41*(3), 541-575.

Bortolini, M., Cascini, A., Gamberi, M., Mora, C., Regattieri, A. (2014a). Sustainable design and life cycle assessment of an innovative multi-functional haymaking agricultural machinery. *Journal of Cleaner Production, 82*, 23-36.

Bortolini, M., Mora, C., Cascini, A., & Gamberi, M. (2014b). Environmental assessment of an innovative agricultural machinery. *International Journal of Operations and Quantitative Management, 20*(3), 243-258.

Bryant, C. E., & Javalgi, R. G. (2014). Global economic integration in developing countries: The role of corruption and human capital investment. *Journal of Business Ethics, 136*(3), 437-450.

Bull, B. (2014). The development of business associations in Central America: The role of international actors and economic integration. *Journal of Public Affairs, 14*(3-4), 331-345.

Clapp, J., & Helleiner, E. (2012). Troubled futures? The global food crisis and the politics of agricultural derivatives regulation. *Review of International Political Economy, 19*(2), 181-207.

Dasgupta, D., Pitigala, N., & Gourdon, J. (2012). South Asia's economic prospects from global rebalancing and integration. In P. Dee (Ed.), *Economic Reform Processes in South Asia: Toward Policy Efficiency* (pp. 23-42). Abington, UK: Routlege.

Ganushchak-Yefimenko, L. M. (2013a). Economic integration as a basis for small and medium enterprises business. *Actual Problems of Economics, 141*(3), 70-77.

Ganushchak-Yefimenko, L. M. (2013b). Management of innovation potential development of small and medium business based on economic integration. *Actual Problems of Economics, 144*(6), 72-79.

Gnedenko, E., Kazmin, M. (2015). Agricultural land and regulation in the transition economy of Russia. *International Advances in Economic Research, 21*(3), 347-348.

Golub, A., Hertel, T. W. (2008). Global economic integration and land-use change. *Journal of Economic Integration, 23*(3), 463-488.

GonÇalves, J. R. B., Madi, M. A. C. (2013). Global economic integration, business expansion and consumer credit in Brazil, 1994-2010. *International Journal of Green Economics, 7*(3), 213-225.

Gong, C., Kim, S. (2013). Economic integration and business cycle synchronization in Asia. *Asian Economic Papers, 12*(1), 76-99.

Huang, H., Yun, Z., You, L., & Wu, J. (2011). Forecast of subsidy for purchasing agricultural machinery based on Life Cycle Theory in China. Paper Presented at International Conference on Management and Service Science, "MASS 2011", August, 12-14, 2011, Wuhan, China.

Khafizova, A.R., Galimardanova, Y. M., Salmina, S.V. (2014). Tax regulation of activity of agricultural commodity producers. *Mediterranean Journal of Social Sciences, 5*(24), 421-425.

Kobrin, S. J. (2015). Is a global nonmarket strategy possible? Economic integration in a multipolar world order. *Journal of World Business, 50*(2), 262-272.

Larionova, A. A., Suslova, I. A., Povorina, E. V., Vinogradova, M. V. (2015). Formation of tourist image of the region. *Mediterranean Journal of Social Sciences, 6*(3), 261-266.

Liu, Y., Hu, W., Jetté-Nantel, S., Tian, Z. (2014). The influence of labor price change on agricultural machinery usage in Chinese agriculture. *Canadian Journal of Agricultural Economics, 62*(2), 219-243.

Morozova, I. A., Litvinova, T. N. (2014). Russian market of agricultural equipment: Challenges and opportunities. *Asian Social Science, 10*(23), 68-77.

Morozova, I. A., Litvinova, T. N., Rodina, E. A., Prosvirkin, N. Y. (2015). Marketing mix in the market of agricultural machinery: Problems and prospects. *Mediterranean Journal of Social Sciences, 6*(36), 19-26.

Mulatu, A., Wossink, A. (2014). Environmental regulation and location of industrialized agricultural production in Europe. *Land Economics, 90*(3), 509-537.

Muzlera, J. (2014). Capitalization strategies and labor in agricultural machinery contractors in Argentina. *Research in Rural Sociology and Development, 20*, 57-74.

Palamarchyk, D. M. (2013). Integration into global production and marketing networks as a factor of influence on national economic development. Actual Problems of Economics, 149 (11), 51-56.

Popkova, E. G., Yurev, V., Stepicheva, O., Denisov, N. (2015). Transformation and concentration of intellectual capital as a factor of economic growth in the modern economy. *Regional and Sectoral Economic Studies, 15*(1), 53-60.

Qobo, M. (2012). Chasing after shadows or strategic integration?: South Africa and global economic governance. *South African Foreign Policy Review, 1*, 257-273.

Rosstat. (2015). *Russia in numbers. Scientific research and innovations 2015: Bulletin of Rosstat.* Retrieved from http://www.gks.ru/free_doc/doc_2015/rusfig/rus-15.pdf

Rugman, A. M., Oh, C. H. (2011). Multinational enterprises and regional economic integration: Rethinking key metrics in international business. In M. N. Jovanović (Ed.), International Handbook on the Economics of Integration (Vol. 3, pp. 73-87). Cheltenham, UK: Edward Elgar Publishing.

Solovchuk, K. O. (2015). Regulation and support for innovations in the agricultural sector of the European Union. *Actual Problems of Economics, 165*(3), 62-68.

Staus, A., Becker, T. (2012). Attributes of overall satisfaction of agricultural machinery dealers using a three-factor model. *Journal of Business and Industrial Marketing, 27*(8), 635-643.

Sung, H. E., Delgado, S., Peña, D., Paladino, A. (2013). Tyrannizing strangers for profit: Wage theft, cross-border migrant workers, and the politics of exclusion in an era of global economic integration. In D. C. Brotherton, D. L. Stageman, S. P. Leyro (Eds.), Outside Justice: Immigration and the criminalizing. Impact of changing policy and practice (pp. 247-267). New York, NY: Springer.

Vinogradova, M. V., Kulyamina, O. S., Koroleva, D. A., Larionova, A. A. (2015). The impact of migration processes on the National Security System of Russia. *Mediterranean Journal of Social Sciences, 6*(3), 161-168.

Vošta, M. (2014). The food market in the CR and its regulation within the framework of the EU agricultural policy. *Agricultural Economics (Zemědělská ekonomika), 60*, 279-286.

Wirtz, J., Tuzovic, S., Ehret, M. (2015). Global business services: Increasing specialization and integration of the world economy as drivers of economic growth. *Journal of Service Management, 26*(4), 565-587.

Yakymenko, O. S. (2013). Peculiarities in strategic management of enterprise development in agricultural machinery sector. *Actual Problems of Economics, 147*(9), 138-144.

Yu, X., Leng, Z., Zhang, H. (2012). Optimal models for impact of agricultural machinery system on agricultural production in Heilongjiang agricultural reclamation area. Paper presented at Proceedings 24th Chinese Control and Decision Conference, "CCDC 2012", May 23-25, 2012, Taiyuan, China.

Yushkevych, O. O. (2013). Regulation mechanisms in the development of agricultural enterprises. *Actual Problems of Economics, 147*(9), 132-137.

Zhovnovach, R. I. (2014). Satisfaction of consumers' demand as the basis for planning competitiveness of agricultural machinery enterprises. *Actual Problems of Economics, 155*(5), 171-180.

10

An Introduction to the Multidimensional Real-Time Economic Modeling

Mario Arturo Ruiz Estrada[1], Vgr Chandran[1], Muhammad Tahir[2]

ABSTRACT

This article proposes a new economic modeling theoretical framework known as multidimensional real-time economic modeling (MRTE-Modeling). The model is an important tool that economists and educators can use to demonstrate the multidimensional aspects of economic behavior. MRTE-Modeling facilitates the analysis of a series of complex and dynamic economic problems that can affect market behavior from a multidimensional perspective. The proposed MRTE-Modeling framework is based on the uses of an alternative mathematical modeling framework, multidimensional graphical modeling approach, and computer algorithm and, thus, allows the possibility to transition from 2-dimensional economic dynamic modeling to multidimensional real-time economic modeling. Therefore, the main objective of using the proposed experimental model in the field of economics is to analyze different macroeconomic scenarios to monitor and provide a warning of possible unexpected economic failure(s). The proposed alternative experimental model is based on the application of Econographicology. Hence, our model is expected to offer policy makers and researchers new analytical tools to study the impact and trend of economic failures in the economy of any country from a new perspective.

KEY WORDS: economic modeling, real-time analysis, multidimensional coordinate spaces, econographicology

[1]Department of Economics, Faculty of Economics and Administration, University of Malaya, Malaysia
[2]Department of Management Sciences, COMSATS Institute of Information Technology, Pakistan

Introduction

This paper aims to illustrate an alternative economic modeling framework to study market behavior as a whole. It is based on the use of a new multidimensional graphical modeling technique coupled with the application of a real-time effect. The proposed modeling framework builds a computer algorithm that can facilitate the input, storage, classification, analysis and visualization of a large number of endogenous variables that can simultaneously affect market behavior. For a long time, academics and scholars depended on the application of 2-dimensional graphical modeling, and now it is time to transition to multidimensional graphical methods given the advancement in computer technology. The simple graphical format of 2-dimensional modeling can show only the visualization of historical and forecasting data in the same graphical space within a limited space of time. However, multidimensional real-time graphical modeling can help researchers observe all possible changes in a large number of variables. The changes in all these variables allow learners to clearly observe the cause and effect of different economic phenomena through the visu-

Correspondence concerning this article should be addressed to: **Mario Arturo Ruiz Estrada,** Department of Economics, Faculty of Economics and Administration, University of Malaya, Kuala Lumpur 50603. E-mail: marioruiz@um.edu.my

alization of multidimensional graphs that permit the observation of a large number of variables in real time. Basically, the transition from 2-dimensional graphical modeling to multidimensional real-time graphical modeling requires researchers to learn how to plot and draw multidimensional graphs using different multidimensional coordinate spaces. Nevertheless, the adaptability to transition from static 2-dimensional graphical modeling to multidimensional real-time graphical modeling takes time. In economic analysis, real economic problems can be identified and incorporated into a multidimensional graph to visualize the movements of variables as simulations of economic variables. Multidimensional graphs can also be used to describe dynamic and multi-functional analyses that represent changes within the total function. Furthermore, multidimensional graphs can also help researchers visualize the changes in all exogenous variables simultaneously.

We suggest the application of Econographication, pioneered by Ruiz Estrada (2007), to learn and understand multidimensional graphs under the application of multidimensional coordinate spaces. Ruiz Estrada contended that the teaching and learning of multidimensional graphs require basic knowledge about the 2-dimensional Cartesian coordinate system, which serves as the foundation in plotting multidimensional graphs in economics. Multidimensional graphs can be constructed in five basic steps: first, the acquisition of basic knowledge of plotting and drawing 2-dimensional graphs in the Cartesian coordinate system; second, the acquisition of basic knowledge of Euler's geometry; third, the attainment of a basic idea of time and space in the graphical space; fourth, the construction of solid prototype(s) using basic materials such as wood, papers, plastics and others; and fifth, the adaptation to learn and understand different dimensions that exist in multidimensional graphs. Before proceeding further, it should be noted that the Omnia Mobilis assumption of Ruiz Estrada (2011a) must be applied to multidimensional graphs to generate the environment of freedom in different dimensions needed for the graphs to work without any restriction or condition. The ***Omnia Mobilis*** assumption suggests applying economic modeling in real time to observe the changes in all variables simultaneously. The ***Omnia Mobilis*** assumption opens a new era in economic theory by applying multidimensional graphs and real-time multidimensional graphical modeling. We can say that the contribution of the ***Ceteris Paribus*** assumption was great in its time, but in the present time, it is not sufficient to simply explain complex and dynamic economic phenomena. The difference between the ***Ceteris paribus*** and ***Omnia Mobilis*** assumptions is that the ***Ceteris Paribus*** assumption takes only a snapshot of the historical moments of some economic phenomena at one time, whereas the ***Omnia Mobilis*** assumption shows video running in real time. The ***Omnia Mobilis*** assumption (everything is moving) was introduced to reduce dependency in the use of the *ceteris paribus* assumption to explain an economic phenomenon. We propose the openness of substantive isolation through the application of the ***Omnia Mobilis*** assumption. Hence, the use of the ceteris paribus assumption is minimal and even relaxed in the application of multidimensional graphical modeling. The ***Omnia Mobilis*** is in contrast to the process of building economic models to explain a complex economic phenomenon in 2 dimensions that begins with the *ceteris paribus* assumption. Marshal (1890) clearly articulated the use of the *ceteris paribus* assumption in economic models. According to Marshall (1890, p. 304),

> "*The element of time is a chief cause of those difficulties in economic investigations which make it necessary for man with his limited powers to go step by step; breaking up a complex question, studying one bit at a time, and at last combining his partial solutions into a more or less complete solution of the whole riddle. In breaking it up, he segregates those disturbing causes, whose wanderings happen to be inconvenient, for the time in a pound called Ceteris Paribus. The study of some group of tendencies is isolated by the assumption other things being equal: the existence of other tendencies is not denied, but their disturbing effect is neglected for a time. The more the issue is thus narrowed, the more exactly can it be handled: but also the less closely does it correspond to real life. Each exact and firm handling of a narrow issue, however, helps towards treating broader issues, in which that narrow issue is contained, more exactly than would otherwise have been possible.*"

Marshall's (1890) approach allows the analyses of complex economic phenomena in parts such that each part of the economic model can be joined to generate an approximation of the real world. This approach can be termed as the Isolation Approach, and according to Marshall (1890) and Schlicht (1985), it originates from two possible isolation clauses. First, the *ceteris paribus* assumption allows some variables to be considered unimportant. This clause is called substantive isolation. Substantive isolation considers that some unimportant variables cannot significantly influence the final result of the economic model. Second, the *ceteris paribus* assumption allows the impact of some important factors to be disregarded. In this case, the application of the *ceteris paribus* assumption is purely hypothetical; therefore, the second clause is called hypothetical isolation. It allows parts of the model to be managed more easily and efficiently. The goal is, therefore, to achieve a parsimonious model that is able to explain the complex real world. The idea is to draw multidimensional graphs that can aid in the visualization of a large number of variables in different spaces on the same graphical space. However, beyond that, multidimensional graphs provide an alternative to Marshall's view of a step-by-step cumulative partial approach to modeling a complex economic phenomenon. To apply the multidimensional real-time economic modeling framework, we generate an effect of movement live or in real time. Hence, the basic premise of the multidimensional real-time graphical modeling framework assumes that markets are in a constant dynamic imbalanced state that experiences constant chaos and high vulnerability. Furthermore, the concept of equilibrium in the multidimensional real-time economic modeling framework is applied to the analysis of market failures. Equilibrium is considered as a leak in the momentum of balance among all variables that can appear at any time. However, we cannot predict exactly when this synchronized balance is going to appear. In the multidimensional real-time economic modeling framework, there is not even a single endogenous variable or single exogenous variable available. Multidimensional real-time economic modeling allows for the observation of a multidimensional graph that is moving different variables in real time in the same graphical space. This multidimensional graph is also capable of showing the regular and irregular behaviors of market failures in the short run. Lastly, multidimensional real-time economic modeling is based on the use of multidimensional partial differentiation.

Law of demand and supply from a multidimensional perspective

Typically, the study of market behavior under the demand and supply law is graphically represented by the traditional demand and supply curves embodied in two-dimensional graphs. In the case of the demand and supply curves in multidimensional form, the ***Dynamic Imbalanced State** (DIS)* (Ruiz & Yap, 2013) must be used under the Omnia Mobilis assumption. The *DIS* permits the demand and supply analysis, which includes internalities and externalities such as economic factors, social factors, political factors, technological factors, environmental factors, institutional factors and other different economic agents and institutional behaviors (e.g., public sector-government, private sector-firms, consumers–households) to explain the real behavior of the market in its whole context. Regarding the application of the analytical graphical method in economics, it is necessary to mention the major contribution of Merritt (1838). Cournot derived the first formula for the rule of supply and demand as a function of price. He was also the first economist to draw supply and demand curves on a graph. This author believed that economists should utilize graphs only to establish probable limits and express less stable facts in more absolute terms. He further held the view that the practical use of mathematics in economics involves not only strict numerical precision but also graphical visualization. In fact, Cournot suggested the application of the first quadrant of the 2-dimensional Cartesian co-ordinate system by drawing two linear functions to represent demand and supply curves in the same graphical space. In addition to Cournot, other innovative economists who contributed to the analytical graph systems in economics over time include Leon Walras, Vilfredo Pareto, Alfred Marshall and Francis Ysidro Edgeworth (McClelland, 1975).

The reason behind applying the demand and supply law to the study of market behavior is to find market equilibrium among a large number of possible combinations between two specific variables followed by the price of the commodity (exogenous variable) and quantity (endogenous variable) in a fixed period of time and space. The mythical part here is how different economic agents (buyers and sellers) react or overreact unconditionally according to the effect of the unexpected behavior of price commodity on the quantity demanded and supplied.

The main reason to visualize demand and supply through the implementation of multidimensional real-time graphical modeling is to explore unknown dimensions of market behavior from a multidimensional perspective. The basic premise is that the market undergoes constant evolution across time and space. This means that markets in each period of history can show different structures, internalities, externalities, institutions, and economic agents can show different behaviors. Hence, the study of market behavior requires alternative economic assumptions and economic models based on each specific period of history. Additionally, we shed some light on the unexpected, irrational and trends that market behavior can experience at any time from a multidimensional perspective. Therefore, the study of market behavior becomes more complicated, demonstrating with low levels of accuracy across the time dimension. In terms of classification, market equilibrium can be either partial or general. Furthermore, partial market equilibrium can be divided into linear and non-linear modeling from the mathematical and graphical perspectives. Basically, partial market equilibrium using the linear modeling approach is based on the analysis of a single commodity and three variables such as the quantity demanded (Q_d), quantity supplied (Q_s) and the price of the commodity (P). This specific model is represented by two linear equations. The main characteristic of the demand linear equation (see expression 1) is that its slope is always negative (downward) because price and quantity demanded move in opposite directions. The slope of the supply linear equation (see expression 2) is positive (upward) because the price and quantity move in the same direction. Furthermore, the price commodity equilibrium (P^*) is a result of the elimination of variables from the identity $Q_d = Q_s$ (see expression 3). Additionally, the quantity equilibrium (Q^*) is a result of replacing the price equilibrium (P^*) with the quantity demanded equation (Q_d) (see expression 4). Finally, market equilibrium (ε) is represented by expression 5.

$$Q_d = \alpha - \beta P \qquad (1)$$

$$Q_s = -\pi + \lambda P \qquad (2)$$

$$Q_d = Q_s \Rightarrow P^* \qquad (3)$$

$$Q^* = Q_d = \alpha - \beta P^* \qquad (4)$$

$$\varepsilon = (P^*, Q^*) \qquad (5)$$

Partial market equilibrium by non-linear modeling is represented by the application of a linear equation (see expression 7) and a non-linear equation (see expression 6). In the first example, we need to identify the price equation by constructing a single equation (see expression 8). Subsequently, we proceed to find the price commodity equilibrium (P^*). It is based on the application of the quadratic formula (see expression 9) to the single equation or price equation. Hence, we consider only the positive final value from the quadratic function because only positive values are economically admissible. The last step is to incorporate the price commodity equilibrium (P^*) into the quantity demanded function (Q_d) to find the obtained equilibrium quantity (Q^*), as shown in expression 10. The final equilibrium is presented in equation 11.

$$Q_d = \alpha - P^2 \qquad (6)$$

$$Q_s = \lambda P - \pi \qquad (7)$$

$$f(P) = Q_d + Q_s \qquad (8)$$

$$P_1^*, P_2^* = \frac{-b \pm (b^2 - 4ac)^{1/2}}{2a} \Rightarrow P_1^*, P_2^* \cap R_+ \qquad (9)$$

$$Q^* = Qd = Q_d = \alpha - (P^*)^2 \qquad (10)$$

$$\varepsilon = (P^*, Q^*) \qquad (11)$$

The analysis between static, dynamic and real time plays an important role in the current era of economic modeling. Initially, we can say that economic modeling in real time does not represent a simple relationship between two variables such as a dependent variable and independent variable(s) that are fixed in a specific period of time. In our case, economic modeling in real time suggests that it is not sufficient to use only static and dynamic economic modeling.

Traditional economic modeling vs. economic modeling in real time

We find that economic modeling in real time can offer an alternative visual approach to observing the behavior of macroeconomic and microeconomic variables that move through a single screen live. To generate this type of modeling, we need to use advanced information technology and multidimensional graphical modeling. Economic modeling in real time allows us to observe different changes in different variables in the same graphical space. All the variables defined in the abovementioned expressions constantly move through different periods of time (years, months, weeks, days, hours, minutes and seconds) and space (different geographical spaces). It is important to mention that economic modeling in real time is an alternative approach to studying economics from a different perspective. We suggest a major transformation in the economic modeling-oriented framework to detect economic failures in a timely manner. We think that it is very difficult to quantify or predict the behavior of any complex economic phenomenon in the long run because domestic factors and externalities in different economies change at different speeds. It is understood that changes in different factors such as factors in the social, economic, technological and political arenas suffer differently in the different world economies. These fast transformations that economies experience cannot be accurately observed in static and dynamic economic modeling or forecasting. Since Smith's approach in 1776 until today, different schemes of economic modeling such as static and dynamic schemes have been used, as evidenced in a large number of essays, articles and books in libraries, the internet and journals. All these documents have used different theoretical approaches such as descriptive, theoretical, experimental and mathematical frameworks including econometrics. Furthermore, they have given us a general idea about some economic phenomenon or behavior in a specific historical moment through a frozen picture in 2 dimensions (X, Y). To analyze an economic phenomenon, we typically focus on selecting a few variables whose impact is expected to be more visible and ignoring the less important variables floating under the application of "*the ceteris paribus assumption*" to support possible unexpected scenarios that cannot be simultaneously included in our analysis. It also seems important to highlight here that partial market equilibrium assumes the use of the ceteris paribus assumption. The doctrine here is to isolate the less important variables from the study of market behavior and focus our attention on two specific variables such as the price of the commodity (P) and the quantity (Q). In fact, the price of the commodity (P) is the only variable that can affect quantity. Nevertheless, general market equilibrium is based on the use of a multi-commodity market. The approach is to include more commodities in our analysis, represented by n-equations in the quantity demanded function (see expression 12) and the quantity supply function (see expression 13). Market equilibrium is represented by expression 14. Lastly, it is important to state that general market equilibrium also rests on the Ceteris Paribus assumption.

$$Qd_i = Qd_i(P_1, P_2, \ldots, P_\infty) \quad i = 1,2,\ldots\infty \tag{12}$$

$$Qs_i = Qs_i(P_1, P_2, \ldots, P_\infty) \quad i = 1,2,\ldots\infty \tag{13}$$

$$\varepsilon_i = (P_1, P_2, \ldots, P_\infty) = 0 \tag{14}$$

After a short review of the demand and supply model, the following question arises: can the classic analysis of demand and supply fully capture the behavior of the market as a whole? However, we suggest that market behavior needs to be studied based on the interaction of a large number of sub-markets. At the same time, all sub-markets should be kept in a permanent dynamic imbalanced state under the application of the Omnia Mobilis assumption. In fact, the market can be considered as a multidimensional system that interacts and works in perfect harmony without any restriction or condition. Our idea of equilibrium is quite different from the traditional classic view because we view equilibrium as an imbalanced synchronization state that can appear in unexpected and unlimited time. The imbalanced synchronization state is considered a fleeting momentum as a result of the relaxation (or lesser instability) of all sub-markets. It depends on the economic, social, political, technological, and environmental factors; market structures; institutions; and economic agents' behavior. In the same context, we suggest the use of the dynamic imbalanced state (DIS), which can help explain possible unexpected market behavior. The dynamic imbalanced state is not a chaotic state; rather, it is the unconditional and unexpected complex sensitive reaction of a large number of sub-markets that is generated by different institutional, economic, political, social, technological, and environmental forces simultaneously under the condition of uncertain non-rational behavior. Therefore, all sub-markets do not necessarily need to be in equilibrium simultaneously because all sub-markets are kept in a dynamic imbalanced state. Moreover, all sub-markets can experience an imbalanced synchronization state at any time. It is a short, fleeting transitional state and is unpredictable and spontaneous. Market equilibrium is not a static and isolated phenomenon; it is a transitional and evolutionary state that cannot be controlled and determined arbitrarily. When studying market equilibrium, we must remember that it is not a natural phenomenon that can be exactly measured or demonstrated by the sciences. In our case, market equilibrium can be considered a dynamic imbalanced state, whereby humans' interactions with each other to satisfy their needs always change according to the different periods of history. The analysis of market behavior under the application of the dynamic imbalanced state can be shown by constructing the quantity demanded equilibrium (Q_d^*) (see expression 15) and quantity supplied equilibrium (Q_s^*, see expression 16). Hence, the interaction between the Q_d^* and Q_s^* identifies the price commodity equilibrium (P^*) for any commodity. The measurement of the quantity demanded equilibrium (Q_d^*) depends on the interaction of a large number of variables without any restriction(s) or classification (see expression 15), while in the case of partial market equilibrium, only the price commodity (P) can affect the quantity (Q). Therefore, we attempt to account for a large number of variables that can influence the quantity demanded equilibrium (Q_d^*).

From a graphical perspective, the quantity demanded equilibrium (Q_d^*) is the vertical axis among all sub-axes located in the bottom part of each sub-level. All these sub-axes at the bottom part of each sub-level are directly connected to the quantity demanded equilibrium (Q_d^*) using straight lines until we can build the demand surface by sub-level, whereby each sub-level represents a specific commodity in the market. A large cylinder can be generated by connecting all sub-levels. It is assumed that each sub-axis in its sub-level shows growth rates (Δ) in real time (*), as depicted in Figure 1. Additionally, we must apply the Omnia Mobilis assumption to generate the relaxation of all variables affecting the demanded quantity equilibrium (Q_d) because we avoid isolating some of the variables that the Ceteris paribus assumption considers less important. However, if all variables suffer because of relaxation, then the umbrella is open and the price imbalance (P≈) becomes lower, according to Figure 2. From a graphical perspective, the price imbalance (P≈) is a vertical axis located between the demand and supply surfaces. Figure 2 shows that each commodity has its own specific sub-level (or commodity) and quantity demanded imbalance (Qd≈) and quantity supplied imbalance (Qs≈) simultaneously in its specific price imbalance (P≈).

$$Qd\approx = Qd\approx (☼\Delta V1, ☼\Delta V2,\ldots,☼\Delta Vn) \quad (15)$$

$$Qs\approx = Qs\approx (☼\Delta V1, ☼\Delta V2,\ldots,☼\Delta Vn) \quad (16)$$

$$☼Qd\approx \approx ☼P\approx \approx ☼Qs\approx \quad (17)$$

Can we provide an alert or forecast of market failures?

This section is devoted to the study of market failures from an economic modeling perspective. It seems important to make a clear distinction between economic forecasting modeling and economic alerting modeling. Economic forecasting modeling is based on the classic use of econometrics under the application of different techniques, methods and models using sophisticated software such as SSPS, SAS, STAT, EVIEWS AREMOS, DATADESK and others. The modern econometrics software always adopts a dynamic modeling approach to analyze time-series, cross-sectional and longitudinal data. Forecasting economic modeling attempts to give us some basic and preliminary reasons behind the cause and effect of any economic phenomenon. In addition, we find that econometric models did not precisely predict market failures in the medium and long run with accuracy or a small margin of error until recently.

Furthermore, forecasting economic modeling under the application of econometrics can have low levels of

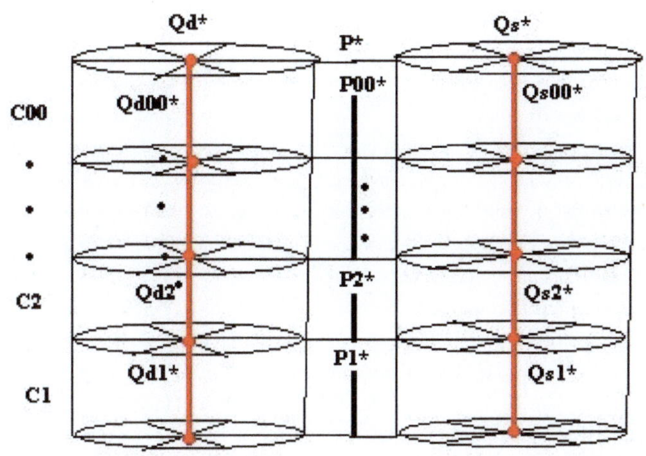

Figure 1. Quantity Demanded Equilibrium (Qd*), Quantity Supplied Equilibrium (Qs*) and Price Commodity Equilibrium (P*) (Ruiz Estrada, Yap, & Nagaraj, 2008)

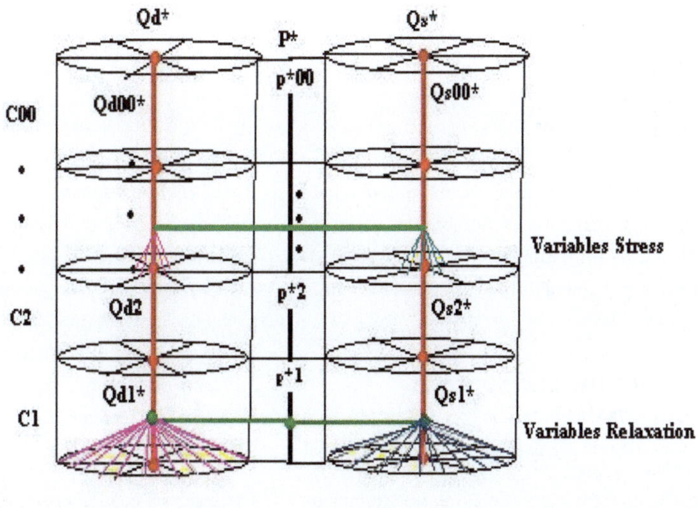

Figure 2. Demand Surface and Supply Surface (Ruiz Estrada et al., 2008)

accuracy and be unclear and unstable scenarios in the long run. Hence, the economic forecasting modeling of market failures in the long run becomes impossible and unrealistic. It can originate from the quickly rising challenges of economic, social, political and technological aspects and institutions in the market. Various factors are responsible for the low level of accuracy in forecasting market failures in the long run. Rapid technological changes, the vulnerability of the world economy due to international trade and investment under the umbrella of globalization, and the unpredictability of natural disasters due to a lack of ability can explain why the forecasting economic models are unable to correctly predict economic crisis in the long run.

By contrast, economic alerting modeling is based on mathematical models and computer programming supported by software and dynamic simulators. This type of economic modeling permits us to observe the behavior of the market as a whole in real time without any restrictions or limitations. Hence, the appearance of unexpected market failures because of an oil crisis, a financial crisis, or an international trade crisis become more difficult to predict than in the past, as market failure shows different signs and behaviors in different periods of time in the history of the world economy. Market failures can appear in different periods of time and retain their unique characteristics before the market experiences a substantial full or partial recovery from a deep or superficial crisis. The magnitude of the final impact of market failures can vary across different periods of time and geographical spaces.

More specifically, the negative impact of any market failure can be accounted for by the fast expansion of unemployment, uncontrolled and galloping inflation, constant economic slowdown, rapid and uncontrolled expansion of poverty, low stock market performance, constant currency depreciations, less international trade, high speculation in real estate and consumer uncertainty. Lastly, economic alerting modeling utilizes multidimensional graphical modeling offered by Econographicology and economic modeling in real time.

The idea of time and space in economic analysis

This section demonstrates that the 2-dimensional space (X, Y) and 3-dimensional space (X, Y, Z) can show only a micro-picture in the visualization of complex and dynamic economic phenomena. The hypothesis of this research paper is that the 2-dimensional and 3-dimensional spaces are micro-slices of the large Mega-space or Universe in a fixed period of time and common space. Therefore, to test the proposed hypothesis, we suggest the application of an alternative multidimensional graphical modeling approach that is called "the Mega-Space Cartesian Plane". For a long time, economists attempted to visualize simple (static) or complex (dynamic) economic phenomena in different periods of time using the same graphical space through the application of 2-dimensional spaces (X, Y) or 3-dimensional spaces (X, Y, Z). The most common dimension applied to economic analysis is the 2-dimensional space (X, Y) to visualize historical data and explain economic theories and results from economic models under the application of econometrics. For example, the graphical visualization of the behavior of any country in response to any economic phenomenon (G.D.P. rates, inflation rates, exports/imports, etc.) is based on the application of the 2-dimensional Cartesian plane (X, Y). Typically, economists attempt to interpret a group of points located in different places according to time and space. All these points are connected by lines to visualize the historical trends from the past until today or possible results from economic models or forecasting models. In fact, the main idea of applying 2-dimensional spaces (X, Y) to economic models or forecasting models is to visualize how an economic phenomenon behaves under the impact of internal and external factors. Hence, economists can search for suitable policies to prevent possible economic failures or possible results of decisions made in the short or long term.

Why do economists use 2-dimensional and 3-dimensional spaces?

Economists use 2-dimensional space (X, Y) or sometimes 3-dimensional space (X, Y, Z) in the graphical representation of complex and dynamic economic problems, and it is important to determine the underlying reasons behind this usage. In our opinion, the following reasons can explain the use of these spaces in the study of economics. .

1. These two graphical models were developed and established in Lafleur's (1960) introduction of the 2-dimensional Cartesian plane. Since then, the application of the 2-dimensional space in economic graphical analysis has been a "**tradition**".
2. The 2-dimensional space is "**easy to apply**" when visualizing basic trends or values in the same graphical space. We randomly selected approximately 5,000 documents (JSTOR and DIRECT SCIENCES -ELSEVIER-, 2013) from different reputable journals and text books in economics, econometrics, business, statistic, mathematic and

sciences. Of all these documents 99.50% used 2-dimensional spaces (X, Y) and only 0.05% used 3-dimensional spaces (X, Y, Z).

3. The logical explanation for the frequent use of 2-dimensional spaces is the ease of plotting, drawing and visualizing any economic phenomenon. Therefore, 2-dimensional spaces can generate a clear visual and mental refraction to graphically present complex and dynamic economic phenomena in the same space and time.
4. It is difficult to find **"alternative and suitable multidimensional graphical models"** to move from 2-dimensional space graphical modeling to graphical modeling of multidimensional spaces. This research paper encountered some difficulties in generating this crucial visual and mental transition from 2-dimensional spaces to multidimensional spaces.

The main consideration of this research paper is that 2-dimensional and 3-dimensional spaces are not able to capture the behavior of the real economic world as a whole. It is understood that the real world is changing constantly and in different spaces and across time. To test this proposition, we assume that inside the Mega-Space or Universe, the number of General-Spaces, Sub-Spaces, Micro-Spaces, Nano-Spaces and JI-Spaces is infinite. All these spaces move differently. The logic behind the plotted points on the 2-dimensional or 3-dimensional Cartesian plane in this research is quite different from the traditional view because a single point plotted on the Cartesian plane is considered a rigid body. The first assumption applied in this research paper is that two rigid bodies cannot occupy the same space simultaneously. Different rigid bodies unfold and contend for different positions in the Mega-Space. The rigid bodies constantly move and generate different graphical reflections. The second assumption is that different rigid bodies in the Mega-Space, General-Spaces, Sub-Spaces, Micro-Spaces, Nano-Spaces and JI-Spaces run at different speeds of time. We assume that there are different types of time and that these times are followed by general times, partial times and constant times. The general time runs in the Mega-Space, but the General-Spaces, Sub-Spaces, Micro-Spaces, Nano-Spaces run under different partial times (see Figure 3). The JI-Spaces runs in constant time. The rigid body hangs on a specific point of the Mega-Space. The rigid body in the economic analysis can be represented by the interaction among fixed values in some specific space through the Cartesian plane. These values can be classified by absolute values (e.g., amounts of money or units of goods) and relative values (e.g., growth rates or percentages). In addition, it is also important to mention the roles of Euclidian geometry and Minkowski's 4-dimensional spaces (Einstein, 1961) in supporting our proposition. Einstein used both geometrical models to explain his theory of relativity. These two geometrical modeling frameworks are strongly supported by his formal mathematical and theoretical frameworks. However, these two geometrical modeling frameworks are not able to provide any graphical modeling to facilitate the visualization of 4-dimensional spaces. Our proposed new multidimensional graphical modeling framework is missing from studies on Euclidian geometry and Minkowski's 4-dimensional spaces. The new multidimensional graphical modeling is based on the application of multidimensional physical spaces (Ruiz Estrada, 2011b).

Introduction to the mega-space coordinate space

We introduce the Mega-Space coordinate system, as shown in Figure 3. Universe (U) is equivalent to the Mega-Space (S). The Mega-space Coordinate System is followed by the General-Spaces (GS), Sub-Spaces (SS), Micro-Spaces (MS), Nano-Spaces (NS) and JI-Spaces (see expression 18). The JI-Space applies formula (18) to plot each JI-Space into its Nano-Space. The JI-Space can be a negative or positive number in its Nano-Space coordinate system, but there is also a possibility that the number "0" is located at the center of all Nano-Space coordinate systems. Hence, the number "0" is a large surface located in the central part of all Micro-Spaces that divides the positive and negative numbers of each JI-Space (see expression 19).

$$U \equiv S = (GS_{i,}\ SS_{i:j,}\ MS_{i:j:k,}\ NS_{i:j:k:l,}\ JI_{i:j:k:l:m}) \qquad (18)$$

$$L = \alpha_h \ x\ \beta_z\ /2 \qquad (19)$$

$$M = [(X<i:j:k:\alpha_h>),(Y<i:j:k:\beta_z>)] \qquad (20)$$

Where i = { 1, 2…∞ }; j = { 1, 2…∞ }; k = { 1, 2…∞ }; h = { 1, 2…∞ } and z = { 1, 2…∞ }

Therefore, the Mega-Space Coordinate System starts from the General-Space "0", as shown in expression 21.

$$U \equiv S = GS_{0,}\ SS_{0:0,}\ MS_{0:0:0,}\ NS_{0:0:0:0}\ ,JI_{0:0:0:0:0} \cdots \quad (21)$$

Until the General-Space, the infinity Space ∞… is expressed by expression 22.

$$GS_{\infty,}\ SS_{\infty:\infty,}\ MS_{\infty:\infty:\infty,}\ NS_{\infty:\infty:\infty:\infty,}\ JI_{\infty:\infty:\infty:\infty:\infty} \cdots \quad (22)$$

$$M = f\ (GS_{i,}\ SS_{i:j,}\ MS_{i:j:k,}\ NS_{L,}\ JI_{m}) \quad (23)$$

The final general function and all partial functions in analyzing the Mega-Space Coordinate System are equal to expressions 24, 25, 26, 27 and 28.

$$S = f\ (GS_{0\boxtimes} GS_{1\boxtimes \ldots} GS_{\infty}) \quad (24)$$

$$GS = f\ (SS_{0\boxtimes} SS_{1\boxtimes \ldots} SS_{\infty}) \quad (25)$$

$$SS = f\ (MS_{0\boxtimes} MS_{1\boxtimes \ldots} MS_{\infty}) \quad (26)$$

$$MS = f\ (NS_{0\boxtimes} NS_{1\boxtimes \ldots} NS_{\infty}) \quad (27)$$

$$NS = f\ (JI_{0\boxtimes} JI_{1\boxtimes \ldots} JI_{\infty}) \quad (28)$$

In fact, when we join all JI-Spaces located in different Nano-Spaces at the same Micro-Space, we observe a single surface in vertical position. Each JI-Space represents a single growth rate and constantly experiences different changes in different proportions compared with its neighbor JI-Spaces in the same Micro-Space. Hence, we can observe a large vertical surface constantly moving in its dimensions. We can determine that all Micro-Spaces move in their Sub-Spaces, that all Sub-Spaces move in their General-Spaces and, finally, that all General-Spaces move in the Mega-Spaces with variable speeds of time. It can be further stated that an economic phenomenon cannot be analyzed in isolation because every economic phenomenon is dynamic and complex by nature. Economic phenomena change dramatically and constantly and, therefore, will be studied from a multidimensional perspective. The traditional economic modeling approach is not able to precisely show the imperceptible changes associated with economic phenomena or behavior in the same graphical space. The multidimensional economic modeling framework can analyze any economic phenomenon from a multidimensional perspective to observe the unknown dimensions that cannot be observed with 2-dimensional modeling. Multidimensional economic modeling requires the use of graphical animation to generate real-time or slow motion visual effects to examine a giant graph move with different speeds of time live.

It will be useful to understand different scenarios that cannot be visualized using 2-dimensional modeling. Our final aim is to propose a powerful multidimensional economic and graphical modeling framework to observe different stages that any economic phenomenon can be experienced in real time or in slow motion.

Definition of time in the mega-space coordinate system

Our basic premise is that the Mega-Space or Universe is multidimensional. The JI-Space is a rigid body (value) that hangs in its Nano-Space. When all JI-Spaces are joined together, a surface in vertical position in the same Micro-Space can be generated. The Mega-space coordinate system applies three different types of time to its graphical modeling including general times (GT), partial times (PT) and constant times (KT), as previously mentioned.

$$S_{GT} = f\ (GS_{i/PT,}\ SS_{i:j/PT,}\ MS_{i:j:k/PT,}\ NS_{i:j:k:l/PT,}\ JI_{i:j:k:l:m/KT}) \quad (29)$$

The Mega-Space runs on a general time, while General-Spaces, Sub-Spaces, Micro-Spaces and Nano-Spaces (see Figure 4) simultaneously run with partial times. The JI-Space hangs in its Micro-Space. A linear or non-linear curve in one Micro-Space can be obtained by joining the JI-Spaces. Expressions 30 and 31 clearly show that the Mega-Space Cartesian plane is applied in three different types of time, as previously mentioned.

$$M_{wt} = f\ (GS_{i/wp,}\ SS_{i:j/wp,}\ MS_{i:j:k/wp,}\ NS_{L/wp,}\ JI_{m/wk}) \quad (30)$$

$$\frac{L_{wp} = \alpha_{h/wk} \text{ x } \beta_{z/wk}}{2} \quad (31)$$

Where

$h = \{1,2\ldots\infty\}$ and $z = \{1,2\ldots\infty\}$

$m_{wk} = [(X<i/wp: j/wp: k/wp: \alpha_{h/wk}>),$

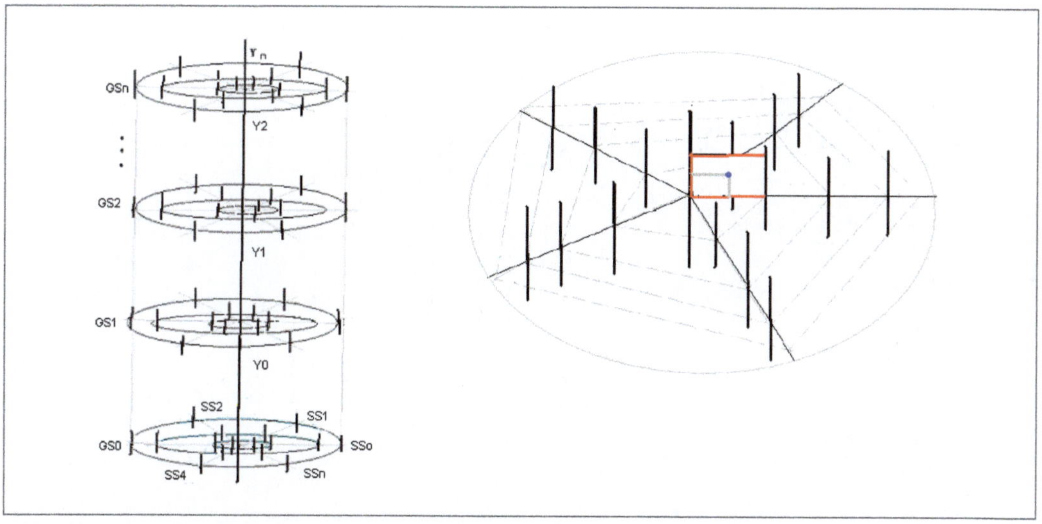

Figure 3. Mega-Space, General Space and Sub-Space (Ruiz Estrada, 2011b)

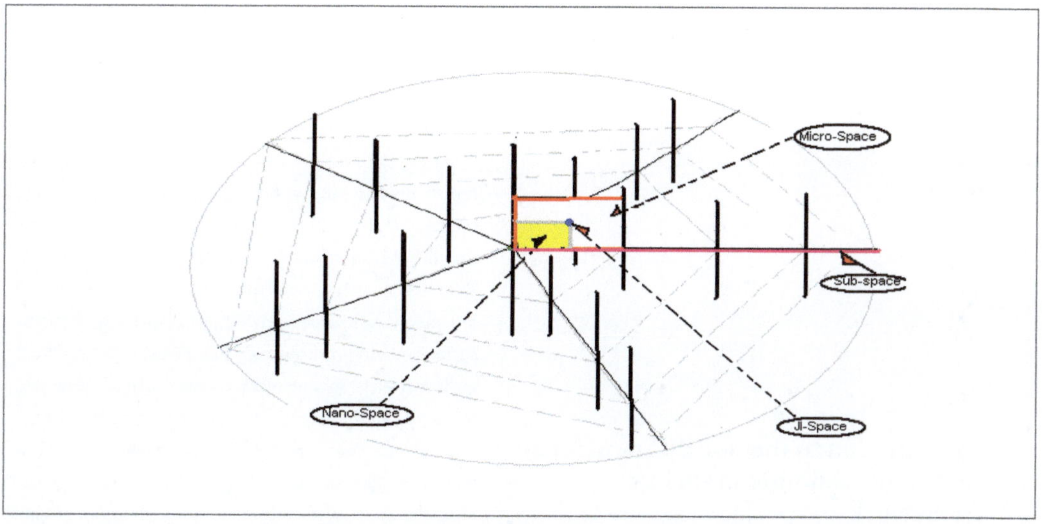

Figure 4. General-Space, Sub-Space, Micro-Space, Nano-Space and JI-Space (Ruiz Estrada, 2011b)

$$(Y<i/wp: j/wp :k/wp :\beta_{z/wk}>)] \quad (32)$$

Where
$i = \{1,2\ldots\infty\}$; $j = \{1,2\ldots\infty\}$ and $k = \{1,2\ldots\infty\}$

How to plot on the mega-space cartesian plane

This section demonstrates how to plot on the Mega-Space. Initially, we apply the Mega-Space Cartesian plane coordinate system that is shown by the following expression.

$$U \equiv M = (GS_{i,}\ SS_{i:j,}\ MS_{i:j:k,}\ NS_{L,}\ JI_{[(X<i:j:k:\alpha h>, (Y<i:j:k:\beta z>)]} \quad (33)$$

$$L = \underline{\alpha_h \times \beta_z} /2 \quad (34)$$

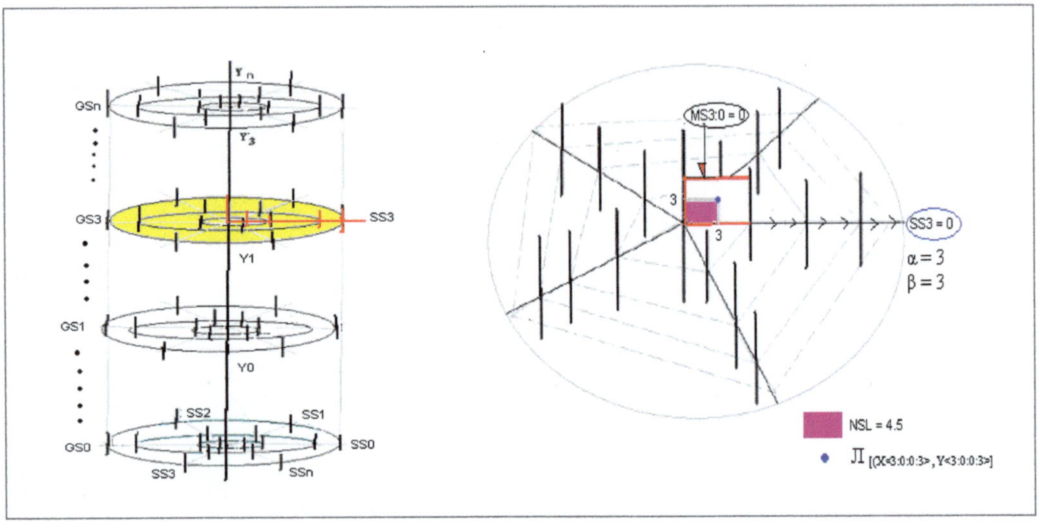

Figure 5. Mega-Space Plotting (Ruiz Estrada, 2011b)

The values that should be used during the process of plotting on the Mega-Space Cartesian plane are shown in Figure 5.

$GS_i = 3$
$SS_3 = 0$
$MS_{3:0} = 0$
$\alpha_h = 3$
$\beta_z = 3$
$NS_L = 4.5$

$JI_{[(X<3:0:0:3>),(Y<3:0:0:3>)]})$

Introduction to the multidimensional real-time economic modeling framework

Economic alerting modeling requires the creation of a data center that is able to save a large amount of information in different databases from different sources such as government agencies, academia, statistical departments and think tanks. The data center can also process a large amount of information in each database and simultaneously plot all the database information in a multidimensional coordinate system such as the mega-surface coordinate system. Similarly, we are also in a position to observe a mega-surface that is moving in real time through a large screen. Lastly, the database can alert us of possible failures in some or all the variables in one mega-surface at the same time. The main idea is to alert and generate special images in real time and slow motion. If we identify exactly which variable(s) is suffering, then we can take action(s) at the appropriate time to prevent more severe damage, for example, a possible major economic crisis in any economy. We assume that the mega-surface does not have a dependent variable; rather, it contains a large surface formed by infinite independent variables moving simultaneously. A mega-surface moving continuously in relation to the different growth rates of independent variables can be generated by adding all these independent variables using straight lines. Furthermore, all these variables are assumed to be independent of each other. The purpose of generating the mega-surface is to study the behavior of several independent variables simultaneously in the same graphical space in real time. We can observe that it is possible to obtain high levels of accuracy and effectiveness to reduce the impact of a possible economic crisis in a timely manner. Our main focus is the ex-present effect in real time instead of the ex-post or ex-ante effect. The objective is to detect failure(s) in some or all independent variables in mega-surface live using the Omnia Mobilis assumption to relax all independent variables in our modeling and, thus, provide an alert of a possible economic crisis at any time.

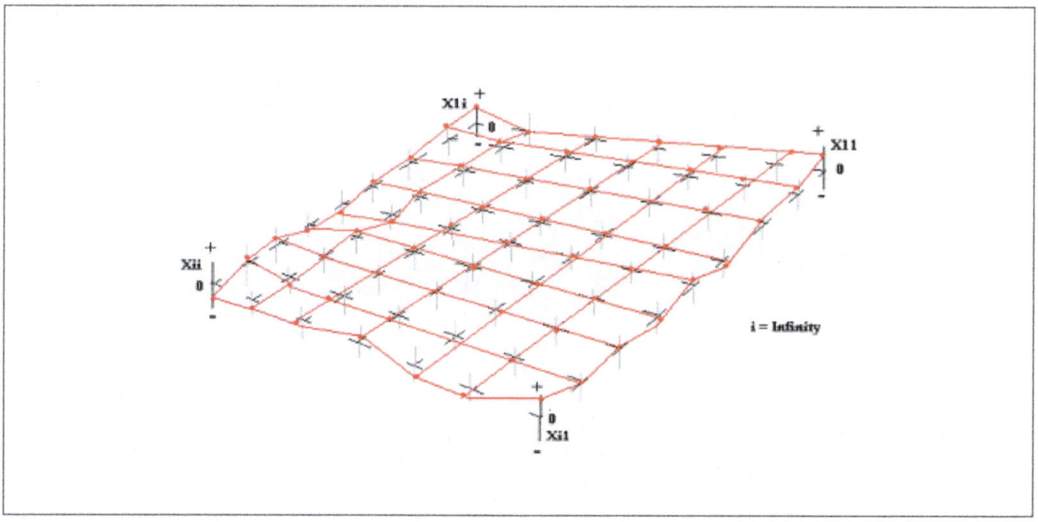

Figure 6. Mega-Surface (Ruiz Estrada, 2011b)

Multidimensional economic modeling

This paper proposes a multidimensional economic modeling framework that is able to generate a large number of simulations in the same graphical space in real time or slow motion to study the behavior of complex and dynamic economic phenomena. We suggest that multidimensional economic modeling requires the use of multidimensional physical spaces. The first assumption of multidimensional economic modeling is that all dimensions run under different speeds of time because any economic phenomenon can adopt a multidimensional behavior across time and space. The second assumption of multidimensional economic modeling is that any economic phenomenon always experiences a dynamic imbalanced state under the application of the Omnia Mobilis assumption. Hence, multidimensional economic modeling never needs to be in a state of equilibrium under the application of the Ceteris Paribus assumption.

Moreover, the idea of time in this model is rather different from that in 2-dimensional linear and non-linear graphical modeling because 2-dimensional modeling refers to a single and unique time standard under the use of the traditional calendar (by months or years) to analyze complex and dynamic economic phenomena or behaviors. In our personal view, the 2-dimensional framework can clearly show analytical inconsistency in the short and long runs. Therefore, we assume that any economic phenomenon can be analyzed from different dimensions because each dimension runs following a different speed of time. Furthermore, any economic phenomenon experiences different speeds of time. If we join different economic phenomena in the same graphical space, then it is possible to observe a series of economic phenomena moving in different directions with variable speeds of time in the same graphical space.

Economic modeling in real time

Economic modeling in real time can be done with the help of Econographicology (Ruiz Estrada, 2007). Econographicology supplies different multidimensional physical spaces to construct multidimensional graphs. The software required for economic modeling in real time follows various steps. First, there must be a standard format to input information on a line daily. Second, all these pieces of information (I) can be transferred to different databases (DB), which are interconnected to a unique information data center. Third, the same software can work immediately to plot different pieces of information (I) from different databases (DB) on the multidimensional physical space. Every observation from a database depends on different data sources such as the central bank, govern-

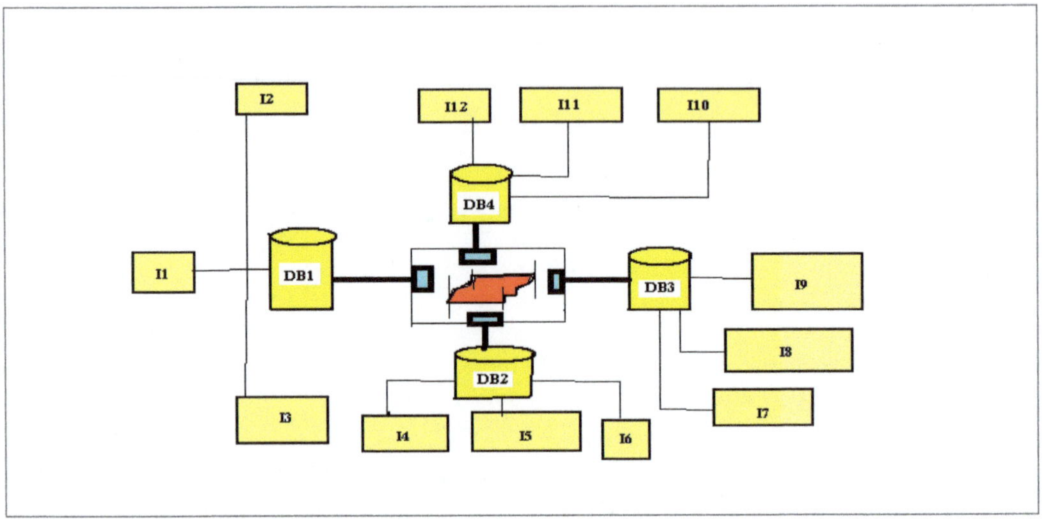

Figure 7. Economic Modeling in Real Time (Ruiz Estrada, 2011b)

ment agencies, private companies, national statistical departments and public and private research institutes, as demonstrated in Figure 6. Each plotted point in the multidimensional physical space is always changing. We use the concept of data changing in real time (see expression 37). Data changes in real time are due to the comparison of pieces of information (I) between two periods of time (the past and the present period of time). Similarly, the data changes in real time are fixed into their coordinate and variable positions all the time. Additionally, we reiterate that all changes in data in real time plotted in the multidimensional physical space are linked together with straight lines that form a single mega-surface in the same physical space (see Figure 6).

Model

Economic modeling in real time routinely starts with the input data function, as shown below:

$$I_{C:R} = Q_1 : Q_2 : \ldots : Q_\infty \qquad (35)$$

I = Input answer **Q** = Question(s) **C** = Column **R** = Row

The next step is the storing the data in the database (DB), which is described with the help of equation 36.

$$DB_{C:R} = \text{☼}SI_{C:R} \text{╬} \ldots \text{╬} \text{☼}SI_{C:R} \ldots \qquad (36)$$

$C = \{1, 2, 3 \ldots n\}$ $n = \infty$

$R = \{1, 2, 3 \ldots n\}$ $n = \infty$

Where DB = Database, **C** = Column, **R** = Row, ☼ = Running information in real time, **SI** = Save Information, and ╬ = Interlink Database

In the case of data changes in real time ($\text{☼}\mathbf{\Delta I}_{C:R}$), we compare the information we received on the previous day (**t-1** = past period of time) and the information received on the current day (**t** = actual period of time), as presented in expression 37.

$$\text{☼}\Delta I_{C:R} = \text{☼}SI(t) - \text{☼}SI(t-1) / \text{☼}SI(t-1) \qquad (37)$$

Finally, the plotting of real-time data is illustrated by expression 38, as follows:

$$Y_{sf} = f\,(\text{☼}\Delta I_{11} \text{╬} \ldots \text{╬} \text{☼}\Delta I_{\infty\infty}) \qquad (38)$$

Next, Figure 7 further clarifies and simplifies the idea discussed above.

The multidimensional graphical signal detection model avoids the use of a single dependent variable. This model suggests replacing a single dependent variable with a single mega-surface. This mega-surface is formed by infinite axes, and each axis is located in a vertical position. An axis shows positive values on the top of the axis and negative values at the bottom of the axis (see Expression 36). Similarly, for each axis, it is possible to observe a point that is pending and moving up and down on its axis constantly. This point represents the behavior of an independent variable on its axis. Furthermore, we need to join each independent variable to its next independent variable neighbor using a straight line. Finally, we can observe that the mega-surface (see expression 37) is formed by joining all independent variables (see Figure 5). The mega-surface is always in constant movement in real time and moving in different directions. The real-time modeling effect generating into the mega-surface depends on the speed of the information reception that directly influences the behavior of each independent variable's growth rate (see Expression 39). We suggest the application of the Omnia Mobilis assumption to relax all independent variables that are moving on their axis in real time. Multidimensional graphical signal detection modeling starts by building the growth rate function of each independent variable, as shown by the following expression:

$$\text{☼}\Delta I_{i;j} = \text{☼}\Delta I(t) - \text{☼}\Delta I(t\text{-}1) / \text{☼}\Delta I(t\text{-}1) \qquad (39)$$

Where the row: i = {1, 2, 3...n} n = ∞; the column: j = {1, 2, 3...n} n = ∞; Δ = Growth rate; ☼ = Running information in real time; t-1 = past period of time and t = actual period of time. Each independent variable in the mega-surface in the coordinate system can be represented as below:

$$\text{☼}\Delta I_{i;j} = (X_{i;j}, Y_{i;j}) \qquad (40)$$

Where X = {-∞ ... -3, -2, -1, 0, 1, 2, 3...∞+} and Y = {-∞ ... -3, -2, -1, 0, 1, 2, 3...∞+}

The next step is to build the final mega-surface given by (i x j).

$$\text{☼}\mathbf{MS} = \begin{pmatrix} \text{☼}\Delta I_{11} \text{╬} \text{☼}\Delta I_{12} \text{╬} \cdots\cdots \text{╬} \text{☼}\Delta I_{1\infty} \\ \text{☼}\Delta I_{21} \text{╬} \text{☼}\Delta I_{22} \text{╬} \cdots\cdots \text{╬} \text{☼}\Delta I_{2\infty} \\ \text{☼}\Delta I_{31} \text{╬} \text{☼}\Delta I_{32} \text{╬} \cdots\cdots \text{╬} \text{☼}\Delta I_{3\infty} \\ . \quad . \quad . \quad . \\ . \quad . \quad . \quad . \\ . \quad . \quad . \quad . \\ \text{☼}\Delta I_{ij} \text{╬} \text{☼}\Delta I_{i+1j+1} \text{╬} \cdots\cdots \text{╬} \text{☼}\Delta I_{\infty\infty} \end{pmatrix} \qquad (41)$$

Where i = {1, 2, 3...∞}; j = {1, 2, 3...∞} and "╬" is equal to the interlinking variables.

Finally, the analysis of the final mega-surface is based on the location of all independent variables in the mega-surface coordinate system. Hence, we obtain the following three possible results:

(1) If $\text{☼}\Delta I_{ij} > 0$, then our mega-surface becomes GREEN in color, indicating good economic performance.
(2) If $\text{☼}\Delta I_{ij} = 0$, then our mega-surface becomes YELLOW, showing that the economy is stagnant.
(3) If $\text{☼}\Delta I_{ij} < 0$, then our mega-surface becomes RED, demonstrating that the economic performance of the economy is poor.

Put simply, the color of the mega-surface can alert us of a possible economic crisis in a timely manner. We would like to state that we cannot stop an economic crisis. Rather, we can only reduce the damage caused by an economic crisis. Therefore, the findings of this paper have serious implications for both researchers and policy makers.

Conclusions

This paper has attempted to develop an alternative modeling approach for researchers to utilize. The traditional 2-dimensional modeling approach is not able to explain complex and dynamic economic problems in real time. We have, therefore, attempted to develop an alternative economic modeling (MRTE-Modeling) framework that is 3-dimensional by construction. Similarly, we believe that alerting economic modeling is more effective than economic forecasting. Now, we are able to observe the behavior of any economic phenomenon as a whole in real time and the timing of possible market failures. However, it should also be noted that we cannot stop market failures; rather, we can only minimize their damage in the short and medium runs. Reducing the damages associated with market failures would certainly help policy makers make their economies more efficient by implementing and executing appropriate policies. The major contribution of this paper to the existing literature on macroeconomic modeling is that it provides solutions for various complex and dynamic economic phenomena in the same graphical space under the application of multi-times framework. We posit that any economic phenomenon needs to be studied from a multidimensional perspective and in real time based on the use of high-performing information technology and the application of multidimensional real time graphical modeling under Econographicology. The proposed modeling framework would enable researchers to observe the behavior of any economic phenomenon live through a screen and to find failures in the market in a timely manner. The idea behind applying multi-times framework is to generate a real-time effect or slow motion visual effect and to identify possible failures that any economic phenomenon can experience in different stages across time and space. Market behavior in the real world is always in a dynamic imbalance state. Therefore, the market does not necessarily need to be in a state of equilibrium in which only the price of the commodity (P) can influence the quantity demanded (Qd) and quantity supplied (Qs). It follows that the real-world market cannot be analyzed using only two variables to explain dynamic and complex market behaviors. In our opinion, the study of the market needs to include a large number of variables that affect demand and supply simultaneously. We, therefore, suggest the use of the price imbalance (P≈) resulting from the relaxation or stress of all variables running into quantity demanded imbalance (Qd≈) and the quantity supplied imbalance (Qs≈) simultaneously.

The proposed modeling framework is sufficiently flexible to include a large number of variables without any restriction or isolation. This is in contrast to the Ceteris Paribus assumption, which imposes restrictions and isolation into partial and general market equilibriums. A market basically consists of a large number of sub-markets in a dynamic imbalanced state. Therefore, if all sub-markets are kept in a dynamic imbalanced state, then the momentum of the imbalanced synchronization state can appear in different sub–markets simultaneously. The momentum of the imbalanced synchronization state is a result of the relaxation of all sub-markets. In fact, the momentum of the imbalanced synchronization state is a fleeting and unpredictable leak momentum that can appear spontaneously in all sub-markets at any time. Furthermore, the price commodity equilibrium (P^*) depends on the relaxation or stress of all the variables that affect the quantity demanded equilibrium (Q_d^*) and the quantity supplied equilibrium (Q_s^*).

References

Einstein, A. (1961). *Relativity: The special and the general theory* (3rd ed.). New York, NY: Three Rivers Press.

Lafleur, L. (1960). *Discourse on method, optics, geometry, and meteorology*. New York, NY: The Liberal Arts Press.

Marshall, A. (1890). *Principles of economics*. London, UK: Macmillan and Co., Ltd.

McClelland, P. D. (1975). *Causal explanation and model building in history, economics, and the new economic history*. Ithaca, NY: Cornell University Press.

Merritt, F. D. (1898). Researches into the Mathematical Principles of the Theory of Wealth Augustin Cournot Nathaniel T. Bacon. *Journal of Political Economy*, 6 (3), 426-430.

Ruiz Estrada, M.A. (2007). Econographicology. *International Journal of Economic Research*, 4 (1), 75-86.

Ruiz Estrada, M. A., Yap, S. F., & Nagaraj, S. (2008). Beyond the ceteris paribus assumption: modeling demand and supply assuming omnia mobilis. *International Journal of Economic Research*, 5 (2), 185-194.

Ruiz Estrada, M. A. (2011a). Policy modeling: definition, classification and evaluation. *Journal of Policy Modeling*, 33 (4), 523-536.

Ruiz Estrada, M. A. (2011b). Multi-dimensional coordinate spaces. *International Journal of Physical Sciences*, 6 (3), 340-357.

Ruiz Estrada, M. A., & Yap, S. F. (2013). The origins and evolution of policy modeling. *Journal of Policy Modeling*, 35 (1), 170-182.

Schlicht, E. (1985). *Isolation and aggregation in economics*. Berlin: Springer-Verlag Publisher.

11

Negative Impacts of the Neo-liberal Policies on the Banking Sector in Bulgaria

Rossitsa Rangelova Pavlova[1], Grigor Sariiski[1]

ABSTRACT

From the beginning of the 1970s until the last global financial and economic crisis in 2008-2009, neo-liberal ideas guided economic policy development. It is worth noting that the Central and Eastern European countries transformed their economies from centrally planned to a market type at the peak of the liberal policies. Bulgaria offers a particularly interesting example because the country encountered a very difficult transition from one extreme of an economic system organization to another. The paper considers the reforms in the Bulgarian banking sector during the transition period from a centrally planned to a market type economy (from 1989 onward) through the implementation of neo-liberal policies. The development of the banking sector and its transformation is analyzed throughout the two main periods: before and after the transition. The latter is divided into two sub-periods (phases) beginning with the early 1990s, followed by the financial and bank crisis in the country, the introduction of a currency board regime in 1997, and stabilization, and ending with the global crisis in 2008-2009. This article summarizes that during the transition period, a modern banking system was established to accumulate profit rather than to promote economic growth. Following a chronological order, the negative effects of the liberalization of the Bulgarian banking sector are specified: the exportation of ownership (and control) upon banking system assets, unfair asset redistribution, the emergence of the local oligarchy, the weak protection of the taxpayers and others.

KEY WORDS: neo-liberal policies, transition from centrally planned to a market type economy, financial sector, Bulgarian banking system

[1] Bulgarian Academy of Sciences - Economic Research Institute, Sofia, Bulgaria

1. Introduction

Neo-liberal ideas emerged a few decades ago. In the early 1970s, an unprecedented boom took place in economic thought. In the mid-1970s, neo-liberals received general admission (founded primarily on the ideas of Friedrich von Hayek and Nobel winner in economics Milton Friedman). Invigorated by the accelerated economic growth, the neo-liberal wave spread among industrial countries. It was reinforced also by the economic crises of the 1970s, which showed that, first, the state and governments could be weak regulators of economic life, and second, a perpetually state-managed economy could not guarantee growth. Various neo-liberal concepts conceived in London, Freiburg and the Chicago School were built on certain principles, such as the primacy of private property, low taxes, limited social policy, and a stable money supply. The uniting thesis postulates the limited state intervention in the economy and undisputed deregulation.

For the past nearly four decades, the neo-liberal ideas implemented in the Washington Consensus have guided

Correspondence concerning this article should be addressed to: **Rossitsa Rangelova Pavlova**, Aksakov, Street No 3, 1040 Sofia, Bulgaria. E-mail: r.rangelova@iki.bas.bg

development policy (Marangos, 2009). This ideology was triumphed throughout the late 1970s; however, it was afterwards evident that it bore a fundamental problem: its proclivity to generate crisis. Throughout the 1990s, the world observed several crises, for example, in Mexico (1994), East Asia (1997), Russia (1998), Brazil (1999), Argentina and Turkey (2000). Another fundamental problem that became evident later is neo-liberalism's policy failure to deliver economic growth. World growth has systematically slowed during the dominance of neo-liberalism, particularly in low- and middle-income countries. A comparative view would show that over the period 1990-1996, the growth was slower than that in 1980-1989, which, in turn, was slower than that in 1965-1980. A third fundamental problem is the tendency to worsen income distribution, be it in the industrialized world or the developing world. Thus, not only has growth slowed during the period of Washington Consensus ascendancy, but there has also been an increase in income inequality within and between the countries. Argentina's recent collapse, for instance, is a typical example of the Washington Consensus model failure. The country followed this model as closely as is ever likely to be possible in the real world of policymaking. The government liberalized the financial markets, eliminated trade barriers, privatized state assets, made its labor markets flexible, tied its currency to the dollar, and pursued monetary and fiscal austerity in the midst of a deep economic slump that bordered on a depression. Argentina's subsequent collapse has irrevocably discredited the neo-liberal ideology and spotlighted the urgent need for a new development paradigm (Palley, 2002). B. Amable (2010) came to the conclusion that the neo-liberal model of economic functioning has historically been exhausted, and the current financial collapse "*is not just a crisis of financial deregulation and of modern finance either. It is a crisis of the neo-liberal model of capitalism*".

Currently, the failure of the neo-liberal ideas has become evident, and it is clear that there is a growing need for a new economic development paradigm. Among the numerous other publications that may be the most concentrated on this subject are the comprehensive studies of A. Kaletsky's (2010) "Capitalism 4.0: The Birth of a New Economy" and J. Stiglitz's (2010) "Freefall. Free Markets and the Sinking of the Global Economy".

Naturally, the neo-liberal model of economic organization is not uniformly applied in each country. Its application is determined by the specific economic level, social attitudes and traditions in the governance. The idea of a specific variation of management was established by the most developed market economies, leading to the belief that neo-liberal policy could be not suitable for other countries. It turned out that the neo-liberal model of economic organization did not work in Scandinavian countries such as Denmark and Sweden because they embraced a qualitatively higher level, which suggested acting in well-developed market environments, policies and practices.

Developed economies have long believed that planning is a necessary evil, and now, they seek options to obtain proper control over the free market. From this point of view, one could, in fact, regard the liberalized market as a step backward from the level of current economic development. This is because neo-liberalism stands for the release of spontaneous market forces as a core value rather than the protection of public interest. In fact, critics of the neo-liberal nature could be found far before its official origin. The worldfamous physicist A. Einstein said back in 1949: "Unlimited competition leads to a huge waste of labor and to that crippling of the social consciousness of individual".

What, then, stimulated Bulgaria to undertake this step towards the implementation of neo-liberal ideology in the early 1990s? What forces led to the unconditional acceptance of these ideas in Bulgaria, which, like the other countries of Central and Eastern Europe (CEE), had been stuck until then in the radically opposite economic doctrine of central planning?

It was in 1989 that the idea of the central planning of economic activity totally collapsed in the socialist system in CEE, including Bulgaria. These countries undertook a transformation that was strongly influenced by the neo-liberal approach. Back in the 1990s, the neo-liberal idea easily found increasingly vigorous supporters, just because a new system was needed to replace the already denied central planning (or, as it was known, the administrative command system). Private ownership was recognized as the only plausible basis for economic life because it promoted a driving motive of profit and competitive markets. At that time, the Asian countries, particularly China (also employing a centrally planned economy at that time), emerged as important players in the global economic scene. Technological revolution, in full swing at that time, was exclusively stimulated by the creation of the global network, which brought about an array of innovation in the financial mechanisms. More visible, and also an unprecedented phenomenon from that time, was the 'demystification' of money (after the collapse of the Bretton Woods international monetary system in the early 1970s). Countries worldwide started using pure paper money without any correlation to gold or other measures of value; that change had significant implications upon financial and economic life. These events influenced the rise of neo-liberal ideas in the world, and most naturally, the same ideas have been selected as the building base in the process of transforming the countries with central planning to a market type economy.

Bulgaria was one of these post-communist countries that adopted an entirely new economic course toward the implementation of the neo-liberal concept after 1989. Perhaps the real problem of the Bulgarian economy and the problem for some of the other CEE countries was that the governments from that time had been making, as a rule, unfavorable decisions from strategic point of view. Thus, the overall effect of the so-called transition now could be regarded as negative in many aspects. It is still early to make such a definitive conclusion, even though it has been over two decades from the start of transformation (Innes, 2014; Kornai, 2006). It has to be taken into account that many benefits could not be possible to achieve in other way (such as free entrepreneurship and the equal treatment of different forms of ownership). On the other hand, the Bulgarian society from that time was definitely ill prepared to fulfill the needs of the process of establishing a fully free market. In the dawn of the transition, there was a total misunderstanding of the market principles not only in Bulgaria but more or less in the other CEE countries, which led to their altered implementation.

The foundation principle in the transition to a market economy is the change of ownership of the dominant state in central planning to private one. The bank's role is primarily directed toward the credit process. Therefore, the development of the banking sector in Bulgaria occupies a primary place in the economic and socio-political processes in the country in the years after 1989. It reflects both the essential processes of transition and its specificity for the country's own, including a number of deformations accompanying this transition.

The article attempts to consider the application of neo-liberal policies in the case of the Bulgarian banking system reforms during the transition period from a centrally planned to a market type economy. To stress the huge difference between the two economic systems, the specificity and development of the banking sector are analyzed before and after the transition to a market type economy, i.e., during the 1980s and from 1989 onward. Following the reform of the banking sector up to the time of the world financial and economic crisis in 2008-2009, the negative effects of the liberalization of Bulgarian banking system are specified.

2. The Bulgarian socialist banking sector legacy

Under the conditions of central planning (up to 1981), the Bulgarian banking system consisted of a handful of state banks, including the *Bulgarian National Bank* (BNB) as the Central Bank, which combined the functions of issuing and commercial banks; the *State Savings Bank* (DSK), serving primarily the savings and credit activities of the population; and *the Bulgarian Foreign Trade Bank,* which specialized in foreign trade operations and the management of foreign reserves. In 1981 was founded *Mineralbank* (transformed in 1982 to *Bank for Economic Initiatives - BSI*). In 1986 and 1987, seven new commercial banks specializing in serving the industry structures were created. Thus, the **first stage of banking reform** was launched in Bulgaria. The new banks (called "associations") were established as joint stock companies; each of them specialized in lending to specific sectors, such as electronics and metallurgy. Although these companies were classified as commercial banks, they were rather like development banks because they granted loans only for long-term investment projects.

The activities performed by BNB were similar to those of a regular commercial bank, including the delivery of credit to businesses. The structure of mediation between savers and borrowers was extremely cumbersome. The majority of savings was gathered through the branches of DSK. From there, they were transferred to BNB.

At the end of 1989 and in 1990, the **second stage of reform** was launched by the conversion of 59 branches of the BNB into commercial banks, some of them with little capital (in large and/or industrial cities throughout Bulgaria). They have been transformed into commercial banks as joint-stock companies, some of them with little capital, and the BNB assigned the lending activities completely to them. Changes have been made in the statutes of the banks to allow the inclusion of private equity. Shares are sold at face value, based on the carrying amount of the authorized capital of the bank on the date of their creation, although the real value was significantly higher. This act initiated the beginning of the transformation of the *National Bank* into an institution with functions typical of the western central banks. A substantial change in the *National Bank* status was carried out as it became more independent from the government and political influence. BNB was no longer subject to supervision by the Council of Ministers. It became responsible directly to the Parliament.

The transition to the market economy (1989 and onwards) imposed substantial structural changes in the banking system, primarily focused upon the destruction of state ownership and the accreditation of the private one (Campos & Fabrizio, 2012). Furthermore, it is aimed toward the creation of a system in which the allocation of funds to the commercial banks and the pricing of assets and liabilities were to be carried out on a market basis. In the field of the financial sector, Bulgaria had to do the following operations to:

- encourage and promote the establishment of new financial instruments as an urgent decision of the system extra liquidity;
- promote the creation of a securities market and its instruments;
- develop the market pricing of capital;
- inspire the establishment of new private banks and financial institutions;
- encourage them to invest in pension funds and in financial assets in general.

The automation of payment and transaction systems and the development of the banking services and capital markets was also needed to facilitate the free trade of goods and services and financial transactions between economic agents.

3. The first phase of transformation to a market type economy (1990-1996)

It could be stated that the starting conditions for the economic reform in Bulgaria were at best unfavorable. The structural distortions were from the very beginning larger than in the other CEE countries because Bulgaria had an overly centralized governance system with almost an entirely state-owned property of assets (nearly 95%), an overly concentrated production structure, relatively low competitiveness of the local goods in foreign markets, an irrational employment structure, and a considerable budget deficit (-4.9% of GDP in 1990). The Bulgarian gross external debt in 1989 was 52.5% of GDP, which was regarded as unacceptably high and provoked the government's moratorium on creditors' repayment. For the sake of comparisons, in the end of 2013H1, despite the very restrictive fiscal policy of the Minister of Finance Simeon Diankov (2009-2013), who was a strong adherent to the neo-liberal policy, the gross external debt reached 95% of GDP. This time, however, it was not considered as huge. The aforementioned initial conditions had a major negative effect on reforms and policies and led to a poor transition progress, particularly in the first half of the 1990s (Fries et al., 2006).

In line with the prime of world economics, at that time, neo-liberal ideas were noted as a natural choice to be followed by the emerging market economies in CEE. Any reluctance or suggestion of other ideas was regarded as a sign of backwardness and a hidden will to keep the status quo of the former socialist reality. The International Monetary Fund (IMF) and the World Bank undertook an active part in the CEE transition to a market economy (Wilczyński, 2011). Their main objective was to discredit the Keynesian model of directed or managed economic policy by the Government and to impose the neo-liberal model of Milton Friedman and the related Chicago School of Economics. The two international organizations encouraged leaders of economically and financially unstable countries to implement a series of economic and social reforms so that communism would be no more. Dozens of countries, not only in the CEE but all over the world, followed the Stabilization and Structural Adjustment Programs of the IMF. The results, however, were far from satisfactory. Among the most recommended were the projects with an allegedly positive effect on GDP growth. Then, the US Agency for International Development (USAID) and the international banks offered "preferential" loans bearing strictly restrictions. By acting as economic consultants in these countries, they and their experts worked out long-run forecasts. Some of the names of the economic consultants in the CEE countries are well known. The "shock therapy" in Poland was organized under the program of Jeffrey

Sachs, who was a young Harvard graduate at that time. For Russia, the name of this consultant was Noreena Hertz, a British economist from the World Bank.

The initial stage of reforms, the basis of the Bulgarian "neo-liberal project" was settled according to the so-called "RahnUtt Plan" (Rahn & Utt, 1990). The Plan set out the main points of the transition to a market economy, in particular the preparation of a privatization program, monetary reform, the free exchange of foreign currencies, the elimination of controls over wages and prices, fiscal reform, commercial law, and the establishment of social policy. This Plan was developed by Prof. Richard Rahn, the chief economist of the US Chamber of Commerce, and his colleague Ronald Utt along with two teams of economic advisors: American and Bulgarian. Drafted from March to August 1990 and accepted by the Grand National Assembly, that Plan outlined the transition of the Bulgarian economy from governmental socialism to neo-liberalism.

The official start of the economic reform in Bulgaria is the 1st of February 1991. It was ambitious, including comprehensive prices, trades and foreign exchange liberalization, the restitution of land and urban property, and the privatization and de-monopolization of specific segments of the large enterprise sector. By radical economic reforms, we refer to the privatization of the stateowned enterprises in Bulgaria, which were envisaged to be only market oriented in contrast to the practice in other emerging market economies, such as Russia or the Czech Republic and Slovakia, where privatization had a stronger social orientation (Miller & Petranov, 2000). Concerning land reform, the Land Law required that restitution of property had to be done *within the real boundaries of land owned in 1946*. This process of land restitution was very complicated and was accompanied by frequent amendments in the Law (35 times within the period 1991-1999), and it lasted nearly ten years.

Stabilization policies were initially successful with respect to the budget deficit and inflation. The newly created environment for private small business fostered the establishment of new private firms, primarily in trade and services. Debt reduction agreements improved to a certain extent Bulgarian external debt situation, but it was still insufficient to ensure economic recovery. The GDP declined for five consecutive years. It was not until 1994 that the growth was restored, but it was for only two years; in 1996, the GDP dropped again by over 10% in comparison to 1995. The relatively improved economic performance in 1994 and 1995 was due to the efforts of the ruling socialist party government to slow the process of the collapse. The cumulative decline in output of over 30% was followed by a rapid increase in unemployment (Table 1).

Table 1. Bulgaria: Main Macroeconomic Indicators (in %), 1990-1995.

INDICATORS	1990	1991	1992	1993	1994	1995
Real GDP (growth rates)	-9.1	-11.7	-7.3	-2.4	1.8	2.5
Real wages (growth rates)	5.3	-39.1	14.9	1.4	-20.5	-7.5
Consumer price index (growth rates)	23.8	338.5	79.4	56.1	87.1	62.2
Employment (growth rates)	-6.1	-13.0	-8.1	-1.6	-2.0	-2.4
Unemployment rate	1.7	11.1	15.3	16.4	12.8	11.1
Real industrial output (growth rates)	-16.8	-22.2	-15.9	-10.9	8.5	4.9
Real personal consumption (growth rates)	-3.3	-15.7	1.0	-0.7	-2.6	-
Budget deficit (share of GDP)	-4.9	-3.8	-5.7	-11.5	-6.6	6.7
Real money (M1; growth rates)	5.8	-48.4	-21.6	-18.2	-4.6	5.5

Note: Adapted from "Main Macroeconomic Indicators, 2007," by National Statistical Institute (2014). Retrieved from http://www.nsi.bg/otrasal-publikaciaen.php?n=156&otr=42

Perhaps one of the main weaknesses of neo-liberal policy was the assumption that the mere placement of the economy to a market basis would lead to its automatic optimization and efficiency improvement. Bulgarian (and not only Bulgarian) practice has shown that this is far from being the whole truth. During the adaptation period (which, in principle, could last for decades), states are virtually defenseless. This situation could be summarized by the words of the president and founder of Intel Corporation, Andy Grove (Palast, 2004, p. 98): "The purpose of new capitalism is to shoot the wounded". The contemporary experience has shown that in addition to the deprivation of the defense mechanisms, the emerging market economies, including Bulgaria could not rely on the adequate protection of international institutions because the voices there belong to the developed economies, which have neither the interest nor the capacity to protect the weaker ones.

4. Privatization of the banking sector

In the early 1990s, BNB was a possessor of 59 banks. It had control in all of them, and the remaining shares were held by primarily state-owned companies. In this manner, the ultimate owner of all the Bulgarian banks was the state.

The banking sector liberalization had been initiated in the beginning of 1990s on a congress of the *Union for Private Economic Enterprise* (SSIG), which made the resolution of the private bank establishment. The founders of SSIG offered to the former party chairman of the *United Democratic Forces* (and, a few months later, the president of the country) Zhelju Zhelev to submit a proposal of the abolition of the state monopoly on the banks for a discussion in Parliament. A few days later, Parliament accepted an amendment of the Constitution art. 13, thus providing a gradual withdraw of BNB from the position of a major shareholder through a sale of its shares.

It was expected that the privatization of the sector and the liberalization of the financial services market would lead to an improvement of market efficiency and that the eight specialized banks eventually would merge with some of the 59 commercial banks. As a result, the country would get an advanced system of money supply and run entirely on a market basis. Initially, the plan was successful. There was a real "license blast". In 1997, the number of banks in Bulgaria reached 87, which was the largest number in comparison with the other former socialist countries. The number of banks was several times larger than in Hungary, Czech Republic, and Poland (Wagner, 2000). In a short time, the count of private banks grew exponentially, but in almost all cases, the resource of equity capital and the purchase of shares were provided by loans from state banks and DSK. From 1990-1995, the DSK granted BGN 70 billion loans and the majority of them were used for that purpose. Hundreds of brokerage houses, exchange bureaus and other financial entities received licenses. Thus, a parallel banking system began to operate in the country.

The lack of regulations was felt not only in the licensing process. In 1990-1991, huge loans were granted without proper collateral (unrecoverable by definition). In fact, the accumulated resource in Bulgarian banks was donated in the form of credit with no idea of its further return to the vaults. In the short period until 1997, the functions of local banks actually degraded to a simple appropriation of society's assets and their further donation to the domestic oligarchs. It should be noted that the main factor that allows this process to happen was actually the lack of adequate regulations.

One could summarize that the withdrawal of the state as an institution contributes not to an increase in financial system efficiency but rather to its destruction. Even after the establishment of legislation, there were so many doors left open in the newly created laws, and the control over their observance was so weak that it was as if they did not exist at all (Minassian, 2013).

Comparing the banking system performance before and after 1997, one could state that at the beginning of the crisis, the private banks were owned by domestic entrepreneurs, and thus, the banking sector was far from any views and standards of the modern banking. The process of bank creation (and not only bank creation) was poorly supervised. Banks' emerging process allowed the assets of a given bank to be used for establishment of another one. It resulted in a number of hollow banks and in the distribution of their loan portfolio between unreliable borrowers. The lending was also poorly controlled. In addition, the Bulgarian population did not display market behavior and thus facilitated the bank or other financial organizations' owners. Before the following crisis in 1996-1997, the entire lending process was associated more with its borrowing part and very rarely with its repayment. This led to the emergence of credit millionaires and ultimately to the national banking crisis.

4.1. The financial crisis 1996-1997: Reasons and consequences

In the discussion of weak regulation, it must be noted that for almost two years in the beginning of the transformation (1991-1993), the banking system was functioning absolutely free, without any interference by the state institutions. In the first half of 1993, the National Bank adopted the main regulations that governed the banking business in Bulgaria. A couple of years later, at the beginning of 1994, it was marked that there were "*certain deficiencies in licensing management by Banking Supervision,*" and on this basis, changes in what was known as Regulation № 2 (for licensing) were proposed. This intervention, however, was late. The country had already developed a hollow structure that did not serve economic circulation but rather exhausted its financial resources (via promises of high interest).

The lack of regulation then led to the creation of parallel quasidepository institutions, or so-called financial pyramids. At the same time (1994), new elections were held, won again by the socialist party. The new government attempted to depart from neo-liberal course by limiting privatization, restoring manufacturing, activating social policies, and increasing public expenditure to improve the quality of education and other sectors, including rehabilitation of economic relations with Russia as a large and traditional market for Bulgaria. The accumulated negatives before that, however, did not allow such policies to be continued. Jobs were shut down, and unemployment and prices increased. Problem loans grew rapidly, and competition from non-banks stimulated sharp raise of the interest rates. Deposit tourism emerged, leading to some prompt migrations of the bank's assets. It led to a serious increase of liquidity problems and to the increase of the potential costs of bank recapitalization.

Data for this period could be found in the secret report prepared in the autumn of 1996 by the National Security Service (Bank Octopus Hidden in the Secret Report "Dobrev", 09.04.2010). According to this report, 44 banks were created and acted within the period 1990-1996, some of which were almost unknown to the public. The authorized capital for their establishment was collected illegally from the vaults and accounts of banks and government offices. At the end of 1995, bad loans of all banks in Bulgaria amounted to 40% of the GDP. In the cited report, it is claimed that through the chain "lobby people-politicians-bank officials and private firms", huge amounts previously condemned as uncollectible loans had expired.

In 1996, the IMF refused a loan to the cabinet of the Prime Minister Jan Videnov. Then, President Zhelju Zhelev returned the proposed budget revision (motivated by an unconstitutional text). The latter among the factors led to resignation of the government, hyperinflation and a disaster of the banking sector. The Bulgarian currency strongly depreciated, affecting the population's deposits. This was an expected consequence of the local application of free market principles in the banking system. The negative effects of the first wave of the neo-liberal policy became obvious. This reform led the country's population to dramatic impoverishment, ineffective business agents and a bank system chocked with uncollectible debts.

This report was commissioned by the Prime Minister Zhan Videnov, after the IMF sent a sharp letter to the government demanding the closure of dubious banks. There is a detailed analysis of the creation of new private commercial banks, their interaction with government financial institutions appointed by a political party bankers and private entrepreneur schemes, in which the vaults were drained by relatives and party firms. It is shown that the set of reasons for the collapse in the financial system has focused almost entirely on the relations between the BNB and commercial banks. These relationships were built on strongly indefinite arrangements, which were inadequate in their liberality and subject only to administrative measures and means of control.

The crisis in our banking system was beneficial for foreign banks that opened branches in the country. Bulgarian citizens relocated much of their withdrawals from foreign currency deposits in ING Bank, Raiffeisen Bank, Drezdenbank. The policy and commitment of the BNB were to maintain a stable exchange rate of the dollar that led to the sale of cheap dollars in the country, and their export abroad was not a problem for licensed foreign banks.

To summarize: The reasons for the negatives, including the very slow recovery and poor economic growth in Bulgaria up to 1997, could be seen as three main factors: (a) inadequate initial conditions for a country with strong central planning to transition to a market type economy in combination with poor economic performance; (b) the adoption of overly radical reforms in all sectors of this economy and their inconsistent implementation; and (c) economic mismanagement. It is hard to favor any of these factors. An equally important role for this crisis was the premature withdrawal of the state from the banking sector along with purely domestic political factors. Bulgaria had an unfavorable combination of neo-liberal views and a specific political environment of dominating influence of the socialist party in an ideological struggle with the opponents, who called themselves democrats and embraced the neo-liberal policy to the letter. In this respect, the frequent change of governments was very indicative. Within seven years (1990-1997), the country went through a line of seven governments of different parties, each of them applying the formula for a political cycle in a very condensed version (because nobody was aware of the duration of their term). Thus, the newly emerging Bulgarian market environment became a combination of the worst aspects of two opposing ideologies, and it allowed the obvious weaknesses of neo-liberalism to be exposed. Conditions in Bulgaria were extremely inappropriate for its implementation because it presupposes the existence of a developed market environment, practices and attitudes that did not exist in the country. Under the slogan of banking sector liberalization, the corruption was widely spread, and the society savings were redistributed in the form of unsecured loans.

The changing philosophy of the reform implemented by different governments over time along with the slow, inconsistent structural reforms impeded the achievements of macroeconomic stabilization. Seven years after the start of the transition, the Bulgarian economy was still in a crucial situation with restricted foreign financing, depressed employment and low investment activity. The lack of structural reforms began to show harmful repercussions on the monetary reform and economic stabilization as a whole. Combined with real currency depreciation, the lack of structural reforms led to the weakening balance of payments and to a decline in foreign reserves. In addition, the impending external debt service obligation enforced an exchange rate crisis. The banking system collapsed. Both high inflation and large exchange rate movements undermined the credibility in economic management.

The reform of the banking sector was not in accordance with transformations in the real (non-financial) sector. This discrepancy had a significant influence on the function of the entire banking sector, and it gradually became a factor that had an adverse effect on the national economy.

This crisis had lasting effects on the banking sector, including the deregulation of the financial sector through the rejection of monetary policy and the introduction of the currency board, the devaluation of debt and the loss of the savings due to hyperinflation. The annual average CPI for the previous year=100 was 121.6% in 1996 and 1058.4% in 1997; afterwards, it sharply slowed down. As a result, the population lost nearly 70% of its savings, impaired assets were intensely redistributed, and the citizens were impoverished, and so on.

Huge losses of the public sector logically led to private sector capitalization. This process generally created opportunities for significant investment in the real sector, but a significant portion of the amount received at that time was used for personal consumption in the private sector, taken out of the country or invested in real estates and financial transactions abroad.

Economists today are convinced that the failure in 1996 of 16 banks completed the first phase of capital accumulation in the country. Then, missing money was invested in the secondary distribution of capital in the privatization. In practice, assets of USD 35 billion were appropriated. Thus, oligarchs and the richest 1% people from the total population were born.

4.2. The second phase of the transformation to a market type economy (1997-2008)

Political and economic changes in the first half of 1997 aimed to stabilize the economy and to restore confidence. The program agreed with the IMF entailed introduction of a currency board regime (from 1 July 1997), price liberalization, and a major acceleration of privatization. In general, the program placed a strong emphasis on structural reforms.

Table 2. Bulgaria: Main Macroeconomic Indicators (in %), 2004-2013

	2004	2005	2006	2007	2008	2009	2010	2011	2012	2013
Growth of real GDP [a]	6.7	6.4	6.5	6.4	6.2	-5.5	0.4	1.8	0.6	0.9[p]
Inflation[b]	6.1	5.0	7.3	8.4	12.3	2.8	2.4	4.2	3.0	0.9
Unemployment	12.0	10.1	9.0	6.9	5.6	6.8	10.2	11.3	12.3	12.9
Cash deficit/surplus, % of GDP [c]	1.7	3.1	3.4	3.3	2.9	0.9	-4.0	-2.0	-0.5	-1.8
Current account balance, % of GDP	-14.0	-11.6	-17.7	-27.2	22.9	-8.9	-1.5	0.1	-0.8	1.9
State debt (Maastricht), % of GDP	37.8	28.9	22.4	17.9	14.2	14.6	16.2	16.3	18.4	18.9

Note: Adapted from "Main Macroeconomic Indicators, 2007," by National Statistical Institute (2014). Retrieved from http://www.nsi.bg/otrasal-publikaciaen.php?n=156&otr=42

[a] previous year = 100

[b] annual average CPI, pervious year =100

[c] unemployment rates of population aged 15 years and over

As a result of adequate policies, although under very difficult conditions, Bulgaria achieved relatively good economic performance in the last four years leading up to 2008 (Table 2). The functioning currency board contributed positive results in the monetary stabilization and adjustment to a process of disinflation and fiscal consolidation. As the IMF reported, the fiscal tightening helped to curb the current account deficit to a level that could be strictly implemented (Aristovnik, 2007), serving to retain labor costs and maintain competitiveness. Structural reforms continued on a wide front: Privatization and enterprise restructuring were accelerated, land restitution was completed, and trade and price liberalization continued (see IMF Staff Country Report, April 2000). In the beginning of 2001, the private sector had already been producing nearly 70% of the gross value added and over 60% of GDP.

From 1997-2001, the government gave a sound commitment to the integration of Bulgaria with the EU structures. It followed a strong Eurodirected strategy. As a result, a budget surplus was achieved in 1998 and 1999, the public debt as a percentage of GDP decreased along with interest rates (Epstein & Jacoby, 2014). All these factors along with the fixed exchange ratio of the national currency brought Bulgaria closer to the requirements for participation in the European Monetary Union (EMU).

The period from 1 July 1997 onward, in the conditions of the currency board arrangements, marks the banking system stabilization. However, its further liberalization continued with the invasion of foreign capital in Bulgarian banks (combined with the inadequate control of the financial intermediation system). A number of banks went bankrupt, and others were merged, thus reducing the number of the banks to 17, the majority of which were foreign. The main effect was initially positive. The foreign investments brought know-how, improved the Bulgarian banks capital adequacy and thus returned the confidence in the system. In a relatively short time (only 3-4 years), the sector has turned to a normal functioning. Because of the implementation of the currency board, however, the state actually gave up its regulating capabilities, and the system was left on its own. The effect of this policy was very noticeable, particularly after 2005, when the credit (and the consumption of imported goods) raised rapidly despite the central bank's attempts to cool down the expansion.

The negative influence of this process soon became apparent. The commercial bank's strategy was focused mostly upon the expansion within the households and the sectors with a quick return, which led to a sharp decrease in the country's competitiveness. It was a logical consequence of the prioritized financing of hotels, restaurants and services on the count of strategic branches with some longer return terms. The last ones could not cover the raised interest costs, and that is why they were left without funding. As a result, the structure of production in the country degenerated (Sariiski & Rangelova, 2013). Bulgaria now produces and ships abroad primarily products with lower value added, which led to a profit decline and hence to further economic deterioration. The second problem was that the credit expansion stimulated a rapid growth of individual consumption in Bulgaria (Sariiski, 2010). This led, on the one hand, to an imports increase (on the count of local goods consumption) and, on the other, to an increase in the living standard and wages of employees. For this reason, the process of relocation that was going until then and supporting at least to some extent the economic development had quickly collapsed.

Furthermore, the negative influence of the intensive banking sector liberalization became apparent later in 2008, when Bulgaria felt the first effects of the global financial crisis. Currently, Bulgaria is one of the five European countries with highest share of bad loans (NPL). Unfortunately, the losses in one way or another are being now absorbed and passed on to the regular banking system consumers, i.e., the population and business (Sariiski, 2011).

The negative consequences of the transition to a market economy had a stimulating effect on the lending in Bulgaria, although it may seem paradoxical. Seizing the savings of the population during the first stage of the transition to 1997 and the loss of jobs due to the closure of state-owned enterprises brought about an unemployment rate of 18% in 2001. The latter, combined with the pumping of the added value by the use of illegal practices (such as the privatization of the input and output of the economic activity) led to the concentration of wealth and economic power in a limited group of individuals with excessively high incomes and consequently to a rapid impoverishment of the rest of the people. Those individuals became unable to compensate for the contraction of income in ways other than the increase of debt. J. Stiglitz (2009) summarizes this very well: "*Increasing inequality means a transfer of money and assets from those at the bottom who can spend it to those at the top who can't. To the people at the bottom we saying that they should continue spending and we continue to lend to them.*" In a normal economic situation, the purchasing power parity decline would lead to a crisis of overproduction and offset the reduced income (albeit at the expense of an increase in debt), which, in turn, would lead to its revival. In Bulgaria, however, the principle was different because most of the production facilities were liquidated in the first phase of transition. That is why the lending stimulated just the import of consumer goods.

Thus, the status quo of the new economic structure was reinforced (Sonin, 2013). Preferences gradually, yet steadily, turned towards the import production; the qualification of employees in the manufacturing sector became permanently lost. The regenerative capacity of the real sector declined. For the banking system, negative consequences of this process occurred a few years later. It is well known that the banking sector could function independently of its foundation, which was the real sector, but the latter was progressively left without the necessary funding. During the period 1999-2006, the share of corporate loans gradually decreased from 81% to less than 60%. A significant stimulating role upon the loans demand at the later stage of transition was played by the expectations that resulted from the forthcoming accession of Bulgaria in the European Union (EU). According to a survey in 2010 on households' budgets, a considerable portion of Bulgarians suffered a permanent deficit (Sariiski, 2010). For more than half of the respondents, the total of debt servicing and the cost of vital minimum provisions (including, e.g., costs for food, utilities, and the provision of housing) are close to 100% or even higher, i.e., part of these budgets maintain a permanent deficit. For this reason, the regular servicing of loans for more than 70% of the respondents is problematic, which reflects the deterioration of the commercial banks' loan portfolio and the contraction of the retail segment.

In fact, the increase in retail lending during the late phase of the transition until the beginning of the global crisis (2008-2009) was fully at the expense of the shrinking of corporate loans' share. What further aggravated the economic potential was the issuance of the bulk of loans to ventures that could not contribute to long-term economic growth (Sariiski & Rangelova, 2013). During the period 2005-2008, quick return was the main priority of financial intermediaries in the process of the distribution of accumulated financial resources. For instance, 30% of loans were granted for trade and repair, 18% were granted for construction, 15% were given for real estate and renting activities. The sectors with a high share of value added by definition (or at least the ones that could contribute to economic growth in the long run), such as telecommunications, education and construction, received less than 1/6 of the credits. It should be noted that from 2005-2008, credit increased its role in the economic life — corporate loans grew from BGN 11.1 bn. (USD 6.7 bn.) to BGN 30.3 bn. (USD 22 bn.). Due to the unfavorable sector structure, the rapid lending growth was reflected primarily in the price increase and inflation of the real estate market's speculative bubble.

The latter created a vicious circle that could not be interrupted. Lending to sectors with fast and high returns led to a growth of the interest rates, and at the end of 2008, they reached 11-12% in the corporate segment and over 15% in consumer loans up to 1 year. As a result, the strategic sectors were deprived of financing. Because those sectors were uncompetitive at such interest rate levels, and because the stock exchange development was weak, they could not seek funding through this channel. The problem here was that the effect, and the liquidation of the economic development potential, occurred only in the medium and long term, when the lending opportunities were shrinking and banks were forced to decrease their business. It is notable that from 2010 onwards, lending rates were low, but households' credit was decreasing. Low incomes and hopes for their upcoming promotion stimulated borrowing again, which would be discontinued in the next economic downturn.

We are still far from the next lending boom. The people taking credit now are primarily desperate households, pressed by creditors such as public utilities and health services. Indicative in this respect is the dynamics of interest rates on consumer loans. It increased continuously from the beginning of 2011, reaching 22% at the end of 2013H1.This would not have happen if government intervention in the considered processes was more active or if there was a functioning mechanism for linking managerial compensation with the long-term performance of their managed entities. Reflection on those aspects of the evolution and development of capitalism are offered by Kaletsky (2010). However, the neoliberal idea is not compatible with such a concept, and it leads to the establishment of an environment that encourages the mandate thinking in corporate governance and state authorities. As Nassim Taleb summarizes: "*We found ourselves in an awkward situation, in which the worst features of capitalism and socialism were combined: profits were privatized and losses were socialized. We taxpayers have the worst*" (Lacqua & O'Donnell, 2009). The contemporary culture of corporate governance and the weak development of corporate social responsibility led to the establishment of a system that maximizes the benefits of those directly involved in management at the expense of long-term company prospects and of the future benefits to its stakeholders. Thus, the compensation asymmetry increases, thereby ignoring the long-term economic development prospects.

The tools for effective shareholder control upon the remuneration of the executive board and its members are practically negligible (Bebchuk & Fried, 2004). This pushes the management principles toward the ideas of short-term maximization of personal benefits and far from focusing upon long-term strategic goals. The entirety of contemporary management can be summarized in one sentence: "*The idea is to get in and get out as fast as you can, and, from the standpoint of someone who's trying to maximize his gain, that's the right strategy*" (Bogle, 2005, p. 762). This is the strategy followed in every deregulated sector, and the negative effects in finance are more than obvious. The former chairman of FED Alan Greenspan stated in October 2008: "*I made a mistake in presuming that the self-interests of organizations, specifically banks and others were such as that they were best capable of protecting their own shareholders and their equity in the firms*". The record was widely spread in the global network with a title "Greenspan Destroys Deregulation in 16 Seconds".

One could summarize that when the banking system ownership in Bulgaria was initially transferred to foreign partners, the overall effect was positive. The foreigners quickly managed to capitalize the banking system, to bring the necessary know-how, to put the banking upon market grounds and to restore the confidence. For a short time after the local crisis, Bulgaria built a modern and well-functioning banking system.

The problem was that other than the banks, no other industry would function well in the country because of the decapitalization process that led to the liquidation of enterprises, the loss of jobs and so on. More serious was the problem of the liquidation of the deterioration of intangible assets, such as primary human capital and confidence in the system. The government institutions have in every way demonstrated that they cannot be a reliable partner in the social contract. A typical example is the dysfunctional health care system, which employs a unilateral obligation to supply funds for health care but without the reciprocal commitment of the state to ensure the specific health status of the population. This reflects very negatively on the banking system as it strengthens the savings motive of the population; this, in turn, deprives the local economy of the recovery potential.

For this reason, the restoration of Bulgarian business depends entirely on the foreign markets' recovery (Jacoby, 2014). Bulgarian business agents are not willing to invest in the activities expansion, adopting a passive attitude in the lending activity. Data for 2013 show that bank loans are maintaining a constant level. The Bulgarian banks succeeded only to compensate their loan portfolios' depreciation, but the overall volume and structures remain unchanged. It should be noted that the totals include a few banks with growth ratios exceeding 30%, i.e., if one excludes such banks from the statistics, the lending actually shrinks.

5. Effect of the world financial crisis of 2008-2009 on the banking sector in Bulgaria

In the period preceding the financial and economic crisis in 2008-2009, a new accumulation of negatives in the banking sector was observed. Commercial banks granted credit to increasingly less reliable customers for the sake of the gain of the market share (Almunia et al, 2010; Erdinç, 2010). The Bulgarian National Bank was unable to control this process because the currency board was strongly limiting its capacity to influence the money supply. Despite several attempts, the Bulgarian National Bank did not succeed in controlling the banks' expansion (Sariiski, 2011). As a result, Bulgaria achieved the fastest pace of lending in the region of CEE during the period 2006-2008. However, it "mined" the sector in the name of winning the market share; the banks gradually lowered their criteria of reliability. The loans from this period are the main reason for the losses from deteriorated exposures. A large portion of the loans past due over 90 days were granted during the period 2005-2007.

Another, even more serious problem of the banking sector was the missing potential for its recovery. The status to which the economy was brought as a result of the transition processes led to a weak realization of financial products. Local businesses are functioning at low profitability rates, and the main part of the value added is created in sectors recovering particularly slowly by definition (such as tourism and real estate). Furthermore, the weak domestic market does not encourage the manufacturing recovery, and it continues to be reflected in the reduction of the business cash flows and difficulties in debt servicing. In addition, strict fiscal discipline contributes to the deterioration of the economic and social environment; the implementation of a restrictive policy to maintain a balanced budget in times of crisis caused by limited demand is not the right approach (Petkov, 2014).

The prevailing attitude of both investors and consumers still remains passive, and this is largely due to a sense of insecurity among economic agents. Throughout the transition period in Bulgaria, the state institutions have repeatedly demonstrated that they lack the capacity to provide a stable environment, and the general direction of their actions is pointed to their withdrawal from economic life.

The state would not commit to any warranties of providing living, educational and health minimums to protect property rights or to implement long-term strategies. The private interests of public officials (or sometimes the absence of interests) lead to a delay of specific measures that would help not only the banking sector but the entire economy, such as the construction of e-government and the access to property registry.

Therefore, the situation at the time actually blocks the money transmission. The insurance motive encourages people to increase their savings. The financial intermediaries, however, are unable to realize cumulated resources because business is not willing to undertake new ventures. Everyone would find themselves losing in this situation because the market was left long enough to itself.

6. Conclusions: Summarizing the negative effects of neo-liberal policies on the Bulgarian financing sector

The failure of neo-liberalism can be summarized in the following way:

First, neo-liberal policy distorts the very idea of a free market because having a monopoly upon the key resources and zero regulation of (in fact) quasi-market practices could not be connected with liberalism; this environment favors development of incorrect and most importantly unproductive practices.

Second, the very focus of neo-liberal ideas, which defend the release of all marketing elements and processes with zero planning, is wrong because it is essentially a return to a stage of development before the emergence of modern society. It should be noted that an entirely unrestricted and unregulated flow of processes are traits of the wilderness.

Third, neo-liberalism creates conditions for state institutions "to play on both sides of the street." If one has to stick tightly to neo-liberal ideas, the state should be engaged primarily with the guarantees of the free market's normal functioning and not interfere in business. Practically, however, the state authorities constantly interfere in the functioning of markets by protecting certain specific private interests. The state officially does not obtrude in the free markets, but it unofficially supports its favorites in various ways, e.g., the direction of the state orders to specific enterprises, timely VAT reimbursement, and excessively close co-operation with selected partners that borders on inappropriate.

The development of the banking sector in Bulgaria in the transition to a market economy shows certain negative effects on the Bulgarian banking sector and the economy as a whole. These effects can be formulated, as follows:

- The first negative effect of neo-liberal policy is the exportation of ownership (and control) upon banking system assets. The most profitable business of utmost importance to the economic development was given to foreign investors, who can now carry out their own policy and, moreover, operate on behalf of others, for instance, on the count of interest-free financing by the European Central Bank.
- The second negative effect is the bringing of the banking system to a condition in which it is deregulated in a position of "self-defense". Introduction of the currency board in 1997 fixed the local currency to the German mark and since the emerging new currency in 1999 to Euro, which, on the one hand, contradicts the exporter's interest, and on the other hand, restricts the regulator and strongly limits its capacity to manage the stability of money supply.
- The third negative effect is the placement of the banking sector before 1997 into the role of mediator in totally unfavorable assets redistribution and the emergence of the local oligarchy. During hyperinflation, household savings were transferred to the so-called credit millionaires. This led to the exhaustion of confidence in the local banking institutions and to their isolation from the economic turnover. It should be noted that for a long time, the transactions in Bulgaria were settled in cash rather than by bank transfer.
- The fourth negative effect concerns the real economy agents as the bank's clients. It is known that the banking sector gains profits primarily from the real economy; however, Bulgaria's case is different. The "regular" companies have low profitability indicators; the majority of the value added is derived from monopolies. Similar is the situation with regular customers, i.e. households and individuals. Although some stabilization of income is formally reported, their personal perception is still about impoverishment and increasing difficulties in loans servicing.
- The fifth negative effect is the elimination of prospects for the long-term growth of the banking sector due to the passive attitude of the state power, which still remains isolated from the banks. Its main tool of management and interference in lending is the Bulgarian Development Bank, but it is more often used to serve private interests rather than for the conduction of a state policy aimed to encourage the financing of strategic projects. The government could use fiscal measures such as tax relief on interest rates for lending to certain sectors, but it fails to do so because it contradicts the neo-liberal idea of non-intervention.
- The sixth negative effect results from the weak protection of the taxpayers. The protection of small savers provided from the *State Fund for Deposit In-*

surance is not reliable because resources in the fund are limited, and their use is regulated in a wishful style. This can lead to a rapid outflow of deposits at the first signs of instability and hence to a liquidity crisis.

- The seventh negative effect is entirely on the count of commercial bank owners. Neoliberal ideas of aggravation of the internal competition determine the mandate thinking in managers, including the maintenance of current profits at the expense of future development prospects. The aftermath of this style of thinking was manifested clearly in the beginning of the last financial crisis of 2008-2009.

In summarizing, the transition period has effectively led to the establishment of a modern banking system in the country, but this system serves only the accumulation of profit (almost all of it belonging to the foreign investors) and does not promote the processes of recovery and growth.

References:

Almunia, M., Bénétrix, A. S., Eichengreen, B. J., O'Rourke K. H., & Rua, G. (2010). From great depression to great credit crisis: similarities, differences and lessons. *Economic Policy*, 25 (62), 219–265.

Amable B. (2010). A change of model requires a new balance of power. In A. Watt & A. Botsch (Eds.), *After the crisis: towards a sustainable growth model* (pp. 151-153). Brussels: European Trade Union Institute.

Aristovnik, A. (2007). Are current account deficits in Eastern Europe and former Soviet Union too high? *Transformations in business & economics*, 6 (1), 32-52.

Bebchuk, L. A., Fried, J. M. (2004). *Pay without performance: The unfulfilled promise of executive compensation*. Cambridge, MA: Harvard University Press.

Bank Octopus hidden in the secret report „Dobrev" [Банков октопод скрит в секретния доклад „Добрев"] (2010, April 9). [Online forum comment]. Retrieved from: http://frognews.bg/news_22026/Bankov_oktopod_skrit_v_sekretniia_doklad_Dobrev/

Bogle, J. C. (2005). The executive compensation system is broken. *Journal of Corporation Law*, 30 (4), 761-765.

Campos, N. F., Coricelli, F. (2012). Financial liberalization and reversals: political and economic determinants. *Economic Policy*, 27 (71), 483-513.

Einstein, A. (1949). Why socialism? *Monthly Review*, 1 (1), 9-15.

Epstein, R. A. & Jacoby, W. (2014). Eastern Enlargement Ten Years On: Transcending the East–West Divide. JCMS: *Journal of Common Market Studies*, 52 (1), 1–16.

Erdinç, D. (2010). Does a credit boom increase bank fragility? *Eastern European Economics*, 48 (3), 68-87.

Fries, S., Neven, D., Seabright, P., & Taci, A. (2006). Market entry, privatization and bank performance in transition. *Economics of Transition*, 14 (4), 579–610.

Greespan, A. (2008, October 23). *Greenspan destroys deregulation in 16 seconds* [Video file]. Retrieved from https://www.youtube.com/watch?v=bAH-o7oEiyY

Innes, A. (2014).The Political Economy of State Capture in Central Europe. *Journal of Common Market Studies*, 52 (1), 88–104.

Jacoby, W. (2014). The EU Factor in Fat Times and in Lean: Did the EU Amplify the Boom and Soften the Bust? *Journal of Common Market Studies*, 52 (1), 52–70.

Kaletsky, A. (2010). *Capitalism 4.0: The birth of a New Economy*. London, UK: Bloomsbury Paperbacks.

Kornai, J. (2006). The great transformation of Central Eastern Europe. *Economics of Transition*, 14 (2), 207–244.

Lacqua, F., & O'Donnell, S. (2009, January 29). Taleb says: *Nationalize banks, you can't trust them* [Press release]. Retrieved from http://www.bloomberg.com/apps/news?pid=newsarchive&sid=asvQUPgW.EZY

Miller, J. B., & Petranov, S. (2000). The first wave of mass privatization in Bulgaria and its immediate aftermath. *Economics of Transition*, 8 (1), 225–250.

Marangos, J. (2009), The evolution of the term 'Washington Consensus', *Journal of Economic Surveys*, 23 (2), 350-384.

Minassian, G. (2013). Bulgarian banking: looking for sustainability. *Contemporary Economics*, 7 (3), 95-114.

National Statistical Institute (2014). Main Macroeconomic Indicators, 2007. Retrieved from http://www.nsi.bg/otrasal-publikaciaen.php?n=156&otr=42

Palast, G. (2004). *The Best Democracy Money Can Buy*. New York, NY: Plume.

Palley, T. I. (2002). *A new development paradigm domestic demand-led growth* [Discussion paper, Foreign Policy in Focus project]. Retrieved from http://www.thomaspalley.com/docs/articles/economic_development/new_development_paradigm.pdf

Petkov, V. S. (2014). Advantages and disadvantages of fiscal discipline in Bulgaria in times of crisis. *Contemporary Economics*, 8 (1), 47-56.

Rahn, R. W., & Utt, R. D. (1990). Paper on the Project on Economic Growth and Transition to a Market Economy in Bulgaria. USA National Chamber Foundation for Republic of Bulgaria, Washington, DC.

Sariiski, G., & Rangelova, R. (2013). Development of the banking activity as an economic growth factor. In *Post-crisis economic development in the EU and Bulgaria: Proceedings of the international conference, Economic Research Institute, Bulgarian Academy of Sciences* (pp. 277-292). Sofia: GorexPress.

Sariiski, G. (2011). *The Global Crisis - Origins and Impact on the Bulgarian Banking System*. Sofia: Economic Policy Institute.

Sariiski, G. (2010). Problems of the Bulgarian households' indebtedness. In M. Trifonova (Ed.), *Competitiveness of the Bulgarian economy: Proceedings of the IV Conference* (pp. 51-63). Sofia: Economic Policy Institute.

Sonin, K. (2013). The end of economic transition. *Economics of Transition*, 21 (1), 1–10.

Stiglitz, J. (2010). Freefall: *Free Markets and the Sinking of the Global Economy*. New York, NY: W. W. Norton & Company.

Stiglitz, J. (2009, March 17). Growing economic inequality lies at root of global crisis. *Shanghai Daily*. Retrieved from http://www.shanghaidaily.com/Opinion/foreign-perspectives/Growing-economic-inequality-lies-at-root-of-global-crisis/shdaily.shtml

Wagner, H. (2000). Central Banking in Transition Countries, *Eastern European Economics*, 38 (4), 6-53.

Wilczyński, R. (2011). Global financial governance: a perspective from the International Monetary Fund. *Contemporary Economics*, 5 (1), 4-16.

12

The Peculiarities of State Regulation of Innovation Activities of Enterprises in the Global Economy

Yuri A. Kolesnikov[1], Tatiana V. Epifanova[2], Anastasia M. Usenko[2], Ekaterina Parshina[2], Victoria N. Ostrovskaya[3]

ABSTRACT

The purposes of this article are to determine the peculiarities of state regulation of the innovational activity of enterprises in the global economy, to determine the level of connection between a country's competitiveness in the global economy and the effectiveness of state regulation of innovational activity in that country, and to develop recommendations for improving the process of state regulation of innovational activity of enterprises in the global economy.

To determine the level of connection between a country's competitiveness in the global economy and the effectiveness of state regulation of innovational activity in that country, this study uses the method of correlation analysis, which calculates the coefficient of correlation using mathematical instruments and program methods (MS Excel and MathCad). To evaluate the effectiveness of state regulation of innovational activity of enterprises in the global economy, this study uses a specially developed proprietary methodology.

As a result of this research, the authors determined the following peculiarities of state regulation of innovational activity of enterprises under the conditions of the global economy: an increased role of the innovational sphere in the development of economies, an accelerated rate of development of innovations, activation of the export of innovations, regulation of the entire economy through regulation of the sphere of innovations, and domination by indirect methods of state regulation of innovational activity of enterprises.

For the purpose of improving the process of state regulation of the innovational activity of enterprises under the conditions of the global economy, the authors of this research offer an optimization model.

KEY WORDS: state regulation, innovational activity, enterprise, global economy, knowledge economy

---

[1] Southern Federal University, Russia; [2] Rostov State Economic University, Russia; [3] Moscow Humanitarian and Economic Institute (Stavropol branch), Russia

Introduction

At present, one of the most important trends in the development of the global economy is the formation of the knowledge economy. The most economically developed countries are in the final stages of this process. Developing countries are focusing their economic development on accelerated formation of their own knowledge economies. Under these conditions, the competition among countries in the global economy is reaching a new level.

While in the pre-industrial economy competition took place in the agrarian sphere, in the industrial

Correspondence concerning this article should be addressed to: **Victoria N. Ostrovskaya**, Department of economics and management of Moscow Humanitarian and Economic Institute (Stavropol branch), 330 Mira St., Stavropol, Russia.
E-mail: ostrovskayav@mail.ru

economy it took place in the sphere of industrial production, and in the post-industrial economy it takes place in the service sphere, in the knowledge economy – as the highest level of the post-industrial economy – competition takes place in the sphere of innovations and scientific research. This requires the development of the sphere of science and education and an increase in the innovational activity of enterprises.

Therefore, issues of state regulation of the innovational activity of enterprises are particularly important in this context. In order to provide the necessary support and stimulation of the innovational activity of enterprises and simultaneously avoid unnecessary expenditures of state budgets, it is essential to determine the peculiarities of state regulation of the innovational activities of enterprises in the modern economy. This is the focus of this article.

On this basis, the authors of this study hypothesize that, in the global economy, the importance of state regulation of innovational activity of enterprises grows, as there is a close connection between a country's competitiveness in the global economy and the effectiveness of state regulation of innovational activity in that country.

The purpose of this article is to verify this hypothesis, which aims to determine the peculiarities of state regulation of innovational activity of enterprises in the global economy, to determine the level of connection between a country's competitiveness in the global economy and the effectiveness of state regulation of innovational activity in that country, and to develop recommendations for improving the process of state regulation of innovational activity of enterprises in the global economy.

Literature review

The theoretical issues underlying state regulation of economies are examined by numerous current authors, in which they substantiate the necessity of state regulation of economic systems, discuss the level of necessary state interference into the workings of market processes, and determine the top-priority spheres of state regulation. Authors who have addressed these issues include (Adigamova, Safiullin, & Tufetulov, 2014; Bagautdinova, Malakhov, Vardanyan, & Shakhnina, 2014; Guerriero, 2013; Veselovsky, Abrashkin, Aleksakhina, & Pogodina, 2014; Zobova, Zagladina, Safiullin, & Malganova, 2014 etc.). Within state regulation of an economy, a policy of freetrading can be implemented, which aims at developing national markets and stimulating free competition (Dzeverina, 2013). A policy of protectionism, aimed at protecting domestic manufacturers from external competition (Ryspekova & Beissekeyeva, 2013), can also be used. Top-priority spheres of state regulation are the defense industry and agriculture (Suntsova, 2012).

Methodological aspects of state regulation of the economy are related to studies of the most important characteristics of the applied and prospective instruments of state economic policy, the peculiarities of applying these instruments in various spheres of the economy under various economic conditions, and methods for evaluating the effectiveness of state interference into economic processes. These topics are addressed in the works of such researchers as (Gataullin, Askarov, Khuzhakhmetova, & Yarkov, 2015; Radu, 2012; Ryazantsev, Karabulatova, Ter-Akopov, Pismennaya, & Bozhenko, 2015; Suntsova, 2013, Tkhakushinov, Zarubin, Nekrasova, Kuizheva, & Ovsyannikova, 2015). Economic methods of regulation include monetary and financial policy (Lan, Pickles, & Zhu, 2015). Administrative methods of economic regulation include such measures as prohibition, permission, and enforcement (Lomeiko, 2015). The effectiveness of state regulation of the economy is determined by the ratio of received economic profit to expenditures on regulations.

Many authors have examined the practical aspects of state regulation of economies using the examples of various countries and regions that have successfully used specific tools of state interference in economies. Some authors have also examined the causes of failure of such interference, obstacles on the path to successful state regulation of economic systems, and possibilities for modeling and forecasting the consequences of state interference with market processes. These authors include (Agénor, Alper, & Pereira da Silva, 2014; Charlot, Malherbet, & Terra, 2015; Nurunnabi, 2015; Popkova, Yurev, Stepicheva, & Denisov, 2015; Uberti, Lemay-Hébert, & Demukaj, 2014; Wang, Zhang, & Zeng, 2016).

Modern Russia uses a state policy of protectionism, within which the state protects internal markets from foreign enterprises (rivals) in order to protect domestic manufacturers (Duncan, 2014). The USA and countries of Western Europe use a policy of free trade, within which the maximum effectiveness of market mechanisms is achieved (Warren & Wood, 2014). The consequences of state interference in economic processes are often modeled, but due to a variety of factors, the forecasts are not always precise (Kim & Kim, 2014).

Many authors have studied the innovational activity of enterprises under modern economic conditions. These authors have determined the most promising directions of innovational initiatives, the most important factors and conditions supporting the development and implementation of innovations at enterprises in various countries around the world, and the national peculiarities of innovational activity. The works of the following scholars should be recognized: (Allan, Crouchley & Robertson, 2012; Anatolyevna & Vladimirivna, 2014; Bayev & Podshivalova, 2013; Nechaev & Antipina, 2015; Ryapukhina, Suprun, Doroshenko, Bukhonova, & Somina, 2015), etc. Innovational activity can improve internal business processes (Imanbekova, 2014) and modify existing ones, or it can lead to the development and manufacture of innovative products (Tovt, 2014). Innovations ensure the development of enterprises and support their competitiveness (Belkin & Belkina, 2013).

A review of the literature on this topic showed that despite extensive discussion of the issues of state regulation of economies and innovational activity of enterprises, there is a lack of complex research into the peculiarities of state regulation of the innovational activity of enterprises in the global economy. This article seeks to fill this gap.

Method

To verify the proposed hypothesis and determine the level of connection between a country's competitiveness in the global economy and the effectiveness of state regulation of innovational activity in that country, this study uses the method of correlation analysis, which calculates coefficients of correlation using mathematical instruments and program methods; in this case, the authors chose MS Excel and MathCad.

With the help of this method, the authors determined the dependence of the value of the index of global competitiveness of countries on the level of effectiveness of state regulation of innovational activity of enterprises in the global economy. For the purpose of evaluating the effectiveness of state regulation of the innovational activity of enterprises in the global economy, this study uses a specially developed proprietary methodology:

$$Ceff=Pinn+Einn/Finn+Rinn \quad (1)$$

where Ceff – coefficient of effectiveness of state regulation of innovational activity of enterprise in the global economy;
Pinn – volume of innovational products, works, and services, USD million;
Einn – export of innovational technologies, USD million;
Finn – state financing of innovational research, USD million;
Rinn – expenditures of business for scientific research and implementation of innovations into production, USD million.

As is seen in formula (1), within this methodology, the coefficient of effectiveness of state regulation of innovational activity of enterprises in the global economy is calculated, which is found as the ratio of the sum of the volume of innovational goods, works, and services and exports of innovational technologies to the ratio of the sum of the volume of state financing of innovational research and expenditures of the business for scientific research and implementation of innovations into production.

Results

On the basis of statistical information regarding development of the innovational sphere, we build a compiled table that contains information on the dynamics of the values of indicators of effectiveness of state regulation of innovational activity of enterprises in the global economy in the USA, France, and Russia for 2010-2014 (Table 1).

This allows calculating the values of the coefficients of effectiveness of state regulation of innovational activity of enterprises in the global economy in the USA, France, and Russia for 2010-2014 (Table 1). Official statistics of the global competitiveness of the USA, France, and Russia for 2010-2014 are shown in Table 2.

By calculating parameters of the function of paired linear regression for characteristics of the dependence of a country's competitiveness in the global economy (y)

Table 1. Dynamics of values of indicators of effectiveness of state regulation of innovational activity of enterprises in the global economy in the USA, France, and Russia for 2010-2014

Year	Values of indicators of effectiveness			
	Pinn	Einn	Finn	Rinn
		USA		
2010	2,401,684.40	89,791.00	58,364.00	37,371.87
2011	3,160,111.05	94,280.55	59,823.10	40,259.78
2012	4,213,481.40	98,994.58	61,318.68	46,955.90
2013	5,745,810.40	103,944.31	62,851.64	53,836.14
2014	7,015,732.00	109,141.52	64,422.94	57,676.74
		France		
2010	849,826.79	8,865.51	20,906.10	34,495.07
2011	1,118,193.14	10,904.58	22,996.71	37,944.57
2012	1,490,924.19	13,412.63	25,296.38	41,739.03
2013	2,033,132.91	16,497.53	27,826.02	45,912.93
2014	2,482,489.78	20,291.97	30,608.62	50,504.22
		Russia		
2010	18,474.50	3,854.57	3,473.26	7,474.37
2011	24,308.55	5,071.80	3,656.06	8,051.96
2012	32,411.40	6,420.00	4,829.22	9,391.18
2013	44,198.54	7,642.86	5,475.69	10,767.23
2014	53,967.17	8,991.60	6,543.10	11,535.35

Source: Adapted from "Russia in numbers. Scientific research and innovations 2015: Bulletin of Rosstat" by Rosstat (2015). Retrieved from Retrieved from http://www.gks.ru/free_doc/doc_2015/rusfig/rus-15.pdf

and the effectiveness of state regulation of innovational activity in that country (x) on the basis of statistical data with the help of the program MathCad, we have the following models:

$y(x)_{USA}=0.91+0.15x.$

$y(x)_{France}=1.39+0.34x.$

$y(x)_{Russia}=1.65+2.84x.$

Let us evaluate the quality of the received regression models. Index b=0.14 shows that with an increase in the effectiveness of state regulation of the innovational activity of an enterprise by 1, the competitiveness of the USA grows by 0.15, of France – by 0.34, and of Russia – by 2.84. Coefficients of correlation for received models - $r_{xy}=0.97$. It is possible to conclude that there is a close correlation between the viewed indicators. Let us calculate the coefficient of determination: $D=r^2_{xy}*100\%=97\%$.

Consequently, the competitiveness of a country in the global economy can be 97% explained by the effectiveness of state regulation of innovational activity in that country. Let us evaluate the model of linear regression through average error of approxi-

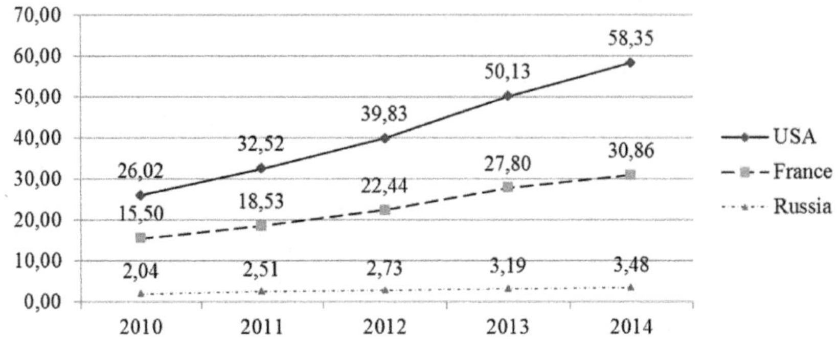

Figure 1. Dynamics of values of the coefficient of effectiveness of state regulation of innovational activity of enterprises in the global economy of the USA, France, and Russia for 2010-2014
Source: Adapted from "Russia in numbers. Scientific research and innovations 2015: Bulletin of Rosstat" by Rosstat (2015). Retrieved from http://www.gks.ru/free_doc/doc_2015/rusfig/rus-15.pdf

Table 2. Statistics of global competitiveness of the USA, France, and Russia for 2010-2014

Year	USA		France		Russia	
	Value of index	Position in rankings	Value of index	Position in rankings	Value of index	Position in rankings
2010	99.091	3	74.372	28	49.318	51
2011	100.00	1	71.394	29	58.376	49
2012	97.755	2	70.003	29	55.159	48
2013	100.000	1	71.327	28	56.809	42
2014	100.000	1	67.941	27	57.997	38

Source: Adapted from "IMD world competitiveness yearbook 2014" by IMD (2014). Retrieved from https://www.imd.org/uupload/IMD.WebSite/wcc/WCYResults/1/scoreboard_2014.pdf

mation, which for this model is 3%. This shows that the model is of high quality.

Under the conditions of the global economy, the sense changes and specific peculiarities of innovational activity of enterprises emerge. Innovations from additional competitive advantages and unique features gradually become inseparable attributes of conducting business and necessary conditions for the successful existence of modern enterprises.

With the accumulation of experience in creating and implementing innovations, sustainable public opinion regarding an innovator's responsibility for his inventions is formed. Modern consumers become more and more knowledgeable and selective regarding innovational products and are interested in the social and ecological responsibility of businesses; they prefer responsible innovations that do no harm but rather produce only profit for the workers who manufacture them and for the surrounding environment and society.

In recent years, both patent law and systems of protection for innovators' interests have been actively developing. This is necessary to support interest in new inventions. At the same time, many innovations are borrowed from multiple rivals after the termination of patents for the purpose of preserving competitiveness, as consumers will not purchase outdated products and will instead choose new goods once innovations are implemented and produced by at least one company in the market.

High-quality transformation of the sphere of innovations predetermines the emergence of certain peculiarities of state regulation of the innovational activity of enterprises in the global economy. First, the innovational activity of enterprises determines national competitiveness, which increases the importance of regulating this type of activity and makes it a top-priority in an economy's development. At present, the attention of governments in developed countries is focused on innovational enterprises, as the entire society is interested in their successful functioning and development.

Second, under the conditions of globalization, there is close cooperation among various economic systems. This ensures favorable conditions for the exchange of accumulated experience and the transfer of knowledge within the general global economic system. Under these conditions, the tendency to export innovations develops, and innovations become the objects of the foreign economic trade relations of various countries.

Here we face a contradiction of interests in countries that export innovations. On the one hand, exporting innovations generates profit, stimulates revenues for the state budget, and contributes to development of the national economy. However, on the other hand, innovations determine the competitive advantages of a country in the global economy, and their export makes innovations generally accessible, which eliminates this advantage.

This contradiction can be partially solved through export not of innovative technologies but rather of innovative goods that are manufactured with the help of these technologies. This allows countries to preserve their competitive advantages and develop exports not of a single technology but of a series of innovative products to various countries around the world.

Third, under the conditions of an innovational economy, new technologies are implemented in all spheres of the economy, so it is possible to regulate the whole economy through regulation of the sphere of innovations. In other words, investments in new technologies positively influence the whole economic system and stimulate its development.

This motivates developing countries to build innovation-oriented economies, which are capable of generating innovations, distributing new knowledge in all spheres of the economy, and ensuring their quick implementation into productive activities of national enterprises.

Fourth, the rate of technology creation is accelerating. While a hundred years ago, the cycle of technological renewal required approximately 30 years, at the beginning of the new millennium, this decreased to 7-10 years, and innovational leaps currently take place each year. This causes a very rapid aging of technologies and equipment and creates a necessity for constant productive modernization.

For this reason, the governments of the most economically developed countries finance investment projects to create new technologies and not to develop manufacturing for innovative products. The efforts of the state are usually directed at realizing long-term research projects, which are prospective but insufficiently attractive for private investors.

Fifth, this study notes the domination of indirect methods of state regulation of the innovational activity of enterprises over methods of direct regulation. This is expressed by a reduction in the state budget in the share of financing for the sphere of science and innovation, the general structure of financing for the innovational activity of enterprises, and the domination of private innovations in this sphere.

This is caused by the increased interest of private investors in the innovational sphere and the goal of saving the assets of the state budget. Moreover, in recent years, under the influence of integration processes and under conditions of global competition, there has been growing interest among enterprises in financing scientific research and implementing innovational technologies into production for the purpose

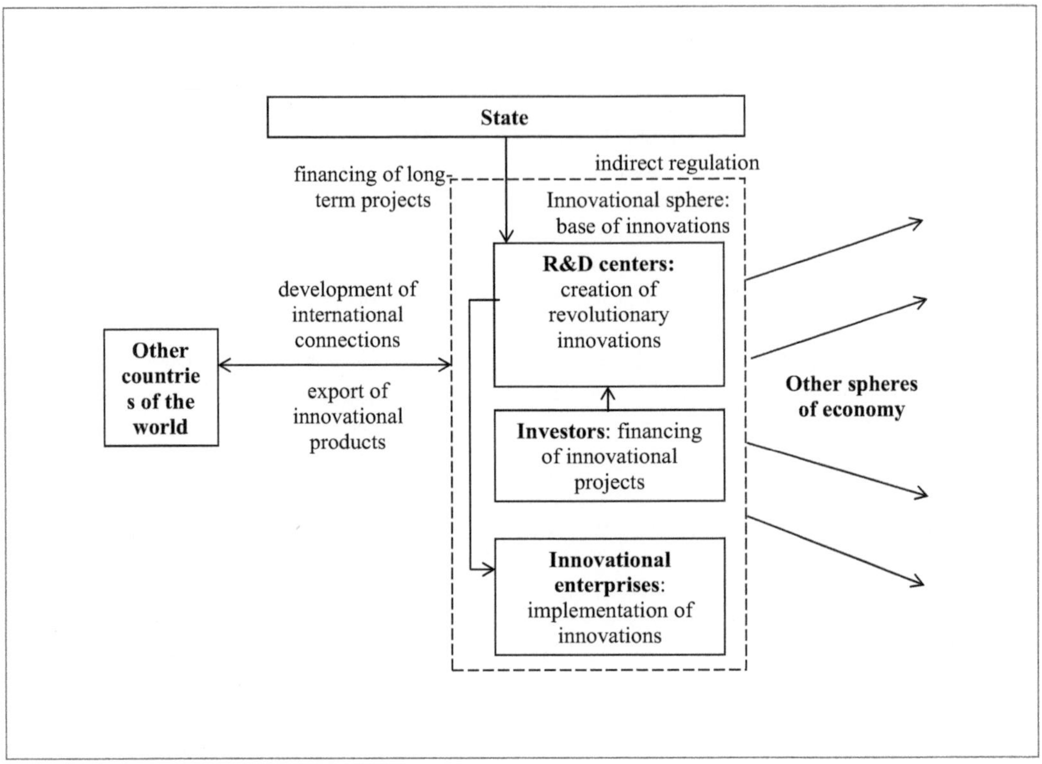

Figure 2. Optimization model of state regulation of innovational activity of enterprises in the global economy

of preserving competitiveness and preserving or increasing market share.

The above features are particular to the global economy as a whole and can be manifested to different extents in various countries, due to national peculiarities and levels of economic development. However, despite differences in the innovational spheres of various countries, they are all interested in their own development. This research offers the following recommendations for improving the process of state regulation of the innovational activity of enterprises in the global economy:

- rejecting the model of overcoming the development of innovations, which supposes the development of evolutionary innovations aimed at improving existing technologies in existing markets and transitioning to the development of revolutionary innovations, which supposes the creation of completely new products and the establishment of new markets;
- formation of the basis of innovation, which should connect innovators, investors, and entrepreneurs. This creates favorable conditions for commercialization of innovations and stimulates their quick integration into productive activities of modern enterprises;
- development of international connections in the sphere of innovations, especially among developing countries. This will allow the exchange of experience and the conduct of joint research to create innovations by means of combining human and financial resources;
- development of institutional bases and infrastructural provisions for the creation and implementation of innovations into production. This is especially important for developing countries, where there are no platforms for the development of innovations; this is a serious barrier to creating innovation-oriented economies in these countries.

To realize the above recommendations, the authors of this research offer an optimization model of state regulation of the innovational activity of enterprises in the global economy (Fig. 2).

Conclusion

As a result of correlation analysis, the close connection between the global competitiveness of countries (in terms of the level of effectiveness of state regulation of innovational activity of enterprises in the global economy) was determined using the examples of the USA, France, and Russia. This proves the hypothesis of this article and shows that in the global economy, the need for state regulation of the innovational activity of enterprises is especially high.

It should be noted that the hypothesis of this article is more applicable to developed countries, as they have more capabilities and opportunities for the creation and implementation of innovations. However, to reduce the gap between various countries in the global economy, it is necessary to intensify innovative activities in developing countries. Taking into account their unfavorable institutional conditions and entrepreneurial climates, the key role in increasing the innovative activity of enterprises in developing countries belongs to the state.

This theory could be further developed due to the strengthening of global competition. The innovational economy is the highest form of economic development. That is why, when conducting further research in this sphere, it is expedient to pay special attention to the development of corresponding institutional and infrastructural environments and to the issue of international economic cooperation in the innovational sphere.

An advantage of this methodology for evaluating the effectiveness of state regulation of the innovational activity of enterprises in the global economy is the simplicity and clarity of its calculations, which sets it apart from the multiple indices prepared by various international organizations. As a result of this evaluation, it was determined that the highest effectiveness of state regulation of innovational activity of enterprises is found in the USA, and the lowest – in Russia.

This is caused by national peculiarities, which include different levels of development of innovations and production and differences in other indicators of competitiveness (which are taken into account in the international rankings). It is also caused by differences in general economic effectiveness, which is related to the different qualities of the institutional infrastructure in these economic systems.

The peculiarities of state regulation of the innovational activity of enterprises in the global economy include the growing role of the innovational sphere in the development of economies, the acceleration of the rates at which innovations are developed, the exports of innovations, the regulation of the whole economy through regulation in the sphere of innovations, and the domination of indirect methods of state regulation of the innovational activity of enterprises.

For the purpose of improving the process of state regulation of the innovational activity of enterprises in the global economy, the authors of this study offer an optimization model that supposes a transition to the development of revolutionary innovations; the formation of innovative bases that connect innovators, investors, and businessmen; the development of international connections in the sphere of innovations; the development of institutional bases; and infrastructural provisions for the creation and implementation of innovations into production.

It can be concluded that the results of correlation analysis are limited by the size of selection and the use of only three studied countries. To obtain more precise results and calculate a global coefficient of correlation that reflects the dependence of the global competitiveness of countries on the level of effectiveness of state regulation of the innovational activity of enterprises in the global economy, it is advisable to conduct further research using examples from other countries around the world.

References

Adigamova F. F., Safiullin M. A., & Tufetulov A. M. (2014). Mechanism of state tax regulation in the global economy. *Mediterranean Journal of Social Sciences, 5*(24), 193-199.

Agénor, P. R., Alper, K. & Pereira da Silva, L. A. (2014). Sudden floods, macroprudential regulation and stability in an open economy. *Journal of International Money and Finance, 48*, 68-100.

Allan, R., Crouchley, R., & Robertson A. (2012). Collaborative and distributed innovation and research in business activity. In A. A. Juan, T. Daradoumis, M. Roca, S. E. Grasman, & J. Faulin (Eds.), *Collaborative and distributed e-research: Innovations in technologies, strategies and applications,* (pp. 310-330). United States of America, USA: Information Science Reference IGI Global.

Anatolyevna, M. I., Vladimirivna, P. L. (2014). The use of subcontracting mechanisms in education as means of the increase of business and innovation activity of higher education institutions. *World Applied Sciences Journal, 31*(5), 884-888.

Bagautdinova, N. G., Malakhov, V. P., Vardanyan, E. A., & Shakhnina, I. Z. (2014). Implementation of state regulation of small enterprises in the modern economy. *Mediterranean Journal of Social Sciences, 5*(18), 11-16.

Bayev, I. A., Podshivalova, M. V. (2013). Tasks of institutional support to increase innovation activity of small business in the region. *Economy of Region, 2013*(1), 189-198.

Belkin, V. N., & Belkina, N. A. (2013). Ways of increasing enterprises' innovation activity. *Economy of Region, 2013*(1), 238-242.

Charlot, O., Malherbet, F., & Terra, C. (2015). Informality in developing economies: Regulation and fiscal policies. *Journal of Economic Dynamics and Control, 51*, 1-27.

Duncan, J. (2014). A political economy of press self-regulation: The case of South Africa. *Media, Culture and Society, 36*(2), 167-182.

Dzeverina, K. S. (2013). Формування інституційного механізму регулювання державно\ власності в національній економіці України. [Institutional mechanism formation for state property regulation within the national economy of Ukraine]. *Actual Problems of Economics, 147*(9), 49-56.

Gataullin, R. F., Askarov, A. A., Khuzhakhmetova, G. N., & Yarkov, N. V. (2015). Organizational and economic forms and effective methods of state regulation of agriculture. *Economy of Region, 42*(2), 271-284.

Guerriero, C. (2013). The political economy of incentive regulation: Theory and evidence from US states. *Journal of Comparative Economics, 41*(1), 91-107.

Imanbekova, M. (2014). The use of foreign experience in forming system state regulation of innovation activities of enterprises in the Republic of Kazakhstan. *World Applied Sciences Journal, 30*(5), 630-634.

IMD (2014). IMD world competitiveness yearbook 2014. Retrieved from https://www.imd.org/uupload/IMD.WebSite/wcc/WCYResults/1/scoreboard_2014.pdf

Kim, I., & Kim, I. (2014). Guest editors' introduction: Financial supervision and regulation with emphasis on Korea and emerging market economies. *Emerging Markets Finance and Trade, 50*(6), 1-4.

Lan, T., Pickles, J., & Zhu, S. (2015). State regulation, economic reform and worker rights: The contingent effects of China's labour contract law. *Journal of Contemporary Asia, 45*(2), 266-293.

Lomeiko, Y. A. (2015). Митне регулювання і контроль у контексті розвитку зовнішньоекономічних відносин в Україні. [Customs regulation and control in the context of external economic relations development in Ukraine]. *Actual Problems of Economics, 166*(4), 75-93.

Nechaev, A., & Antipina, O. (2015). Tax stimulation of innovation activities enterprises. *Mediterranean Journal of Social Sciences, 6*(1S2), 42-47.

Nurunnabi, M. (2015). Tensions between politico-institutional factors and accounting regulation in a developing economy: Insights from institutional theory. *Business Ethics, 24*(4), 398-424.

Popkova, E. G., Yurev, V., Stepicheva, O., & Denisov, N. (2015). Transformation and concentration of intellectual capital as a factor of economic growth in the modern economy. *Regional and Sectoral Economic Studies, 15*(1), 53-60.

Radu, L. D. (2012). Economic growth through eco-efficient methods and strategies: Regulations and achievements in Romania. Paper presented at Proceedings of the 18th *International Business Information Management Association Conference,* May 10-12, 2012. Istanbul, Turkey.

Rosstat. (2015). Russia in numbers. Scientific research and innovations 2015: Bulletin of Rosstat. Retrieved from http://www.gks.ru/free_doc/doc_2015/rusfig/rus-15.pdf

Ryapukhina, V. N., Suprun, E. V., Doroshenko, Y. A., Bukhonova, S. M., Somina, I. V. (2015). Strategy of effective management for small businesses at different stages of innovation activity. *Journal of Applied Engineering Science, 13*(2), 117-125.

Ryazantsev, S. V., Karabulatova, I. S., Ter-Akopov, A. A., Pismennaya, E. E., & Bozhenko, V. V. (2015). The specificity of the differential regulation of economic integration in the context of contemporary labor migration. *Mediterranean Journal of Social Sciences, 6*(3), 96-102.

Ryspekova, M. O., & Beissekeyeva, A. K. (2013). Analysis and ways of state regulation of social security system in the Republic of Kazakhstan under economy modernization. *Actual Problems of Economics, 148*(10), 456-463.

Suntsova, A. O. (2012). Методологічні засади оцінювання ефективності макроекономічного регулювання розвитку національного господарства. [Methodological grounds for efficiency evaluation of state regulation of national economy development]. *Actual Problems of Economics, 134*(8), 139-145.

Suntsova, A. O. (2013). Фінансові методи в регулюванні економічного розвитку країни. [Financial methods in regulation of economic development of a country]. *Actual Problems of Economics, 140*(2), 29-33.

Tkhakushinov, E. K., Zarubin, V. I., Nekrasova, S. O., Kuizheva, S. K., & Ovsyannikova, T. A. (2015). Algorithm for organizing the process of ecological and economic system regulation of the territorial unit. *Asian Social Science, 11*(14), 297-305

Tovt, T. I. (2014). Regulation mechanism for investment support of innovation activities of enterprises. *Actual Problems of Economics, 152*(2), 211-218.

Uberti, L. J., Lemay-Hébert, N., & Demukaj, V. (2014). Introduction: The political economy of regulation in post-war Kosovo: intended and unintended consequences of external actors' involvement. *East European Politics, 30*(4), 429-435.

Yakovlevich Veselovsky, M., Sergeevich Abrashkin, M., Griegorievna Aleksakhina, V., Vitalievna Pogodina, T. (2014). Features of state regulation of the economy in terms of its transition to innovative way of development. *Asian Social Science, 11*(1), 288-296.

Wang, Z., Zhang, B., & Zeng, H. (2016). The effect of environmental regulation on external trade: Empirical evidences from Chinese economy. *Journal of Cleaner Production, 144*, 55-61.

Warren, P. L., & Wood, D. H. (2014). The political economy of regulation in markets with naïve consumers. *Journal of the European Economic Association, 12*(6), 1617-1642.

Zobova, I.Y, Zagladina, E. N., Safiullin, L. N., & Malganova, I. G. (2014). Institutional aspects of state regulation in cyclic development of economy conditions. *Mediterranean Journal of Social Sciences, 5*(28), 40-44.

13

Measuring Business Cycles

Marinko Škare[1], Saša Stjepanović[1]

ABSTRACT This article summarizes the main findings on problems related to the measurement and identification of business cycles. The aim of this study is to define and identify the determinants of business cycles. This paper provides an overview of the methodology and its future course. Our investigation suggests that some methodological frameworks are available in the literature, but none is perfect. A new development in the field lies in spectral analysis methods for measuring business cycles, which may have advantages over existing methodologies (nonlinearity, stationarity issues). We feel that fractional integration is important in the proper monitoring and explanation of business cycles. Spectral analysis techniques have also proved to be useful for addressing the problems of stationarity and structural breaks in time series when analyzing business cycles. Another important issue that is excluded when studying business cycles is that the link between cycles and economic growth is presumed to be non-existent, implying money neutrality.

KEY WORDS: economic growth, cycles, contraction, recession, total factor productivity

[1]Juraj Dobrila University of Pula - Faculty of economics and Tourism "Dr. Mijo Mirkovic", Croatia

Introduction

Economic expansions and slowdowns are inherent in economic systems. Finding mechanisms through which to prolong expansions and limit, or at least alleviate, recessions is in the focus of macroeconomic theory and policy. That the recent financial crisis came as a surprise to a majority of economic experts reemphasizes to those in the economic discipline the necessity of identifying turning points in the economy.

The process of measuring business cycle requires defining the cycle, defining criteria for distinguishing between business cycles and other similar fluctuations, defining procedures for the detection of business cycles and defining methods for measuring business cycles. The main aim of today's macroeconomic policy is to understand the functioning of the business cycle.

The terms business cycle or economic cycle refer to a change in the economic activity of a country during a particular period. Changes in economic activity can occur in two directions: a period of relatively rapid economic growth and expansion or a period of decline and contraction. The real gross domestic product (GDP) is a common way of measuring and determining the strength of a business cycle.

In 1819, the dominant theory was the theory of general equilibrium. That year, a paper entitled Nouveaux principes d'économie politique by Jean Charles Léonard de Sismondi was published, which studied the existence of periodic economic crises that form business cycles. Before this work, classical economists had denied the existence of business cycles. Classical

Correspondence concerning this article should be addressed to: **Marinko Škare,** Juraj Dobrila University of Pula - Faculty of economics and Tourism "Dr. Mijo Mirkovic", Preradoviceva 1/1 Pula Istarska zupanija 52100, Croatia, E-mail: mskare@unipu.hr

economists blamed war as a leading cause of business cycles in the economy. However, Sismondi was the first to discover the existence of cycles by examining an economic crises that occurred during peacetime.

In recent years, economic theory has addressed monitoring and measuring economic fluctuations rather than measuring business cycles. Recent studies that used spectral analysis methods have proved the existence of business cycles in world GDP.

In this paper, we show how the theory and measurement of business cycles were developed over the years, we will define business cycles, we will show what causes business cycles, and we will assess the future of business cycle measurement.

In section 2, definitions of the business cycle are reviewed based on various theoretical and empirical explanations. Section 3 investigates the primary sources of business cycles, while section 4 present different methods for measuring cycles. Section 5 provide concluding remarks on open questions in measuring business cycles, providing new insights into how these issues can be addressed to expand knowledge in the business cycles literature.

Defining the Business Cycle

The idea that the market economy functions under recurring fluctuations depending on a number of variables was formalized by Mitchell (1927), Burns and Mitchell (1946) as follows:

> *" Business cycles are a type of fluctuation found in the aggregate economic activity of nations that organize their work mainly in business enterprises: a cycle consists of expansions occurring at about the same time in many economic activities, followed by similarly general recessions, contractions and revivals which merge into the expansion phase of the next cycle; this sequence of changes is recurrent but not periodic; in duration business cycles vary from more than one year to ten or twelve years; they are not divisible into shorter cycles of similar character with amplitudes approximating their own.".*

Today, this definition serves as the foundation of modern thinking about business cycles, in so far as it concerns the measurement of business cycles or the construction of cyclical fluctuation models. Burns and Mitchell have noted that this definition creates many new issues. For example, if we look at the fluctuations in the overall economic activity of a nation, then we should take into account the differences between business cycles in different regions. Further, questions arise as to whether business cycles should be studied in an international or national context, whether there is a historical nature of business cycles, and whether business cycles change over time. Likewise, if we take into account Burns and Mitchell's remark that "expansion that occurs in many economic activities", we need to define and aggregate the activities. The fact that economic activities occur at around the same time suggests the possibility that some macroeconomic variables are formed before (leading) and after some cycles (lagging). Looking at these "recurring changes", we need to determine how we should address seasonal changes, random fluctuations and secular trends. Furthermore, the comments relating to the duration and amplitude of business cycles are based on actual observations of cyclical phenomena and the rules for excluding irregular movement and other similar changes.

The National Bureau of Economic Research has access to data that allow the identification of the business cycle, which occurs in two steps: first, find the cyclical peaks and troughs in the observed economic variables and, second, determine whether these changes are common enough through all the observed series. If the answer to the second question is affirmative, then the aggregate business cycle or reference cycle is identified. Once the reference dates are found, the cyclical behavior of each series is discussed as the reference cycle. As a part of this analysis, the duration, time and amplitude of each cycle are compared to those of the reference period. In its method of studying business cycles, the NBER identifies business cycles based on (absolute) declines or changes in the general level of production. Such an approach is known as a classic example of the business cycle. There are alternative approaches that consider whether the fall in the series originated as a deviation from its long-term trend, which in Zarnowitz's terminology (1992), are known as growth cycles. Note that one advantage of using the growth cycle is that expansion and contraction of the business cycle are of approximately the same duration.

In classic cycles, the recession is usually shorter than the expansion due to growth effects.

If we decide to use growth cycles, the question arises as how to identify the cyclical component of a particular series. According to King et al. (1991), models of the real business cycle (RBC), which enable a trend in technological shocks, imply that growth and business cycles are mutually determined. The practice of separating the trend and cyclical components using linear time series methods are well established. There are several approaches to de-trending economic time series. One approach is to use linear de-trending procedures that assume that the observed series has a deterministic time trend. An alternative approach is to assume that the stochastic trend is modeled with a unit root in the time series. The major contribution of Nelson and Plosser (1982) to this analysis is, in fact, that they have proved that economic time series, such as those of real GDP, usually have a unit root. However, Stock and Watson (1998) argue that linear time trends or first differentiation to eliminate the unit root do not provide satisfactory results for identifying the cyclical component series of the observed data. Note that while the first approach to linear time trends leads to the generation of false effects of business cycles in de-trending series, in the second, first differentiation exacerbates the role of short-term noise.

Several alternative approaches have been recently proposed in the business cycles literature to address the separation of the trend from the cyclical components of the time series. One of these approaches is the so-called Hodrick–Prescott (HP) filter, which minimizes the quadratic form to determine the trend component in a given series:

$$y_t = \tau_t + c_t \quad (1)$$

where τ_t represents the trend component, and c_t represents the cyclical component. τ_t may be non-stationary and may contain a deterministic and stochastic trend. The primary objective was to assess c_t, a stationary cyclical component that is derived from stochastic cycles of different periods of time. The trend component is calculated as $\tau_t = y_t - c_t$.

The properties of the HP filter are studied by many authors, including Singleton (1988), King and Rebelo (2000), and Cogley and Nason (1995). Cogley and Nason claim, in particular, that dynamic business cycles obtained using HP de-trending methods depend on the characteristics of the studied data. If they are stationary, then the de-trending procedure has favorable characteristics. If the observed data are non-stationary, the HP filter produces spurious business cycle fluctuations.

The second approach is based on the spectral analysis of economic time series. The band-pass filter, which filters and traces the long-term trend of the high-frequency changes in a observed time series, was developed by Baxter and King (1999). The approach maintains the components that are associated with the periodicity of a typical business cycle. Usually, this periodicity is between six quarter and eight years. The band-pass filter of Baxter and King (1999) is obtained by applying the Kth order moving average of a given time series:

$$y_t^* = \sum_{k=K}^{K} \alpha_k y_{t-k}, \quad (2)$$

where the ratio of the moving average is selected to be symmetrical, $a_k = a_{-k}$ for $k = 1, \ldots\ldots, K$, showing that if the sum of the coefficients of the moving average is zero, $\sum_{k=K}^{K} \alpha_k = 0$, then there is a characteristic of trend elimination.

The Baxter-King filter will eliminate deterministic quadratic trends, or it will produce a stationary series that is integrated of order two or less. This filter is designed to have a range of other features, including that the results should not depend on the sample size and not change the relationship between time series at any frequency. Baxter and King created a band-pass filter, taking into account low-pass and high-pass filters with the required properties.

The various methodologies used by scholars in defining business cycles are evident from Table 1.

The Origins of Cycles

One of the most common and challenging questions in macroeconomics is related to the business cycle: Which shocks cause business fluctuations? In economic theory, most responses to this question implicate monetary and fiscal policies or oil shocks. To that list, Prescott (1986) adds the impact of technological shocks and argues that technological shocks in the post-war period were, in more than 75 % of

Table 1. Methods for Identifying Business Cycles

Authors	Methods for defining business cycles
Burns and Wesley (1946)	Business cycles are a type of fluctuation in aggregate economic activity
NBER (2010)	Business cycles are based on two parts: cyclical peaks and bottoms
Zarnowitz (1992)	Considers growth cycles where the fall in the series is determined by the deviation from the long-term trend.
King, Plosser and Stock (1991)	Using a model of real business cycle, they implied that growth and business cycles are mutually determined
Singleton (1988), King and Rebelo (1998), Cogley and Nason (1995)	An alternative approach for defining business cycles using the Hodrick-Prescott filter
Baxter and King (1999)	Another alternative approach for defining business cycles using spectral analysis of time series

Table 2. Key Determinants of Business Cycles

Authors	What causes business cycles?
Prescott (1986)	Considers the impact uncertainty of technological shocks in the post -war period
Norrbin (1988)	Measures TFP (total factor productivity) using military spending
Evans (1992)	Measures TFP using indicators of monetary policy
Gali (1999), King et al. (1991), Nelson and Plosser (1982), King and Rebelo (1999)	Discuss the importance of technology shocks as pulses in business cycles
Kim and Lougani (1992), Rotemberg and Woodford (1996), Finn (2000)	Consider shocks in the oil industry instead of technological progress as the main variable that causes business cycles
Christiano and Eichenbaum (1992), Baxter and King (1999), Braun (1994) and McGrattan (1994)	Consider fiscal shocks instead of technological progress as the main variable that causes business cycles
Ramey and Shapiro (1998), Burnside et al. (1996) and Fisher (2003)	Take into account the effects of changes in government spending on business cycles
Bernanke, Gertler and Gilchrist (1996), Dixit and Stiglitz (1977)	Consider monetary shocks instead of technological progress as the main variable that causes business cycles
Farmer (1999)	Takes the basic RBC model as starting point to model multiple equilibria for determining causes of business cycles

cases, the causes of business fluctuations. The idea of technology shocks as a main driver of business cycles is among the more controversial ideas. Prescott calculates total factor productivity (TFP) and treats this as a measure of exogenous technology shocks. However, there are reasons to distrust that TFP measures real shocks in technology. TFP can be forecast using military spending, as conducted by Norrbin (1988), or using indicators of monetary policy, as conducted by Evans (1992). In both modes, observed variables are unlikely to have an impact on the rate of technical progress. This evidence suggests that TFP, which Prescott calculates, is not the pure exogenous shock he observes. Instead, they already include endogenous components. The utilization of capital variable observed by Basu (1996), and Burnside, Eichenbaum and Rebelo (1996); changes in use of labor, which are studied by Burnside, Eichenbaum and Rebelo (1993); and changes in the rates of income, which Jaimovich and Floetotto (2008) examined, all show significant differences between TFP and actual technology shocks. These differences imply that the magnitude of the real technology shock will be much smaller than that of the TFP shocks used by Prescott.

Key determinants of business cycles on growth issues, as analyzed by various authors, can be seen in Table 2.

Burnside et al. (1996), King and Rebelo (1999), Jaimovich and Floetotto (2008), argue that the fact that actual technological shocks are smaller than TFP shocks does not imply that technological shocks irrelevant. If we introduce mechanisms such as capacity utilization and revenue diversity into models of real business cycles, we obtain two effects. First, these mechanisms make technological shocks less volatile than TFP shocks. Second, they significantly increase the impact of technology shocks. This enhancement allows models with these mechanisms that generate volatility in output that are similar to the data for which we have far fewer technological shocks.

Another controversial aspect of the real business cycle model is the usage of technology shocks in generating a recession. NBER (2010) defines a 'a significant decline in the economic activity spread across the country, lasting more than a few months, normally visible in real gross domestic product (GDP) growth, real personal income, employment (non-farm payrolls), industrial production, and wholesale-retail sales. If we look at total output in the United States for the period from 1947 to 2005, we see that it dropped by 12%. Most models of real business cycles require a decline in TFP to replicate the decrease in output that we observe in this period. Macroeconomists agree that an increase in production, at least over the medium and long term, is driven by the increase in TFP derived by technological progress. In contrast, the claim that a collapse of TFP causes recessions has been met with skepticism. Simply speaking, this means that in the recession, we have technological setbacks rather than progression.

Gali (1999) prompted a discussion about the importance of technology shocks as pulses in the business cycle. Gali estimates a structural VAR model, assuming that technological shocks are the only source of long-term changes in labor productivity. He discovered that over the short run, there is a decrease in the number of hours worked in response to positive shocks to technology. This finding is in direct contradiction with the fundamentals of real business cycle models. King, Plosser and Rebelo (1988) and Baxter and King (1999) detailed the capacity of positive technological shocks to increase the number of hours worked in the real business cycle models. Christiano, Eichenbaum and Vigfusson (2003) found that Gali's results are not robust to VAR specifications for which the data are in levels rather than as first differences. Chari, Kehoe and McGrattan (2004) used a model of the real business cycle that showed that Gail's research was derived from incorrect model specifications.

The debate about the role of technology shocks in business cycles has influenced and inspired research on models in which technological shocks are less significant or play no role. These studies have strongly influenced the methods and ideas developed in the literature on real business cycle models. In fact, in most of these alternative theories, the starting point of the new models is the fundamental model of real business cycles (Khorunzhina, 2015). Shakina and Barajas (2014) explore the interesting link between firm's intellectual capital and cycles.

One of the variables that is observed instead of technological progress is a shock in the oil industry. Changes in the prices of oil and oil products are poorly linked to US recessions. Kim and Lougani (1992), Rotemberg and Woodford (1996) and Finn (2000) studied the effects of shocks in the prices of energy and real business cycle models. These shocks have facilitated the success of models of real business cycles, but they have also showed that these are not the primary causes of fluctuations in output. Although energy prices are very volatile, energy costs represent too small a share of the added value of changes in the price of energy to have a significant impact on economic activity (Lee and Mukoyama, 2015).

Another observed effect is the effect of fiscal shocks. Christiano and Eichenbaum (1992), Baxter and King (1999), Braun (1994) and McGrattan (1994), among others, have studied the impact of shocks in tax rates and government spending on real business cycle models. These fiscal shocks enhance the ability of real business cycle models to replicate the variability of consumption and hours of operation and the low correlation between hours worked and average labor productivity. Fiscal shocks also have increased volatility in output that is generated in real business cycle models. The effects of financial contagion and economic crisis on major financial markets are discussed in Dajčman (2014), showing that contagion is not strongly connected to the crisis. Fiscal stimulus can speed up economic recovery by attracting foreign direct investments, but it is supported by other non-fiscal factors, mainly infrastructure and political stability (Rădulescu and Druica, 2014).

However, there is a lack of cyclical variation in taxes and government spending for fiscal shocks to be the primary cause of business fluctuations. Cyclical movements in public expenditures are relatively small; during periods of war there is usually a temporary increase in government spending. Ohanian (1997) shows that models of real business cycles can explain the main macroeconomic elements of war episodes: a moderate decrease in consumption, a substantial decline in investment, and a significant increase in working hours. These features occur naturally in real business cycle models in which government spending is financed by lump-sum taxes. Additional government spending must eventually be funded from taxes. The wealth of households declines as the corporate taxes grows. In response to this reduction, households reduce their consumption and increase their number of working hours, reducing the number of hours used for leisure. This increase in working hours creates a moderate increase in production. Because the current marginal propensity to consume is reduced, households prefer to pay taxes related to war, so as to reduce consumption today and in the future. Because such spending cuts today occur with an increase in output, which is smaller than the increased government spending, there is a reduction in investment. Cooley and Ohanian (1997) use a model of the real business cycle to compare the social implications of different strategies of war financing. Ramey and Shapiro (1998) take into account the effects of changes in government spending. Burnside, Eichenbaum and Fisher (2004) study the impact of a large current increase in government expenditures in the presence of a taxation distortion. A possible link between labor markets and business cycles is explored in Tomić (2014).

The following observed effect is the impact of specific investments in technological change. One of the natural alternatives to technological shocks is an investment, in particular, in technological change. In the standard model of the real business cycle, positive technology shocks make both work and existing capital more productive. In contrast, specific investments in technological advances do not affect the productivity of old capital goods. Instead, new capital allows greater productivity and lower costs, resulting in an increase in the real rate of return on investment. We can measure the pace of specific investments in technological change by the relative price of investment goods in terms of consumption goods. According to the data constructed by Gordon (1990), relative prices have dramatically declined over the past forty years. Based on these observations, Greenwood, Hercowitz and Krusell (2000) use growth accounting methods to claim that 60 percent of post-war growth in the output per worker-hour ratio is derived from investments in particular technological changes. Using VAR, which is identified with long-term restrictions, Fisher (2003) believes that investing in particular technological changes affects 50 percent of the variation in hours worked and 40 percent of the variation in the quantity of output. On the contrary, he believes that technological shocks affect less than 10 percent of the variation in output and hours worked. Because of Greenwood, Hercowitz and Krusell (1997), investments in technological change, in particular, have become one of the standard shocks included in real business cycle models.

The following observed effect is the impact of monetary shocks. There are some studies on the impact of monetary shocks on real business cycle models that are extended to contain additional elements of real and nominal friction. Researchers such as Bernanke, Gertler, and Gilchrist (1996) emphasize the role of credit friction in response to the technological economy and monetary shocks. Another important element is monopolistic competition, modeled according to Dixit and Stiglitz (1977). In basic models of the real business cycle, companies and employees have acquired prices from perfectly competitive markets. Such an environment is less meaningful to observe the enterprise than are those in which they choose their prices or employees as those who want the reward (performance-based pay). Introducing monopolistic competition to the production and labor markets gives workers and enterprises the ability to make decisions on prices.

The most significant nominal frictions that have been introduced in basic RBC monetary model are sticky prices and wages. In these models, prices are determined by companies that are committed to offer goods at those prices, and salaries are determined by employees who are committed to provide their work for those wages. Wages and prices can only be changed periodically or at a cost. Firms and workers look ahead because they take into account that it might be impossible or too expensive to change prices or wages over the short term in their determinations of prices and salaries. Macroeconomic shocks also register important effects on business cycles dynamics (Cavallo and Ribba, 2015). Fluctuations in aggregate demand through the wealth effect also impact business cycles (Guo, Sirbu, & Weder, 2015). Monetary policy and inflation targeting are also accounted for, at least for the US (Araújo, 2015).

This new generation of basic RBC monetary models can generate impulse response functions to monetary shocks that are similar to the estimated responses obtained from the VAR technique. In many of these models, technological shocks are still significant, but financial forces play an increasingly important role in creating the economic response to technology shocks. In fact, Altig et al. (2011) and Gali, Lopez-Salido and Valles (2003) found in their models that the sizeable short-term impact of technology shocks requires that monetary policy be flexible.

The following observed effect is the impact that created multiple equilibrium models. Many papers examine models that show balance in multiple equilibrium expectations. Early studies of multiple equilibria rely heavily on models that extend for several generations, partly because these models can be explored without resorting to numerical methods. The latest works related to multiple equilibria are discussed by Farmer (1999). They take the basic RBC model as a starting point for their research and then look for the most appropriate modifications that will generate multiple equilibria.

In basic RBC models, we can calculate the competitive equilibrium as a solution to a concave planning problem. This problem has a unique solution, and therefore, a competitive equilibrium of the same kind. When we introduce additions to the model, such as externalities, increasing yields of return or monopolistic competition, we cannot calculate the competitive equilibrium for the concave planning problem. Therefore, these new features, which have been added to the model, open up the possibility of multiple equilibria.

Models that allow multiple equilibria have two attractive features. The first is that human beliefs and their fulfillment can generate business cycles. If participants in the economy become more pessimistic and think that the economy is in recession or will go into a recession, the economy will slow down. Second, these models have strong inner persistence, and therefore, these do not need serial correlation of shocks to generate persistence in macroeconomic time series. Starting from a model that has a unique equilibrium and introducing multiplicity implies reducing the absolute value of the characteristic root from over one to below one.

One of the drawbacks of current models of multiple equilibria is that they imply volatile beliefs, but these are coordinated through all market participants. Thus, operators have to change their view of the future continually, but they do have to coordinate that change among themselves.

Measuring Business Cycles

Measuring business cycles provides a reference point for assessing macroeconomic theory and policy. The process of measuring the business cycle takes place in several steps. First, we must define and detect a cycle, and second, we must determine the turning point. The next phase of measuring the business cycle is determining the appropriate procedures of models that are commonly used. Further, it is essential to measure cycle features. Finally, we need to define and detect business cycles using multivariate information and automatic construction of the reference cycle. As a last resort, it is necessary to determine the underlying procedures in the model for the definition, determination and extraction of the reference cycle.

In their classic paper, *Measuring Business Cycles,* Burns and Mitchell (1946) define the specific cycles in the series y_t and have since used it as a turning point for the display of the business cycle. This part is the first step in measuring the business cycle; it represents the definition and detection of the cycle. When we talk about business cycles, Burns and Mitchell simply describe y_t as the level of aggregate economic activity, although it would be correct to say that this series shows that the logarithm economic activities at the turning point of cycles equal the logarithm of overall economic activity. Some, e.g., the Institute for Economic Business Cycles, have studied tilting point in cycles as opposed to Δy_t data. At the time when Mitchell began his work on alternative views of y_t, which is seen as a periodic component, the sine and cosine represent waves:

$$y_t = \sum_{j=1}^{m} \alpha_j \cos \lambda_j t + \beta_j \sin \lambda_j t , \quad (3)$$

where λ_j is the frequency rate, and j represents the oscillation. If m=1, then there is only one periodic cycle. The problem of this representation is that it has small economic time series that shows evidence of periodicity.

As mentioned above, the next step in measuring business cycles is to locate the turning point. To be able to locate the turning points in a particular series, some way to identify them in a time series should be defined and created. One of the most practical solutions is that the peaks are local maxima in the time series y_t. In this case, if the carets $\vee_t(\wedge_t)$ are binary variables, having value 1 as local extrema and zero otherwise. Formally, we obtain the following (Harding and Pagan, 2004):

$$\begin{aligned} \vee_t &= 1(y_t < y_{t\pm j}, 1 \le j \le k) \\ \wedge_t &= 1(y_t > y_{tj\pm}, 1 \le j \le k) \end{aligned} . \quad (4)$$

Turning points can also be located through alternative methods. An alternative approach for locating the turning points is based on the fundamental processes in the model. The above procedure does not require any knowledge of the process generating the y_t data. An alternative approach is to apply the model using Δy_t, which is then used for the location of tipping point. Today, such models are parametric and feature two modes. One of the most popular parametric models is that of Hamilton (1989), where the growth rate is treated with a Markov switching process of the form:

$$\Delta y_t = \mu_0(1-\xi_t) + \mu_1 \xi + e_t , \quad (5)$$

where μ_j represents the growth rates in the regimes, and they are indexed by latent binary state ξ_t, with e_t as a normally distributed, zero mean error term μ0. This model represents a state of low growth rates, and μ_1 represents a state of high growth rates. The model is completed in a manner that specifies the probability of transition from a state $\xi_{t-1} = 0$ or 1 to a state $\xi_t = 1$ or 0. The model may be more complex, and the extra dynamics and different variances of each of the arrangement thus enable the probability of transition to depend on the observed data.

Measuring cycle features is the next step in the procedure. The process of locating the turning point separates the time series into stages. The expansion phase starts from the next peak; the contraction phase extends from the peak to the next base. What follows in the model is most easily described as a derivation of the information in the extension.

Two fundamental pieces of data are required in the growth stages: duration and amplitude. The length of the expansion stage represents the number of periods between the bottom and top, whereas the amplitude is a measure that shows changes in y_t from bottom to top. In many cases, the y_t logarithm of some variable, such as GDP or industrial production, is used, and in such cases, the amplitude is explained as the percentage change in y_t between the bottom and top. Connecting the bottom and the top yields the hypotenuse. If $y_t = \ln Y_t$, then the hypotenuse represents the path followed by the variable that shows steady growth during the expansion. If this is taken into consideration, then it is instructive to study the movement of the actual data on the path of constant growth that is represented by the hypotenuse.

Burns and Mitchell's famous definition of the business cycle includes two aspects. First, we need to identify the aggregate economic activity, and the second requirement is the existence of synchronization among different variables during certain phases of the business cycle. The authors consider that GDP is a good measure of economic activity, although others, such as Moore and Zarnowitz (1986), prefer to have a weighted average of several series and not just one series. Given that GDP as a measure was not available to Burns and Mitchell, there were no data for the period that they needed, so it is natural that they have given emphasis to the second component of their definition of business cycles, i.e., the synchronization of cycle-specific series representing economic activity. Burns and Mitchell determined the turning points in number of series and then determined the reference cycle in a way that sets the dates around which peaks and troughs of business cycles revolve. Moreover, at the end of the process, it is necessary to know the extent to which each particular cycle is synchronized with aggregate cycles.

Conclusion

In this paper, we presented a history of business cycles measurement and the problems associated with that process. In the first part, we have explained the concept and definition of the business cycle. Through the definition of the business cycle, we reached some new and unresolved issues that have emerged out of the definition. In the second part, we have addressed causes such as exogenous effects of technology shocks on business cycles. We have also considered the ratio of total factor productivity and technology shocks and emphasized the exogenous and endogenous effect of technology shocks. We have subsequently presented some other shocks (the influence of oil shocks, monetary shocks, and fiscal shocks) that can replace technological shocks in measuring business cycles. The paper also presents an overview of new models of business cycles showing differences in steps; determining the turning points, peaks and troughs of business cycles; developing the hypotenuse and automatic connection between trough and peak; and decomposing the business cycle curve.

Although Burns and Mitchell represented a relatively significant discovery in the measurement of business cycles, their findings were not initially accepted in academic circles. Today, this has changed an increasing number of people and scholars accept their method for several reasons, the most important being that today it is much easier to estimate turning points in the business cycle with individual models – an important step in their analysis. Further, it should be noted that today there enough emerging research facilitating advances through tools that simulate data much more accurately than previously possible. From our study, we can conclude that there is no one solution for measuring business cycles that would be accepted by the profession. All of the above solutions have their shortcomings, which are objectively presented in this paper.

As for the future, there are many areas that are being investigated and solutions that are being looked into. We have attempted a new approach to measuring business cycles that tries to address these shortcomings. We introduce multi-regime Markov switching VAR, HP (Hedrick Prescott) filters and spectral analysis as the latest developments in the study of business cycle movements. We are of the opinion that fractional integration is also important for proper business cycles monitoring and explanation (Škare & Stjepanovic, 2013) and that the impact of information and prices from the firm perspective also plays a role in business cycle dynamics (Mäkinen & Ohl, 2015).

References

Altig, D., Christiano, L. J., Eichenbaum, M., & Linde, J. (2011). Firm-Specific Capital, Nominal Rigidities and the Business Cycle. *Review of Economic Dynamics*, 14 (2), 225-247.

Araújo, E. (2015). Monetary policy objectives and Money's role in U.S. business cycles. *Journal of Macroeconomics*, 45, 85-107.

Basu, S. (1996). Procyclical Productivity, Increasing Returns of Cyclical Utilization? *Quarterly Journal of Economics*, 111 (3), 719-751.

Baxter, M., King, R. (1999). Fiscal Policy in General Equilibrium. *American Economic Review*, 83 (3), 315-334.

Bernanke, B., Gertler, M., Gilchrist, S. (1996). The Financial Accelerator in a Quantitative Business Cycle Framework. *Review of Economics and Statistics*, 78 (1), 1-15.

Braun, R. A. (1994). Tax Disturbances and Real Economic Activity in the Postwar United States. *Journal of Monetary Economics*, 33 (3), 441–462.

Burns, A., Mitchell, W. C. (1946). *Measuring Business Cycles* (Vol. 2). New York, NY: National Bureau of Economic Research.

Burnside, C., Eichenbaum, M., & Rebelo, S. (1993). Labour Hoarding and the Business Cycle. *Journal of Political Economy*, 101 (2), 245-273.

Burnside, C., Eichenbaum, M., & Rebelo, S. (1996). Sectoral Solow Residuals. *European Economic Review*, 40 (3-5), 861-869.

Burnside, C., Eichenbaum, M., & Fisher, J. (2004). Fiscal shocks and their consequences. *Journal of Economic Theory*, 115 (1), 89-117.

Cavallo, A., Ribba, A. (2015). Common macroeconomic shocks and business cycle fluctuations in Euro area countries. *International Review of Economics & Finance*, 38, 377-392.

Chari, V., Kehoe, P., McGrattan, E. (2004). *Are structural VARs with long-run restrictions useful in developing business cycle theory?* (Staff Report No. 364). Federal Reserve Bank of Minneapolis.

Christiano, L. J., Eichenbaum, M. (1992). Current real-business-cycle theories and aggregate labor-market fluctuations. *The American Economic Review,* 82 (3), 430-450.

Christiano, L. J., Eichenbaum, M., & Vigfusson, R. (2003). *What happens after a technology shock?* (Working Paper No. 9819). National Bureau of Economic Research.

Cogley, T., Nason, J. (1995). Output Dynamics in Real Business Cycle Models. *American Economic Review,* 85 (3), 492-511.

Cooley, T. F., Ohanian, L. E. (1997). Postwar British economic growth and the legacy of Keynes. *Journal of Political Economy,* 105 (3), 439-472.

Dajčman, S. (2014). Was there a contagion between major European and Croatian stock markets? An analysis of co-exceedances. *Economic Research-Ekonomska Istraživanja,* 27 (1), 155-168.

Dixit, A., Stiglitz, J. (1977). Monopolistic Competition and Optimum Product Diversity. *American Economic Review,* 67 (3), 298-308.

Evans, L. (1992). Productivity Shocks and Real Business Cycles. *Journal of Monetary Economics,* 29 (2), 191-208.

Farmer, R. (1999). *Macroeconomics of Self-fulfilling Prophecies* (2nd ed.). Cambridge, MA: MIT Press.

Finn, M. (2000). Perfect Competition and the Effects of Energy Price Increases on Economic Activity, *Journal of Money, Credit and Banking,* 32 (3), 400-416.

Fisher, J. (2003). *Technology Shocks Matter* (Working Paper No. 02-14). Federal Reserve Bank of Chicago.

Gali, J. (1999). Technology, Employment and the Business Cycle: Do Technology Shocks Explain Aggregate Fluctuations? *American Economic Review,* 89 (1), 249-271.

Gali, J., Lopez-Salido, J. D., Valles, J. (2003). Technology Shocks and Monetary Policy: Assessing the Feds Performance. *Journal of Monetary Economics,* 50 (4), 723-743.

Gordon, R. (1990). *The Measurement of Durable Goods Prices.* Chicago, IL: University of Chicago Press.

Greenwood, J., Hercowitz, Z., & Krusell, P. (2000). The Role of Investment-Specific Technological Change in the Business Cycle. *European Economic Review,* 44 (1), 91-115.

Greenwood, J., Hercowitz, Z., & Krusell, P. (1997). Long-Run Implications of Investment-Specific Technological Change. *American Economic Review,* 87 (3), 342-362.

Guo, J. T., Sirbu, A. I., Weder, M. (2015). News About Aggregate Demand and the Business Cycle. *Journal of Monetary Economics,* 72, 83-96.

Hamilton, J. D. (1989). A new approach to the economic analysis of nonstationary time series and the business cycle. *Econometrica,* 57 (2), 357–384.

Harding, D., Pagan, A. (2006). *Measurement of Business Cycles.* University of Melbourne, Department of Economics Research Paper 966

Jaimovich, N., Floetotto, M. (2008). Firm Dynamics, Markup Variations, and the Business Cycle. *Journal of Monetary Economics,* 55 (7), 1238-1252.

Khorunzhina, N. (2015). Real Business-Cycle Model with Habits: Empirical Investigation. *Economic Modelling,* 46, 61-69.

Kim, I. M., Loungani, P. (1992). The Role of Energy in Real Business Cycle Models. *Journal of Monetary Economics,* 29 (2), 173-189.

King, R. G., Plosser, C. I., Rebelo, S. T. (1988). Production, growth, and business cycles I: The basic neoclassical model. *Journal of Monetary Economics,* 21 (2-3), 195-232.

King, R., Plosser, C., Stock, J., Watson, M. (1991). Stochastic Trends and Economic Fluctuations. *The American Economic Review,* 81 (4), 819-840.

King, R. G., Rebelo, S. T. (1999). Resuscitating real business cycles in Handbook of macroeconomics. In J. B. Taylor & M. Woodford (Eds.), *Handbook of Macroeconomics* (Vol. 1, pp. 927-1007). Amsterdam: Elsevier.

King, R., Rebelo, S. (2000). *Resuscitating Real Business Cycles* (Working Paper No. 7534). National Bureau of Economic Research.

Lee, Y., Mukoyama, T. (2015). Entry and Exit of Manufacturing Plants Over the Business Cycle, *European Economic Review,* 77, 20-27.

Mäkinen, T., Ohl, B. (2015). Information Acquisition and Learning from Prices Over the Business Cycle. *Journal of Economic Theory,* 158, 585-633.

McGrattan, E. R. (1994). The Macroeconomic Effects of Distortionary Taxation. *Journal of Monetary Economics,* 33 (3), 573–601.

Mitchell, W. C. (1927). *Business Cycles: The Problem and Its Setting*. New York, NY: National Bureau of Economic Research.

Moore, G. H., Zarnowitz, V. (1986). Major Changes in Cyclical Behavior. In R. J. Gordon (Ed.), *The American Business Cycle: Continuity and Change* (pp. 519-582). Chicago, IL: University of Chicago Press.

National Bureau of Economic Research, *Business Cycle Dating Commitee* (2010). Available at http://www.nber.org/cycles/sept2010.html

Nelson, C., Plosser, C. (1982). Trends and Random Walks in Macroeconomic Time Series: Some Evidence and Implications. *Journal of Monetary Economics*, 10 (2), 139-162.

Norrbin, S. C. (1988). The Relation Between Price and Marginal Cost in U.S. Industry. A Contradiction. *Journal of Political Economy*, 101 (6), 1149-1164.

Ohanian, L. (1997). The Macroeconomic Effects of War Finance in the United States: World War II and the Korean War. *American Economic Review*, 87 (1), 23-40.

Prescott, E. (1986). *Theory Ahead of Business-Cycle Measurement* (Staff Report No. 102). Federal Reserve Bank of Minneapolis.

Rădulescu, M., Druica, E. (2014). The Impact of Fiscal Policy on Foreign Direct Investments. Empiric Evidence from Romania. *Economic Research-Ekonomska Istraživanja*, 27 (1), 86-106.

Ramey, V., Shapiro, M. (1998). *Costly Capital Reallocation and the Effects of Government Spending*. Carnegie-Rochester Conference Series on Public Policy, 48 (1), 145-194.

Rotemberg, J. J., Woodford, M. (1996). Real-business-cycle models and the forecastable movements in output, hours, and consumption. *The American Economic Review*, 86 (1), 71-89.

Shakina, E., Barajas, A. (2014). The Dynamics of Intellectual Resources During the Economic Crisis. *Economic Research-Ekonomska Istraživanja*, 27 (1), 861-881.

Singleton, K. (1988). Econometric issues in the analysis of equilibrium business cycle models. *Journal of Monetary Economics*, 21 (2-3), 361-386.

Škare, M., Stjepanović, S. (2013). A Fractionally Integrated Model for the Croatian Aggregate Output (GDP) *Series. Ekonomska istraživanja - Economic Research*, 26 (2), 289-330.

Stock, J., Watson, M. (1999). Business Cycle Fluctuations in U.S.Macroeconomic Time Series. In J. B. Taylor, & M. Woodford (Eds.), *Handbook of Macroeconomics* (Vol. 1, pp. 3-65). Amsterdam: Elsevier.

Tomić, I. (2014). Structural Unemployment in Croatia – How Important Is the Occupational Mismatch? *Economic Research-Ekonomska Istraživanja*, 27 (1), 346-365.

Zarnowitz, V. (1992). *Business Cycles Theory, History, Indicators and Forecasting*. Chicago, IL: The University of Chicago Press.

14

Aggregate matching in Spain. Time series analysis using cointegration techniques

Ewa Gałecka-Burdziak[1]

ABSTRACT I analyze the matching process in the Spanish labor market from 1994-2005. I use monthly registered unemployment data and refer solely to public employment intermediation. This period reflects an upward movement along a downward sloping Beveridge curve; therefore, major changes in the process efficiency should not be observed. I narrow the considerations to a job queuing model, which is the most relevant description of the labor market matching process in Spain, according to the literature. I apply various quantitative methods to address the problem of non-stationary data. The Engle-Granger estimates emphasize the crucial role of the demand in generating the outflows from unemployment to employment. The ECT coefficient confirms that the model efficiently approaches the new equilibrium. These findings confirm that job seekers find themselves on the disadvantaged side of the market and compete for scarce job offers, which, in turn, are ascribed randomly to the workers. The diagnostic tests of the VAR models question the relevance of a multivariate space analysis because the outflow from unemployment to employment appears to be the sole endogenous variable.

KEY WORDS: labor market matching, job queuing model, time series analysis, Spanish labor market

[1] Department of Economics I, Warsaw School of Economics, Poland

Introduction

Trade occurs constantly in a labor market and leads to matches between job seekers and vacancies. Trade occurs randomly or non-randomly and can be formally presented by a matching function. In this article, I focus on a technical perspective of the matching process. Most often, the log-linear specification (with constant returns to scale restriction imposed) is assumed, and the coefficients are estimated by the OLS estimator (Petrongolo & Pissarides 2001). Soininen (2006) notes that empirical research relatively rarely refers econometrically to a non-stationary time series. Among the few papers using Engle-Granger or Johansen approaches, one can distinguish, for example: (Albaek & Hansen, 2004; Archambault & Fortin, 2001; Blanchard & Diamond, 1989; de Francesco, 1999; Soininen, 2006), and for Spain, in particular, Bell (1997) and Gałecka-Burdziak (2013).

I use various econometric methods, including cointegration techniques, to contribute to the robustness of the results that concern the matching process in Spain. I begin with the single equation model using Engle-

Correspondence concerning this article should be addressed to: **Ewa Gałecka-Burdziak**, Department of Economics I, Warsaw School of Economics, ul. Madalińskiego 6/8, 02-513 Warsaw, Poland E-mail: ewa.galecka-burdziak@sgh.waw.pl

Granger and Engle-Yoo procedures. The estimated coefficients can be interpreted as the outflow elasticities with respect to unemployment or vacancy pools that are of main interest in the matching function analysis. Next, I extend the analysis to the multivariate perspective. I develop VAR models to analyze the interdependence among the variables to describe the labor market matching process. I choose a country from the Iberian Peninsula because the data characteristics allow for a precise public employment intermediation description. I choose the time span, 1994-2005, which reflects an upward movement along a downward sloping Beveridge curve. Thus, we can expect homogenous trade technology with no major changes in the trade process efficiency. The recession, which Spain experienced at the beginning of the 1990s, ended in 1993. In May 2005, a new methodology of gathering data was implemented; this introduces a breakthrough in the data (since then, there have been no comparable data on vacancies registered at public employment offices because each offer can consist of the numerous job posts).

The Spanish labor market has endured fundamental changes concerning legal conditions because the implementation of the new constitution in 1978. Spain joined the European Economic Community in 1986 and implemented a series of reforms with the objective of increasing the elasticity of the market, encouraging companies to create better quality jobs and hiring workers on permanent contracts (e.g., reforms implemented in 1984, 1994, 1997 and 2001). Among the outcomes of these changes, one can list the duality of the labor market; this originates from the extensive use of temporary contracts (approximately 25% in 2010) and the high volatility of (un)employment. Petrongolo and Pissarides (2008) prove that both unemployment inflow and outflow contribute to high unemployment volatility.

One can find a few literature surveys that concern the matching function estimates for the Spanish labor market, for example: (Alujas Ruiz, 2002; Álvarez de Toledo, Núñez and Usabiaga, 2004; 2008; Núñez, 2006; Núñez & Usabiaga, 2007). The main qualitative conclusions arise from using registered data. Antolín (1994) proposes a method to recalculate the vacancy data for the entire economy (but for a stock-based model). The analyses imply that vacancies are the driving force of the outflow from unemployment to employment creation. Moreover, the findings indicate that the job queuing model, which assumes random matching between unemployment stock and vacancy inflow, most properly describes the public employment intermediation in Spain.

This paper is organized as follows. In section 2, I present data. Section 3 includes a univariate space analysis using Engle-Granger and Engle-Yoo techniques. I refer to the job queuing model to present matching between the stock of the job seekers and the inflow of new vacancies. I extend the dimension of the analysis in section 4, in which I apply the Johansen approach. In section 5, I interpret the results and compile concluding remarks in section 6.

Data characteristics

I base quantitative analysis on the registered unemployment and vacancy data from public employment offices (*Servicio Público de Empleo Estatal).* These time series possess certain valuable features. Companies are obliged to register each job offer (as a vacancy or as a covered job post). The outflow from unemployment to employment can be directly assigned to public employment intermediation, which refers to the job offers registered at public employment offices. Once we compare this time series with the total hires, we can assess the fraction of the total job creation that arises from public employment offices intermediation.

Table 1 compiles summary statistics for the selected variables: the outflow from unemployment to employment generated through public employment intermediation (M), unemployment stock (U), total job seekers stock (J), unemployment inflow (u) and vacancy variables, stock (V) and inflow (v). The time series are seasonally adjusted.

Job seeker stocks possess distinctions from the other variables features. These time series decrease during the chosen time span, whereas the others generally rise. The means are higher than the medians for the job seekers stocks, and both time series are right skewed. The other variables are left skewed, excluding the vacancy stock, which is nearly symmetric. The coefficient of variation is the lowest for job seekers stocks. A relatively low variation is further confirmed by the turnover indices. Vacancies are more volatile and should enjoy a lower expected duration. The time series display a high degree of persistence.

Table 1. Main statistical properties of the variables, 1994-2005

	$O \rightarrow E$	U	J	u^{a}	V	v
mean	152296	1906811	3540272	392099	94560	168378
median	172814	1682303	3196175	404939	102657	199315
min	27211	1509629	2944337	224557	16010	27861
max	247456	2705753	4766034	491944	215337	264115
stand. dev.	55528	376350	559615	58272	51387	65009
coef. of variation	0.365	0.197	0.158	0.149	0.543	0.389
monthly autocor.	0.945	0.981	0.979	0.937	0.958	0.950
average turnover						
$\frac{\text{unempl. inflow}}{\text{unempl. stock}}$	–	0.22	0.12	–	–	
$\frac{\text{vacancy inflow}}{\text{vacancy stock}}$	–	–	–	–	2.05	
no. of observations	136	136	136	136	136	136

[a] – data re-estimated (compare Álvarez de Toledo et al. (2008)).
Source: Author`s own calculation on the basis of Database published by Servicio Público de Empleo Estatal (2012).

Table 2. Unit root tests results

	M	U	J	u^{b}	V	v
ADF	-2.18	-2.98	-3.72	-1.92	-1.46	-2.23
(p-value)	(0.22)	(0.04)	(0.00)	(0.32)	(0.55)	(0.20)
ADF[a]	-14.94	-1.94	-1.95	-15.03	-10.90	-14.09
(p-value)	(0.00)	(0.05)	(0.05)	(0.00)	(0.00)	(0.00)
Phillips-Perron	-2.21	-3.17	-3.55	-2.08	-1.50	-2.14
(p-value)	(0.20)	(0.02)	(0.01)	(0.26)	(0.53)	(0.23)
Phillips-Perron[a]	-14.65	-6.38	-4.76	-15.08	-10.85	-14.11
(p-value)	(0.00)	(0.00)	(0.00)	(0.00)	(0.00)	(0.00)

[a] – calculated for first differences, [b] – data re-estimated (compare Álvarez de Toledo et al. (2008)).

Table 2 compiles the unit root tests results for the particular variables. I apply ADF and Phillips-Perron tests. The ADF test results indicate that the time series are I(1), excluding the unemployment stock and total job seekers stock, which appear to be I(0). This inference is enhanced by the Phillips-Perron test results.

A single equation model

The empirical research of the matching function focuses on determining the values of the outflow from unemployment to employment elasticities with respect to the job seekers and vacancies. This focus allows the identification of the matching process character and the indication of the impact of the other variables on the trade process efficiency, e.g., means of the active labor market policy.

Shapiro and Stiglitz (1984) specify the job queuing model of the labor market matching process. The idea of the trade process is based on the unemployment queue. Workers possess perfect information regarding job opportunities. However, workers must wait for new job posts because there is an insufficient number of vacancies. Once new offers are announced, job seekers are randomly assigned to new job posts. The randomness is justified by the large discrepancy between demand and supply. Formally, the matching function takes the form:

$$M_t = m(U_{t-1}, v_t)$$

where:

M_t – outflow from unemployment to employment during month t;

U_{t-1} – unemployment stock at the end of month $t-1$, or J_{t-1} – total job seekers stock at the end of month $t-1$; and

v_t – vacancy inflow during month t.

I estimate the job queuing matching function using the OLS estimator. The results suffer from high autocorrelation, which is addressed by using the AR(1)

Table 3. Job queuing model estimates, 1994-2005

Independent variable / statistics	Parameters estimates (t-student statistics)					
	I	I[a]	I ECM	II	II[a]	II ECM
lnU_{t-1}	0.330 (4.67)	0.237 (2.32)	-	-	-	-
lnJ_{t-1}	-	-	-	0.382 (4.51)	0.265 (2.16)	-
lnv_t	1.069 (41.85)	1.033 (27.78)	-	1.061 (42.88)	1.025 (28.38)	-
$dlnv_t$	-	-	0.897 (18.35)	-	-	0.895 (18.25)
ECT parameter	-	-	-0.619 (-8.01)	-	-	-0.612 (-7.92)
R^2 (adj. R^2)	0.985 0.985	0.986 0.986	0.745 0.743	0.985 0.985	0.986 0.986	0.743 0.741
ADF test for residuals (p-value)	-3.95 (0.00)	-4.97 (0.00)	-4.82 (0.00)	-3.87 (0.00)	-4.93 (0.00)	-4.72 (0.00)

[a] – equation includes AR(1), dependent variable – outflow from unemployment to employment, ECT - error correction term
t-Statistics presented in parentheses

Table 4. VAR models' diagnostic tests results

	VAR model (job seekers stocks = unemployment stock)	VAR model (job seekers stocks = total job seekers stock)
Lag structure (AIC criterion)	4	2
LM autocorrelation p-value	0.01 (5th degree)	0.21 (3rd degree)
Doornik-Hansen normality test (skewness, joint p-value)	0.32	0.11

The models comprise dummy variables.

Table 5. Cointegration and Granger block exogeneity tests results

	VAR model (job seekers stocks = unemployment stock)	VAR model (job seekers stocks = total job seekers stock)
Cointegration Rank Test (trace): no. of cointegrating equations	2	1
Granger block exogeneity Wald test, dependent variable χ^2 (p-value):		
• matches	18.66 (0.02)	10.63 (0.03)
• unemployment stock	12.95 (0.11)	-
• total job seekers stock	-	6.56 (0.16)
• vacancy inflow	11.98 (0.15)	3.55 (0.47)

term; the corrected specifications do not provide qualitatively different results. Short-term and long-term multipliers are estimated using Engle-Granger and Engle-Yoo procedures. Model I (in Table 3) refers to the regular job queuing equation; I[a] contains the AR(1) term, and I ECM checks for a long-term relation and the speed of approaching a new equilibrium. The supply is approximated by the unemployment stock. Models II, II[a] and II ECM are analogous; however, they contain total job seekers stock as a supply approximation. All the results for the ADF test show that, at the 5% significance level, the null hypothesis of the unit root test in the disturbance term should be rejected; therefore, the model approaches long run equilibrium. Overall, the model specifications fit the data reasonably well.

The coefficients express a higher impact of the vacancy inflow on the number of matches than the job seekers pools. This conclusion applies to both long-term and short-term perspectives, in which the vacancy inflow is the sole statistically significant variable that describes the trade between demand and supply. The results do not differ due to the variable approximation of different job seekers pools. The estimated coefficients of the error correction term (ECT) indicate a high speed of achieving equilibrium. On average, equilibrium occurs in less than two months. The Engle-Yoo procedure does not change the results.

A multivariate space analysis

I develop two VAR models to express the possible trade between the job seekers pools and the vacancies: $M = f(U,v)$ and $M = f(J,v)$. I use the logarithms of the outflow from unemployment to employment, vacancy inflow and job seekers pools (unemployment stock or job seekers stock). The final model specifications are based on the respective diagnostic tests (compare Table 4). I analyze the lag structure, the inverse roots of the characteristic AR polynomial and the residuals.

The stability condition is satisfied for both models. The model with the unemployment stock requires 4 lags; the model with total job seekers stock requires 2 lags. The LM autocorrelation tests imply no serial correlation (at the 1% significance level for the unemployment stock model and at the 5% significance level for the other model). The Doornik-Hansen skewness test indicates multivariate normal distribution of the residuals.

Next, I perform a cointegration test and a Granger block exogeneity test (compare Table 5). The unemployment stock model experiences 2 cointegrating vectors. The total job seekers stock model experiences one cointegrating vector. The Granger block exogeneity test implies that, in both specifications, only the variable that presents the number of matches should be treated as the endogenous variable. The others are exogenous. Pairwise Granger causality tests indicate, at the 5% significance level, that the unemployment stock influences the outflow from unemployment to employment as does the vacancy inflow. Nevertheless, the job seekers stock does not influence the outflow from unemployment to employment and the inverse relation does not hold. Then, the results question the relevance of a multivariate space analysis.

Discussion

I have encountered two papers that refer to non-stationary data in analyzing labor market matching in Spain. Bell (1997) performs comparative analysis of the matching process in three European countries, including Spain. She adopts a general dynamic error correction regression specification with differences and lagged levels of the dependent and explanatory variables. Gałecka-Burdziak (2013) uses two-step Engle-Granger and three-step Engle-Yoo procedures. In both papers, the unemployment negatively influences the matching process, whereas the impact of vacancies is positive.

The diagnostic tests of the VAR models question the analysis of a public intermediation matching process in the Spanish labor market. It appears that the outflows from unemployment are explained by the number of agents present in the labor market; however, the inverse relation does not hold.

Thus, the single equation model estimates appear to provide consistent results. However, one must remember that the Engle-Granger procedure provides one cointegrating vector. If there are more such vectors, the outcome may constitute a linear combination of the basis vectors (Welfe 2009). The quantitative results show that demand appears to be the driving force in the job creation process that occurs through public employment intermediation, which is in accordance with previous analyses. ECT estimates express the high efficiency of the market. For a comparison, we can recall the Berman (1997) and Gałecka-Burdziak (2013) analyses. Berman (1997) performs estimates and simulations of the matching process in the Israeli labor market. He finds the job search process to be extremely efficient; the labor market absorbs shocks within less than a few months. Gałecka-Burdziak (2013) obtains comparable results (less than a few months) for the Polish and Spanish labor markets. The equilibrium in the matching function concept is defined by the equity of inflows and outflows from unemployment. High efficiency may reflect the large volatility of the market and a permanent adjustment process.

Conclusions

I conduct quantitative analysis of the labor market matching process in Spain during the 1994-2005 time period. This time span reflects an upward movement along a Beveridge curve; therefore, we can expect homogenous trade technology. I refer solely to public employment intermediation by using registered unemployment data. I focus on the problem of non-stationary data. I conduct multivariate space analysis and use a single equation model. The results are, in general, consistent with the literature findings.

The number of matches, the outflow from unemployment to employment, increases when new job offers are registered at public employment offices. The demand role in generating matches is unquestionable. However, it should be emphasized that the number of matches is computed on the basis of the number of covered job posts.

Supply's role is much smaller; therefore, the workers exert a higher congestion effect on each other. Job seekers compete for job offers. The relevance of the job queuing model confirms that job seekers are randomly ascribed to new job offers. There arises the need to increase the number of job offers available to match to improve the public employment intermediation matching process.

References

Albaek, K., Handen, H. (2004). The rise in Danish unemployment: reallocation or mismatch? *Oxford Bulletin of Economics and Statistics*, 66 (4), 515–536.

Alujas Ruiz, J. A. (2002). Politicas activas de Mercado de trabajo en Espana 1985 - 2000 [Active labor market policies in Spain 1985 - 2000] (Doctoral thesis, University of Barcelona, Barcelona, Spain).

Álvarez de Toledo, P., Núñez, F., & Usabiaga, C. (2004). *Los datos de la Estadística de Empleo del INEM y la estimación de la función de emparejamiento para la economía española* [INEM data and the matching function estimates for the Spanish economy] (Working Paper No E2004/09) Fundación Centro de Estudios Andaluces.

Álvarez de Toledo, P., Núñez, F., & Usabiaga, C. (2008). La función de emparejamiento en el mercado de trabajo español [The matching function in the Spanish labor market]. *Revista de Economia Aplicada*, 16 (48), 5–35.

Antolín, P. (1994). Unemployment flows and vacancies in Spain (Working Paper No. 94-05). The *Valencian Institute* of Economic Research. Retrieved from http://www.ivie.es/downloads/docs/wpasec/wpasec-1994-05.pdf

Archambault, R., Fortin M. (2001). The Beveridge curve and unemployment fluctuation in Canada. *Canadian Journal of Economics*, 34 (1), 58–81.

Bell, U. (1997). *A Comparative Analysis of the Aggregate Matching Process in France, Great Britain and Spain* (Working Paper No. 9721). Central Bank of Spain.

Berman, E. (1997). Help wanted, job needed: estimates of a matching function from employment service data. *Journal of Labor Economics*, 15 (1), 251–292.

Blanchard, O., Diamond, P. (1989). The Beveridge Curve. *Brookings Papers on Economic Activity*, 20 (1), 1–76.

de Francesco, A. (1999). The relationship between unemployment and vacancies in Australia. *Applied Economics*, 31 (5), 641–652.

Gałecka-Burdziak, E. (2013). Mechanisms of labour market matching of job seekers and vacancies (Doctoral thesis, Warsaw School of Economics, Warsaw, Poland).

Núñez, F. (2006). Análisis *Macroeconómico de los mercados de trabajo Español y Andaluz: La curva de Beveridge y la función de emparejamiento* [The macroeconomic analysis of the labor markets in Spain and Andalusia. The Beveridge curve and the matching function] (Doctoral thesis, University of Seville, Seville, Spain).

Núñez, F., Usabiaga C. (2007). *La Curva de Beveridge y la Función de Emparejamiento: Revisión de Sus Fundamentos Teóricos y de la Literatura Empírica, con Especial Énfasis en el Caso Español* [The Beveridge curve and the matching function. The theoretical and empirical literature review, with the focus on the Spanish case]. Seville: Fundación Centro de Estudios Andaluces.

Petrongolo, B., Pissarides, C. (2001). Looking into the black box: a survey of the matching function. *Journal of Economic Literature*, 39 (2), 390–431.

Petrongolo, B., Pissarides, C. (2008). *The ins and outs of European unemployment* (IZA Discussion Paper No. 3315). Institute for the Study of Labor.

Servicio Público de Empleo Estatal (2012). Database. Available at: http://www.sepe.es/contenidos/que_es_el_sepe/estadisticas/index.html

Shapiro, C., Stiglitz, J. (1984). Equilibrium unemployment as a worker discipline device. *The American Economic Review*, 74 (3), 433–444.

Soininen, H. (2006). *Empirical Studies on Labor Market Matching*. (Doctoral thesis, Swedish School of Economics and Business Administration, Department of Economics, Helsinki, Finland). Retrieved from https://helda.helsinki.fi/bitstream/handle/10227/61/159-951-555-917-0.pdf?sequence=1

Welfe, A. (2009). *Ekonometria. Metody i ich zastosowanie* [Econometrics. Methods and application]. Warszaw: Polskie Wydawnictwo Ekonomiczne.

15

Types of agglomeration economies: effects on business innovation

Enrique Claver-Cortés[1], Bartolome Marco-Lajara[1], Encarnacion Manresa-Marhuenda[1]

ABSTRACT A review of the literature does not provide conclusive results about the effects caused by firm agglomeration on innovation. In order to shed light on this issue, this paper draws a distinction among three kinds of agglomeration economies and empirically tests their respective impact on business innovation. The advantage that external knowledge generated through concentration can bring to each company depends on its absorptive capacity. Hence, it is posited that this dynamic capability acts as a mediator in the relationship between agglomeration and innovation. Using data from a survey conducted in 2013 by the Technological Innovation Panel (PITEC), an analysis of these ideas was performed using a sample of 2,906 high and medium-high technology companies. The results obtained indicate that several types of agglomeration economies exist and that the net effect each one of them has on innovation is different. More specifically, only urbanization economies favor innovation. Additionally, all of our findings reveal that firms increase their greater absorptive capacity in the context of agglomeration.

KEY WORDS: Innovation, Agglomeration, Externalities, Absorptive Capacity

[1] Department of Management, University of Alicante, Spain

1. Introduction

Given that innovation –which generates growth, efficiency and profit in today's world– constitutes a key element in competitiveness, firms must innovate if they want to survive (Beugelsdijk, 2007). According to the Oslo Manual, innovation refers to the conception and implementation of significant changes in products, marketing, technical processes, and organizational processes for the purpose of improving firm performance (OECD/Eurostat, 2005).

Correspondence concerning this article should be addressed to: **Bartolome Marco-Lajara**, Department of Management, University of Alicante, P.O. Box 99, E-03080 Alicante, Spain. E-mail: bartolome.marco@ua.es

However, the complexity that characterizes the environment of many industries forces companies not only to cooperate but also to exploit external knowledge and combine it with internal sources of knowledge (Chesbrough, 2003).

Although access to external knowledge may prove difficult, the physical proximity of firms favors their mutual interactions as does the existence of a set of common standards and values that enable the exchange and transfer of (tacit) knowledge. The latter is linked to the agglomeration of firms and institutions in a geographical area, i.e., agglomeration economies (Marshall, 1920). In this sense, a line of research forecasts a positive effect of localization in agglomerations on firm innovation and performance.

Regarding the impact of location on business innovation, the dynamic capabilities approach indicates that the effect varies across companies, depending on the individual capabilities of each company (Maskell & Malmberg, 1999; Stuart & Sorenson, 2003), especially that of one of the most often analyzed capabilities in recent years, namely, absorptive capacity (Giuliani & Bell, 2005; Molina-Morales, García-Villaverde, & Parra-Requena, 2014). Dynamic capabilities are defined as organizational skills that allow firms to integrate, reconfigure, renew, and create internal and external resources to develop and maintain competitive advantages as a response to the constant and increasing changes in the business environment (Teece, Pisano, & Shuen, 1997; Winter, 2003). From this perspective, the aim of this paper is to analyze and provide empirical evidence of the role that absorptive capacity (AC) plays in the relationship between agglomeration and business innovation.

This dynamic capability was described by Cohen and Levinthal (1990) as representing "a firm's ability to value, assimilate, and apply new knowledge." In turn, Kim (1998) defines absorptive capacity as "the ability to learn and solve problems," whereas Zahra and George (2002) contend that it is "a set of organizational processes and routines whereby firms acquire, assimilate, transform, and exploit knowledge in order to produce a dynamic organizational capability." Other researchers, such as Lane, Koka and Pathak (2006, p. 856), have broadened the concept by defining it as "a firm's ability to utilize external knowledge through a sequential exploratory, transformative, and exploitative learning process." Thus, AC is envisaged as a source of competitive advantage that plays a central role in the development of competences, capabilities, and innovations and in the creation of knowledge (Cohen & Levinthal, 1990), insofar as increased AC implies greater skill with respect to external knowledge achievement and implementation, thereby extending their possibilities compared to firms that, in the best of cases, can only exploit internal knowledge.

Seeking to achieve our aims, the literature review provided in Section 2 contributes to the task of hypothesis formulation, and Section 3 explains the methodology applied in the empirical research. After presenting the results of our study in Section 4, the conclusions drawn from our research are summarized in Section 5.

2. Literature review

2.1. Effects of agglomeration economies on business innovation

According to studies on agglomeration, the concentration of economic activity generates different types of externalities (Anselin, Varga, & Acs, 1997; Audretsch, 2003). These external economies, also known as economies of agglomeration, assume that the profits of a firm located near other firms increase as the number of firms in the same location increases (Appold, 1995). However, recent studies find that agglomeration can also have negative effects on business profits because greater competition exists among companies to obtain necessary inputs, such as land, employees, etc. (Arikan & Schilling, 2010; Flyer & Shaver, 2003; Folta, Cooper, & Baik, 2006; Glaesmeier, 1991; Pouder & St. John, 1996; Prevezer, 1997).

The purpose of this paper is to clarify the ambiguity surrounding the relationship between agglomeration and innovation. We begin by distinguishing among the three types of agglomeration economies that may prove beneficial for innovation depending on the type of co-located firms, namely, urbanization economies, localization economies, and knowledge-intensive economies.

Urbanization economies (Jacobs, 1969) are those derived from the concentration of companies that develop various economic activities in a particular area or region. This plurality of technological and commercial realities carries multiple and varied types of knowledge that firms can share and combine, thus enhancing innovation (Frenken, van Oort, & Verburg, 2007). It is in this context that inter-firm cooperation becomes feasible and allows for the generation of new knowledge, insofar as these firms are not rivals because they come from different industrial sectors. Moreover, creativity and innovation are likely to be favored through the combination of heterogeneous knowledge stemming from various industrial and commercial environments. As such a spatial concentration of activities without sectorial or industrial specialization is also characterized by a wider range of infrastructures, specialized services, and agents that act as middlemen and are responsible, to some extent, for the investment attraction effect. A first hypothesis is formulated based on these thoughts.

Hypothesis 1: Business innovation increases with urbanization economies.

Localization economies (Glaeser, Kallal, Scheinkman, & Shleifer, 1992; Marshall, 1920) are those derived from the concentration of companies that develop the same economic activity in a specific area or region. This geographical concentration produces externalities that allow firms to learn from each other. In this case, apart from the transmission of knowledge and ideas across companies, the use of the same language, together with the existence of a common knowledge base, permits greater interaction among firms and generates greater possibilities for new knowledge creation. Thus, we present the following hypothesis:

Hypothesis 2a: Business innovation increases with localization economies.

Conversely, a higher concentration of potential competitors in the same place implies a greater relative shortage of resources, particularly that of valuable knowledge. In other words, although it is true that knowledge is not necessarily exhausted, it stops being valuable once it becomes indiscriminately accessible to any rival. That is why, within a context of physical proximity characterized by greater exposure to possible imitators, those firms that generate and take advantage of external knowledge must invest in the protection of that knowledge. This reallocation of resources meant for isolation and protection will most probably prove detrimental to investments in innovation.

Furthermore, in this regard, aside from the risk of being plundered by imitators, those firms that are best equipped in terms of knowledge will choose not to be located in places characterized by the concentration of competitors.

Taking into account both lines of reasoning allows us to conclude that being located in an environment with a higher concentration of firms belonging to the same industrial sector favors innovation up to a certain level of agglomeration after which saturation becomes excessive and the net effect on innovation then becomes negative (Marco-Lajara, Claver-Cortés, Úbeda-García, & Zaragoza-Sáez, 2016; Melo, Graham, & Noland, 2009; Sorensen & Sorenson, 2003). Consequently, we advance the following hypothesis:

Hypothesis 2b: An inverted U-shaped relationship exists between business innovation and localization economies.

Knowledge-intensive economies (Knoben, Raspe, Arikan, & Oort, 2016) arise in locations next to firms and/or organizations that produce knowledge, in an environment where knowledge is valued, transferred, and generated. This knowledge-intensity is an essential feature of regions without industry specialization and where innovative and knowledge-oriented agents are located. Thus, we formulate Hypothesis 3.

Hypothesis 3: Business innovation increases with knowledge-intensive economies.

2.2. The mediation effect of absorptive capacity

Even though a large number of firms may actually be exposed to identical environmental conditions, not all of them are able to convert outside knowledge into results with the same levels of success because they differ in their abilities to use these sources of knowledge (Caloghirou, Kastelli, & Tsakanikas, 2004; Rothaermel & Hess, 2007).

In fact, the existence of more external sources of potentially useful knowledge increases the possible combinations of knowledge and, therefore, the complexity of its management. As a result, the inability of firms to manage and exploit that knowledge can limit their possibilities for innovation (Henderson & Clark, 1990; Laursen & Salter, 2006), which is why it is necessary to highlight the role of AC (Cohen & Levinthal, 1990). This capability, as related to the firm's ability to learn, constitutes a multidimensional construct that makes knowledge acquisition, assimilation, transformation, and exploitation possible.

Several authors suggest breaking AC down into two dimensions (Jansen, Van Den Bosch, & Volberda, 2005) that are related to one another through mutual influences (Katila & Ahuja, 2002), namely, potential absorptive capacity (PAC) and realized absorptive capacity (RAC). PAC allows a firm to be receptive to knowledge coming from the outside and is influenced by, among other things, the prior knowledge owned by the firm and its participation in alliances, whereas RAC represents the ability to generate and apply new knowledge by taking the existing knowledge as a reference and investing in regenerating and updating that knowledge. Furthermore, bearing in mind that knowledge has a cumulative nature, RAC may depend on the level of education, experience, and training of employees. In this respect, the greater this training is, the greater is the ability to implement and profit from the knowledge that has been absorbed.

In relation to the link between AC and innovation, it has been found that AC positively impacts the chances for technological innovation (Cepeda-Carrión, Cegarra-Navarro, & Jiménez-Jiménez, 2012), process and organizational innovation (Murovec & Prodan, 2009), product innovation (George, Zahra, Wheatley, & Khan, 2001), patenting (Sørensen & Stuart, 2000), etc. Thus, the following hypothesis is posed:

Hypothesis 4: AC has a positive effect on business innovation.

The agglomeration of firms encourages their participation in networks and alliances. Such collaboration occurs in various ways. For example, collaboration can be established between non-rival firms seeking knowledge complementarity, between rival companies' intent on creating mutually valuable knowledge, and between firms and other organizations interested in knowledge generation.

In any case, this interaction appears to be a determining factor of AC (Caloghirou *et al.*, 2004) as both the learning and the accumulation of the knowledge that lies at the base of AC are gradual processes of an interactive and social nature. Accordingly, AC depends on the external context where it develops.

It is also important to emphasize that apart from fostering the generation of a skilled labor market, geographic concentration also contributes to creating knowledge and skills for the workers of agglomerated firms, as this labor market ensures a certain base of knowledge and skills that positively impacts organizational AC when employed (Tallman, Jenkins, Henry, & Pinch, 2004).

Finally, the literature mentions other drivers, such as the level of previous internal knowledge (number of patents), employee skills, periodical investments in innovation (R&D, training), etc., and highlights the importance that corresponds to the allocation of resources. This allocation depends on the expectations of potentially profitable external knowledge. Moreover, those expectations are greater in those environments where access to external knowledge and learning are more likely and more profitable from the perspective of their exploitation (Kaiser, 2002; Veugelers, 1997). Based on these ideas, we formulate the following hypothesis:

Hypothesis 5: Agglomeration economies have a positive effect on AC.

Together, Hypotheses 4 and 5 lead to another hypothesis that predicts a mediating effect of AC on the link between agglomeration and innovation:

Hypothesis 6: AC mediates the relationship between agglomeration and business innovation.

3. Empirical research

3.1. Methodology

Although the present study tests the hypotheses using a multiple linear regression, a variety of models are estimated because not all hypotheses can be tested in the same way. H1, H2a, and H3 predict a direct effect of the independent variable (agglomeration) on the dependent variable (innovation); H4, H5, and H6 forecast a mediating effect; and H2b predicts a non-linear effect.

Furthermore, with respect to H1, H2a, and H3, the model exhibits a general formulation such that $Y = \beta_{10} + \beta_{11} * X + \beta_{12} * C$, where Y is the dependent variable, X is the independent variable, and C is the control variable.

According to Judd and Kenny (1981) and Baron and Kenny (1986), the analysis of the mediating effect requires the formulation of three equations. In the first equation, the dependent variable is estimated using independent and control variables, and the equation is the same as that of the direct effect. In the second equation, the mediator variable is estimated using independent and control variables. Regarding the third, the dependent variable is simultaneously estimated using the independent, mediator, and control variables:

$$Y = \beta_{10} + \beta_{11} * X + \beta_{12} * C + \varepsilon_1$$

$$Me = \alpha_{20} + \alpha_{21} * X + \alpha_{22} * C + \varepsilon_2$$

$$Y = \beta_{30} + \beta_{31} * X + \beta_{32} * Me + \beta_{33} * C + \varepsilon_3$$

Several requirements must be fulfilled to verify the mediating effect, specifically, a statistically significant and non-zero independent variable coefficient in all three equations; a statistically significant and non-zero mediator variable coefficient in the last equation; the absolute value corresponding to the residual effect of the independent variable on the dependent variable, after granting the mediating indirect effect is less than the absolute value of the total effect. In other words, $\beta_{11} \neq 0$, $\alpha_{21} \neq 0$, $\beta_{32} \neq 0$ and $/\beta_{31}/</\beta_{11}/$ -all of these coefficients must be statistically significant.

Considering all of the study variables, the verification model is expressed as follows:

$$INNOVATION = \beta_{10} + \beta_{11} * AGGLOMERATION + + \beta_{12} * CONTROL\ VAR. + \varepsilon_1$$

$$AC = \alpha_{20} + \alpha_{21} * AGGLOMERATION + + \alpha_{22} * CONTROL\ VAR. + \varepsilon_2$$

$$INNOVATION = \beta_{30} + \beta_{31} * AGGLOMERATION + + \beta_{32} * AC + \beta_{33} * CONTROL\ VAR. + \varepsilon_3$$

where $\beta_{11} \neq 0$, $\alpha_{21} \neq 0$, $\beta_{31} \neq 0$ and $/\beta_{31}/</\beta_{11}/$. All of these coefficients must be statistically significant.

Our final task is to verify H2b using a non-linear or quadratic equation. The estimating model adopts the following formulation:

$$Y = \beta_{40} + \beta_{41} * X + \beta_{42} * X^2 + \beta_{43} * C + \varepsilon_4$$

$$INNOVATION=\beta_{40}+\beta_{41}*AGGLOMERATION+ +\beta_{42}*AGGLOMERATION^2+\beta_{43}*CONTROL\ VAR+\varepsilon_4$$

The verification of H2b requires that $\beta_{42}<0$ and be statistically significant.

The IBM Statistical Package for the Social Sciences (SPSS) version 23 was used to conduct the calculations.

3.2. Measurement of variables

The work performed to measure all the variables specified in the equations is supported by the PITEC (*Panel de Innovación Tecnológica*) database, elaborated using a questionnaire about innovation in business.

3.2.1. Dependent variable

Two approaches were considered when estimating INNOVATION. One of the commonly used measures refers to the number of patents for which a company has filed an application (Dutta & Weiss, 1997; Henderson & Cockburn, 1994; Squicciarini, 2008; 2009; Vásquez-Urriago, Barge-Gil, Modrego-Rico, & Paraskevopoulou, 2014). Therefore, our proposal includes the PATNUM variable, which measures the number of patent applications filed between 2011 and 2013. However, one of the drawbacks to this this index is that it fails to consider that not all firms register their innovations with patents.

Furthermore, the term innovation can be measured in a broader sense, which led us to check whether the firm had innovated or modernized products, technical processes, organizational practices, or commercial strategies between 2011 and 2013. Accordingly, the values of thirteen dichotomous variables from the PITEC database, which evaluates the different types of innovations in each firm, allowed us to calculate the variable INNOVA, which aggregates the data for each firm (PITEC, 2013). The value of this variable ranges between 0, indicating the firm has not innovated, and 13, indicating it has innovated in every business area (Montoro-Sánchez, Mora-Valentín, & Ortiz-de-Urbina-Criado, 2012).

A principal components factor analysis was applied with both approaches, which explains 65.55% of variance.

3.2.2. Independent variables

URB.AGGL. represents urbanization economies generated in cities and urban areas. The problem lies in the fact that the PITEC database does not provide any information about the city where the firm's R&D area is located. Hence, we use a proxy variable to indicate whether the firm is located in a scientific and technologic park (STP). This dichotomous variable takes either a 1 if located in an STP or a 0 value otherwise.

STPs are comprised of an agglomeration of firms from several and different industries and other organizations. Cooperation between businesses and organizations is fostered in such locations, and a physical as well as social infrastructure exists that stimulates the creation, access, and acquisition of external knowledge. Accordingly, innovation is encouraged in such locations (Squicciarini, 2008; 2009; Siegel, Westhead, & Wright, 2003).

LOC.AGGL. Localization economies result from the geographic concentration of similar firms in a given area, an autonomous region in our case. The fact that many firms are located in several regions caused us to adopt a criterion when determining the autonomous region associated with each company, more precisely, the place where each firm develops its internal R&D. In this sense, it was decided that this place corresponds to the physical location of R&D workers. The data reveal that 59.73% (1,736) of the firms in our sample have staff who develop their professional activity in R&D on a full-time basis and that 92.74% (1,610) of those firms concentrate their R&D personnel in a single autonomous region, whereas the remaining 126 own assets in several regions.

Bearing all this information in mind, the proportion of high and medium-high technology firms to the total number of firms in each autonomous region enabled us to estimate the LOC.AGGL variable (the data correspond to 2013).

KNOW.AGGL. Knowledge-intensive economies underscore the importance of orientation to innovation, as exhibited by an area or region, on performance with respect to the degree of innovation implemented by the firms located in the specific area or region. Autonomous regions were also chosen as reference geographical areas. Using data provided by the *INE* [Spanish National Statistics Institute], the following variables that indicate the propensity of an autonomous region to innovation were considered: innovation intensity corresponding to the total number of companies (= spending in innovative activities x 100/sales volume); percentage of sales in new or improved products; percentage of employees with higher education; and percentage of innovative firms. A principal components factor analysis explaining 81.61% of the variance for the KNOW.AGGL variable was applied with those four indices.

ABSORPTIVE CAPACITY (AC). AC is a function of the knowledge to which firms can gain access combined with the means used to exploit that knowledge. Therefore, this multidimensional construct results from combining potential absorptive capacity (PAC) and realized absorptive capacity (RAC).

With respect to PAC, the variable EXTSOURC scores the number of external sources of knowledge (machine suppliers, clients/customers, competitors, consultants, private laboratories, universities, public research bodies, technology centers, conferences, fairs or exhibitions, scientific journals, industrial and professional associations) that can be assessed as being of high importance by firms. The value of EXTSOURC ranges from 0 to 9. The opportunity for each firm to access external knowledge through successful alliances, for which the variable SUCCALL was estimated, was also considered. SUCCALL receives a score of 1 if the firm has engaged in developing or innovating products, technological processes, organizational practices, or commercial strategies with other firms or institutions. A principal components factor analysis performed with these two variables enabled us to extract one factor that explains 60.46% of the PAC variance.

As for RAC, the literature often uses measures related to R&D expenditure. Therefore, our study focused on the percentage of internal expenditure R&D over the total expenditure in R&D (INTR&D). RAC not only depends on the implementation of such investments, but its use as an indicator could actually penalize the importance of smaller-sized organizations that are unable to carry out R&D activities on a regular basis. Perhaps for this reason, several studies ultimately stressed the importance of human resources when identifying and assessing this capability (Mangematin & Nesta, 1999). In keeping with the previous line of reasoning, the following indicators were considered: the relative importance of research staff with respect to the entire staff –denoted by the variable RESTAFF– and whether the RAC has a twofold dimension depending on the source of information, i.e., scientific or market-related, on which it is supported (Caloghirou *et al.*, 2004; Murovec & Prodan, 2009). Hence our decision to take two variables into account, namely, R&DSTAFF (percentage of R&D staff employed in internal R&D) and HIGHEDU (percentage of employees who have completed higher education). A principal components factor analysis performed with the aforementioned four variables allowed us to extract a

Table 1. Sample firm distribution by activity sector

CNAE 2009	HIGH & MEDIUM-HIGH TECHNOLOGY SECTOR	N*
	High-Tech Manufacturing Sector	**376**
21	Pharmaceutical	128
26	Computer, Electronic and Optical	230
30.3	Aircraft and Spacecraft and Related Machinery	18
	Medium-High Technology Manufacturing Sector	**1,555**
20	Chemicals and Chemical Products	488
27-28-29	Electrical Equipment; General-Purpose Machinery; Motor Vehicles, Trailers and Semi-Trailers	1,020
30-30.1	Manufacture of other transport equipment; Building of ships and boats	47
	High-Tech Service Sector	**975**
59-58-60-61-62-63	Motion Picture, Video and Television Program Production, Sound Recording and Music Publishing; Programming and Broadcasting; Telecommunications; Computer Programming, Consultancy and Related; Information Service	777
72	Scientific Research and Development	198
	TOTAL	2,906

*Number of firms
Source: PITEC (2013)

factor that explains 77.81% of the RAC variance. Finally, the measure that represents the AC was obtained from a factorial analysis of these two factors (PAC and RAC), which explains 73.35% of the variance.

3.2.3. Control variables

AGE. The number of years during which a firm has been operating since its foundation can influence innovation both positively and negatively. Indeed, greater experience is likely to permit a higher accumulation of knowledge, but it may also become an inertia-generating source that hinders both adaptation and the introduction of novelties in products and processes.

SIZE. Size is significantly correlated with innovation, even though no consensus exists as to whether this relationship is positive or negative. On the one hand, larger firms can be more innovative due to their greater financial holdings, but on the other hand, the higher flexibility and the better communication level actually allows smaller-sized firms to be the most innovative (Damanpour & Gopalakrishnan, 1998). A dichotomous variable, SIZE200, which shows whether the firm is defined as large because it has over 200 employees or is not large, was added to our model to assess this effect.

GEOGRAPHIC SCOPE. The greater or lesser predisposition to innovate may additionally be determined by sales expectations, which in turn are going to depend on the breadth of the geographical markets that constitute the product or service target (Löfsten & Lindelöf, 2003). Thus, sales dispersion will also most likely encourage innovation because of the need to adapt products to the local demand and to the regulations of foreign markets (Vernon, 1966). Based on the information presented herein and following other works such as that authored by Urgal, Quintás and Arévalo-Tomé (2011), the categorical variable GEOGSCOPE was included with three possible situations or values, namely, the local, national, and international markets.

BUSINESS GROUP. Every firm's need to acquire external knowledge, and ultimately to innovate, depends on its affiliation to a business group (Barge-Gil, Vásquez, & Rico, 2011). This was measured by means of a dummy variable that takes the value 1 if it belongs to a business group and 0 otherwise.

3.3. *Population and sample*

The study object of this paper is formed by those firms that have innovated, that is, firms that have engaged in any activity oriented to achieve new or significantly improved products or processes. Previous studies suggest that the dynamism or the technological turbulence typical of each industry is a variable that can largely influence not only greater or lesser proneness to innovation but also other variables relevant for this study, such as AC (Martínez-Senra, Quintás, Sartal, & Vázquez, 2013). This led us to complete our analysis with the innovative firms belonging to sectors that exhibit similar degrees of technological turbulence, more precisely, medium-technology and high-technology sectors. Following the classification adopted by *INE*, medium-technology and high-technology sectors may include both manufacture and service sectors. INE's estimates for 2013 placed the number of firms belonging to these two sectors at 4,823 in Spain.

With regard to the sample, the PITEC database served as the basis for our work. The survey conducted by PITEC in 2013 included the responses of 10,074 firms, 2,906 of which (just above 28.84%) belonged to the medium-high technology and high technology sectors. Table 1 displays the distribution of firms by activity sectors.

4. Results

The following tables summarize the results of all the models estimated.[1] As presented in Table 2, H1, H4 (this effect is included in every table), and H5 were verified when considering the urbanization economies generated in a STP. Moreover, confirmation was equally obtained for H6, according to which AC mediates the influence of agglomeration on business innovation.

Instead, Tables 3 and 4 test the effect of localization economies on business innovation (H2a and H2b). The absence of a direct and significant effect becomes evident, which means that neither H2a nor H2b are verified. It can, however, be proved that these economies directly and significantly impact the AC of firms (H5). An additional regression was performed in which the relationship between AC and the localization economies was non-linear. The results of that regression indicate that AC increases up to a certain level of agglomeration at which point it then begins to decrease. This is the effect as predicted by H2b for business innovation.

Finally, knowledge-intensive economies exhibit the same patterns as do the other types of economies (Table 5). Moreover, they do not have a direct and significant effect on innovation, which prevents us from validating H3 and H6, but they do cause such an effect on AC (H5).

With regard to control variables, despite the fact that none of the control variables has a significant effect on absolute value as none of the estimated coefficients exceeds one, all but AGE cause a positive effect and are statistically significant in every estimated equation.

5. Discussion, conclusions, and future lines of research

Part of the literature dedicated to studying the effect of location on business profits has traditionally identified location and agglomeration as determining factors of business innovation. However, this literature does not provide conclusive results regarding the extent to which firm agglomeration influences innovation. Seeking to provide insight on this issue, the present paper distinguishes three types of agglomeration economies, namely, urbanization economies, localization economies, and knowledge-intensive economies, and empirically tests the effect that each of these economies has on business innovation.

Each one of the three externalities has some bearing on innovation for reasons associated with knowledge externalities, that is, the external knowledge of a collective nature that firms access, acquire, and use to improve their profits. Nevertheless, the exploitation of this location effect is far from symmetrical or similar. Considering the dynamic capabilities approach as a reference, the literature review has allowed us to highlight that absorptive capacity played a key role in the relationship between location and

Table 2. Testing the Mediating and Direct Effects of URG.AGGL and AC on INNOVATION

			DIRECT EFFECT	MEDIATING EFFECT	
	DEPENDENT VARIABLE	**INNOVATION**	**INNOVATION**	**AC**	**INNOVATION**
INDEPENDENT VARIABLES	URG.AGGL		0.513***	0.708***	0.243***
	AC				0.381***
	AGE	0.001	0.002**	0.002	0.002*
	GROUP	0.102***	0.107***	0.087**	0.074**
	SIZE200	0.539***	0.523***	0.124**	0.475***
	GEOGSCOPE	0.257***	0.250***	0.328***	0.125***
	Constant	-0.866***	-0.921***	-1.055***	-0.519***
	R^2	0.079	0.098	0.078	0.232

*p < 0.1; **p < 0.05; ***p < 0.01.

Table 3. Testing the Mediating and Direct Effects of LOC.AGGL and AC on INNOVATION

			DIRECT EFFECT	MEDIATING EFFECT	
	DEPENDENT VARIABLE	**INNOVATION**	**INNOVATION**	**AC**	**INNOVATION**
INDEPENDENT VARIABLES	LOC.AGGL		-0.220	0.323**	-0.326*
	AC				0.327***
	AGE	0.001	0.001	-0.002**	0.002
	GROUP	0.102***	0.068	-0.021	0.075*
	SIZE200	0.539***	0.461***	0.025	0.453***
	GEOGSCOPE	0.257***	0.175***	0.067*	0.153***
	Constant	-0.866***	-0.341**	0.462***	-0.492***
	R^2	0.079	0.074	0.007	0.151

*p < 0.1; **p < 0.05; ***p < 0.01.

Table 4. Testing the Mediating and Direct Effects of LOC.AGGL² and AC on INNOVATION

			DIRECT EFFECT	MEDIATING EFFECT	
	DEPENDENT VARIABLE	INNOVATION	INNOVATION	AC	INNOVATION
INDEPENDENT VARIABLES	$LOC.AGGL^2$		-0.385	0.458**	-0.535*
	AC				0.327***
	AGE	0.001	0.001	-0.002**	0.002
	GROUP	0.102***	0.068	-0.019	0.074*
	SIZE200	0.539***	0.461***	0.024	0.453***
	GEOGSCOPE	0.257***	0.174***	0.067*	0.152***
	Constant	-0.866***	-0.341**	0.504***	-0.527***
	R^2	0.079	0.074	0.006	0.150

*p < 0.1; **p < 0.05; ***p < 0.01.

Table 5. Testing the Mediating and Direct Effects of KNOW.AGGL and AC on INNOVATION

			DIRECT EFFECT	MEDIATING EFFECT	
	DEPENDENT VARIABLE	INNOVATION	INNOVATION	AC	INNOVATION
INDEPENDENT VARIABLES	KNOW.AGGL		-0.029	0.032*	-0.039**
	AC				0.327***
	AGE	0.001	0.001	-0.002**	0.002
	GROUP	0.102***	0.069	-0.020	0.076*
	SIZE200	0.539***	0.462***	0.023	0.454***
	GEOGSCOPE	0.257***	0.175***	0.065*	0.154***
	Constant	-0.866***	-0.392***	0.540***	-0.568***
	R^2	0.079	0.074	0.006	0.151

*p < 0.1; **p < 0.05; ***p < 0.01.

innovation, as this is what determines the acquisition and use of external knowledge.

An empirical study based on a sample of 2,906 firms in high and medium-high technology sectors with data provided by PITEC (2013) was performed to delve deeper into the analysis of agglomeration, AC, and business innovation.

The results obtained allow us to conclude that only urbanization economies, estimated using localization in a STP, and AC cause direct and significant impacts on innovation and that, moreover, the mediating effect is only met in these agglomeration economies. No unanimity can be found, however, regarding the existing empirical evidence, and there is no consensus on the influence location in a STP has on innovation (Colombo & Delmastro, 2002; Felsenstein, 1994; Ferguson & Olofsson, 2004; Jiménez-Moreno, Martínez-Cañas, Ruiz-Palomino, & Sáez-Martínez, 2013; Löfsten & Lindelöf, 2001; Siegel *et al.*, 2003; Squicciarini, 2008; 2009; Sofoulli & Vonortas, 2007; Westhead, 1997; Yang, Motohashi, & Chen, 2009). In addition to methodological inequalities, an explanation of these discrepancies is found in the socioeconomic context that characterizes each country. Thus, the conditions existing inside and outside the parks in a number of countries, such as Sweden and the United Kingdom, are quite similar and, therefore, being located inside these parks does not provide significant additional advantages. Rather, there are nations, such as Italy and Spain, where being located in a TSP favors firm innovation because it provides a varied environment where interaction and/or learning becomes much more likely.

Meanwhile, with respect to the rest of the economies (localization and knowledge-intensive), and unlike what could be expected, it was impossible for us to validate a direct effect on innovation; in other words, our study cannot validate that being located in an agglomeration of firms belonging to the same industrial sector or next to agents that value knowledge has a favorable impact on innovation. This outcome is consistent with the findings of other authors (Alcácer & Chung, 2014; Boschma & Ter Wal, 2007; Díez-Vial & Fernández-Olmos, 2015; Huang, Yu, & Seetoo, 2012; Morrison & Rabelloti, 2009) and may be explained in a variety of ways.

One explanation would revolve around the fact that rivalry between agents may result in competition for external knowledge or for participation in the networks within which such knowledge flows. For example, in the context of industrial districts, Breschi and Lissoni (2001) point out that specialized knowledge does not circulate openly; instead, its creation, access, and use seem to be restricted to certain specific communities or networks inside the district. In this way, knowledge remains external to each one of the firms; it cannot be stated that it is freely disseminated across the district, becoming a *club* asset (Morrison, 2008). This makes us reflect not only on the fact that being located near sources of external knowledge does not guarantee access to it but also on the importance of developing the ability to establish and manage alliances as well as on the extent to which this influences the generation of and access to external valuable knowledge resulting from cooperation.

It could also be assumed that firms characterized for being more autonomous and self-sufficient from the knowledge point of view depend to a lesser extent on the advantages that location in agglomerations can bring and that they have a stronger need for protection against exposure and potential imitation. This probably justifies why they seem less willing to be located close to other rival firms or to those for which external knowledge really is a must. Being able to prove this argument would allow us to state that the appeal of agglomerations is much greater for firms that are more strongly dependent on external knowledge.

Finally, it would be of interest to verify whether firms put in place more sophisticated knowledge protection mechanisms when they interact with potentially more dangerous firms or those showing a higher AC (Alcácer & Chung, 2014). This might result in part of the resources dedicated to innovation being allocated elsewhere, with the corresponding deleterious effect on innovative outcomes.

In any case, what the results obtained do allow us to state is that the location in contexts where agglomeration economies arise (urbanization, localization, and knowledge-intensive) actually has an impact on innovation or, at least, on the ability to acquire, assimilate, transform, and exploit the knowledge that makes this innovation. As a matter of fact, the development achieved in AC not only positively correlates with the location in places characterized by agglomeration but also depends on the level thereof.

In addition to the possible contributions made with this study, our work has a number of limitations. The first problem which deserves to be mentioned has to do with the causality involved in the relationship between some variables because that causality was imposed by the researchers. This led us to wonder if the positive relationship between AC and agglomeration economies occurs because the former comes as a consequence of the latter or if it is the other way round. In other words, if it is the agglomeration that favors a greater development of AC or, alternatively, if it is the higher level of development achieved in AC that determines the location in agglomeration areas for the purpose of gaining access to knowledge spillovers. The implementation of other more robust analysis techniques in the future might help to clarify this aspect.

As for the empirical results obtained, potential reasonable improvements can equally be suggested by using primary data specifically built for the interests of this research, together with other indicators to represent variables, constructs, etc. Furthermore, it should not be forgotten that each agglomeration (either in a country or in an autonomous region, an industrial district, or a STP) is different, insofar as the socio-economic conditions, the stage of the life cycle, the degree of agglomeration, or the diversity of firms, managers -amongst other things- vary, which has different implications for the firms located therein. Consequently, including the "individuality" of each agglomeration could prove interesting for a future line of research in which the characteristics of the agglomerations that determine whether firms are more profitable due to their location would be more easily identified.

References

Alcácer, J., & Chung, W. (2014). Location strategies and knowledge spillovers. *Management Science, 53*(5), 760-776.

Anselin, L., Varga, A. & Acs, Z. J. (1997). Local geographic spillovers between university research and high technology innovations. *Journal of Urban Economics, 42*(3), 422-448.

Appold, S. J. (1995). Agglomeration, interorganizational networks, and competitive performance in the US metalworking sector. *Economic Geography, 71*(1), 27-54.

Arikan, A. T., & Schilling, M. A. (2010). Structure and governance in industrial districts: Implications for competitive advantage. *Journal of Management Studies, 48*(4), 772-803.

Audretsch, D. B. (2003). Innovation and spatial externalities. *International Regional Science Review, 26*(2), 167-174.

Barge-Gil, A., Vásquez-Urriago, A. & Modrego-Rico, A., (2011). El impacto de los parques científicos y tecnológicos españoles sobre la innovación empresarial según distintos tipos de empresas. La innovación como factor de competitividad de la empresa española [The impact of the Spanish science and technology parks on business innovation according to different types of firms. Innovation as a factor in the competitiveness of the Spanish firm]. *ICE: Revista de economía*, 860, 73-88.

Baron, R. M., & Kenny, D. A. (1986). The moderator-mediator variable distinction in social psychological research: Conceptual, strategic and statistical considerations. *Journal of Personality and Social Psychology, 51*(6), 1173-1182.

Beugelsdijk, S. (2007). The regional environment and a firm´s innovative performance: A plea for a multilevel interactionist approach. *Economic Geography, 83*(2), 181-199.

Boschma, R. A. & Ter Wal, A. L. J. (2007). Knowledge networks and innovative performance in an industrial district: The case of a footwear district in the south of Italy. *Industry and Innovation, 14*(2), 177-199.

Breschi, S., & Lissoni, F. (2001). Knowledge spillovers and local innovation systems: a critical survey. *Industrial and Corporate Change, 10*(4), 975-1005.

Caloghirou, Y., Kastelli, I., & Tsakanikas, A. (2004). Internal capabilities and external knowledge sources: complements or substitutes for innovative performance? *Technovation, 24*(1), 29-39.

Cepeda-Carrión, G., Cegarra-Navarro, J. G., & Jiménez-Jiménez, D. (2012). The effects of absorptive capacity on innovativeness: context and information systems capability as catalysts. *British Journal of Management, 23*(1), 110-129.

Chesbrough, H. W. (2003). The logic of open innovation: managing intellectual property. *California Management Review, 45*(3), 33-58.

Cohen, W. M., & Levinthal, D. A. (1990). Absorptive capacity: a new perspective on learning and innovation. *Administrative Science Quarterly, 35*(1), 128-152.

Colombo, M. G., & Delmastro, M. (2002). How effective are technology incubators? evidence from Italy. *Research Policy, 31*(7), 1103-1122.

Damanpour, F., & Gopalakrishnan, S. (1998). Theories of organizational structure and innovation adoption: the role of environmental change. *Journal of Engineering and Technology Management, 15*(1), 1-24.

Díez-Vial, I., & Fernández-Olmos, M. (2015). Knowledge spillovers in science and technology parks: how can firms benefit most? *The Journal of Technology Transfer, 40*(1), 70-84.

Dutta, S., & Weiss A. M. (1997). The relationship between a firm's level of technological innovativeness and its pattern of partnership agreements. *Management Science, 43*(3), 343-356.

Felsenstein, D. (1994). University-related science parks - 'seedbeds' or 'enclaves' of innovation? *Technovation, 14*(2), 93-110.

Ferguson, R., & Olofsson, C. (2004). Science parks and the development of NTBFs-location, survival and growth. *The Journal of Technology Transfer*, 29(1), 5-17.

Flyer, F., & Shaver, J. M. (2003). Location choices under agglomeration externalities and strategic interaction. In J. A. C. Baum, O. Sorenson (Eds.), *Advances in Strategic Management: Geography and Strategy* (Vol. 20, pp. 193-214). Amsterdam: Elsevier JAI.

Folta, T. B., Cooper, A. C., & Baik, Y. (2006). Geographic cluster size and firm performance. *Journal of Business Venturing, 21*(2), 217-242.

Frenken, K., van Oort, F., & Verburg, T. (2007). Relate variety, unrelated variety and regional economic growth. *Regional Studies*, 41(5), 685-697.

George, G., Zahra, S. A., Wheatley, K., & Khan, R. (2001), The effects of alliance portfolio characteristics and absorptive capacity on performance: a study of biotechnology firms. *Journal of High Technology Management Research, 12*(2), 205-227.

Giuliani, E., & Bell, M. (2005). The micro-determinants of meso-level learning and innovation: evidence from a Chilean wine cluster. *Research Policy, 34*(1), 47-68.

Glaeser, E. L., Kallal, H. D., Scheinkman, J. A., & Shleifer A. (1992). Growth in Cities. *The Journal of Political Economy, 100*(6), 1126-1152.

Glasmeier, A. K. (1991). Technological discontinuities and flexible production networks: the case of Switzerland and the world watch industry. *Research Policy, 20*(5), 469-485.

Henderson, R. M. & Clark, K. B. (1990). Architectural innovation: the reconfiguration of existing product technologies and the failure of established firms. *Administrative Science Quarterly, 35*(1), 9-30.

Henderson, R., & Cockburn, I. (1994). Measuring competence? Exploring firm effects in pharmaceutical research. *Strategic Management Journal, 15*, 63-84.

Huang, K. F., Yu, C. M., & Seetoo, D. H. (2012). Firm innovation in policy-driven parks and spontaneous clusters: the smaller firm the better? *The Journal of Technology Transfer, 37*(5), 715-731.

Jacobs, J. (1969). *The Economy of Cities*. New York, NY: Random House.

Jansen, J. J. P., Van Den Bosch, F. A. J., & Volberda, H. W. (2005). Managing potential and realized absorptive capacity: how do organizational antecedents matter? *Academy Management Journal, 48*(6), 999-1015.

Jiménez-Moreno, J. J, Martínez-Cañas, R., Ruiz-Palomino, P., & Sáez-Martínez, F. J. (2013). The role of science and technology parks in the generation of firm level social capital through university–firm relations: an empirical study in Spain. In J. J. M. Ferreira, M. Raposo, R. Rutten, & A. Varga (Eds.), *Cooperation, clusters, and knowledge transfer* (pp. 19-34). Berlin: Springer.

Judd, C. M., & Kenny, D. A. (1981). Process analysis: Estimating mediation in treatment evaluation. *Evaluation Review*, 5, 602-619.

Kaiser, U. (2002). An empirical test of models explaining research expenditures and research cooperation: evidence for the German service sector. *International Journal of Industrial Organization, 20*(6), 747-774.

Katila, R., & Ahuja, G. (2002). Something old, something new: A longitudinal study of search behavior and new product introduction. *Academy of Management Journal, 45*(6), 1183-1194.

Kim, L. (1998). Crisis construction and organizational learning: Capability building in catching up at Hyundai Motor. *Organization Science*, 9(4), 506-521.

Knoben, J., Raspe, O., Arikan, A. & Oort, F. (2016). Agglomeration and firm performance: One firm's medicine is another firm's poison. *Environment and Planning, 48*(1), 132-153.

Lane, P., Koka, B., & Pathak, S. (2006). The reification of absorptive capacity: a critical review and rejuvenation of the construct. *The Academy Management Review*, 31(4), 833-863.

Laursen, K., & Salter, A. (2006). Open for innovation: The role of openness in explaining innovation performance among U.K. manufacturing firms. *Strategic Management Journal, 27*(2), 131-150.

Löfsten, H., & Lindelöf, P. (2001). Science parks in Sweden - industrial renewal and development? *R&D Management, 31*(3), 309-322.

Löfsten, H., & Lindelöf, P. (2003). Determinants for an entrepreneurial milieu: Science parks and business policy in growing firms. *Technovation*, 23(1), 51-64.

Mangematin, V., & Nesta, L. (1999). What kind of knowledge can a firm absorb? *International Journal of Technology Management*, 18(3-4), 149-172.

Marco-Lajara, B., Claver-Cortés, E., Úbeda-García, M., & Zaragoza-Sáez, P. C. (2016). Hotel Performance and Agglomeration of Tourist Districts. *Regional Studies, 50*(6), 1016-1035.

Marshall, A. (1920). Principles of Economics (8th ed.). London, UK: MacMillan.

Martínez-Senra, A. I., Quintás, M. A., Sartal, A., & Vázquez, X. H. (2013). Es rentable "pensar por pensar"? Evidencia sobre innovación en España [Is it profitable 'thinking by thinking'? Evidence on innovation in Spain]. *Cuadernos de Economía y Dirección de la Empresa, 16*, 142-153.

Maskell, P., & Malmberg, A. (1999). Localised learning and industrial competitiveness. *Cambridge Journal of Economics, 23*(2), 167-185.

Melo, P. C., Graham, D. J., & Noland, R. B. (2009). A meta-analysis of estimates of urban agglomeration economies. *Regional Science and Urban Economics*, 39(3), 332-342.

Molina-Morales, F. X., García-Villaverde, P. M., & Parra-Requena, G. (2014). Geographical and cognitive proximity effects on innovation performance in SMEs: a way through knowledge acquisition. *International Entrepreneurship and Management Journal, 10*(2), 231-251.

Montoro-Sánchez, M. A., Mora-Valentín, E. M., & Ortiz-de-Urbina-Criado, M. (2012). Localización en parques científicos y tecnológicos y cooperación en I+D+i como factores determinantes de la innovación [Science and technology parks location and R+D+i cooperation as determinant factors of innovation]. *Revista Europea de Dirección y Economía de la Empresa*, 21(2), 182-190.

Morrison, A. (2008). Gatekeepers of knowledge within industrial districts: Who they are, how do they interact? *Regional Studies, 42*(6), 817-835.

Morrison, A., & Rabellotti, R (2009). Knowledge and information networks in an Italian wine cluster. *European Planning Studies*, 17(7), 983-1006.

Murovec, N., & Prodan, I. (2009). Absorptive capacity, its determinants, and influence on innovation output: Cross-cultural validation of the structural model. *Technovation, 29*(12), 859-872.

OECD/Eurostat. (2005). *Oslo Manual: Guidelines for collecting and interpreting innovation data* (3rd ed.). Paris: OECD Publishing. Available from http://www.oecd-ilibrary.org/science-and-technology/oslo-manual_9789264013100-en

PITEC (2013). *Panel de Innovación Tecnológica [Technological Innovation Panel]. Madrid:* Instituto Nacional de Estadística y Fundación Española para la Ciencia y la Tecnología.

Pouder, R., & St. John C. H. (1996). Hot spots and blind spots: Geographical clusters of firms and innovation. *Academy of Management Review, 21*(4), 1192-1225.

Prevezer, M. (1997). The dynamics of industrial clustering in biotechnology. *Small Business Economics, 9*(3), 255-271.

Rothaemel, F. T., & Hess, A. M. (2007). Building dynamic capabilities: Innovation driven by individual-, firm-, and network-level effects. *Organization Science, 18*(6), 898-921.

Siegel, D. S., Westhead, P., & Wright, M. (2003). Assessing the impact of science parks on research productivity: Exploratory firm-level evidence from the United Kingdom. *International Journal of Industrial Organization, 21*(9), 1357-1369.

Sofoulli, E., & Vonortas, N. (2007). S&T parks and business incubator in middle-sized countries: The case of Greece. *The Journal of Technology Transfer, 32(5)*, 525-544.

Squicciarini, M. (2008). Science parks' tenants versus out-of-park firms: Who innovates more? A Duration Model," *Journal of Technology Transfer, 33*(1), 45-71.

Squicciarini, M. (2009). Science parks: Seedbeds of innovation? A duration analysis of firms' patenting activity. *Small Business Economics 32*(2), 169-190.

Sørensen, J. B., & Stuart, T. (2000). Aging, obsolescence and organizational innovation. *Administrative Science Quarterly, 45*(1), 81-112.

Stuart, T. & Sorenson, O. (2003). The geography of opportunity: spatial heterogeneity in founding rates and the performance of biotechnology firms. *Research Policy, 32*(2), 229-253.

Tallman, S., Jenkins, M., Henry, N., & Pinch, S. (2004). Knowledge, clusters and competitive advantage. *The Academy of Management Review, 29*(2), 258-271.

Teece, D. J., Pisano, G., & Shuen, A. (1997). Dynamic capabilities and strategic management. *Strategic Management Journal, 18*(7), 509-533.

Urgal, B., Quintás, M. A. & Arévalo-Tomé, R. (2011). Conocimiento tecnológico, capacidad de innovación y desempeño innovador: el rol moderador del ambiente interno de la empresa [Technological knowledge, innovation capability and innovative performance: the moderating role of the behavioural environment of the firm]. *Cuadernos de Economía y Dirección de la Empresa, 14(*1), 53-66.

Vásquez-Urriago, A. R., Barge-Gil, A., Modrego-Rico, A., & Paraskevopoulou, E. (2014). The impact of science and technology parks on firms' product innovation: empirical evidence from Spain. *Journal of Evolutionary Economics, 24*(4), 835-873.

Vernon, R. (1966). International investment and international trade in the product cycle. *Quarterly Journal of Economics, 80*(2), 190-207.

Veugelers, R. (1997). Internal R&D expenditures and external technology sourcing. *Research Policy, 26*(3), 303-315.

Westhead, P. (1997). R&D "inputs" and "outputs" of technology-based firms located on and off science parks. *R&D Management, 27*(1), 45-62.

Winter, S. G. (2003). Understanding dynamic capabilities. *Strategic Management Journal, 24*(10), 991-995.

Yang, C. H., Motohashi, K., & Chen, J. R. (2009). Are new technology-based firms located on science parks really more innovative, Evidence from Taiwan. *Research Policy, 38*(1), 77-85.

Zahra, S. A., & George, G. (2002). Absorptive capacity: A review, reconceptualization, and extension. *The Academy Management Review, 27*(2), 185-203.

Endnotes

1 *An estimate was carried out that included only the possible effect of a type of agglomeration economies because the simultaneous inclusion of all three types causes multicollinearity problems.*

16

Complementary Person-Environment Fit as a Predictor of Job Pursuit Intentions in the Service Industry

Marlena A. Bednarska[1]

ABSTRACT

There is an intrinsic link between the success of service firms and the availability of appropriate labor resources, making employee attraction and retention a critical concern for service organizations. Effects of recruitment efforts are influenced by applicants' subjective person-environment (P-E) fit, referring to the compatibility between an individual and a work environment. The purpose of this paper is to examine the role of employer attractiveness in the relationship between potential employees' perceptions of P-E fit and job pursuit intentions in the service industry. This study was conducted with a group of 335 undergraduates and graduates enrolled in tourism and hospitality studies in Poznan. Data were collected through group-administered questionnaires. Research revealed that students generally did not believe that a career in the hospitality sector would fulfill their needs, rating job attributes slightly higher than organization attributes. Regression analyses showed that both person-job (P-J) fit and person-organization (P-O) fit were positively related to intentions to apply for a job, with the former being a stronger predictor. The relationship under study was fully mediated by the perceived attractiveness of hospitality employers. The findings contribute to an improved understanding of the influence of P-J and P-O fit on work-related attitudes and intentions of Generation Y prospective employees in the hospitality industry.

KEY WORDS: person-environment fit, employer attractiveness, job pursuit intentions, service industry, potential employees

[1] Faculty of International Business and Economics, Poznan University of Economics and Business, Poland

Introduction

There is a broad consensus that the success of service firms in general and high-contact service firms in particular lies to a great extent in the quality of their human resources. It has been argued that the ultimate source of value creation is operant resources – employees' knowledge, skills, and abilities utilized to create a differentiated and valued offering in the marketplace (Andreassen & Lanseng, 2010; Lusch, Vargo, & O'Brien, 2007). Therefore, the issue of attracting and retaining qualified and engaged employees is of critical importance for service organizations. The perception of organization attractiveness as a workplace is determined by job searchers' subjective appraisal of the interaction between them and the work environment. If potential employees find value congruence and a match between

Correspondence concerning this article should be addressed to: **Marlena A. Bednarska** Faculty of International Business and Economics, Poznan University of Economics and Business, Poland Al. Niepodleglosci 10, 61-875 Poznan, Poland
E-mail: m.bednarska@ue.poznan.pl

their personal abilities and needs and the job and organization demands and supplies, they are more likely to have positive attitudes towards being employed by a company, to declare an acceptance intention if a job were to be offered, and to make the decision to pursue a firm as a place of work (Cable & Judge, 1996; Carless, 2005; Kristof-Brown, Zimmerman, & Johnson, 2005).

Given the importance of person-environment (P-E) fit for the success of an organization's recruitment efforts, it is essential for service enterprises to obtain a clear picture of the preferences of future workers and locate any incorrect beliefs that potential employees might hold. Furthermore, due to growing generational diversity among the current workforce, with Generation Y making up an increasingly larger percentage of employees, service companies should find solutions for attracting Millennial candidates. Accommodating the needs of this cohort seems to be a challenge, as this group is believed to approach employment in a manner different from that of their predecessors (Bednarska & Olszewski, 2014; Hershatter & Epstein, 2010). Nevertheless, understanding the values that younger generations bring to work appears essential for those who wish to remain competitive in attracting qualified applicants (Cogin, 2012). Although P-E fit has received much interest from researchers over the past several decades, the understanding of the phenomenon is based primarily on studies conducted in North America (Oh et al., 2014). Additionally, greater attention has been paid to exploring the consequences of fit during post-hire stages (Jansen & Kristof-Brown, 2006). The present paper addresses these shortcomings by investigating the role of P-E fit in the job choice process of Generation Y in the context of Poland.

The objective of the paper is to examine the role of employer attractiveness in the relationship between potential employees' perceptions of complementary P-E fit and job pursuit intentions in the service industry. The empirical investigation is limited to a single industry, namely, hospitality. To reach the objective proposed, the paper proceeds as follows. First, the concept of P-E fit and its outcomes are discussed on the basis of the existing literature. Next, the research methodology and findings of the study on students' attitudes and intentions towards careers in the hospitality industry are presented. Finally, implications and guidelines for future research are proposed.

Literature review and hypothesis development

The domain of interaction between workers and the environments in which they function has been prevalent in management research for decades. In general, P-E fit refers to the congruence, match, or similarity between the person and the environment. These terms denote the proximity of the person and the environment to each other (Edwards, 2008). The broad construct of P-E fit can be distinguished in terms of supplementary fit and complementary fit (Kristof, 1996). Supplementary fit exists when the person possesses characteristics that are similar to others in the environment. Complementary fit occurs when the person's characteristics fill a gap in the environment or vice versa. It encompasses both the need-supply fit, defined as the degree to which the needs of the individual are fulfilled by rewards in the environment, and the demand-ability fit, defined as the degree to which the needs of the environment are fulfilled by the capabilities of the individual (Kristof, 1996).

Strategies for fit operationalization also vary widely. Edwards et al. (2006) distinguish three basic approaches to studying P-E fit: atomistic, molecular, and molar. The atomistic approach examines perceptions of the person and the environment as separate entities and then compares them. The molecular approach concerns the perceived discrepancy between the person and the environment and preserves the direction of the difference. The molar approach focuses on the perceived similarity between the person and the environment and disregards the direction of the difference. As noted by Kristof-Brown et al. (2005), P-E fit can be assessed directly, based on perceived compatibility, or indirectly, based on actual compatibility of separately rated variables. The latter can be differentiated into subjective fit, if the variables are reported by a single source, and objective fit, if the variables are reported by different sources.

P-E fit has been the subject of a large number of studies. However, as both people and the environments they inhabit are multidimensional, researchers have been faced with the problem of capturing all the fit forms (Edwards & Billsberry, 2010). Scholars investigated the fit between employees and their vocations (Feij et al., 1999; Marcus & Wagner, 2015), jobs (Babakus, Yavas, & Ashill, 2011; Chen, Yen, &

Tsai, 2014), teams (Glew, 2012), work groups (Seong & Kristof-Brown, 2012; Werbel & Johnson, 2001), supervisors (Kim & Kim, 2013), organizations (Piasentin & Chapman, 2007; Swider, Zimmerman, & Barrick, 2015), cultures (Nazir, 2005), and locations (Solnet et al., 2014). Consequently, P-E fit is generally considered to be a multidimensional concept (Edwards & Billsberry, 2010; Jansen & Kristof-Brown, 2006; Wheeler et al., 2005).

The substantial stream of research on the compatibility between individuals and their work environments used two-factor conceptualization and focused on person-job (P-J) and person-organization (P-O) fits. P-J fit refers to the relationship between the individual's characteristics and those of the tasks that are performed at work. P-O fit addresses the compatibility between the individual and the organization as a whole (Kristof-Brown et al., 2005).

A growing body of empirical evidence supports the notion that fit between employees and their work environments affects both pre-entry and post-entry attitudes, intentions, and behaviors in the workplace. Recent meta-analytic studies (Kristof-Brown et al., 2005; Oh et al., 2014) confirmed that P-J and P-O fit had a significant relationship with outcomes reported by prospective employees (organizational attraction and job acceptance), employing organizations (intent to hire and job offers), and actual employees (job satisfaction, organizational identification, organizational commitment, job performance, and intent to quit).

The focus of this paper is on the complementary form of need-supply fit, which was found to have the greatest impact on individual attitudes and behaviors (Kristof-Brown et al., 2005; Schmidt, Chapman, & Jones, 2015). The primary mechanism by which need-supply fit shapes attitudinal outcomes can be explained by theories of psychological need fulfillment (Cable & Edwards, 2004). These theories posit that employees' attitudes are affected by a cognitive comparison of the desired amount of reward relative to the amount that is perceived to be supplied in the work environment. As the degree to which employees' desires are met increases, the positive attitudes they will experience towards the employer increase.

Another theoretical guide for investigating complementary fit outcomes is offered by the theory of reasoned action and the theory of planned behavior, with the latter being the extension of the former (Ajzen, 1991; Fishbein & Ajzen, 1975). In general, these theories assume that an individual's beliefs about an object manifest into attitudes towards behaviors related to this object; attitudes are then expected to influence intentions to engage in these behaviors, which predict subsequent behaviors. Applied to the job choice context, the primary antecedent of job pursuit behavior is the intention to pursue the job in question. The intention to apply for the job in a given company, in turn, is a function of the perception of this company's attractiveness as an employer, which is affected by subjective assessment of the match between the individual and the work environment.

The outcome variables that have received the most attention in research on pre-entry fit perceptions are employer attraction (attractiveness) and job pursuit intentions. The former construct reflects the degree to which a prospective employee finds an employer a desirable place to work, and the latter, his or her willingness to enter or stay in the applicant pool. Although some researchers combine attitudinal and intentional measures to assess applicant attraction (e.g., Judge & Cable, 1997; Harold & Ployhart, 2008), for the purpose of this study, the attractiveness of the employer and the intentions to pursue a job are treated as distinct constructs. While attractiveness refers to a passive affect towards a potential relationship with a company as a place of employment, job pursuit intentions require an active engagement of an applicant (Aiman-Smith, Bauer, & Cable, 2001; Highhouse, Lievens, & Sinar, 2003).

Based on the above discussion, the following hypotheses are developed:

Hypothesis 1: P-E fit is positively related to employer attractiveness.

Hypothesis 2: Employer attractiveness is positively related to job pursuit intentions.

Hypothesis 3: Employer attractiveness mediates the effect of P-E fit on job pursuit intentions.

These hypotheses are summarized in the model presented in Figure 1.

In early recruitment stages, applicants have only some elementary knowledge of potential jobs and organizations, which they generate for future consideration. Consequently, initial intentions to pursue employment opportunities at a particular firm are based on

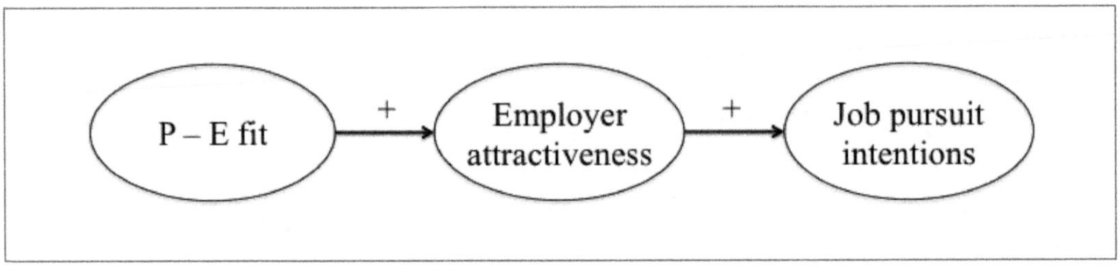

Figure 1. Hypothesized model

Table 1. Respondent profile

Variable	Category	N	Share [%]
Gender	Female	230	68.9
	Male	104	31.1
Age	20 and younger	120	35.9
	21-22	125	37.4
	23-24	67	20.1
	25 and older	22	6.6
Study degree	Bachelor's	256	76.6
	Master's	78	23.4
Study mode	Full time	273	81.7
	Part time	61	18.3
Type of school	Public	251	74.9
	Non-public	84	25.1
Work experience	Yes	275	82.1
	No	60	17.9
Work experience in hospitality	Yes	167	50.0
	No	167	50.0

general impressions of employer attractiveness, which are affected by the industry in which the firm operates. Additionally, as the applicants' familiarity with a company decreases, the frequency with which they use general industry perceptions to form impressions of a specific organization increases (Burmann, Schaefer, & Maloney, 2008; Wilden, Gudergan, & Lings, 2010). This situation is fairly common in service sectors, which are fragmented and dominated by small- and medium-sized enterprises. Given the importance of the industry image in regard to the evaluation of potential employers, the need to explore prospective employees' beliefs about their fit with jobs and organizations in a particular industry is becoming evident.

Research method

To reach the objective of the study, field investigation was conducted. The target population comprised undergraduates and graduates enrolled in tourism and hospitality studies in universities in Poznan, Poland. At the time of data collection (academic year 2012/2013), eight public and private higher

Table 2. Factor loadings for items

Items	Factor loadings	
	1.	2.
Stable employment conditions	.822	
Feeling of trust and cooperation in the workplace	.796	
Friendly atmosphere	.781	
Opportunities of enhancing qualifications	.780	
Integration and belonging	.769	
Work-life balance	.751	
Attractive fringe benefits	.734	
Good prospects for promotion within the organization	.723	
Good prospects for long-term professional development	.712	
Competent supervisors	.696	
High salary	.686	
Experience for future employment	.538	
Challenging tasks		.837
Matching individual interests		.768
Variety of work activities		.617

Table 3. Summary of exploratory factor analysis

Factors	Number of items	Eigenvalue	Variance explained	Cronbach's alpha
1. Person-organization fit	12	7.825	44.26%	.935
2. Person-job fit	3	1.268	16.36%	.691

education institutions in Poznan offered bachelor's and master's degrees in tourism, and a total of 4150 students took tourism and hospitality courses. To obtain a representative subset of the target population, a random sampling process was employed, specifically, a single-stage cluster sampling. Tourism and hospitality course providers were contacted, and they all agreed to facilitate access to their students. Data were collected through group-administered paper-based questionnaires distributed during a regularly scheduled class period. The sample accounted for 348 respondents, yielding a response rate of 66%. Due to incomplete or incoherent information, 13 questionnaires were excluded, which resulted in 335 usable questionnaires for further analysis. The sample was demographically diverse – the age span of the respondents was 18 to 45 years old, with a mean age of 22, and 69% of them were female. Of the respondents, 77% were pursuing a bachelor's degree, and the sample was dominated by full-time students (82%). The majority of students had work experience (82%), and 50% of them worked in the hospitality industry. Table 1 shows descriptive statistics for the sample.

A questionnaire designed for the purpose of this study was developed based on a review of previous investigations on complementary P-E fit and employer attractiveness. Measures used in the survey were adapted from multiple resources (Bednarska & Olszewski, 2013; Boon et al., 2011; Cable & Edwards, 2004; Schlager et al., 2011).

Table 4. Variable descriptive statistics and correlations

Variables	M	SD	Correlations					
			1.	2.	3.	4.	5.	6.
1. Age	21.632	2.553						
2. Gender	0.689	0.464	-.105					
3. Experience in hospitality	0.500	0.501	.130*	.022				
4. Person-organization fit	-1.199	1.020	-.207**	-.018	-.052			
5. Person-job fit	-1.018	1.290	-.091	.052	.054	.523**		
6. Employer attractiveness	4.643	1.474	-.080	.137*	.211**	.362**	.530**	
7. Job pursuit intentions	4.223	1.830	-.139*	.103	.185**	.281**	.402**	.658**

Note: Gender: 0=male, 1=female; Experience in hospitality: 0=no, 1=yes
Significant at * $p<0.05$; ** $p<0.01$ (2-tailed).

The research instrument consisted of four main components. Respondents were requested first to imagine an ideal employer for whom they would choose to work and to evaluate 15 job and organizational attributes based on their expectations. Afterwards, they were asked to assess the analyzed attributes regarding employers in the hospitality industry. This approach allows an evaluation of the need-supply fit, and it is in line with an atomistic strategy for measuring fit. The data enabled the computation of the gaps between preferred and perceived job/organization attributes, which were independent variables in the study. The gap was calculated as a difference between perception and expectation for desired attributes and as a difference between expectation and perception for undesired attributes (Bednarska & Olszewski, 2013). Accordingly, a positive number denotes exceeded expectations, and a negative number denotes unmet expectations. In the third section, two outcomes of P-E fit were investigated – the hospitality industry's attractiveness as an employer and the intention to apply for a job in the hospitality industry. Both outcomes were assessed using single-item measures ("I find being employed in the hospitality industry an interesting option" and "I plan to apply for a job in the hospitality industry"). Although the validity of single-item scales is a subject of constant debate, such measures are deemed appropriate for concrete objects and attributes of the underlying construct (Bergkvist & Rossiter, 2007). The inquiry form contained closed-ended questions, and for gradations of opinions, a seven-point Likert scale was utilized, ranging from "strongly disagree" (1) to "strongly agree" (7). In the final section, demographic data were collected.

Analysis and results

In order to confirm the dimensionality of the questionnaire and to guarantee that each variable constituted an independent construct, an exploratory factor analysis was conducted, using principal component extraction with varimax rotation. Both the Kaiser-Meyer-Olkin measure of sampling adequacy (0.92) and Bartlett's test of sphericity (χ^2=1195.88, $p<0.001$) suggested that factor analysis was appropriate for the data collected. The results of this procedure are reported in Tables 2 and 3. The analysis produced two factors with eigenvalues greater than 1.0, which explained 61% of the total variance. Although a reliability coefficient (Cronbach's alpha) for P-J fit was lower than the generally accepted minimum level of 0.7, the construct was retained, as for scales with a small number of items, a smaller alpha is considered permissible (Nunnally & Bernstein, 1994).

Means, standard deviations, and correlations between the variables of interest are presented in Table 4. The independent variables scores were computed by averaging the items that constitute the relevant dimension. The picture that emerges from the table is that the students generally did not believe that a career in the hospitality sector would fulfill their needs,

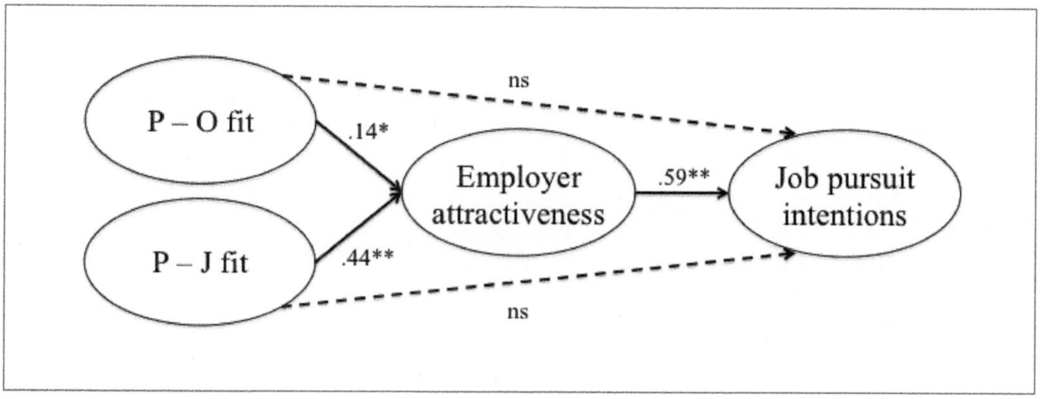

Figure 2. Research model results
Standardized beta coefficients are provided
Significant at * p<0.05; ** p<0.01; ns = non-significant

with job attributes being rated slightly higher than organization attributes. Both P-J and P-O fit showed statistically significant positive correlations with industry attractiveness as an employer and with job pursuit intentions, with P-J fit displaying a stronger relationship with them.

To investigate the outcomes of P-E fit, multiple regression analyses were performed. Specifically, to test hypothesis 1, employer attractiveness was regressed on P-J and P-O fit; to test hypothesis 2, job pursuit intentions were regressed on employer attractiveness. In both cases, demographic variables were entered in the first step of the analysis to control for the potentially confounding effects of age, gender, and work experience gained in the hospitality industry. As shown in Table 5, the results indicated that there were significant positive relations between employer attractiveness and P-J and P-O fit (model 1) and between job pursuit intentions and employer attractiveness (model 2) after controlling for demographics. Thus, hypotheses 1 and 2 were supported.

Additionally, this study tested the hypothesis that employer attractiveness mediates the positive relationship between complementary P-J and P-O fit and the intention to apply for a job. To test the mediating effects of perceived employer attractiveness, Baron and Kenny's (1986) recommended procedures were applied. First, the relationship between P-J and P-O fit (predictors) and job pursuit intentions (outcome) was examined. Second, employer attractiveness (mediator) was related both to P-J and P-O fit and to job pursuit intentions (hypothesis 1 and 2 testing). Finally, the effects of P-J and P-O fit on job pursuit intentions, controlling for employer attractiveness, were tested. The results of regression analyses are displayed in Table 6. As shown in model 1, both P-J and P-O fit were significantly and positively related to intentions to apply for a job, with the former being a stronger predictor. As presented in model 2, when perceived employer attractiveness was added to the regression model, the antecedents explained 44% of the variance in intentions to apply for a job (compared to 21% without a mediator), and relationships between P-J and P-O fit and job pursuit intentions were no longer significant. Thus, the findings reveal that the conditions for full mediation were met. The Sobel test ($Z= 2.48$, $p<0.05$, for P-O fit; $Z= 6.70$, $p<0.001$, for P-J fit) indicates that the indirect effects under study were significant, thus providing support for hypothesis 3. The results are illustrated in Figure 2.

In summary, the empirical evidence supports positive indirect links between the complementary P-E fit and job pursuit intentions of Generation Y in the hospitality industry. That is, P-E fit must first increase perceived employer attractiveness in order to then strengthen the intentions to apply for a job.

Discussion

Although abundant research involved various areas of fit between employees and their work environments, relatively few studies to date have focused on

Table 5. Results of regression analyses: employer attractiveness as a dependent variable (model 1) and as an independent variable (model 2)

Variables	**Model 1 Employer attractiveness**		**Model 2 Job pursuit intentions**	
	1.	2.	1.	2.
Step 1 – control variables				
Age	-.093+	-.021	-.159**	-.098*
Gender	.126*	.107*	.092+	.014
Experience in hospitality	.226**	.203**	.209**	.067
Step 2 – study variables				
Person-organization fit		.138*		
Person-job fit		.439**		
Employer attractiveness				.636**
R^2	.074	.344	.073	.448
Adj. R^2	.065	.334	.064	.442
ΔR^2		.270**		.375**
F	8.631**	33.777**	8.556**	66.032**

Note: Standardized beta coefficients are provided
Significant at + $p<0.1$; * $p<0.05$; ** $p<0.01$.

pre-entry P-E fit perceptions and their consequences for the job search behavior of Millennials. Additionally, despite calls for a multidimensional approach to studying fit, the majority of past research evaluated the fit between an individual and a single aspect of the work environment (Jansen & Kristof-Brown, 2006). The present study, therefore, aims to address this gap by investigating the simultaneous effects of complementary P-J and P-O fit perceived by prospective employees from Generation Y on job pursuit intentions in one of the service industries – hospitality. Moreover, unlike most empirical research on the topic, this study does not consider beliefs, attitudes, and intentions related to the specific organization but rather to the industry as a career field.

The findings provide empirical validation for the proposed model; in particular, the results showed that subjective P-E fit influenced intentions to apply for a job indirectly via employer attractiveness. As the degree to which the needs of prospective employees were perceived to be fulfilled by rewards in the given industry increased, the industry was found to be more attractive as a potential place for employment. As candidates' opinion of the industry as an employer became more favorable, their intentions to apply for a job in that industry strengthened. The relations between the variables are consistent with the propositions of theories of reasoned action and planned behavior. The results correspond with those obtained in prior research conducted among actual job applicants (Carless, 2005; Phillips et al., 2014).

The study's findings also showed that complementary P-J fit tended to display a stronger relationship with the perceived attractiveness of the industry as a workplace and job pursuit intentions, compared to P-O fit. This finding suggests that Millennial potential employees are more interested in ensuring that the job they choose is congruent with their requirements rather than working in an organization that satisfies their needs. This observation is in line with Jansen and Kristof-Brown's (2006) proposition, which claims that the salience of fit with different aspects of the environment is affected by the temporal stage of work experience. At early stages of the pre-hire phase, P-J fit is more salient than P-O fit. Similar findings in the graduate applicant context were reported by Carless (2005).

Table 6. Results of regression analyses: employer attractiveness as a mediating variable

Variables	Model 1 Job pursuit intentions		Model 2 Job pursuit intentions	
	1.	2.	1.	2.
Step 1 – control variables				
Age	-.159**	-.106*	-.157**	-.091*
Gender	.085	.075	.088	.012
Experience in hospitality	.216**	.196**	.217**	.078+
Step 2 – study variables				
Person-organization fit		.104+		.015
Person-job fit		.324**		.072
Employer attractiveness				.591**
R^2	.074	.222	.075	.454
Adj. R^2	.065	.210	.066	.443
ΔR^2		.148**		.379**
F	8.647**	18.433**	8.704**	44.288**

Note: Standardized beta coefficients are provided
Significant at + $p<0.1$; * $p<0.05$; ** $p<0.01$.

The findings of the present investigation have both research and practical implications. From a theoretical standpoint, the study demonstrates a vital function of the fit construct in the job search process; thus, it may bring added value to existing knowledge about the antecedents of potential employees' work-related attitudes and behavioral intentions in service industries. Additionally, the results extend current P-E fit research by addressing the notion of complementary fit and its outcomes at the industry level. Concerning suggestions for managerial practice, the results emphasize the importance of developing recruitment practices that are targeted to a specific group of candidates. It is critical for employers to be aware of age dissimilarities within the workforce and to realize that new entrants have different values and expectations. Service organizations seeking to attract Generation Y employees should ensure that applicants have sufficient information about the job to be able to evaluate their P-J fit. As the degree of perceived fit between an individual's characteristics and those of the tasks that are performed at work increases, the quantity of applicant pools increases and, consequently, the likelihood of recruiting high-quality candidates who would contribute to performance enhancement strengthens. If employers fail to deliver information that can be used to determine fit, they risk losing job seekers who self-select out of the recruitment process.

The results of this study should be considered in light of its limitations. Although the use of a group-administered survey was appropriate, given the objective of the investigation, it raises concerns about common method bias. Field study data were delivered by respondents, and self-reported data are prone to response bias, especially social desirability. In addition, all variables were measured based on the same source, which resulted in the subjective assessment of fit. However, it is argued that the subjective perception of match is particularly relevant in the context of job choice, as it represents an individual's direct judgment of how well he or she would fit in the work environment (Judge & Cable, 1997). Another issue to keep in mind when interpreting the results is that this study used cross-sectional data to test the hypotheses, which means that the direction of causality cannot be unambiguously determined. However, this concern is mitigated in this context because the hypothesized relationships were based on logical grounds and on previous research relying on longitudinal data. In addition, the model focused on employer attractiveness as a mediating link. It would be of value to explore other possible mediating mechanisms between complementary fit and job pursuit intentions. It should also be noted that the outcome variables were measured with single-item scales, which is a source of a reliability assessment problem and may have attenuated observed relationships. Finally, a potential weakness of this inquiry arises from the unique characteristics of the population. Research was carried out in only one city among undergraduates and graduates enrolled in tourism and hospitality studies. Consequently, the findings may not be generalizable to a sample of other prospective employees who have more work experience and are in other stages of their careers. They also may not be wholly transferable to service environments not considered here. Therefore, further studies are needed to verify or repudiate these findings within different contexts.

References

Aiman-Smith, L., Bauer, T. N., & Cable, D. M. (2001). Are you attracted? Do you intend to pursue? A recruiting policy-capturing study. *Journal of Business and Psychology*, 16 (2), 219–237.

Ajzen, I. (1991). The theory of planned behavior. *Organizational behavior and human Decision Processes*, 50 (2), 179–211.

Andreassen, T. W., & Lanseng, E. J. (2010). Service differentiation: A self-image congruency perspective on brand building in the labor market. *Journal of Service Management*, 21 (2), 212–236.

Babakus, E., Yavas, U., & Ashill, N. J. (2011). Service worker burnout and turnover intentions: Roles of person-job fit, servant leadership, and customer orientation. *Services Marketing Quarterly*, 32 (1), 17–31.

Baron, R. M., & Kenny, D. A. (1986). The moderator–mediator variable distinction in social psychological research: Conceptual, strategic, and statistical considerations. *Journal of Personality and Social Psychology*, 51 (6), 1173–1182.

Bednarska, M., & Olszewski, M. (2014). Pokolenie Y na turystycznym rynku pracy [Generation Y in the tourism labour market]. In B. Krakowiak & J. Latosińska (Eds.), *Przeszłość, teraźniejszość i przyszłość turystyki: warsztaty z geografii turyzmu* [Past, present and future of tourism: Workshop in tourism geography] (pp. 279–291). Łódź: Wydawnictwo Uniwersytetu Łódzkiego,

Bednarska, M. A., & Olszewski, M. (2013). Organisational determinants of employer image: A case of the tourism industry in Poland. *Anuario Turismo Y Sociedad*, 14, 17–31.

Bergkvist, L. I., & Rossiter, J. R. (2007). The predictive validity of multiple-item versus single-item measures of the same constructs. *Journal of Marketing Research*, 44 (2), 175–184.

Boon, C., Den Hartog, D. N., Boselie, P., & Paauwe, J. (2011). The relationship between perceptions of HR practices and employee outcomes: Examining the role of person–organisation and person–job fit. *International Journal of Human Resource Management*, 22 (1), 138–162.

Burmann, C., Schaefer, K., & Maloney, P. (2008). Industry image: Its impact on the brand image of potential employees. *Journal of Brand Management*, 15 (3), 157–176.

Cable, D. M., & Edwards, J. R. (2004). Complementary and supplementary fit: A theoretical and empirical integration. *Journal of Applied Psychology*, 89 (5), 822–834.

Cable, D. M., & Judge, T. A. (1996). Person – organization fit, job choice decision, and organizational entry. *Organizational Behavior and Human Decision Processes*, 67 (3), 294–311.

Carless, S. A. (2005). Person-job fit versus person-organization fit as predictors of organizational attraction and job acceptance intentions: A longitudinal study. *Journal of Occupational and Organizational Psychology*, 78 (3), 411–429.

Chen, C. Y., Yen, C. H., & Tsai, F. C. (2014). Job crafting and job engagement: The mediating role of person-job fit. *International Journal of Hospitality Management*, 37, 21–28.

Cogin, J. (2012). Are generational differences in work values fact or fiction ? Multi-country evidence and implications. *International Journal of Human Resource Management*, 23 (11), 2268–2294.

Edwards, J. A., & Billsberry, J. (2010). Testing a multidimensional theory of person-environment fit. *Journal of Managerial Issues*, 22 (4), 476–493.

Edwards, J. R. (2008). Person–environment fit in organizations: An assessment of theoretical progress. *Academy of Management Annals*, 2 (1), 167–230.

Edwards, J. R., Cable, D. M., Williamson, I. O., Lambert, L. S., & Shipp, A. J. (2006). The phenomenology of fit: Linking the person and environment to the subjective experience of person-environment fit. *Journal of Applied Psychology*, 91 (4), 802–27.

Feij, J. A., van der Velde, M. E. G., Taris, R., & Taris, T. W. (1999). The development of person-vocation fit: A longitudinal study among young employees. *International Journal of Selection and Assessment*, 7 (1), 12–25.

Fishbein, M., & Ajzen, I. (1975). *Belief, attitude, intention, and behavior: An introduction to theory and research*. Reading, MA: Addison-Wesley.

Glew, D. J. (2012). Effects of interdependence and social interaction-based person-team fit. *Administrative Sciences*, 2 (1), 26–46.

Harold, C. M., & Ployhart, R. E. (2008). What do applicants want? Examining changes in attribute judgments over time. *Journal of Occupational and Organizational Psychology*, 81 (2), 191–218.

Hershatter, A., & Epstein, M. (2010). Millennials and the world of work: An organization and management perspective. *Journal of Business and Psychology*, 25 (2), 211–223.

Highhouse, S., Lievens, F., & Sinar, E. F. (2003). Measuring attraction to organizations. *Educational and Psychological Measurement*, 63 (6), 986–1001.

Jansen, K. J., & Kristof-Brown, A. (2006). Toward a multidimensional theory of person-environment fit. *Journal of Managerial Issues*, 18 (2), 193–212.

Judge, T. A., & Cable, D. M. (1997). Applicant personality, organizational culture, and organization attraction. *Personnel Psychology*, 50 (2), 359–394.

Kim, T.-Y., & Kim, M. (2013). Leaders' moral competence and employee outcomes: The effects of psychological empowerment and person–supervisor fit. *Journal of Business Ethics*, 112 (1), 155–166.

Kristof, A. L. (1996). Person-organization fit: An integrative review of its conceptualizations, measurement, and implications. *Personnel Psychology*, 49 (1), 1–49.

Kristof-Brown, A. L., Zimmerman, R. D., & Johnson, E. C. (2005). Consequences of individuals' fit at work: A meta-analysis of person-job, person-organization, person-group, and person-supervisor fit. *Personnel Psychology*, 58 (2), 281–342.

Lusch, R. F., Vargo, S. L., & O'Brien, M. (2007). Competing through service: Insights from service-dominant logic. *Journal of Retailing*, 83 (1), 5–18.

Marcus, B., & Wagner, U. (2015). What do you want to be? Criterion-related validity of attained vocational aspirations versus inventoried person–vocation fit. *Journal of Business and Psychology*, 30 (1), 51–62.

Nazir, N. A. (2005). Person-culture fit and employee commitment in banks. *Vikalpa*, 30 (3), 39–51.

Nunnally, J. C., & Bernstein, I. H. (1994). *Psychometric theory* (3rd ed.). New York, NY: McGraw-Hill.

Oh, I.-S., Guay, R. P., Kim, K., Harold, C. M., Lee, J. H., Heo, C. G., & Shin, K. H. (2014). Fit happens globally: A meta-analytic comparison of the relationships of person-environment fit dimensions with work attitudes and performance across East Asia, Europe, and North America. *Personnel Psychology*, 67 (1), 99–152.

Piasentin, K. A., & Chapman, D. S. (2007). Perceived similarity and complementarity as predictors of subjective person-organization fit. *Journal of Occupational and Organizational Psychology*, 80 (2), 341–354.

Phillips, J. M., Gully, S. M., McCarthy, J. E., Castellano, W. G., & Kim, M. S. (2014). Recruiting global travelers: The role of global travel recruitment messages and individual differences in perceived fit, attraction, and job pursuit intentions. *Personnel Psychology*, 67 (1), 153–201.

Schlager, T., Bodderas, M., Maas, P., & Cachelin, J. L. (2011). The influence of the employer brand on employee attitudes relevant for service branding: An empirical investigation. *Journal of Services Marketing*, 25 (7), 497–508.

Schmidt, J. A., Chapman, D. S., & Jones, D. A. (2015). Does emphasizing different types of person–environment fit in online job ads influence application behavior and applicant quality? Evidence from a field experiment. *Journal of Business and Psychology*, 30, 267–282.

Seong, J. Y., & Kristof-Brown, A. L. (2012). Testing multidimensional models of person-group fit. *Journal of Managerial Psychology*, 27 (6), 536–556.

Solnet, D. J., Ford, R. C., Robinson, R. N. S., Ritchie, B. W., & Olsen, M. (2014). Modeling locational factors for tourism employment. *Annals of Tourism Research*, 45, 30–45.

Swider, B. W., Zimmerman, R. D., & Barrick M. R. (2015), Searching for the right fit: Development of applicant person-organization fit perceptions during the recruitment process. *Journal of Applied Psychology*, 100 (3) 880–93.

Werbel, J. D., & Johnson, D. J. (2001). The use of person–group fit for employment selection: A missing link in person–environment fit. *Human Resources Management*, 40 (3) 227–240.

Wheeler, A. R., Buckley, M. R., Halbesleben, J. R. B., Brouer, R. L., & Ferris, G. R. (2005). "The elusive criterion of fit" revisited: Toward an integrative theory of multidimensional fit. *Research in Personnel and Human Resources Management*, 24, 265–304.

Wilden, R., Gudergan, S., & Lings, I. N. (2010). Employer branding: Strategic implications for staff recruitment. *Journal of Marketing Management*, 26 (1-2), 56–73.

17

Innovational Development for Transitional Economy – Russia Case Study

Valeria A. Arsenyeva[1], Svetlana A. Litvinova[1], Valentina N. Parakhina[2], Zinaida N. Kozenko[3], Mikhail Y. Denisov[4]

ABSTRACT

The purpose of this article is to develop mechanisms of innovational development for countries with transitional economies. The methodological base of the research consists of a factor analysis of the structure of GDP adapted to the analysis of the innovational development of countries with a transitional economy, distinguishing the innovational sphere of the economy, the structure of manufactured innovational goods, the structure of the creation of leading production technologies, and the structure of the leading production technologies.

During the course of the research, the authors determined the key problems inhibiting innovational development in Russia and other countries with transitional economies, determined the most important preconditions of Russia's transition to an innovation-oriented type of economic development, and offered instruments for Russia's transition to an innovation-oriented type of economic development. As a result, the authors developed working mechanisms of the innovational development of countries with a transitional economy.

The authors come to the conclusion that the innovational development of an economy is an important condition for the adaptation of countries with a transitional economy to new market conditions because it allows the private manufacturing of products that are competitive in global markets. High innovational activity is one of the most important features of a market economy compared to an administrative & command economic system; thus, without the development of innovations, transitioning to a new type of economic system is impossible for countries with a transitional economy.

KEY WORDS: **innovational development, countries with transitional economy, leading production technologies, modern Russia**

[1]South-Russian Institute of Management – Branch of Russian Presidential Academy of National Economy and Public Administration, Russia; [2]North Caucasus Federal University, Russia; [3]Volgograd State Agrarian University, Russia; [4]Rostov State Economic University (RINH), Russia

Introduction

Major participants in international economic relations and important components of the global economy are countries with transitional economies, which possess unique capabilities related to the transitional nature of their economic systems that are caused by changes in the management type and foundations of the conduct of economic activities.

Although these countries comprise a large and separate block of the modern global economic system, they do not contribute much to its development because they are mainly concentrated on solving internal prob-

Correspondence concerning this article should be addressed to: Valeria Arsenyeva, South-Russian Institute of Management – Branch of Russian Presidential Academy of National Economy and Public Administration 70 Pushkinskaya St. , Rostov-on-Don 344002, Russian Federation. Email: valeria-arsenyeva@rambler.ru

lems related to the stabilization of economic development and termination of the transitional period.

Multiple examples prove that innovations make it possible to overcome crises in the economy. The transitional period of economic development can also be considered a type of crisis of an economic system. A country may not fully realize its existing potential due to periodic systemic errors, a lack of clear rules that are understandable to all members of the economic system, and a lack of cooperation between various institutes.

According to the expectations of most modern economists, innovational development will help countries with a transitional economy pass to a new stage and end the transitional period. The main problem is insufficiently high levels of innovational development and a lack of working mechanisms for the activation of innovational activity in countries with a transitional economy.

It is important to note that such countries require special mechanisms that are adapted to the specifics of their nation, the level of development of their institutional environment and the general social mood in their society and business environment. This determines the actuality of the development of such mechanisms, which is studied in this research. The purpose of this article is to develop mechanisms of innovational development for countries with a transitional economy by using the example of modern Russia.

This goal is achieved by determining the foundations and tendencies of current innovational development in countries with a transitional economy, determining key problems and preconditions of the transition of countries with a transitional economy to an innovation-oriented type of economic development, and developing the corresponding instruments.

Literature review

The theoretical base of the research includes works of modern authors in the sphere of economic growth on substantiating the necessity and importance of the growth of economic systems to achieve the development of the global economy; determining the preconditions and factors of economic growth; and determining obstacles to the growth and development of the modern global economy and the means and methods of their elimination. Such authors include (Bartolini & Sarracino, 2015; González-Pernía & Peña-Legazkue, 2015; Odhiambo, 2015; Pogosov, 2015; Popkova, Yurev, Stepicheva, & Denisov, 2005; Zeira & Zoabi, 2015). Economic growth is very important and necessary for the development of the global economy (Choi & Shin, 2015). A precondition of economic growth is high entrepreneurial and innovational economic activity (Lee & Oh, 2015). The state can stimulate economic growth by financing scientific research, creating favorable conditions for business, and attracting foreign investments (Castiglione, Infante, & Smirnova, 2015).

This article also uses the theoretical research of economists in the sphere of innovational development of economic systems, in which the role of innovations in the development of economic systems is studied, the role of state regulation and the initiatives of private business in the provision of economic innovational development is determined, and regularities and terms of innovational development are analyzed. Such authors include (Appe, 2015; Imanbekova, 2014; Solovchuk, 2015). Despite the state financing of science and education, innovations are implemented by private business, which is a ley source of innovations in the economy (Zhao & Sun, 2014). Innovational development can be evolutional, via the implementation of insignificant improvements (Baldwin, Black, & O'Leary, 2014), or revolutionary, via the establishment of completely new technological modes (Tovt, 2014).

In addition, the work uses the studies of scientists assessing the methodical and practical aspects of economic growth and mechanisms of innovational development of the economies of modern countries, in which the effectiveness of various innovational tools is determined and issues of the use of various models of innovational development are viewed with the example of countries and regions. These authors include (Castellacci, 2015; Coccia, 2015; Donate, Peña, & Sánchez de Pablo, 2015; Rumyantsev, 2015; Scherer & Voegtlin, 2015; Vasin & Gamidullaeva, 2015). In Russia, the state is the member of economic relations that has the most initiative and expresses an interest in the creation and implementation of innovations (Lillis, Szwejczewski, & Goffin, 2015).

This is caused by the relative isolation of the economy of modern Russia and a low level of competition (Kolychev & Prokhorov, 2015). In developed countries, competition creates stimuli for the implementation of innovations for private enterprises (Ng, Kanagasundram, Wong, & Chandran, 2015). The authors also use the works of various researchers studying the peculiarities of the development of countries with transitional economies, which are known as transit economies, as well as those studying the most important aspects of the functioning of an economy during transitional periods from an administrative & command system to a market system and determining preconditions for the end of transitional periods. Such works include (Akimov, 2015; Andres & Round, 2015; Askarov & Doucouliagos, 2015; Borgersen & King, 2015; Makanyeza & Du Toit, 2015; Mutlu, Zhan, Peng, & Lin, 2015). Countries with a transitional economy include countries of the former USSR, one of which is modern Russia (Boermans & Roelfsema, 2015). The transitional character of the economy supposes refusal from administrative and command state management and the transition to the development of a market economic system (Hong, Hong, Wang, Xu, & Zhao, 2015). Currently, countries of the former USSR have not yet come to the end of the transitional period (Dovlatyan, Makeeva, Oboymova, & Cherkesova, 2015)

Method

The methodological basis of the research is comprised of factor analysis, adapted to the analysis of innovational development of countries with a transitional economy. Within this approach, the initial point of conduct of the analysis is the development of an economic model. This research builds a structural model of GDP with the allocation of the innovational sphere of the economy, which has the following form:

$$GDP_i=IP_i+AP_i+SS_i+IN_i \quad (1)$$

where GDP – gross domestic product in a certain year;
IP – volume of industrial production of industrial products that are not innovational in a certain year;
AP – volume of agricultural production of food products that are not innovational in a certain year;
SS – volume of provision of services that are not innovational within the sphere of service and trade in a certain year;
IN – volume of innovational products manufactured in all spheres of economy in a certain year; and
i – studied period of time (year).

The next stage of the factor analysis is the collection of statistical information to determine the value of indicators in both the studied year and the year prior. Then, a calculation table is built, into which the values of the indicator for the studied two-year period are entered in a special way. The upper and first lines of the table consist of statistical data for the previous year, the second line consists of the same information replaced with the value of the indicators of the IN data for current year, and the third line consists of the indicators' values for previous year.

The final stage of the factor analysis is to determine the contribution of the studied factor or several studied factors in the innovational development of countries with a transitional economy using the following formula:

$$\Delta GDP(IN)=GDP_{IN}-GDP_{i-1} \quad (2)$$

In equation (2), GDP_{IN} is the growth of GDP by means of an increase in the volume of manufactured innovational products. That is, all components of GDP are taken for the previous year, and the indicator of innovational activity is taken for the current (studied) year. This difference is significant because it makes it possible to determine the contribution of the factor of innovational activity to the growth of GDP in the current year.

In addition to the determination of contribution of innovations to the formation of GDP of a country with a transitional economy, the complex analysis of its innovational development requires a factor analysis of the structure of manufactured innovational goods. For this, the authors of this research offer the following model:

$$IP_i=ME_i+PP_i+DE_i+CM_i+CT_i+OS_i \quad (3)$$

Where IP – total volume of manufactured innovational products in a certain year;
ME – volume of manufactured innovational goods in a certain year in the sphere of minerals extraction;
PP – volume of manufactured innovational goods in a certain year in the sphere of processing production;
DE – volume of manufactured innovational goods in a certain year in the sphere of the production and distribution of electricity, gas, and water;

CM – volume of manufactured innovational goods in a certain year in the sphere of telecommunications;
CT – volume of manufactured innovational goods in a certain year in the sphere of computational technics use and informational technologies; and
OS – volume of manufactured innovational goods in a certain year in the sphere of the provision of other types of services.

Within this, a calculation model is built, into which the values of the indicators for the studied two-year period are entered in a special way. The upper and first lines of the table include statistical information on previous year; the second, third, fourth, fifth, sixth, and seventh lines include the same information replaced with the values of the targeted studied indicators for the studied year; and the last, eighth, line includes information for the current year.

To create a general notion on the nature of innovational development of a country with a transitional economy, it is important to know the structure of the creation of leading production technologies. We use the following model:

$$LPT_i=NGC_i+CNT_i+UPI_i \quad (4)$$

where LPT – total number of developed leading production technologies in a certain year;
NGC – number of leading production technologies that are new for the given country, in a certain year;
CNT – number of completely new leading production technologies in a certain year; and
UPI – number of new leading production technologies with the use of patented inventions with the development of technology in a certain year.

Finally, it is necessary to determine the structure of the used leading production technologies according to the following formula:

$$UPT_i=TDP_i+TFP_i \quad (5)$$

where UPT – total number of leading production technologies used in this country in a certain year;
TDP – number of leading production technologies of domestic production used in this country in a certain year; and
TFP – total number of leading production technologies of foreign production used in this country in a certain year.

For this model, the data are shown in the following table.

Results

The largest representative of countries with a transitional economy is the Russian Federation. Considering the similar features of such countries, it suffices to view tendencies of innovational development of modern Russia because they can later be applied, with a high level of authenticity and representation, to other countries with a transitional economy. To determine the sense and tendencies of current innovational development in Russia, let us conduct a factor analysis on the basis of the compiled models (Table 1-4).

As seen from the results of the factor analysis, the increase in the manufacturing of innovational products stimulated the growth of the Russian GDP in 2014, compared to 2013, by RUB 574.3 billion (6%). Thus, the growth of innovational products contributed only slightly to the development of national production, reflecting a low level of innovational development of the modern Russian economy.

The largest growth of innovational products in 2014, compared to 2013, was observed in the sphere of processing productions (95%), and the contribution of each other sphere to the growth in the volume of manufactured innovational goods constituted less than 1%. The largest share in the structure of created innovations in 2013-2014 belonged to innovations that are new for Russia but not new for the world. In 2014, the volume of created innovations decreased compared to the level of 2013.

The number of implemented foreign investments significantly exceeded the number of implemented foreign investments in Russia in 2013-2014. The total volume of innovations, implemented into production, decreased over the studied period. Among the key problems of innovational development of Russia and other countries with a transitional economy, it is possible to distinguish the following:

- the creation of innovations that are a novelty only for this country and have long been known around the world;

Table 1. Summarized calculation table for conduct of factor analysis of the role of innovations in formation of GDP of countries with a transitional economy, RUB billion

	IP	AP	SS	IN	GDP
GDP_{2013}	42,155.3	5,140.9	66,945.8	2,588.9	116,831.0
GDP_{IN}	42,155.3	5,140.9	66,945.8	3,163.2	117,405.3
GDP_{2014}	45,395.4	5,536.0	72,091.4	3,163.2	126,186.0

Source: Adapted from "Russia in numbers. Scientific research and innovations 2015: Bulletin of Rosstat" by Rosstat (2015). Retrieved from Retrieved from http://www.gks.ru/free_doc/doc_2015/rusfig/rus-15.pdf

Table 2. Summarized calculation table for a factor analysis of innovational development for countries with a transitional economy, RUB million

	ME	PP	DE	CM	CT	OS	IP
IP_{2013}	522,890.9	1,973,535.6	13,177.9	41,444.1	14,648.1	23,251.3	2,588,948
IP_{ME}	523,210.5	1,973,535.6	13,177.9	41,444.1	14,648.1	23,251.3	2,589,268
IP_{PP}	522,890.9	2,518,618	13,177.9	41,444.1	14,648.1	23,251.3	3,134,030
IP_{DE}	522,890.9	1,973,535.6	30,702.2	41,444.1	14,648.1	23,251.3	2,606,472
IP_{CM}	522,890.9	1,973,535.6	13,177.9	31,535.7	14,648.1	23,251.3	2,579,040
IP_{CT}	522,890.9	1,973,535.6	13,177.9	41,444.1	39,558.7	23,251.3	2,613,859
IP_{OS}	522,890.9	1,973,535.6	13,177.9	41,444.1	14,648.1	19,590.8	2,585,287
IP_{2014}	523,210.5	2,518,618	30,702.2	31,535.7	39,558.7	19,590.8	3,163,216

Source: Adapted from "Russia in numbers. Scientific research and innovations 2015: Bulletin of Rosstat" by Rosstat (2015). Retrieved from Retrieved from http://www.gks.ru/free_doc/doc_2015/rusfig/rus-15.pdf

Table 3. Summarized calculation table for a factor analysis of the developed leading production technologies in countries with a transitional economy

	NGC	CNT	UPI	LPT
LPT_{2013}	1,276	153	694	2,123
LPT_{NGC}	1,245	153	694	2,092
LPT_{CNT}	1,276	164	694	2,134
LPT_{UPI}	1,276	153	712	2,141
LPT_{2014}	1,245	164	712	2,121

Source: Adapted from "Russia in numbers. Scientific research and innovations 2015: Bulletin of Rosstat" by Rosstat (2015). Retrieved from Retrieved from http://www.gks.ru/free_doc/doc_2015/rusfig/rus-15.pdf

Table 4. Summarized calculation table for a factor analysis of the leading production technologies in countries with a transitional economy

	TDP	TFP	UPT
UPT_{2013}	117,697	40,544	158,241
UPT_{TDP}	110,037	40,544	150,581
UPT_{TFP}	117,697	48,068	165,765
UPT_{2014}	110,037	48,068	158,105

Source: Adapted from "Russia in numbers. Scientific research and innovations 2015: Bulletin of Rosstat" by Rosstat (2015). Retrieved from Retrieved from http://www.gks.ru/free_doc/doc_2015/rusfig/rus-15.pdf

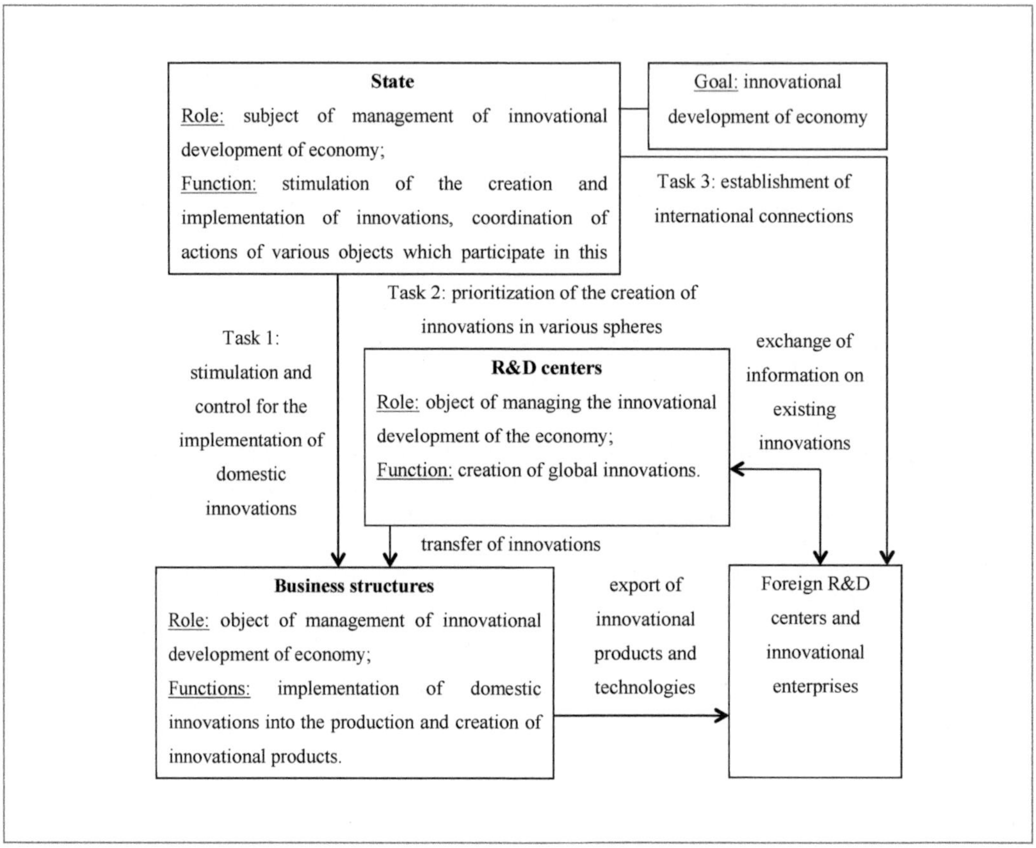

Figure 1. Mechanisms of innovational development of countries with a transitional economy

- the concentration of created innovations in the spheres of economy that develop actively, which contradicts the idea of diversification; and
- an excessive orientation towards the use of foreign investments and refusal to implement new domestic developments into production.

The most important preconditions of Russia's transition to an innovation-oriented type of economic development include the following:

- society's realization of the necessity, social readiness, and approval of a transition to an innovational path of economic development;
- significant accumulated scientific and technical potential of the economy; and
- the development of the resource component of production.

The following mechanisms are offered in this research as instruments for Russia's transition to an innovation-oriented type of economic development (Fig. 1):

- the establishment of international connections for acquaintance with popular innovations – for the purpose of preventing their repeated invention;
- the creation of an international committee for the evaluation of the level of innovativeness of new developments throughout the world;
- the establishment of priorities for the creation of innovations in new spheres of the economy for its diversification; and
- the stimulation of the implementation of domestic innovations through the provision of tax concessions.

The offered mechanisms of innovational development of countries with a transitional economy are given in Fig. 1.

Conclusion

As a result of this research, the set goal was achieved by using the set tasks. The offered mechanisms of innovational development in countries with a transitional economy are aimed at state stimulation and control for the implementation of domestic innovations, the prioritization of the creation of innovations in various spheres, and the establishment of international connections to increase the quantity and quality (level of novelty for the world) of created innovations and to create favorable conditions for the implementation of domestic innovations in production.

These mechanisms make it possible to overcome the existing problems in the way of the Russian economy's transition to innovational development. The subject of management within the developed mechanisms is the state, and the object of management is R&D centers in the country and domestic business structures.

It is important to note that the innovational development of an economy is an important condition for the adaptation of countries with a transitional economy to new market conditions because they enable the development of private manufacturing of products that are competitive in the global markets. High innovational activity is one of the most important peculiarities of a market economy compared to an administrative and command economic system. Without the development of innovations, transition to the new type of economic system of countries with a transitional economy is impossible.

It should be noted that this article does not study all of the characteristics of innovational development for countries with a transitional economy but focuses instead on only the main ones. This limitation, which affects the results of the conducted research, is due to the limited length of the article. During further research in the sphere of innovational development in countries with a transitional economy, it would be expedient to view other aspects.

References

Akimov, A. (2015). The Political Economy of Financial Reforms in Authoritarian Transition Economies: A Comparative Studies in Kazakhstan and Uzbekistan. In K. Ruziev & N. Perdikis (Eds.), *Development and Financial Reform in Emerging Economies* (pp. 125–147). United Kingdom, UK: Pickering and Chatto.

Andres, L., & Round, J. (2015). The creative economy in a context of transition: A review of the mechanisms of micro-resilience. *Cities, 45*, 1-6.

Appe, S. (2015). Government mapping of the third sector: a government innovation for regulation and coordination? Perspectives from the third sector. *International Journal of Public Administration, 38*(10), 724-733.

Askarov, Z., & Doucouliagos, H. (2015). Aid and institutions in transition economies. *European Journal of Political Economy, 38*, 55-70.

Baldwin, R., Black, J., & O'Leary, G. (2014). Risk regulation and transnationality: institutional accountability as a driver of innovation. *Transnational Environmental Law, 3*(2), 373-390.

Bartolini, S., & Sarracino, F. (2015). The dark side of Chinese growth: Declining social capital and well-Being in times of economic boom. *World Development, 74*, 333-351.

Boermans, M. A., & Roelfsema, H. (2015). The effects of internationalization on innovation: Firm-level evidence for transition economies. *Open Economies Review, 26*(2), 333-350.

Borgersen, T. A., & King, R. M. (2015). Endogenous supply side constraints to export-led growth and aggregate growth implications in transition economies. *Structural Change and Economic Dynamics, 33*, 96-109.

Castellacci, F. (2015). Institutional voids or organizational resilience? Business groups, innovation, and market development in Latin America. *World Development, 70*, 43-58.

Castiglione, C., Infante, D., & Smirnova, J. (2015). Environment and economic growth: Is the rule of law the go-between? The case of high-income countries. *Energy, Sustainability and Society, 5*(26). doi:10.1186/s13705-015-0054-8.

Choi, K. H., & Shin, S. (2015). Population aging, economic growth, and the social transmission of human capital: An analysis with an overlapping generations model. *Economic Modelling, 50*, 138-147.

Coccia, M. (2015). General sources of general purpose technologies in complex societies: Theory of global leadership-driven innovation, warfare and human development. *Technology in Society, 42*, 199-226.

Donate, M. J., Peña, I., & Sánchez de Pablo, J. D. (2016). HRM practices for human and social capital development: Effects on innovation capabilities. *The International Journal of Human Resource Management, 27*(9), 928-953.

Dovlatyan, G. P., Makeeva, E. I., Oboymova, N. T., & Cherkesova, E. Y. (2015). Potential for use of foreign experience in evaluation of strategic sustainability of enterprises relating to transition of Russia's economy to strategic path of development. *Asian Social Science, 11*(20), 56-65.

González-Pernía, J. L., & Peña-Legazkue, I. (2015). Export-oriented entrepreneurship and regional economic growth. *Small Business Economics, 45*(3), 505-522.

Hong, J., Hong, S., Wang, L., Xu, Y., & Zhao, D. (2015). Government grants, private R&D funding and innovation efficiency in transition economy. *Technology Analysis and Strategic Management, 27*(9), 1068-1096.

Imanbekova, M. (2014). The use of foreign experience in forming system state regulation of innovation activities of enterprises in the Republic of Kazakhstan. *World Applied Sciences Journal, 30*(5), 630-634.

Kolychev, V. D., & Prokhorov, I. V. (2015). Conception, technology and methods of development of university system of innovation projects commercialization based on effectuation. *Asian Social Science, 11*(8), 44-51.

Lee, S., & Oh, D.W. (2015). Economic growth and the environment in China: Empirical evidence using prefecture level data. *China Economic Review, 36*, 73-85.

Lillis, B., Szwejczewski, M., & Goffin, K. (2015). The development of innovation capability in services: research propositions and management implications. *Operations Management Research, 8*(1), 48-68.

Makanyeza, C., & Du Toit, F. (2015). Examining the measurement and dimensionality of the construct of consumer awareness in a developing and transition economy. *SA Journal of Industrial Psychology, 41*(1). doi: 10.4102/sajip.v41i1.1250

Mutlu, C. C., Zhan, W., Peng, M.W., & Lin, Z. J. (2015). Competing in (and out of) transition economies. *Asia Pacific Journal of Management, 32*(3), 571-596.

Ng, B. K., Kanagasundram, T., Wong, C. Y., & Chandran, V. G. R. (2015). Innovation for inclusive development in Southeast Asia: The roles of regional coordination mechanisms. *The Pacific Review, 2*(1), 1- 30.

Odhiambo, N. M. (2015). Government expenditure and economic growth in South Africa: An empirical envestigation. *Atlantic Economic Journal, 43*(3), 393-406.

Pogosov, I.A. (2015). Factors of long-term economic growth: Scientific and technical progress and capital intensity of production. *Studies on Russian Economic Development, 26*(5), 423-433.

Popkova, E. G., Yurev, V., Stepicheva, O., & Denisov, N. (2015). Transformation and concentration of intellectual capital as a factor of economic growth in the modern economy. *Regional and Sectoral Economic Studies, 15*(1), 53-60.

Rosstat. (2015). Russia in numbers. Scientific research and innovations 2015: Bulletin of Rosstat. Retrieved from http://www.gks.ru/free_doc/doc_2015/rusfig/rus-15.pdf

Rumyantsev, A. A. (2015). Science and innovation space of a macroregion: Prospects of innovative territorial development. *Studies on Russian Economic Development, 26*(4), 379-387

Solovchuk, K. O. (2015). Регулювання і підтримка інноваційної діяльності у сфері АПК в країнах Європейського Союзу. [Regulation and support for innovations in the agricultural sector of the European Union]. *Actual Problems of Economics, 165*(3), 62-68.

Tovt, T. I. (2014). Regulation mechanism for investment support of innovation activities of enterprises. *Actual Problems of Economics, 152*(2), 211-218.

Vasin, S. M., & Gamidullaeva, L. A. (2015). Development a basic model of the innovation system. *Review of European Studies, 7*(11), 175-183.

Voegtlin, C., & Scherer, A. G. (2015). Responsible innovation and the innovation of responsibility: Governing sustainable development in a globalized world. *Journal of Business Ethics*. Doi: 10.1007/s10551-015-2769-z.

Zeira, J., & Zoabi, H. (2015). Economic growth and sector dynamics. *European Economic Review, 79*, 1-15.

Zhao, X., & Sun, B. (2014). The influence of Chinese environmental regulation on corporation innovation and competitiveness. *Journal of Cleaner Production, 112*, 1523-1236.

Permissions

All chapters in this book were first published in Contemporary Economics, by University of Finance and Management, Warsaw; Vistula University; hereby published with permission under the Creative Commons Attribution License or equivalent. Every chapter published in this book has been scrutinized by our experts. Their significance has been extensively debated. The topics covered herein carry significant findings which will fuel the growth of the discipline. They may even be implemented as practical applications or may be referred to as a beginning point for another development.

The contributors of this book come from diverse backgrounds, making this book a truly international effort. This book will bring forth new frontiers with its revolutionizing research information and detailed analysis of the nascent developments around the world.

We would like to thank all the contributing authors for lending their expertise to make the book truly unique. They have played a crucial role in the development of this book. Without their invaluable contributions this book wouldn't have been possible. They have made vital efforts to compile up to date information on the varied aspects of this subject to make this book a valuable addition to the collection of many professionals and students.

This book was conceptualized with the vision of imparting up-to-date information and advanced data in this field. To ensure the same, a matchless editorial board was set up. Every individual on the board went through rigorous rounds of assessment to prove their worth. After which they invested a large part of their time researching and compiling the most relevant data for our readers.

The editorial board has been involved in producing this book since its inception. They have spent rigorous hours researching and exploring the diverse topics which have resulted in the successful publishing of this book. They have passed on their knowledge of decades through this book. To expedite this challenging task, the publisher supported the team at every step. A small team of assistant editors was also appointed to further simplify the editing procedure and attain best results for the readers.

Apart from the editorial board, the designing team has also invested a significant amount of their time in understanding the subject and creating the most relevant covers. They scrutinized every image to scout for the most suitable representation of the subject and create an appropriate cover for the book.

The publishing team has been an ardent support to the editorial, designing and production team. Their endless efforts to recruit the best for this project, has resulted in the accomplishment of this book. They are a veteran in the field of academics and their pool of knowledge is as vast as their experience in printing. Their expertise and guidance has proved useful at every step. Their uncompromising quality standards have made this book an exceptional effort. Their encouragement from time to time has been an inspiration for everyone.

The publisher and the editorial board hope that this book will prove to be a valuable piece of knowledge for researchers, students, practitioners and scholars across the globe.

List of Contributors

Hankyeung Choi
Ministry of Strategy and Finance, Sejong Special Self-Governing City, Republic of Korea

David J. Leatham and Kunlapath Sukcharoen
Department of Agricultural Economics, Texas A&M University, USA

Agata Sierpińska-Sawicz
Poznan University of Economics, Poland

Sok-Gee Chan
Department of Finance and Banking, Faculty of Business and Accountancy, Universiti of Malaya, Malaysia

Mohd. Zaini Abd. Karim
Othman Yeop Abdullah Graduate School of Business, Universiti Utara Malaysia, Malaysia

Agata Sierpińska-Sawicz
Poznań University of Economics - Department of Controlling, Financial Analysis and Valuation, Poland

Patrycja Barbara Bąk
AGH University of Science and Technology - Department of Economics and Management in Industry, Poland

Elena Popkova
Volgograd State Technical University, Russian Federation

Svetlana Meshkova
Perm Institute of Economics and Finance, Russian Federation

Evgeniya Karpunina
G.R. Derzhavin Tambov State University, Russian Federation

Elena Karpushko
Volgograd State University of Architecture and Civil Engineering, Russian Federation

Marina Karpushko
Perm National Research Polytechnic University, Russian Federation

Anselm Komla Abotsi
National Institute of Development Administration - Department of Development Economics, Bangkok, Thailand
University of Education, Winneba Department of Economics, Ghana

Tongyai Iyavarakul
National Institute of Development Administration - Department of Development Economics, Bangkok, Thailand

Egor V. Dudukalov
Russian Presidential Academy of National Economy and Public Administration, Russia

Natalia D. Rodionova
Rostov State Economic University (RINH), Russia

Yana E. Sivakova
Institute of Management - Branch of Russian Presidential Academy of National Economy and Public Administration, Russia

Elena Vyugova
Institute of Economics and Finance, Russia

Irina V. Cheryomushkina
Voronezh State University of Engineering Technologies, Russia

Elena G. Popkova
Volgograd State Technical University, Russia

Mario Arturo Ruiz Estrada
University of Malaya - Economics, Malaysia

Evangelos Koutronas
University of Malaya - Social Security Research Centre (SSRC), Malaysia

Ross Knippenberg
American Veterinary Medical Association - Economics, United States

Tatiana N. Litvinova
Volgograd State Agricultural University, Russia

Galina A. Khmeleva
Samara State University of Economics, Russia
Samara National Research University, Russia

Lilia V. Ermolina
Samara State Technical University, Russia

Tatiana V. Alferova
Perm State National Research University, Russia

Irina V. Cheryomushkina
Federal State Budget Educational Institution of Higher Education "Voronezh State University of Engineering Technologies", Russia

Mario Arturo Ruiz Estrada and Vgr Chandran
Department of Economics, Faculty of Economics and Administration, University of Malaya, Malaysia

Muhammad Tahir
Department of Management Sciences, COMSATS Institute of Information Technology, Pakistan

Rossitsa Rangelova Pavlova and Grigor Sariiski
Bulgarian Academy of Sciences - Economic Research Institute, Sofia, Bulgaria

Yuri A. Kolesnikov
Southern Federal University, Russia

Tatiana V. Epifanova, Anastasia M. Usenko and Ekaterina Parshina
Rostov State Economic University, Russia

Victoria N. Ostrovskaya
Moscow Humanitarian and Economic Institute (Stavropol branch), Russia

Marinko Škare and Saša Stjepanović
Juraj Dobrila University of Pula - Faculty of economics and Tourism "Dr. Mijo Mirkovic", Croatia

Ewa Gałecka-Burdziak
Department of Economics I, Warsaw School of Economics, Poland

Enrique Claver-Cortés, Bartolome Marco-Lajara and Encarnacion Manresa-Marhuenda
Department of Management, University of Alicante, Spain

Marlena A. Bednarska
Faculty of International Business and Economics, Poznan University of Economics and Business, Poland

Valeria A. Arsenyeva and Svetlana A. Litvinova
South-Russian Institute of Management – Branch of Russian Presidential Academy of National Economy and Public Administration, Russia

Valentina N. Parakhina
North Caucasus Federal University, Russia

Zinaida N. Kozenko
Volgograd State Agrarian University, Russia

Mikhail Y. Denisov
Rostov State Economic University (RINH), Russia

Index